**ORACLE®**

Oracle Press

# Oracle8 Certified Professional DBA Practice Exams

## About the Author

Jason S. Couchman is a database consultant and the co-author of *Oracle Certified Professional DBA Certification Exam Guide*, also from Oracle Press. He is a regular presenter on Oracle and OCP at international Oracle user conferences and meetings. His work has been published by *Oracle Magazine,* Harvard Business School Publishing, and Gannett Newspapers, among others.

**ORACLE®**

*Oracle Press*™

# Oracle8 Certified Professional DBA Practice Exams

Jason S. Couchman

Osborne/**McGraw-Hill**

Berkeley  New York  St. Louis  San Francisco
Auckland  Bogotá  Hamburg  London  Madrid
Mexico City  Milan  Montreal  New Delhi  Panama City
Paris  São Paulo  Singapore  Sydney  Tokyo  Toronto

Osborne/**McGraw-Hill**
2600 Tenth Street
Berkeley, California 94710
U.S.A.

For information on translations or book distributors outside the U.S.A., or to arrange bulk purchase discounts for sales promotions, premiums, or fund-raisers, please contact Osborne/**McGraw-Hill** at the above address.

### Oracle8 Certified Professional DBA Practice Exams

Copyright © 2000 by The McGraw-Hill Companies, Inc. (Publisher). All rights reserved. Printed in the United States of America. Except as permitted under the Copyright Act of 1976, no part of this publication may be reproduced or distributed in any form or by any means, or stored in a database or retrieval system, without the prior written permission of Publisher.

Oracle is a registered trademark and Oracle8*i* is a trademark or registered trademark of Oracle Corporation.

1234567890 AGM AGM 019876543210
Book P/N 0-07-212699-X   and   CD. P/N 0-07-212698-1
parts of

ISBN 0-07-212700-7

**Publisher**
  Brandon A. Nordin

**Vice President & Associate Publisher**
  Scott Rogers

**Acquisitions Editor**
  Jeremy Judson

**Project Editor**
  LeeAnn Pickrell

**Acquisitions Coordinators**
  Monika Faltiss
  Ross Doll

**Technical Editor**
  Ulrike Schwinn

**Copy Editor**
  Dennis Weaver

**Proofreaders**
  Stefany Otis
  Linda Medoff
  Paul Medoff

**Indexer**
  Jack Lewis

**Computer Designers**
  Jani Beckwith
  Elizabeth Jang

**Illustrators**
  Robert Hansen
  Michael Mueller
  Beth E. Young

**Series Design**
  Jani Beckwith

**Cover Design**
  William Voss

This book was composed with Corel VENTURA ™ Publisher.

Information has been obtained by Publisher from sources believed to be reliable. However, because of the possibility of human or mechanical error by our sources, Publisher, or others, Publisher does not guarantee to the accuracy, adequacy, or completeness of any information included in this work and is not responsible for any errors or omissions or the results obtained from the use of such information.

**To My Siblings**

**ORACLE®**
Certified Professional

## About the Oracle Certification Exams

The expertise of Oracle database administrators (DBAs) is integral to the success of today's increasingly complex system environments. The best DBAs operate primarily behind the scenes, looking for ways to fine-tune day-to-day performance to prevent unscheduled crises, and hours of expensive downtime. They know they stand between optimal performance and a crisis that could bring a company to a standstill. The Oracle Certified Database Administrator Track provides DBAs with tangible evidence of their skills with the Oracle database.

The Oracle Certified Professional (OCP) Program was developed by Oracle to recognize technical professionals who can demonstrate the depth of knowledge and hands-on skills required to maximize Oracle's core products according to a rigorous standard established by Oracle. By earning professional certification, you can translate the impressive knowledge and skill you have worked so hard to accumulate into a tangible credential that can lead to greater job security or more challenging, better-paying opportunities.

Oracle Certified Professionals are eligible to receive use of the Oracle Certified Professional logo and a certificate for framing.

## Requirements for Certification

To become an Oracle Certified Database Administrator, you must pass five tests. These exams cover knowledge of the essential aspects of the SQL language, Oracle administration, backup and recovery, and performance tuning of systems. The certification process requires that you pass the following five exams:

- Exam 1: Introduction to Oracle: SQL and PL/SQL
- Exam 2: Oracle8 Database Administration
- Exam 3: Oracle8 Backup and Recovery
- Exam 4: Oracle8 Performance Tuning
- Exam 5: Network Administration

If you fail a test, you must wait at least 30 days before you retake that exam. You may attempt a particular test up to three times in a twelve-month period.

## Recertification

Oracle announces the requirements for upgrading your certification based on the release of new products and upgrades. Oracle will give six-months' notice announcing when an exam version is expiring.

## Exam Format

The computer-based exams are multiple-choice tests, consisting of 60-90 questions that must be completed in 90 minutes.

## Special 10% Exam Discount Offer

You can qualify for a special 10% discount when you register for the OCP exam by contacting the number listed below. You must specifically request the discount and mention extension 27. Offer valid through January 30, 2000. To register for an Oracle test and be eligible for the 10% discount, call Sylvan Prometric at:

1-800-891-EXAM, ext. 27 (1-800-891-3926, ext. 27)
Outside the U.S. call +1.612.820.5000

Contact your local Oracle Education Representative for exam preparation courses and materials. Or download the *Candidate Guide* at **http://education.oracle.com/certification** for specific exam objectives and preparation methods.

# Contents at a Glance

## PART I
## OCP Practice Exams

1 OCP Exam 1: Introduction to SQL and PL/SQL ..................... 3
2 OCP Exam 2: Database Administration ............................ 79
3 OCP Exam 3: Backup and Recovery Workshop ..................... 149
4 OCP Exam 4: Performance Tuning Workshop ...................... 213
5 OCP Exam 5: Network Administration ............................ 279
6 OCP Oracle8i Upgrade Exam: New Features for Administrators ......... 331

## PART II
## OCP Key Terms and Concepts

7 OCP Exam 1 Terms and Concepts ................................ 399
8 OCP Exam 2 Terms and Concepts ................................ 415
9 OCP Exam 3 Terms and Concepts ................................ 437

| 10 | OCP Exam 4 Terms and Concepts | 455 |
| 11 | OCP Exam 5 Terms and Concepts | 473 |
| 12 | OCP Oracle8*i* Upgrade Exam Terms and Concepts | 487 |
|  | Index | 521 |

# Contents

PREFACE .................................................. XV
ACKNOWLEDGMENTS ...................................... XVII
INTRODUCTION ............................................ XIX

## PART I
## OCP Practice Exams

**1 OCP Exam 1: Introduction to SQL and PL/SQL** ................ 3
   OCP Exam 1 Topic Areas ................................. 4
   Practice Exam 1 ........................................ 9
   Practice Exam 2 ....................................... 27
   Answers to Practice Exam 1 ............................. 49
   Answers to Practice Exam 2 ............................. 63

**2 OCP Exam 2: Database Administration** ..................... 79
   OCP Exam 2 Topic Areas ................................ 80
   Practice Exam 1 ....................................... 85
   Practice Exam 2 ...................................... 102
   Answers to Practice Exam 1 ............................ 118
   Answers to Practice Exam 2 ............................ 133

## 3 OCP Exam 3: Backup and Recovery Workshop ... 149
OCP Exam 3 Topic Areas ... 150
Practice Exam 1 ... 154
Practice Exam 2 ... 170
Answers to Practice Exam 1 ... 186
Answers to Practice Exam 2 ... 199

## 4 OCP Exam 4: Performance Tuning Workshop ... 213
OCP Exam 4 Topic Areas ... 214
Practice Exam 1 ... 218
Practice Exam 2 ... 234
Answers to Practice Exam 1 ... 250
Answers to Practice Exam 2 ... 264

## 5 OCP Exam 5: Network Administration ... 279
OCP Exam 5 Topic Areas ... 280
Practice Exam 1 ... 282
Practice Exam 2 ... 294
Answers to Practice Exam 1 ... 308
Answers to Practice Exam 2 ... 320

## 6 OCP Oracle8i Upgrade Exam: New Features for Administrators ... 331
OCP Upgrade Exam Topic Areas ... 332
Practice Exam 1 ... 339
Practice Exam 2 ... 355
Answers to Practice Exam 1 ... 370
Answers to Practice Exam 2 ... 386

# PART II
# OCP Key Terms and Concepts

## 7 OCP Exam 1 Terms and Concepts ... 399
Overview of Relational Databases, SQL and PL/SQL ... 400
Writing Basic SQL Statements ... 401
Restricting and Sorting Data ... 402
Single-Row Functions ... 402
Displaying Data from Multiple Tables ... 403
Aggregating Data Using Group Functions ... 404
Subqueries ... 404
Multiple-Column Subqueries ... 405
Producing Readable Output from SQL*Plus ... 405
Manipulating Data ... 406
Creating and Managing Tables ... 406
Including Constraints ... 407

| | | |
|---|---|---:|
| | Creating Views | 408 |
| | Oracle Data Dictionary | 410 |
| | Other Database Objects | 410 |
| | Controlling User Access | 411 |
| | Declaring Variables | 412 |
| | Write Executable Statements | 412 |
| | Interacting with the Oracle Server | 413 |
| | Writing Control Structures | 413 |
| | Working with Composite Datatypes | 413 |
| | Writing Explicit Cursors | 414 |
| | Advanced Explicit Cursor Concepts | 414 |
| | Handling Exceptions | 414 |
| **8** | **OCP Exam 2 Terms and Concepts** | **415** |
| | Oracle Architectural Components | 416 |
| | Using Administrative Tools | 417 |
| | Managing an Oracle Instance | 418 |
| | Creating a Database | 419 |
| | Data Dictionary Views and Standard Packages | 420 |
| | Maintaining the Control File | 421 |
| | Maintaining Redo Log Files | 421 |
| | Managing Tablespaces and Datafiles | 422 |
| | Storage Structures and Relationships | 422 |
| | Managing Rollback Segments | 423 |
| | Managing Temporary Segments | 424 |
| | Managing Tables | 424 |
| | Managing Indexes | 426 |
| | Maintaining Data Integrity | 426 |
| | Using Clusters and Index-Organized Tables | 427 |
| | Loading and Reorganizing Data | 429 |
| | Managing Users | 430 |
| | Managing Profiles | 431 |
| | Managing Privileges | 432 |
| | Managing Roles | 434 |
| | Auditing | 435 |
| | Using National Language Support | 436 |
| **9** | **OCP Exam 3 Terms and Concepts** | **437** |
| | Backup and Recovery Considerations | 438 |
| | Oracle Recovery Structures and Processes | 439 |
| | Oracle Backup and Recovery Configuration | 439 |
| | Oracle Recovery Manager Overview | 440 |
| | Oracle Recovery Catalog Maintenance | 441 |

|        |                                                              |     |
|--------|--------------------------------------------------------------|-----|
|        | Physical Backups Without Oracle Recovery Manager             | 442 |
|        | Physical Backups Using Oracle Recovery Manager               | 444 |
|        | Types of Failures and Troubleshooting                        | 445 |
|        | Oracle Recovery Without Archiving                            | 446 |
|        | Complete Oracle Recovery with Archiving                      | 447 |
|        | Incomplete Oracle Recovery with Archiving                    | 449 |
|        | Oracle Export and Import Utilities                           | 450 |
|        | Additional Oracle Recovery Issues                            | 451 |
| **10** | **OCP Exam 4 Terms and Concepts**                            | **455** |
|        | Business Requirements and Tuning                             | 456 |
|        | Oracle Alert, Trace Files, and Events                        | 456 |
|        | Utilities and Dynamic Performance Views                      | 457 |
|        | Tuning Considerations for Different Applications             | 458 |
|        | SQL Tuning                                                   | 459 |
|        | Generic Operating System Tuning Issues and Oracle            | 462 |
|        | Tuning the Shared Pool                                       | 462 |
|        | Tuning the Buffer Cache                                      | 463 |
|        | Tuning the Redo Log Buffer                                   | 464 |
|        | Database Configuration and I/O issues                        | 465 |
|        | Using Oracle Blocks Efficiently                              | 467 |
|        | Optimizing Sort Operations                                   | 467 |
|        | Rollback Segment Tuning                                      | 468 |
|        | Monitoring and Detecting Lock Contention                     | 469 |
|        | Latch and Contention Issues                                  | 470 |
|        | Tuning with Oracle Expert                                    | 471 |
| **11** | **OCP Exam 5 Terms and Concepts**                            | **473** |
|        | Overview                                                     | 474 |
|        | Basic Net8 Architecture                                      | 474 |
|        | Basic Net8 Server-Side Configuration                         | 476 |
|        | Basic Net8 Client-Side Configuration                         | 477 |
|        | Usage and Configuration of Oracle Names                      | 478 |
|        | Usage and Configuration of Oracle Intelligent Agent for OEM  | 479 |
|        | Usage and Configuration of the Multithreaded Server          | 479 |
|        | Usage and Configuration of Connection Manager                | 480 |
|        | Troubleshoot the Network Environment                         | 482 |
|        | Security in the Network Environment                          | 485 |
| **12** | **OCP Oracle8i Upgrade Exam Terms and Concepts**             | **487** |
|        | Oracle8i New Features                                        | 488 |
|        | Java in the Database                                         | 488 |
|        | Memory Management                                            | 490 |

| | |
|---|---|
| Optimizer and Query Improvements | 491 |
| Summary Management | 492 |
| Indexes and Index-Organized Tables | 494 |
| Defining Object Relational Features | 496 |
| Manage Large Objects | 497 |
| Basic Partitioning Concepts | 498 |
| Partition Maintenance Operations | 500 |
| Composite Partitioning | 501 |
| Parallel DDL, Parallel DML, and Parallel Queries | 501 |
| Installation, Configuration, and Migration | 503 |
| Tablespace Management | 505 |
| Database Resource Manager | 506 |
| Miscellaneous Manageability Features | 507 |
| Recovery Manager | 508 |
| Miscellaneous Availability and Recoverability Features | 511 |
| Features of Net8 | 513 |
| SQL*Plus, PL/SQL, and National Language Support | 514 |
| Advanced Queuing | 515 |
| Database Security | 516 |
| Oracle Enterprise Manager Version 2 | 517 |
| Constraints | 518 |
| Index | 521 |

# Preface

My interest in Oracle certification began in 1996 when I read about the Oracle DBA certificate offered by the Chauncey Group. I found it difficult to prepare for that certification exam for two reasons. First, there was an absence of practice questions readily available. Second, preparation for the exam involved reviewing six or seven different manuals and Oracle Press books, none of which were particularly suited to the task. Judging from the response to the *Oracle8 Certified Professional DBA Certification Exam Guide* so far, it would seem others have had similar experiences.

This book, the *Oracle8 Certified Professional DBA Practice Exams,* is divided into two parts, the first of which contains practice exams for all five of the tests in the Oracle8 core DBA certification track from Oracle, plus the Oracle8*i* DBA upgrade exam. The first five chapters of core DBA practice exams are also suitable for preparing for the new Oracle8*i* DBA core exams. Explanations should clearly delineate both the Oracle8 and Oracle8*i* functionality, and how the functionality being tested has changed between Oracle8 and Oracle8*i*. I believe you will find this book to be a low-cost complement to the Oracle Certified Professional DBA Certification Exam Guides from Oracle Press or to any certification preparation plan.

The second part contains crib notes that will assist you in preparing for the real OCP DBA exam. The notes are broken out by section according to the OCP DBA Candidate

Guide, published by Oracle Corporation on the **http://education.oracle.com/ certification** Web site.

To get the most from this book, you need to answer the following question: what is your level of Oracle experience? To start assessing that question, take the first practice exam in the section. For those questions you get wrong, review background information to better understand the topic area. Then, when you feel more comfortable with the material, attempt the second exam. With a lot of practice (and a little luck!), you should be ready to tackle the real exam.

Finally, a note about errata. Because OCP covers such vast ground in a short time, this has become a living text. If you feel you have encountered difficulties due to errors, you can either check out **www.exampilot.com** to find the latest errata, or send me e-mail directly at **jcouchman@mindspring.com**.

Good luck!

# Acknowledgments

There are many people I would like to thank for their help with writing this book. My first and most heartfelt thanks goes to the dedicated readers of all of my other books, who took time out of their busy schedules to send feedback on those books. I have listened to your praise and constructive criticism and made every effort to correct and amplify my work based on the points you made. Please, keep the e-mail coming—it is by far the most effective way to make the books better!

Next, a note of gratitude to the folks at Oracle who make the book possible. Thanks to Julia Johnson and Ulrike Schwinn for their feedback and assistance with the technical content review and with the material covering Oracle8 and Oracle8*i*. Thanks also to the fine folks at Osborne—Scott Rogers, Jeremy Judson, and Monika Faltiss. Special thanks to the folks in editorial services and production as well—Ron Hull, LeeAnn Pickrell, Dennis Weaver, Stefany Otis, and Jenn Tust, for giving that page proof the rigorous looking over it needed.

This book is especially dedicated to my wonderful siblings. Deb, if I could point to a single person who made me the computer professional I am today, it would be you. Tony, I'm still grateful for that word processor you bought me before college—it was my first "writer's tool." Thanks also to my parents, Mom, Dad, Ele, and Ron, for all they have made possible for me. As always, thanks to my wonderful wife who tended to numerous details while I wrote. Stacy, you really are the greatest thing that ever happened to me.

Finally, I want to extend a warm gesture of thanks to a great group of folks at the Stonebridge Technologies Houston office and in the South Central service line, who made the months of June and July 2000 a lot of fun. Tim, Mike, Karen, Dave, S.K., Delores, Magda, Merina, Cortes, Don, Bryan, Bernadette, Harold, Jim B., Jim P., Ian, Travis, Matt, Laura, and Rigo—we will meet again. Special note for Cortes—I'll be looking for your name in bookstores nationwide … don't let me down!

# Introduction

The Oracle Certified Professional DBA certification exam series is the latest knowledge good from Oracle Corporation. Called OCP, it represents the culmination of many people's request for objective standards in one of the hottest markets in the software field, Oracle database administration. The presence of OCP on the market indicates an important reality about Oracle as a career path. Oracle is mature, robust, and stable for enterprise-wide information management. However, corporations facing a severe shortage of qualified Oracle professionals need a measurement for Oracle expertise.

The OCP certification core track for DBAs consists of five tests in the following areas of Oracle8: SQL and PL/SQL, database administration, performance tuning, network administration, and backup/recovery. As of this printing, each test consists of about 60 multiple choice questions pertaining to the recommended usage of Oracle databases. You have about 90 minutes to take each exam. The current content of those five exams covers Oracle through version 8.0. A sixth exam is available to test DBAs on the new features available in Oracle8*i*. Obtaining certification for Oracle8 through the core track is contingent on taking and passing *all five* core examinations, while certification on the upgrade track for Oracle8 and Oracle8*i* requires taking and passing the Oracle8 and Oracle8*i* new features exams.

## Why Get Certified?

If you are already an Oracle professional, you may wonder, "Why should I get certified?" Perhaps you have a successful career as an Oracle DBA, enjoying the instant prestige your resume gets with that one magic word on it. With market forces currently in your favor, you're right to wonder. But, while no one is saying you don't know Oracle when you put the magic word on your resume, can you prove how well you *do* know Oracle without undergoing a technical interview? I started asking myself that question last year when Oracle certification began to emerge. I was surprised to find out that, after years of using Oracle, developing Oracle applications, and administering Oracle databases for Fortune 500 companies, there were a lot of things about Oracle I *didn't* know. And the only reason I know them now is because I took the time and effort to become certified.

If you're looking for another reason to become certified in Oracle, consider the example of computer professionals with Novell NetWare experience in the late 1980s and early 1990s. It seemed that anyone with even a little experience in Novell could count on a fantastic job offer. Then Novell introduced its CNE/CNA programs. At first, employers were fine hiring professionals with or without the certificate. As time went on, however, employers no longer asked for computer professionals with Novell NetWare experience—they asked for CNEs and CNAs. A similar phenomenon can be witnessed in the arena of Microsoft Windows NT and 2000, where the MCSE has already become the standard by which those professionals are measuring their skills. If you want to stay competitive in the field of Oracle database administration, your real question shouldn't be *whether* you should become certified, but *when*.

If you are not in the field of Oracle database management, or if you want to advance your career using Oracle, there has never been a better time to do so. OCP is already altering the playing field for DBAs by changing the focus of the Oracle skill set from "how many years have you used it" to "*how well* do you know how to use it?" That shift benefits organizations using Oracle as much as it benefits the professionals who use Oracle because the emphasis is on *performance*, not attrition.

Managers who are faced with the task of hiring Oracle professionals can breathe a sigh of relief with the debut of OCP as well. By seeking professionals who are certified, managers can spend less time trying to determine if the candidate knows Oracle well enough to do the job and more time assessing the candidate's work habits and compatibility with the team.

## How Should You Prepare for the Exam?

If you spend your free time studying things like the name of the dynamic performance view that helps a DBA estimate the effect of adding buffers to the buffer cache, you are probably ready to take the OCP DBA exams now. For the rest of us, Oracle and other companies offer classroom- and computer-based training options to learn Oracle. Now, users have another option—the Oracle8 Certified Professional DBA Certification Exam Guides and this book! By selecting this book, you demonstrate two excellent characteristics—that you are committed to a superior career in the field of Oracle database administration, and that you care about preparing for the exam correctly and thoroughly. And by the way, the name of the dynamic performance view that helps a DBA estimate the effect of adding buffers to the buffer cache is V$CURRENT_BUCKET, and it is on the OCP DBA exam. That fact, along with thousands of others, is tested extensively in this book to help you prepare for, and pass, the OCP DBA certification exam.

## DBA Certification Past and Present

Oracle certification started in the mid 1990s with the involvement of the Chauncey Group International, a division of Educational Testing Service. With the help of many Oracle DBAs, Chauncey put together an objective, fact-based and scenario-based examination on Oracle database administration. This test did an excellent job of measuring knowledge of Oracle7, versions 7.0 to 7.2. Consisting of 60 questions, Chauncey's exam covered several different topic areas, including backup and recovery, security, administration, and performance tuning, all in one test.

Oracle Corporation has taken DBA certification several giant leaps ahead with the advent of OCP. Their certification examination is actually five tests, each consisting of about 60 questions. By quintupling the number of questions you must answer, Oracle requires that you have unprecedented depth of knowledge in Oracle database administration. Oracle has also committed to including scenario-based questions on the OCP examinations, and preparation material for these new questions is included in this book as well. Scenario-based questions require you not only to know the facts about Oracle, but also to understand how to apply those facts in real-life situations.

Oracle's final contribution to the area of Oracle certification is a commitment to reviewing and updating the material presented in the certification exams. Oracle-certified DBAs will be required to maintain their certification by retaking the certification exams periodically—meaning that those who certify will stay on the cutting edge of the Oracle database better than those who do not.

## Taking the Oracle Assessment Test

It is essential that you begin your preparation for the OCP DBA certification exams by taking the Oracle assessment test. The Oracle assessment test is a mock-up of the real exam, with questions designed to help you identify your personal areas of strength and weakness with Oracle. You can load the Oracle assessment test from the Oracle

Education Web site; its URL is **http://education.oracle.com/ certification**. You should load it onto your Windows-based computer and take the exams to determine which areas you need to study. You should also download the OCP Candidate Guide for the DBA 8.0 track, which publishes the topic areas for each exam.

Figure 1 is a diagram of the assessment test graphical user interface. The features of the interface are indicated in the figure. Several of the main features of the assessment test interface are explained here. The assessment test interface is similar to the actual Sylvan Prometric OCP DBA test driver, with a few exceptions as noted. At the top of the test, you can see how much time has elapsed and the number of questions you have answered. On the actual OCP exam, there is also a check box in the upper left-hand corner of the interface. You can use this check box to mark questions you would like to review later. The main window of the interface contains the actual question, along with the choices. The interface generally allows the user to select only one answer, unless the question directs you to select more answers. In this case, the interface will allow you to select only as many answers as the question requests. After answering a question, or marking the question for later review, the candidate can move onto the next question by clicking the appropriate button in the lower left-hand corner. The next button on the bottom allows you either to print the assessment test or to return to the previous question on the OCP exam. For the assessment test only, you can score your questions at any time by pressing the Grade Now button on the bottom right-hand side. Another feature worth noting is the Exhibit button. In some cases, you may need to view an exhibit to answer a question. If the question does not require use of an exhibit, the button will be grayed out.

The assessment test indicates your performance in a Grade Report window, like the one displayed in Figure 2. It details the number of questions you answered correctly, along with your percentage score based on 100 percent. Finally, a bar graph indicates how your performance compares to the maximum score possible on the exam. The OCP Exam reports your score immediately after you exit the exam, so you will know right then whether you pass or not in a similar fashion as the assessment test. Both interfaces offer you the ability to print a report of your score.

# Taking the OCP Exams

The score range for each OCP Exam is between 200 and 800. Since there is a 600-point range for potential scores, and typically there are 60 questions, each question is worth about 10 points. Given the recent use of questions with two or even three correct answers on OCP exams, the scoring method for actual OCP exams may differ somewhat from my explanation. There is no penalty for wrong answers. The OCP examinations required for the DBA track are listed next. The OCP DBA certification exam is administered at Sylvan Prometric test centers. To schedule your OCP Exam in the United States, call Sylvan Prometric at **1-800-891-EXAM**. For contact information

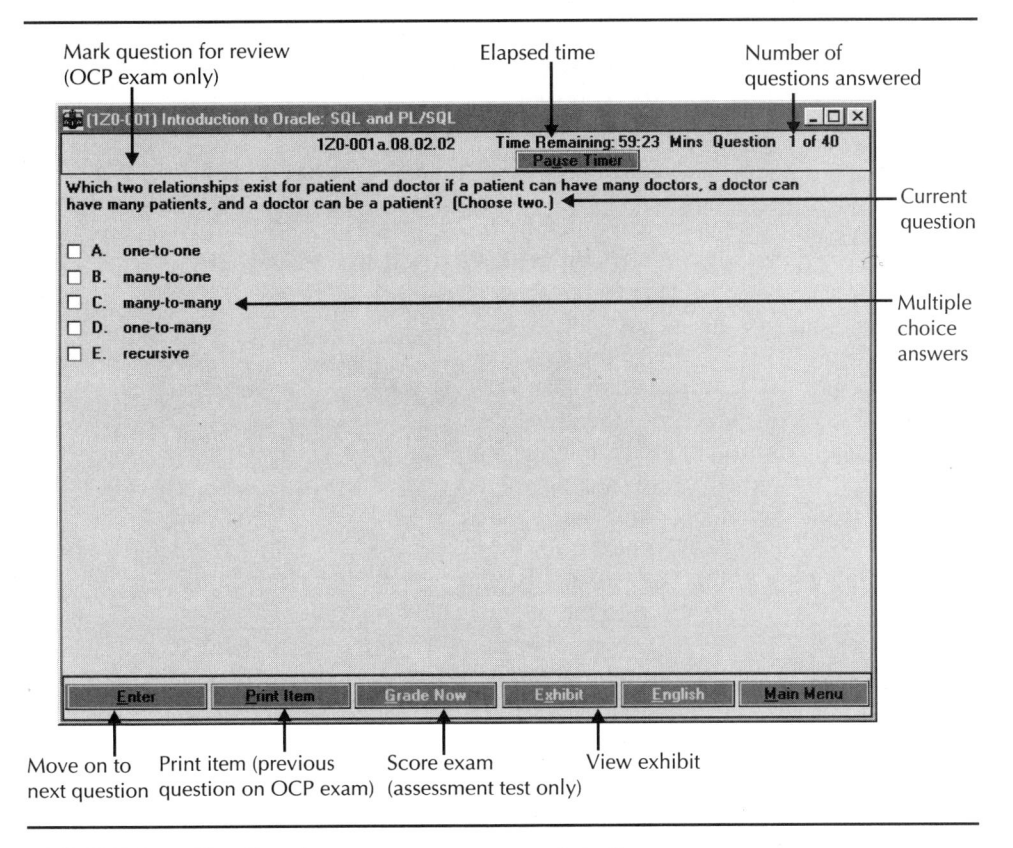

**FIGURE 1.** *The Oracle assessment test user interface*

outside the USA, refer to the assessment test software. For Oracle's official information about OCP Certification, visit **http://education.oracle.com/certification**. The exams in the OCP DBA series are as follows:

1. Oracle8: SQL and PL/SQL
2. Oracle8: Database Administration
3. Oracle8: Backup and Recovery
4. Oracle8: Performance Tuning
5. Oracle8: Network Administration
6. Oracle8i: New Features for Administrators (not required for Oracle8 Certification)

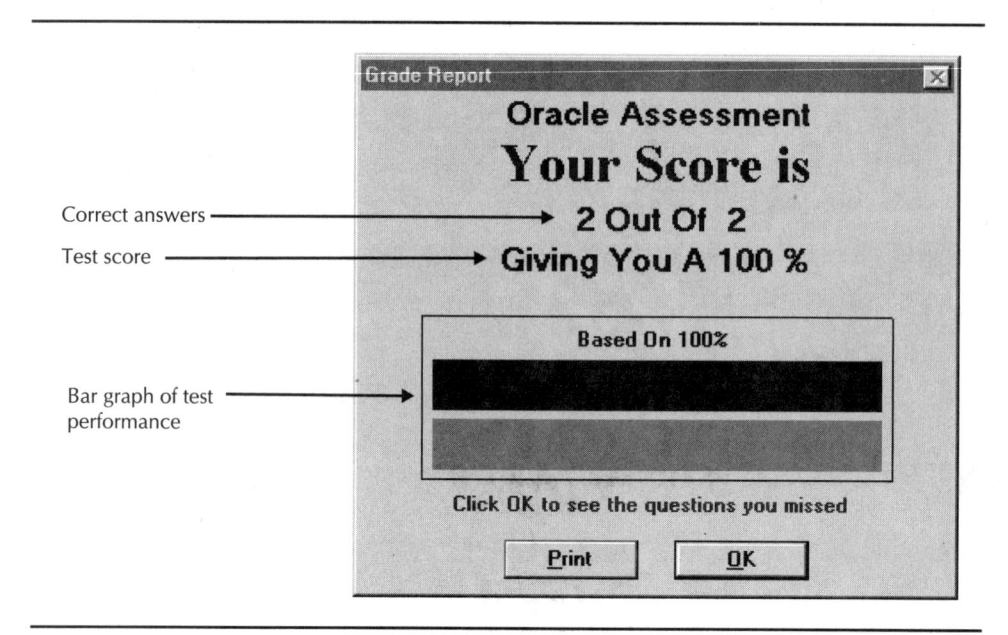

**FIGURE 2.** *Grading your test performance*

Here's some advice on taking the OCP exams. The first tip is, *don't wait until you're the world's foremost authority on Oracle to take the OCP Exam.* The passing score for most exams is approximately 650. You have to get 45–50 questions right, or about 75 to 80 percent of the exam. So, if you are getting about four out of five questions right on the assessment test or in the chapters, you should consider taking the OCP exam. Remember, you're certified if you pass with a 650 or an 800.

The next item is, *if you can't answer the question within 30 seconds, mark the check box in the upper left-hand corner of the OCP interface for review later.* The most significant difference between the OCP interface and the assessment test interface is a special screen appearing after you answer all the questions. This screen displays all your answers, along with a special indicator next to the questions you marked for review. This screen also displays a button to click in order to review the questions you marked. You should use this feature extensively. If you spend only 30 seconds answering each question in your first pass on the exam, you will have at least an hour to review the questions you're unsure of, with the added bonus of knowing you answered all the questions that were easiest first.

Third, *there is no penalty for guessing.* If you answer the question correctly, your score goes up ten points, if not, your score does not change. If you can eliminate any choices on a question, you should take the chance in the interest of improving your score. In some questions, the OCP exam requires you to specify two or even three choices—this can work in your favor, meaning you need to eliminate fewer choices to get the question right.

Finally, unless your level of expertise with Oracle is high in a particular area, *it is recommended that you take the exams in the sequential order listed previously.* This is especially recommended for readers whose background in Oracle is more on the beginner/intermediate level. This is even more important if you are using the Oracle8 Certified Professional DBA Exam Guides and this book to prepare for the exam. This is because each subsequent chapter of the Guides builds on information presented in the previous chapters. As such, you should read the Guides from beginning to end, and take the tests accordingly. Taking the exams in this manner will maximize your use of the Guides and your results on the tests.

# The New Scenario-Based Questions on the OCP Exam

Oracle Corporation has announced its intention to include scenario-based questions in the OCP DBA certification exam series. These questions require you to take the facts about Oracle and apply those facts to real-life situations portrayed on the exam—complete with exhibits and documents to substantiate the example—and determine the correct answer based on those exhibits and documents. In order to assist you better in preparation for these new test questions, the questions in this book have been designed to replicate scenario-based exam questions.

Finally, if you have comments about the book or would like to contact me about it, please do so by e-mail at **jcouchman@mindspring.com**. You can also find related information, such as posted corrections and amplifications, at **www.exampilot.com**.

# PART I

## OCP Practice Exams

# CHAPTER 1

## OCP Exam 1: Introduction to SQL and PL/SQL

OCP Exam 1 in the Oracle DBA track covers concepts and practices around the use of SQL and PL/SQL commands. To pass this exam, you need to demonstrate an understanding of the basic SQL constructs available in Oracle, including built-in functions. You should also understand the basic concepts behind an Oracle relational database management system. In more recent editions of OCP Exam 1, the focus has included understanding the use of the PL/SQL programming language. In addition, new features in PL/SQL introduced in Oracle8*i* are tested, so you should also be sure you understand these new features.

## OCP Exam I Topic Areas

The following topic areas are covered in OCP Exam 1. Note that these concepts are taken directly from the Oracle OCP Candidate Guide for OCP Exam 1, and are current as of the publication of this book. The topics and subtopics are as follows:

1. Overview of Relational Databases, SQL, and PL/SQL
    1.1. Discuss the theoretical and physical aspects of a relational database
    1.2. Describe the Oracle implementation of the RDBMS and ORDBMS
    1.3. Describe the use and benefits of PL/SQL
2. Writing Basic SQL Statements
    2.1. List the capabilities of SQL SELECT statements
    2.2. Execute a basic SELECT statement
    2.3. Differentiate between SQL statements and SQL*Plus commands
3. Restricting and Sorting Data
    3.1. Limit the rows retrieved by a query
    3.2. Sort the rows retrieved by a query
4. Single-Row Functions
    4.1. Describe various types of functions available in SQL
    4.2. Use character, number, and date functions in select statements
    4.3. Describe the use of conversion functions

**5.** Displaying Data from Multiple Tables

- **5.1.** Write SELECT statements to access data from more than one table using equality and nonequality joins
- **5.2.** View data that generally does not meet a join condition by using outer joins
- **5.3.** Join a table to itself

**6.** Aggregating Data Using Group Functions

- **6.1.** Identify the available group functions
- **6.2.** Describe the use of group functions
- **6.3.** Group data using the GROUP BY clause
- **6.4.** Include or exclude grouped rows using the HAVING clause

**7.** Subqueries

- **7.1.** Describe the types of problems that subqueries can solve
- **7.2.** Define subqueries
- **7.3.** List types of subqueries
- **7.4.** Write single-row and multiple-row subqueries

**8.** Multiple-Column Subqueries

- **8.1.** Write multiple-column subqueries
- **8.2.** Describe and maintain the behavior of subqueries when NULL values are retrieved
- **8.3.** Write subqueries in a FROM clause

**9.** Producing Readable Output from SQL*Plus

- **9.1.** Produce queries that require an input variable
- **9.2.** Customize the SQL*Plus environment
- **9.3.** Produce more readable output
- **9.4.** Create and execute script files
- **9.5.** Save customizations

10. Manipulating Data
    - 10.1. Describe each DML statement
    - 10.2. INSERT rows into a table
    - 10.3. UPDATE rows in a table
    - 10.4. DELETE rows from a table
    - 10.5. Control transactions
11. Creating and Managing Tables
    - 11.1. Describe the main database objects
    - 11.2. Create tables
    - 11.3. Describe the datatypes that can be used when specifying column definition
    - 11.4. Alter table definitions
    - 11.5. Drop, rename, and truncate tables
12. Including Constraints
    - 12.1. Describe constraints
    - 12.2. Create and maintain constraints
13. Creating Views
    - 13.1. Describe a view
    - 13.2. Create a view
    - 13.3. Retrieve data through a view
    - 13.4. INSERT, UPDATE, or DELETE data through a view
    - 13.5. Drop a view
14. Oracle Data Dictionary
    - 14.1. Describe the data dictionary views a user may access
    - 14.2. Query data from the data dictionary
15. Other Database Objects
    - 15.1. Describe database objects and their uses
    - 15.2. Create, maintain, and use sequences

## Chapter 1: OCP Exam 1: Introduction to SQL and PL/SQL

- **15.3.** Create and maintain indexes
- **15.4.** Create public and private synonyms

**16.** Controlling User Access
- **16.1.** Create users
- **16.2.** Create roles to ease setup and maintenance of the security model
- **16.3.** Use the GRANT and REVOKE commands to grant and revoke object privileges

**17.** Declaring variables
- **17.1.** List the benefits of PL/SQL
- **17.2.** Describe the basic PL/SQL block and its sections
- **17.3.** Describe the significance of variables in PL/SQL
- **17.4.** Declare PL/SQL variables
- **17.5.** Execute a PL/SQL block

**18.** Write Executable Statements
- **18.1.** Describe the significance of the executable section
- **18.2.** Write statements in the executable section
- **18.3.** Describe the rules of nested blocks
- **18.4.** Execute and test a PL/SQL block
- **18.5.** Use coding conventions

**19.** Interacting with the Oracle Server
- **19.1.** Write a successful SELECT statement in PL/SQL
- **19.2.** Declare the datatype and size of the PL/SQL variable dynamically
- **19.3.** Write DML statements in PL/SQL
- **19.4.** Control transactions in PL/SQL
- **19.5.** Determine the outcome of SQL statements

**20.** Writing Control Structures
- **20.1.** Identify the uses and types of control structures
- **20.2.** Construct an IF statement

- 20.3. Construct and identify different loop statements
- 20.4. Use logic tables
- 20.5. Control block flow using nested loops and labels

21. Working with Composite Datatypes
    - 21.1. Create user-defined PL/SQL records
    - 21.2. Create a record with the %ROWTYPE attribute
    - 21.3. Create a PL/SQL table
    - 21.4. Create a PL/SQL table of records
    - 21.5. Describe the difference between records, tables, and tables of records

22. Writing Explicit Cursors
    - 22.1. Distinguish between an implicit and an explicit cursor
    - 22.2. Use a PL/SQL record variable
    - 22.3. Write a CURSOR FOR loop

23. Advanced Explicit Cursor Concepts
    - 23.1. Write a cursor that uses parameters
    - 23.2. Determine when a FOR UPDATE clause in a cursor is required
    - 23.3. Determine when to use the WHERE CURRENT OF clause
    - 23.4. Write a cursor that uses a subquery

24. Handling Exceptions
    - 24.1. Define PL/SQL exceptions
    - 24.2. Recognize unhandled exceptions
    - 24.3. List and use different types of PL/SQL exception handlers
    - 24.4. Trap unanticipated errors
    - 24.5. Describe the effect of exception propagation in nested blocks
    - 24.6. Customize PL/SQL exception messages

# Practice Exam 1

1. You are formulating a SQL statement to retrieve data from Oracle. Which of the following SQL statements are invalid?

    **A.** SELECT NAME, JERSEY_NO WHERE JERSEY_NO = 6;

    **B.** SELECT NAME, JERSEY_NO FROM PLAYERS;

    **C.** SELECT * FROM PLAYERS WHERE JERSEY_NO = 6;

    **D.** SELECT JERSEY_NO FROM PLAYERS;

2. You can use the PL/SQL block example to answer the following question.

    ```
    DECLARE
    CURSOR My_Employees IS
    SELECT name, title FROM employee;
    My_Name VARCHAR2(30);
    My_Title VARCHAR2(30);
    BEGIN
    OPEN My_Employees;
    LOOP
    FETCH My_Employees INTO My_Name, My_Title;
    EXIT WHEN My_Employees%NOTFOUND;
    INSERT INTO MY_EMPS (MY_EMPNAME, MY_EMPTITLE)
    VALUES (My_Name, My_Title);
    END LOOP;
    CLOSE My_Employees;
    END;
    ```

    If you were rewriting this block of PL/SQL, which of the following types of loops would you use if you wanted to use the smallest amount of code?

    **A.** LOOP ... EXIT WHEN

    **B.** WHILE ... LOOP

    **C.** LOOP ... END LOOP

    **D.** CURSOR FOR LOOP

3. You are coding a complex PL/SQL block where several procedures call other procedures. You have one outermost procedure that calls all other procedures. If you wanted to prevent the user of the outermost procedure from having the procedure fail due to an unanticipated problem, you would include which of the following exceptions?

A. NO_DATA_FOUND

B. OTHERS

C. ZERO_DIVIDE

D. TOO_MANY_ROWS

4. You are attempting to develop a more robust PL/SQL application. Which of the following keywords allow you to associate a user-defined error message with an exception condition?

   A. PRAGMA

   B. OTHERS

   C. RAISE_APPLICATION_ERROR

   D. EXCEPTION

5. You are processing some data changes in your SQL*Plus session as part of one transaction. Which of the following choices does not typically indicate the end of a transaction?

   A. Issuing an UPDATE statement

   B. Issuing a COMMIT statement

   C. Issuing a ROLLBACK statement

   D. Ending your session

6. You have just removed 1,700 rows from a table that were no longer needed. In order to save the changes you've made to the database, which of the following statements are used?

   A. SAVEPOINT

   B. COMMIT

   C. ROLLBACK

   D. SET TRANSACTION

7. To identify the columns that are indexed exclusively as the result of their inclusion in a constraint, which of the following dictionary views would be appropriate?

   A. USER_INDEXES

   B. USER_TAB_COLUMNS

C. USER_COLUMNS

D. USER_CONS_COLUMNS

8. You are creating some tables in your database as part of the logical data model. Which of the following constraints have an index associated with them that is generated automatically by Oracle?

   A. Unique
   B. Foreign-key
   C. Check
   D. NOT NULL

9. You have a table with three associated indexes, two triggers, two references to that table from other tables, and a view. You issue the DROP TABLE CASCADE CONSTRAINTS statement. Which of the following objects will still remain after the statement is issued?

   A. The triggers
   B. The indexes
   C. The foreign keys in the other tables
   D. The view

10. All of the following DATE functions return a DATE datatype, except one. Which one is it?

    A. NEW_TIME
    B. LAST_DAY
    C. ADD_MONTHS
    D. MONTHS_BETWEEN

11. You issue a SELECT statement on the BANK_ACCT table containing the ORDER BY clause. Which of the following uses of the ORDER BY clause would produce an error?

    A. ORDER BY acctno DESC;
    B. ORDER BY 1;
    C. ORDER BY sqrt(1);
    D. ORDER BY acctno ASC;

12. You execute the query SELECT 5 + 4 FROM DUAL. You have never inserted data into the DUAL table before. Which of the following statements best describes the DUAL table?

    A. Dictionary view containing two schema names

    B. Table with one column and one row used in various operations

    C. Dictionary view containing two index names

    D. Table with two columns and no rows used in various operations

13. You issue the following statement:
    ```
    SELECT DECODE(ACCTNO, 123456, 'CLOSED', 654321, 'SEIZED',
    590395, 'TRANSFER','ACTIVE') FROM BANK_ACCT;
    ```
    If the value for ACCTNO is 503952, what information will this statement display?

    A. ACTIVE

    B. TRANSFER

    C. SEIZED

    D. CLOSED

14. You are entering several dozen rows of data into the BANK_ACCT table. Which of the following statements will enable you to execute the same statement again and again, entering different values for variables at statement runtime?

    A. INSERT INTO BANK_ACCT (ACCTNO, NAME) VALUES (123456,'SMITH');

    B. INSERT INTO BANK_ACCT (ACCTNO, NAME) VALUES (VAR1, VAR2);

    C. INSERT INTO BANK_ACCT (ACCTNO, NAME) VALUES (&VAR1, '&VAR2');

    D. INSERT INTO BANK_ACCT (SELECT ACCTNO, NAME FROM EMP_BANK_ACCTS);

15. You execute the following SQL statement: SELECT ADD_MONTHS ('28-APR-97',120) FROM DUAL. What will Oracle return?

    A. 28-APR-03

    B. 28-APR-07

    C. 28-APR-13

**D.** 28-APR-17

16. On Monday, June 26, 2037, at 10:30 at night, you issue the following statement against an Oracle database:

```
ALTER SESSION SET NLS_DATE_FORMAT =
'DAY MONTH DD, YYYY: HH:MIAM';
```

Then, you issue the following statement:

```
SELECT SYSDATE FROM DUAL;
```

**What will Oracle return?**

**A.** 26-JUN-37

**B.** June 26, 2037, 22:30

**C.** 26-JUN-2037

**D.** MONDAY JUNE 26, 2037: 10:30PM

17. You wish to join the data from two tables, A and B, into one result set and display that set in your session. Tables A and B have a common column, called C in both tables. Which of the following choices correctly displays the WHERE clause you would use if you wanted to see the data in table A where the value in column C = 5, even when there was no corresponding value in table B?

**A.** WHERE A.C = 5 AND A.C = B.C;

**B.** WHERE A.C = 5 AND A.C = B.C (+);

**C.** WHERE A.C = 5 AND A.C (+) = B.C(+);

**D.** WHERE A.C = 5;

18. Each of the following statements is true about referential integrity, except one. Which is it?

**A.** The referencing column in the child table must correspond with a primary key in the parent.

**B.** All values in the referenced column in the parent table must be present in the referencing column in the child.

**C.** The datatype of the referenced column in the parent table must be identical to the referencing column in the child.

**D.** All values in the referencing column in the child table must be present in the referenced column in the parent.

19. You have a group of values from a column in a table, and you would like to perform a group operation on them. Each of the following functions

operate on data from all rows as a group, except for which of the following choices?

A. AVG

B. SQRT

C. COUNT

D. STDDEV

20. You have a situation where you need to use the NVL function. All the following statements about the NVL function are true except one. Which is it?

A. NVL returns the second value passed if the first value is NULL.

B. NVL handles values of many different datatypes.

C. NVL returns NULL if the first value is not equal to the second.

D. Both the values passed for NVL must be the same datatype.

21. You are developing a stored procedure that handles table data. The %ROWTYPE expression in PL/SQL allows you to declare which of the following kinds of variables?

A. Records

B. VARCHAR2s

C. PLS_INTEGERs

D. NUMBERs

22. You create a sequence with the following statement:

```
CREATE SEQUENCE MY_SEQ
START WITH 394
INCREMENT BY 12
NOMINVALUE
NOMAXVALUE
NOCACHE
NOCYCLE;
```

Two users have already issued SQL statements to obtain NEXTVAL, and four more have issued SQL statements to obtain CURRVAL. If you issue a SQL statement to obtain the CURRVAL, what will Oracle return?

A. 406

B. 418

C. 430

D. 442

23. Table EMP has 17,394,430 rows in it. You issue a DELETE FROM EMP statement, followed by a COMMIT. Then, you issue a SELECT COUNT(*) to find out how many rows there are in the table. Several minutes later, Oracle returns 0. Why did it take so long for Oracle to obtain this information?

    A. The table was not empty.

    B. The high-water mark was not reset.

    C. Oracle always performs slowly after a COMMIT is issued.

    D. The table data did not exist to be counted anymore.

24. After creating a view, you realize that several columns were left out. Which of the following statements would you issue in order to add some columns to your view?

    A. ALTER VIEW

    B. CREATE OR REPLACE VIEW

    C. INSERT INTO VIEW

    D. CREATE VIEW

25. You are testing several SQL statements for accuracy and usefulness. A SQL statement will result in a Cartesian product as the result of which of the following items?

    A. A join statement without a WHERE clause

    B. The result of the SUM operation

    C. SELECT * FROM DUAL

    D. The result of the AVG operation

26. In order to set your SQL*Plus session so that your NLS_DATE_FORMAT information is altered in a specific way every time you log into Oracle, what method would be used?

    A. Setting preferences in the appropriate menu option

    B. Creating an appropriate LOGIN.SQL file

**C.** Issuing the ALTER USER statement

**D.** Issuing the ALTER TABLE statement

27. The EMP_SALARY table has two columns, EMP_USER and SALARY. EMP_USER is set to be the same as the Oracle username. To support user MARTHA, the salary administrator, you create a view with the following statement:

```
CREATE VIEW EMP_SAL_VW
AS SELECT EMP_USER, SALARY
FROM EMP_SALARY
WHERE EMP_USER <> 'MARTHA';
```

MARTHA is supposed to be able to view and update anyone in the company's salary except her own through this view. Which of the following clauses do you need to add to your view creation statement in order to implement this functionality?

**A.** WITH ADMIN OPTION

**B.** WITH GRANT OPTION

**C.** WITH SECURITY OPTION

**D.** WITH CHECK OPTION

28. You are developing PL/SQL code to manipulate and store data in an Oracle table. All of the following numeric datatypes in PL/SQL can be stored in an Oracle database, except one. Which is it?

**A.** NUMBER

**B.** RAW

**C.** DATE

**D.** INTEGER

29. You are performing some conversion operations in your PL/SQL programs. To convert a date value into a text string, you would use which of the following conversion functions?

**A.** CONVERT

**B.** TO_CHAR

**C.** TO_NUMBER

**D.** TO_DATE

Chapter 1: OCP Exam 1: Introduction to SQL and PL/SQL  17

30. Your attempt to read the view creation code stored in the Oracle data dictionary has encountered a problem. The view code appears to be getting cut off at the end. In order to resolve this problem, which of the following measures are appropriate?

    A. Increase the size of the dictionary view.

    B. Increase your user view allotment with the ALTER USER statement.

    C. Use the SET LONG statement.

    D. Use the SET NLS_DATE_FORMAT statement.

31. You issue the following UPDATE statement against the Oracle database:

    ```
    UPDATE BANK_ACCT SET NAME = 'SHAW';
    ```

    **Which records will be updated in that table?**

    A. The first record only

    B. All records

    C. The last record only

    D. None of the records

32. You are coding a complex PL/SQL block where several procedures call other procedures. You have one outermost procedure that calls all other procedures. If you only wanted to prevent the procedure from failing due to a situation where a SELECT INTO statement received two or more records, you would include which of the following exceptions?

    A. TOO_MANY_ROWS

    B. OTHERS

    C. ZERO_DIVIDE

    D. NO_DATA_FOUND

33. You create a table but then subsequently realize you needed a few new columns. To add those columns later, you would issue which of the following statements?

    A. CREATE OR REPLACE TABLE

    B. ALTER TABLE

    C. CREATE TABLE

    D. TRUNCATE TABLE

34. You are busy creating your tables based on an LDM. Which of the following constraints require the REFERENCES privilege in order to be created?

    A. Unique

    B. Foreign-key

    C. Check

    D. NOT NULL

35. The INVENTORY table has three columns: UPC_CODE, UNITS, and DELIV_DATE. The primary key is UPC_CODE. New records are added daily through a view. The view was created using the following code:

    ```
    CREATE VIEW DAY_INVENTORY_VW
    AS SELECT UPC_CODE, UNITS, DELIV_DATE
    FROM INVENTORY
    WHERE DELIV_DATE = SYSDATE
    WITH CHECK OPTION;
    ```

    What happens when a user tries to INSERT a record with duplicate UPC_CODE?

    A. The statement fails due to WITH CHECK OPTION clause.

    B. The statement will succeed.

    C. The statement fails due to primary-key constraint.

    D. The statement will INSERT everything except the date.

36. You need to search for text data in a column, but you only remember part of the string. Which of the following SQL operations allows the use of wildcard comparisons?

    A. IN

    B. EXISTS

    C. BETWEEN

    D. LIKE

37. You have a script you plan to run using SQL*Plus that contains one SQL statement that INSERTs data into one table. Which of the following options is the easiest way for this script to allow you to specify values for variables once in the script, in a way where there is no user interaction?

**A.** Use DEFINE to capture value

   **B.** Use ACCEPT to capture value for each run

   **C.** Using & to specify values at runtime for the statement

   **D.** Hardcoded values in the statement

38. You join data from two tables, EXPNS and EMP, into one result set and display that set in your session. The tables have a common column called EMPID. Which of the following choices correctly displays the WHERE clause you would use if you wanted to see the data in table EMP where the value in column EMPID = 39284, but only when there is a corresponding value in table EXPNS?

    **A.** WHERE EMP.EMPID = 39284 AND EMP.EMPID = EXPNS.EMPID;

    **B.** WHERE EMP.EMPID = 39284 (+) AND EMP.EMPID = EXPNS.EMPID;

    **C.** WHERE EMP.EMPID = EXPNS.EMPID;

    **D.** WHERE EMP.EMPID = 39284 AND EMP.EMPID = EXPNS.EMPID (+);

39. The %TYPE expression in PL/SQL can be used to declare which of the following kinds of variables?

    **A.** DATE variables

    **B.** TEXT variables

    **C.** PLS_INTEGER variables

    **D.** REAL variables

40. Review the following transcript of a SQL*Plus session:

    ```
    INSERT INTO INVENTORY (UPC_CODE, PRODUCT )
    VALUES (503949353,'HAZELNUT COFFEE');
    INSERT INTO INVENTORY (UPC_CODE, PRODUCT)
    VALUES (593923506,'SKIM MILK');
    INSERT INTO INVENTORY (UPC_CODE, PRODUCT)
    VALUES (402392340,'CANDY BAR');
    SAVEPOINT INV1;
    UPDATE INVENTORY SET UPC_CODE = 50393950
    WHERE UPC_CODE = 402392340;
    UPDATE INVENTORY SET UPC_CODE = 4104930504
    WHERE UPC_CODE = 402392340;
    ```

```
COMMIT;
UPDATE INVENTORY SET PRODUCT = (
SELECT PRODUCT FROM INVENTORY
WHERE UPC_CODE = 50393950)
WHERE UPC_CODE = 593923506;
ROLLBACK;
```

Which of the following UPC codes will not have records in the INVENTORY table as a result of this series of operations?

**A.** 593923506

**B.** 503949353

**C.** 4104930504

**D.** 50393950

41. You are cleaning information out of the Oracle database. Which of the following statements will get rid of all views that use a table at the same time you eliminate the table from the database?

   **A.** DROP VIEW

   **B.** ALTER TABLE

   **C.** DROP INDEX

   **D.** ALTER TABLE DROP CONSTRAINT

42. You want to join data from four tables into one result set and display that set in your session. Table A has a column in common with table B, table B with table C, and table C with table D. You want to further restrict data returned from the tables by only returning data where values in the common column shared by A and B equals 5. How many conditions should you have in the WHERE clause of your SELECT statement?

   **A.** 2

   **B.** 3

   **C.** 4

   **D.** 5

43. You are developing some code in PL/SQL. If you wanted to declare variables that could be used to store table column values, but didn't know the actual datatype of that column, PL/SQL allows you to declare which of the following kinds of variables?

A. %ROWTYPE variables

B. %TYPE variables

C. FLOAT variables

D. VARCHAR2 variables

44. You are attempting to explain the Oracle security model for an Oracle database to the new security administrator. What are two components of the Oracle database security model?

    A. Password authentication and granting privileges

    B. Password authentication and creating database objects

    C. Creating database objects and creating users

    D. Creating users and password authentication

45. You have a script you plan to run using SQL*Plus that contains several SQL statements that manage milk inventory in several different tables based on various bits of information. You want the output to go into a file for review later. Which command would you use?

    A. PROMPT

    B. ECHO

    C. SPOOL

    D. DEFINE

46. Your application's business logic aligns closely with an Oracle internal error. If you wanted to associate that internal error with a named exception for handling in your application, in which of the following areas in your procedure code must you include some support of this exception?

    A. DECLARATION and EXCEPTION only.

    B. DECLARATION, EXECUTION, and EXCEPTION.

    C. EXCEPTION only.

    D. No coding, definition, or exception handler are required to raise this exception.

47. You have a table called TEST_SCORE that stores test results by student personal ID number, test location, and date the test was taken. Tests given in various locations throughout the country are stored in this table. A student is not allowed to take a test for 30 days after failing it the first

time, and there is a check in the application preventing the student from taking a test twice in 30 days at the same location. Recently, it has come to everyone's attention that students are able to circumvent the 30-day rule by taking a test in a different location. Which of the following SQL statements would be useful for identifying the students who have done so?

**A.** SELECT A.STUDENT_ID, A.LOCATION, B.LOCATION FROM TEST_SCORE A, TEST_SCORE B WHERE A.STUDENT_ID = B.STUDENT_ID AND A.LOCATION = B.LOCATION AND TRUNC(A.TEST_DATE)+30 <= TRUNC(B.TEST_DATE) AND TRUNC(A.TEST_DATE)-30 >= TRUNC(B.TEST_DATE);

**B.** SELECT A.STUDENT_ID, A.LOCATION, B.LOCATION FROM TEST_SCORE A, TEST_SCORE B WHERE A.STUDENT_ID = B.STUDENT_ID AND A.LOCATION <> B.LOCATION AND TRUNC(A.TEST_DATE)+30 >= TRUNC(B.TEST_DATE) AND TRUNC(A.TEST_DATE)-30 <= TRUNC(B.TEST_DATE);

**C.** SELECT A.STUDENT_ID, A.LOCATION, B.LOCATION FROM TEST_SCORE A, TEST_SCORE B WHERE A.STUDENT_ID = B.STUDENT_ID AND A.LOCATION = B.LOCATION AND TRUNC(A.TEST_DATE)+30 >= TRUNC(B.TEST_DATE) AND TRUNC(A.TEST_DATE)-30 <= TRUNC(B.TEST_DATE);

**D.** SELECT A.STUDENT_ID, A.LOCATION, B.LOCATION FROM TEST_SCORE A, TEST_SCORE B WHERE A.STUDENT_ID = B.STUDENT_ID AND A.LOCATION <> B.LOCATION AND TRUNC(A.TEST_DATE)+30 <= TRUNC(B.TEST_DATE) AND TRUNC(A.TEST_DATE)-30 >= TRUNC(B.TEST_DATE);

48. In an expense application, you are searching for employee information in the EMPLOYEE table corresponding to an invoice number you have. The INVOICE table contains EMPID, the primary key for EMPLOYEE. Which of the following options is appropriate for obtaining data from EMPLOYEE using your invoice number?

    **A.** select * from EMPLOYEE where empid = &empid;

    **B.** select * from EMPLOYEE where empid = 69494;

    **C.** select * from EMPLOYEE where empid = (select empid from invoice where invoice_no = 4399485);

    **D.** select * from EMPLOYEE;

49. Which of the following uses does NOT describe an appropriate use of the HAVING clause?

    A. To put returned data into sorted order

    B. To exclude certain data groups based on known criteria

    C. To include certain data groups based on unknown criteria

    D. To include certain data groups based on known criteria

50. You are managing data access for an application with 163 tables and 10,000 users. Which of the following objects would assist in managing access in this application by grouping privileges into an object that can be granted to users at once?

    A. Sequences

    B. Tables

    C. Indexes

    D. Roles

51. After logging on to Oracle the first time to access table EMP, user SNOW is told to change his password. Which of the following statements allows him to do so?

    A. ALTER USER

    B. ALTER TABLE

    C. ALTER ROLE

    D. ALTER INDEX

52. User SNOW executes the following statement: SELECT * FROM EMP. This statement executes successfully, and SNOW can see the output. Table EMP is owned by user REED. What object would be required in order for this scenario to happen?

    A. User SNOW would need the role to view table EMP.

    B. User SNOW would need the privileges to view table EMP.

    C. User SNOW would need a synonym for table EMP.

    D. User SNOW would need the password for table EMP.

53. You develop a PL/SQL block containing a complex series of data changes. A user then executes your PL/SQL block. At what point will the data changes made be committed to the database?

   A. When the PL/SQL block finishes

   B. After each individual update

   C. Whenever the COMMIT command is issued

   D. When you, the creator of the PL/SQL block, disconnect from your session

54. If you would like to code your PL/SQL block to select some data from a table, and then run through each row of output and perform some work, which of the following choices best identifies how you would do so?

   A. Implicit cursors with a CURSOR FOR loop

   B. Implicit cursors with implicit cursor attributes

   C. Explicit cursors with a CURSOR FOR loop

   D. Explicit cursors with implicit cursor attributes

55. You have the following code block declaration in PL/SQL:

    ```
    DECLARE
    CURSOR EMP_1 IS
    SELECT * FROM EMP
    WHERE EMPID = '40593';
    CURSOR EMP_2 IS
    SELECT * FROM EMP
    WHERE EMPID = '50694';
    BEGIN...
    ```

    How could you rewrite this declaration block to reduce the number of explicit cursors used in your program?

   A. Using CURSOR FOR loops

   B. Using %ROWTYPE

   C. Using %NOTFOUND

   D. Passing EMPID values as parameters to the cursor

56. You issue the following statement in Oracle:

    ```
    SELECT * FROM EMP WHERE DEPT IN
    (SELECT DEPT FROM VALID_DEPTS
    WHERE DEPT_HEAD = 'SALLY'
    ORDER BY DEPT);
    ```

**Which of the following choices best indicates how Oracle will respond to this SQL statement?**

   **A.** Oracle returns the data selected

   **B.** Oracle returns data from EMP but not VALID_DEPTS

   **C.** Oracle returns data from VALID_DEPTS but not EMP

   **D.** Oracle returns an error

57. **You would like to reference a table in your PL/SQL block. What special syntactic attribute must you precede the SQL statement with in order to make the PL/SQL block compile?**

   **A.** Put a colon in front of all variables.

   **B.** Use /* */ to surround the SQL code.

   **C.** Prefix the command EXEC SQL in front of the statement.

   **D.** No special syntax is required.

58. **You are coding SQL statements in SQL*Plus. Which of the following is a valid SQL statement?**

   **A.** SELECT nvl(sqrt(59483)) FROM DUAL;

   **B.** SELECT to_char(nvl(sqrt(59483), '0')) FROM DUAL;

   **C.** SELECT TO_CHAR(nvl(sqrt(59483), 'VALID')) FROM DUAL;

   **D.** SELECT (to_char(nvl(sqrt(59483), '0')) FROM DUAL;

59. **The following output is from a SQL*Plus session:**

```
select PLAY_NAME||', ' || AUTHOR play_table from PLAYS;
My Plays and Authors
--------------------------------------
Midsummer Night's Dream, SHAKESPEARE
Waiting For Godot, BECKETT
The Glass Menagerie, WILLIAMS
```

   **Which of the following SQL*Plus commands produced it?**

   **A.** column PLAY_TABLE alias "My Plays and Authors"

   **B.** column PLAY_TABLE format a12

   **C.** column PLAY_TABLE heading "My Plays and Authors"

   **D.** column PLAY_TABLE as "My Plays and Authors"

**60. You create a view with the following statement:**

```
CREATE VIEW BASEBALL_TEAM_VW
AS SELECT B.JERSEY_NUM, B.POSITION, B.NAME
FROM BASEBALL_TEAM B
WHERE B.NAME = USER;
```

**What will happen when user JONES attempts to SELECT a listing for user SMITH?**

A. The SELECT will receive an error.

B. The SELECT will succeed.

C. The SELECT will receive NO ROWS SELECTED.

D. The SELECT will add data only to BASEBALL_TEAM.

# Practice Exam 2

1. Which of the following choices identifies a PL/SQL block containing the correct version of a CURSOR FOR loop?

    **A.**
    ```
    DECLARE
        CURSOR My_Employees IS
          SELECT * FROM employee;
        My_NameVARCHAR2(30);
        My_Title VARCHAR2(30);
    BEGIN
        OPEN My_Employees;
         FOR csr_rec IN My_Employees LOOP
            INSERT INTO MY_EMPS (MY_EMPNAME, MY_EMPTITLE)
            VALUES (My_Name, My_Title);
           END LOOP;
        CLOSE My_Employees;
    END;
    ```

    **B.**
    ```
    DECLARE
        CURSOR My_Employees IS
          SELECT * FROM employee;
        csr_rec VARCHAR2(30);
    BEGIN
       FOR csr_rec IN My_Employees LOOP
          EXIT WHEN My_Employees%NOTFOUND;
             INSERT INTO MY_EMPS (MY_EMPNAME, MY_EMPTITLE)
             VALUES (csr_rec.name, csr_rec.title);
           END LOOP;
    END;
    ```

    **C.**
    ```
    DECLARE
        CURSOR My_Employees IS
          SELECT name, title FROM employee;
    BEGIN
       FOR csr_rec IN My_Employees LOOP
             INSERT INTO MY_EMPS (MY_EMPNAME, MY_EMPTITLE)
             VALUES (csr_rec.name, csr_rec.title);
           END LOOP;
    END;
    ```

    **D.**
    ```
    DECLARE
        CURSOR My_Employees IS
          SELECT name, title FROM employee;
    ```

```
        My_Name VARCHAR2(30);
        My_Title VARCHAR2(30);
    BEGIN
        OPEN My_Employees;
         LOOP
            FETCH My_Employees INTO My_Name, My_Title;
            EXIT WHEN My_Employees%NOTFOUND;
            INSERT INTO MY_EMPS (MY_EMPNAME, MY_EMPTITLE)
            VALUES (My_Name, My_Title);
           END LOOP;
        CLOSE My_Employees;
    END;
```

2. Your attempt to read the trigger creation code stored in the Oracle data dictionary has encountered a problem. The view code appears to be getting cut off at the end. In order to resolve this problem, which of the following measures are appropriate?

    **A.** Increase the size of the dictionary view.

    **B.** Increase your user view allotment with the ALTER USER statement.

    **C.** Use the SET LONG statement.

    **D.** Use the SET NLS_DATE_FORMAT statement.

3. Inspect the following SQL statement:
```
SELECT FARM_NAME, COW_NAME,
COUNT(CARTON) AS NUMBER_OF_CARTONS
FROM COW_MILK
GROUP BY COW_NAME;
```
   Which of the following choices contains the line with the error?

    **A.** SELECT FARM_NAME, COW_NAME,

    **B.** COUNT(CARTON) AS NUMBER_OF_CARTONS

    **C.** FROM COW_MILK

    **D.** GROUP BY COW_NAME;

    **E.** There are no errors in the statement.

4. All of the following types of PL/SQL blocks are stored within the Oracle database for reusability, except for one type. Which type is it?

    **A.** Functions

- **B.** Procedures
- **C.** Package specs
- **D.** Package bodies
- **E.** Anonymous blocks
- **F.** Triggers

5. Inspect the following SQL statement:

```
SELECT COW_NAME,
  MOD(CARTON, FILL_STATUS)
FROM COW_MILK
GROUP BY COW_NAME;
```

   **Which of the following lines contains an error?**

   - **A.** SELECT COW_NAME,
   - **B.** MOD(CARTON, FILL_STATUS)
   - **C.** FROM COW_MILK
   - **D.** GROUP BY COW_NAME;
   - **E.** There are no errors in this statement.

6. You are writing queries against an Oracle database. Which of the following queries takes advantage of an inline view?

   - **A.** SELECT * FROM EMP_VW WHERE EMPID = (SELECT EMPID FROM INVOICE WHERE INV_NUM = 5506934);
   - **B.** SELECT A.LASTNAME, B.DEPT_NO FROM EMP A, (SELECT EMPID, DEPT_NO FROM DEPT) B WHERE A.EMPID = B.EMPID;
   - **C.** SELECT * FROM EMP WHERE EMPID IN (SELECT EMPID FROM INVOICE WHERE INV_NUM > 23);
   - **D.** SELECT 'SELECT * FROM EMP_VW WHERE EMPID IS NOT NULL;' FROM USER_TABLES;

7. For the following question, assume that before the following PL/SQL block is executed, table MY_TAB contains one column called 'COLUMN1', and one row with the value 'FLIBBERJIBBER'.

```
DECLARE
 VAR1 VARCHAR2(1);
 VAR2 VARCHAR2(1);
IS
```

```
BEGIN
  SELECT TO_CHAR(CEIL(SQRT(40)))
  INTO VAR2
  FROM DUAL;
  SELECT SUBSTR(COLUMN1,4,1)
  INTO VAR1
  FROM MY_TAB;
  IF VAR1 = 'J' THEN
     VAR2 := '5';
  ELSIF VAR2 = '7' THEN
     VAR2 := 'L';
  ELSE
     VAR2 = '9';
  END IF;
  INSERT INTO MY_TAB VALUES (VAR2);
  COMMIT;
END;
```

**What is the value of COLUMN1 after executing this code block?**

**A.** 5

**B.** 7

**C.** L

**D.** 9

**E.** J

8. **You create the following PL/SQL block:**

```
DECLARE
  VAR1 CONSTANT NUMBER := 90;
  VAR2 NUMBER := 0;
BEGIN
  SELECT ACCTNO
  INTO VAR2
  FROM BANK_ACCT
  WHERE NAME = 'LEWIS';
   VAR1 := VAR2 + 3049;
END;
```

**Which of the following lines in this block of PL/SQL code will produce an error?**

**A.** VAR2 NUMBER := 0;

**B.** INTO VAR2

C. WHERE NAME = 'LEWIS';

D. VAR1 := VAR2 + 3049;

E. There are no errors in this PL/SQL block.

9. You are preparing to compile a block of PL/SQL code. The lines in the block are shown in the choices below:

```
CREATE FUNCTION FOO (VAR1 IN VARCHAR2) IS
  VAR2 VARCHAR2(1);
BEGIN
  SELECT GENDER INTO VAR2 FROM EMP
    WHERE LASTNAME = 'SMITHERS';
  IF VAR1 = 6 THEN RETURN (6) ELSE RETURN (8);
END;
```

Which of the lines of PL/SQL code contain an error?

A. CREATE FUNCTION FOO (VAR1 IN VARCHAR2) IS

B. SELECT GENDER INTO VAR2 FROM EMP

C. WHERE LASTNAME = 'SMITHERS';

D. IF VAR1 = 6 THEN RETURN (6) ELSE RETURN (8);

E. There are no errors in this PL/SQL block.

10. You have several indexes on a table that you want to remove. You want to avoid the indexes associated with constraints, however. Each of the following statements will work for removing an index associated with a constraint, except one. Which choice is it?

A. DROP INDEX

B. ALTER TABLE DROP PRIMARY KEY CASCADE

C. ALTER TABLE DROP CONSTRAINT

D. DROP TABLE

11. You are managing constraints on a table in Oracle. Which of the following choices correctly identifies the limitations on CHECK constraints?

A. Values must be obtained from a lookup table

B. Values must be part of a fixed set defined by CREATE or ALTER TABLE

C. Values must include reserved words like SYSDATE and USER

D. Column cannot contain a NULL value

**12.** Review the following statement:

```
CREATE TABLE FOOBAR
( MOO VARCHAR2(3),
  BOO NUMBER);
```

This table contains 60,000,000 rows. You issue the following statement:

```
SELECT MOO, BOO FROM FOOBAR WHERE MOO = 'ABC'
```

This value appears in column MOO less than 10 percent of the time. Yet, the query takes several minutes to resolve. Which of the following explanations is the best reason why?

**A.** Oracle didn't use the existing primary key index.

**B.** SELECT statements that do not use views take longer to resolve.

**C.** Table FOOBAR has no primary key, and therefore no index on MOO.

**D.** The table had been dropped and re-created.

**13.** You have created a table called EMP with a primary key called EMP_PK_01. In order to identify any objects that may be associated with that table and primary key, what dictionary views and characteristics would you look for?

**A.** USER_SEQUENCES, sequences created at the same time

**B.** USER_TABLES, tables with the same number of columns

**C.** USER_IND_COLUMNS, constraints with the same name as the table

**D.** USER_INDEXES, indexes with the same name as the constraint

**14.** You are designing your database, and you are attempting to determine the best method for indexing your tables. Identify a main advantage for using bitmap indexes on a database.

**A.** To improve performance on columns with many unique values

**B.** To improve performance on columns with few unique values

**C.** To improve performance on columns with all unique values

**D.** To improve performance on sequences with all unique values

**15.** You can use the PL/SQL block example to answer the following question.

```
DECLARE
  CURSOR CARTON_CRSR IS
  SELECT CARTON FROM MILK;
  MY_CARTON MILK.CARTON%TYPE;
BEGIN
```

```
    OPEN CARTON_CRSR;
    LOOP
        FETCH CARTON_CRSR INTO MY_CARTON;
        INSERT INTO MY_MILK_CRATE (CARTON)
        VALUES (MY_CARTON);
    END LOOP;
    CLOSE CARTON_CRSR;
END;
```

**What is wrong with this PL/SQL block?**

**A.** It will not work unless the loop is rewritten as a CURSOR FOR loop.

**B.** The exception handler must be defined if cursor is not declared.

**C.** The user does not have permission to execute the block.

**D.** A loop exit condition must be defined.

**E.** There are no errors in this code block.

16. **Your PL/SQL block includes the following statement:**

```
SELECT EMP_ID
INTO MY_EMPID
FROM EMPLOYEE
WHEN LASTNAME = 'FRANKLIN';
```

**You want Oracle to process the situation where no data is retrieved for that LASTNAME value. Which of the following actions should be taken?**

**A.** Include the %FOUND implicit cursor attribute

**B.** Include the %NOTFOUND implicit cursor attribute

**C.** Include the WHEN ROWTYPE_MISMATCH exception

**D.** Nothing, Oracle raises this as an exception automatically.

17. **User JANKO would like to insert a row into the EMPLOYEE table that has three columns: EMPID, LASTNAME, and SALARY. The user would like to enter data for EMPID 59694, LASTNAME Harris, but no salary. Which statement would work best?**

**A.** insert into EMPLOYEE values (59694,'HARRIS', NULL);

**B.** insert into EMPLOYEE values (59694,'HARRIS');

**C.** insert into EMPLOYEE (EMPID, LASTNAME, SALARY) values (59694,'HARRIS');

**D.** insert into EMPLOYEE (select 59694 from 'HARRIS');

18. You join data from two tables, COW_MILK (C) and CARTON_CRATE (C1), into one result set and display that set in your session. The tables have a common column, called CARTON_NUM in both tables. Which of the following choices correctly displays the WHERE clause you would use if you wanted to see the data in table COW_MILK for BESS the cow and all corresponding information in CARTON_CRATE, where if there is no data in CARTON_NUM, you don't want to see the data in COW_MILK?

    A. WHERE C.COW_NAME <> 'BESS' AND C.CARTON_NUM = C1.CARTON_NUM;

    B. WHERE C.CARTON_NUM = C1.CARTON_NUM;

    C. WHERE C.COW_NAME = 'BESS';

    D. WHERE C.COW_NAME = 'BESS' AND C.CARTON_NUM = C1.CARTON_NUM;

    E. WHERE C.COW_NAME = 'BESS' AND C.CARTON_NUM = C1.CARTON_NUM (+);

19. You create a table with a primary key that is populated on INSERT with a value from a sequence, then add several hundred rows to the table. You then drop and re-create the sequence with the original sequence code. Suddenly, your users are getting constraint violations. Which of the following explanations is most likely the cause?

    A. Dropping a sequence also removes any associated primary keys.

    B. Any cached sequence values before it was dropped are unusable.

    C. The table is read only.

    D. The INSERTs contain duplicate data due to the reset sequence.

20. You are developing SQL statements for the application. Which of the following SQL operations requires the use of a subquery?

    A. IN

    B. EXISTS

    C. BETWEEN

    D. LIKE

21. Review the following transcript from a SQL*Plus session:

```
SELECT CEIL(4093.505) FROM DUAL;
CEIL(4093.505)
```

```
------------------
          4094
```

Which single-row function could not be used to produce 4093 from the number passed to the CEIL function?

- **A.** ROUND
- **B.** TRUNC
- **C.** FLOOR
- **D.** ABS

22. You have a script you plan to run using SQL*Plus that contains several SQL statements that update banking information for one person in several different tables based on name. Since the script only changes information for one person, you want the ability to enter the name only once, and have that information reused throughout the script. Which of the following options is the best way to accomplish this goal in such a way that you don't have to modify the script each time you want to run it?

- **A.** Use DEFINE to capture name value for each run
- **B.** Use ACCEPT to capture name value for each run
- **C.** Using the & character to specify lexical substitution for names at runtime
- **D.** Hardcode names in all SQL statements, and change the value each run

23. You need to undo some data changes. Which of the following data changes cannot be undone using the ROLLBACK command?

- **A.** UPDATE
- **B.** TRUNCATE
- **C.** DELETE
- **D.** INSERT

24. You are developing some code to handle transaction processing. Each of the following items signifies the beginning of a new transaction, except one. Which is it?

- **A.** SAVEPOINT
- **B.** SET TRANSACTION
- **C.** Opening a new session
- **D.** COMMIT

**25.** The following SQL statement is invalid:

```
SELECT   PRODUCT, BRAND
WHERE UPC_CODE = '650-35365656-34453453454-45';
```

Which of the following choices indicate an area of change that would make this statement valid?

**A.** A SELECT clause

**B.** A FROM clause

**C.** A WHERE clause

**D.** An ORDER BY clause

**26.** You can use the PL/SQL block example to answer the following question.

```
DECLARE
   CURSOR UPC_CODE_CRSR IS
     SELECT UPC_CODE FROM INVENTORY;
   MY_UPC_CODE INVENTORY%ROWTYPE;
BEGIN
    OPEN UPC_CODE_CRSR;
      LOOP
         FETCH UPC_CODE_CRSR INTO MY_UPC_CODE;
         EXIT WHEN UPC_CODE_CRSR%NOTFOUND;
         INSERT INTO MY_SHOPPING_CART (UPC_CODE)
         VALUES (UPC_CODE_CRSR);
       END LOOP;
    CLOSE UPC_CODE_CRSR;
END;
```

What is wrong with this PL/SQL block?

**A.** It will not work unless loop is rewritten as a CURSOR FOR loop.

**B.** The exception handler must be defined if cursor is not declared.

**C.** The user does not have permission to execute the block.

**D.** Values from a cursor cannot be referenced directly.

**27.** You are coding a PL/SQL block. PROC_A calls PROC_B, which then calls PROC_C, and PROC_B has no exception handler. If you wanted to prevent the PROC_A procedure from failing due to a situation in PROC_B where the divisor in a division statement was zero, how would you address this in your code?

A. Use an IF %ZERODIVIDE statement immediately following the math operation.

B. Code a WHEN ZERO_DIVIDE exception handler in PROC_C.

C. Code a WHEN OTHERS exception handler in PROC_A.

D. Code a WHEN OTHERS exception handler in PROC_C.

28. If you wanted to define an exception that caused no Oracle errors but represented a violation of some business rule in your application, in which of the following areas in your procedure code must you include some support of this exception?

    A. DECLARATION and EXCEPTION only

    B. DECLARATION, EXECUTION, and EXCEPTION

    C. EXCEPTION only

    D. No coding or definition is required to raise this exception.

29. You are at the beginning of your current transaction, and want to prevent your transaction from being able to change data in the database. To prevent any statements in the current transaction from altering database tables, which statement is used?

    A. SET TRANSACTION

    B. ROLLBACK

    C. COMMIT

    D. SAVEPOINT

30. Your application searches for data in the EMP table on the database on a nullable column indicating whether a person is male or female. To improve performance, you decide to index it. The table contains over 2,000,000 rows, and the column contains few NULL values. Which of the following indexes would be most appropriate?

    A. Nonunique B-tree index

    B. Unique B-tree index

    C. Bitmap index

    D. Primary-key indexes

**31.** Your employee expense application stores information for invoices in one table. Each invoice can have several items, which is stored in another table. Each invoice may have one or more items, or none at all, but every item must correspond to one invoice. The relationship between the invoice table and invoice item table is best marked as what kind of relationship on a logical data model?

   **A.** Optional, one-to-many

   **B.** Mandatory, one-to-many

   **C.** Mandatory, one-to-one

   **D.** Optional, one-to-one

**32.** You issue the following statement:

```
SELECT DECODE(UPC_CODE, 40390, 'DISCONTINUED', 65421, 'STALE',
90395, 'BROKEN', 'ACTIVE') FROM INVENTORY;
```

   If the value for ACCTNO is 20395, what information will this statement display?

   **A.** DISCONTINUED

   **B.** STALE

   **C.** BROKEN

   **D.** ACTIVE

**33.** In considering the logical aspects to physical aspects of a database, which of the following choices best represents the mapping of physical datafiles to their logical counterparts?

   **A.** Extents

   **B.** Tablespaces

   **C.** Segments

   **D.** Blocks

**34.** You are comparing the storage implementation strategy employed by Oracle to the strategy for storage implementation used in hierarchical database systems like IMS. Which three of the following choices represent advantages of the RDBMS implementation that are not present in hierarchical databases?

   **A.** RDBMS requires that you define how to obtain data

B. RDBMS defines how to obtain data for you

C. RDBMS can model master-detail relationships

D. RDBMS allows flexibility in changing data relationships

E. RDBMS is able to model relationships other than master-detail

35. Which of the following choices does not identify a benefit for using PL/SQL that a developer might want to employ in an Oracle RDBMS application?

A. Ease of accessing data stored in Oracle

B. Ease of integrating programs written in different languages

C. Ability to manipulate cursor data

D. Ability to handle errors without explicit conditional operations

36. You are developing advanced queries for an Oracle database. Which of the following WHERE clauses makes use of Oracle's ability to logically test values against a set of results returned without explicitly knowing what the set is before executing the query?

A. WHERE COL_A = 6

B. WHERE COL_A IN (6,7,8,9,10)

C. WHERE COL_A BETWEEN 6 AND 10

D. WHERE COL_A IN (SELECT NUM FROM TAB_OF_NUMS)

37. You are developing a multiple-row query to handle a complex and dynamic comparison operation in the Olympics. Two tables are involved. CONTESTANT lists all contestants from every country, and MEDALS lists every country and the number of gold, silver, and bronze medals they have. If a country has not received one of the three types of medals, a zero appears in the column. Thus, a query will always return data, even for countries that haven't won a medal. Which of the following queries shows only the contestants from countries with more than 10 medallists of any type?

A. SELECT NAME FROM CONTESTANT C, MEDALS M WHERE C.COUNTRY = M.COUNTRY;

B. SELECT NAME FROM CONTESTANT WHERE COUNTRY C IN (SELECT COUNTRY FROM MEDALS M WHERE C.COUNTRY = M.COUNTRY)

C. SELECT NAME FROM CONTESTANT WHERE COUNTRY C = (SELECT COUNTRY FROM MEDALS M WHERE C.COUNTRY = M.COUNTRY)

D. SELECT NAME FROM CONTESTANT WHERE COUNTRY IN (SELECT COUNTRY FROM MEDALS WHERE NUM_GOLD + NUM_SILVER + NUM_BRONZE > 10)

38. You issue the following query in a SQL*Plus session:

```
SELECT NAME, AGE, COUNTRY FROM CONTESTANT
WHERE (COUNTRY, AGE) IN ( SELECT COUNTRY, MIN(AGE)
FROM CONTESTANT GROUP BY COUNTRY);
```

Which of the following choices identifies both the type of query and the expected result from the Oracle database?

A. Single-row subquery, the youngest contestant from one country

B. Multiple-row subquery, the youngest contestant from all countries

C. Multiple-column subquery, the youngest contestant from all countries

D. Multiple-column subquery, Oracle will return an error because '=' should replace 'IN'

39. The contents of the CONTESTANTS table are listed as follows:

```
NAME              AGE             COUNTRY
---------------   -------------   ---------------
BERTRAND          24              FRANCE
GONZALEZ          29              SPAIN
HEINRICH          25              GERMANY
TAN               39              CHINA
SVENSKY           30              RUSSIA
SOO               21
```

You issue the following query against this table:

```
SELECT NAME FROM CONTESTANT
WHERE (COUNTRY, AGE) IN ( SELECT COUNTRY, MIN(AGE)
FROM CONTESTANT GROUP BY COUNTRY);
```

What is the result?

A. SOO

B. HEINRICH

C. BERTRAND

D. GONZALEZ

**Chapter 1: OCP Exam 1: Introduction to SQL and PL/SQL** **41**

40. An object in Oracle contains many columns that are functionally dependent on the key column for that object. The object requires segments to be stored in areas of the database other than the data dictionary. The object in question is correctly referred to as which of the following objects?

    **A.** CURSOR

    **B.** TABLE

    **C.** SEQUENCE

    **D.** VIEW

41. You are defining where to place information in a PL/SQL block. If you wanted the block to contain a conditional operation that determined whether a portion of code would be executed based on the value returned from a query, which section of the PL/SQL block would you write the code into?

    **A.** Declaration

    **B.** Executable

    **C.** Exception

    **D.** Package specification

42. You can use the following PL/SQL block to answer this question:

    ```
    DECLARE
      CURSOR UPC_CODE_CRSR IS
        SELECT UPC_CODE FROM INVENTORY;
    BEGIN
       MY_UPC_CODE INVENTORY%ROWTYPE;
       OPEN UPC_CODE_CRSR;
         LOOP
            FETCH UPC_CODE_CRSR INTO MY_UPC_CODE;
            EXIT WHEN UPC_CODE_CRSR%NOTFOUND;
            INSERT INTO MY_SHOPPING_CART (UPC_CODE)
            VALUES (UPC_CODE_CRSR);
         END LOOP;
       CLOSE UPC_CODE_CRSR;
    END;
    ```

    **What is wrong with this code block?**

    **A.** The variable is declared incorrectly.

    **B.** Appropriate looping values are not used.

C. The INSERT statement is incorrectly defined.

D. The loop must be closed in the exception handler.

43. You need to execute a PL/SQL procedure. Which of the following choices does not represent a way to do so?

    A. With the EXECUTE command from SQL*Plus

    B. From within a procedure

    C. From within a SELECT statement

    D. Using the START command

44. You are declaring variables in PL/SQL. Which two of the following choices are not methods that can be used to define variables with an initial value?

    A. VAR_1 CONSTANT NUMBER(3) :=96;

    B. VAR_1 NUMBER(3) :=96;

    C. VAR_1 NUMBER(3) DEFAULT 96;

    D. VAR_1 NUMBER(3) INITIAL 96;

45. You are developing a PL/SQL block in Oracle. Which of the following standard parts of a PL/SQL block are required for proper compilation and use?

    A. Declaration section

    B. Exception section

    C. Execution section

    D. Parameter passing

46. You may use the following PL/SQL block to answer this question:

```
DECLARE
PROCEDURE UPDATE_EMP_SAL ( P_EMPID IN NUMBER, P_SAL IN NUMBER) IS BEGIN
UPDATE EMP SET SALARY = SAL WHERE EMPID = P_EMPID;
END;
MY_EMPID NUMBER := 12345;
MY_SAL NUMBER DEFAULT 50000;
BEGIN
UPDATE_EMP_SAL (MY_EMPID, MY_SAL);
END;
```

**What is wrong with this PL/SQL block?**

**A.** Blocks containing named subprograms must also be named.

**B.** Variables passed as parameters must have the same name as the parameter.

**C.** The nested block must be defined after variables used in the main block.

**D.** The DEFAULT keyword is invalid in PL/SQL.

**47.** Your application uses database objects in distributed systems owned by many users. In masking complexity added by referencing those various objects, which of the following choices identify a situation where use of synonyms is not permitted?

**A.** Package constants in the local procedure

**B.** Procedures in a remote system

**C.** Procedures owned by another user

**D.** Tables owned by another user in a remote system

**48.** You are developing a complex PL/SQL routine. Which of the following control structures in PL/SQL can be used for unconditional branching to a particular area of the code block?

**A.** IF TRUE THEN

**B.** LOOP

**C.** IF-THEN-ELSE

**D.** GOTO

**49.** The contents of the CONTESTANTS table are listed as follows:

```
NAME                AGE             COUNTRY
----------------    --------------  ---------------
BERTRAND            24              FRANCE
GONZALEZ            29              SPAIN
HEINRICH            22              GERMANY
TAN                 39              CHINA
SVENSKY             30              RUSSIA
SOO                 21
```

Use the following PL/SQL block to answer the question:

```
DECLARE
 VAR1 VARCHAR2(20);
 VAR2 NUMBER := 0;
```

```
BEGIN
 SELECT NAME INTO VAR1 FROM CONTESTANT
 WHERE COUNTRY = 'JAPAN';
 IF VAR1 = 'GERMANY' THEN
    VAR2 := LENGTH(VAR1);
ELSIF VAR1 = 'RUSSIA' THEN
 VAR2 := LENGTH(VAR1) + 15;
ELSIF VAR1 = 'FRANCE' THEN
 VAR2 := LENGTH(VAR1) + 25;
ELSIF VAR1 = 'GERMANY' THEN
 VAR2 := LENGTH(VAR1) + 35;
ELSIF VAR1 = 'CHINA' THEN
 VAR2 := LENGTH(VAR1) + 45;
ELSE
   VAR2 := LENGTH(VAR1) + 55;
END IF;
END;
```

**What is the value of VAR2 at the end of this code block?**

**A.** 7

**B.** 21

**C.** 55

**D.** NULL

**50.** The contents of the CONTESTANTS table are listed as follows:

```
NAME                    AGE             COUNTRY
----------------        ----------      ---------------
BERTRAND                 24             FRANCE
GONZALEZ                 29             SPAIN
HEINRICH                 22             GERMANY
TAN                      39             CHINA
SVENSKY                  30             RUSSIA
SOO                      21
```

**You may use the following PL/SQL block to answer this question:**

```
DECLARE
   JUNK VARCHAR2(20);
   i PLS_INTEGER := 0;
BEGIN
SELECT NAME INTO JUNK FROM CONTESTANT
WHERE COUNTRY = 'RUSSIA';
 FOR i IN 1..50 LOOP
    IF JUNK = 'SVENSKY' THEN
```

```
      GOTO END_LOOP;
  END IF;
    JUNK := 'RIZENFRANZ';
 <<end_loop>>
 end loop;
END;
```

**What is wrong with this statement?**

**A.** The label is not followed by an executable statement.

**B.** The endless loop must be modified.

**C.** The looping variable must be assigned a default value.

**D.** There is nothing wrong with this statement.

51. **You want to create a user-defined record corresponding to the columns in table CONTESTANT. The columns in this table include:**

```
NAME - VARCHAR2(20)
AGE - NUMBER(5)
COUNTRY - VARCHAR2(30)
```

**Which of the following code fragments handle this declaration properly?**

**A.** ```
CONTESTANT_RECORD_NAME VARCHAR2(20);
CONTESTANT_RECORD_AGE NUMBER(5);
CONTESTANT_RECORD_COUNTRY VARCHAR2(30);
```

**B.** ```
TYPE cont_rec IS (
NAME VARCHAR2(20),
AGE NUMBER(5),
COUNTRY VARCHAR2(30));
CONTESTANT_RECORD cont_rec;
```

**C.** `CONTESTANT_RECORD CONTESTANT%ROWTYPE;`

**D.** `CONTESTANT_RECORD RECORD OF TABLE CONTESTANT;`

52. **You are loading data into the CONTESTANTS table, which contains the following columns:**

```
NAME - VARCHAR2(20)
AGE - NUMBER(5)
COUNTRY - VARCHAR2(30)
```

**To use a PL/SQL table for doing so, which of the following code fragments identifies how you would declare it?**

**A.** CONTESTANT_TABLE IS TABLE OF VARCHAR2(20), NUMBER(5), VARCHAR2(30) INDEX BY BINARY_INTEGER;

**B.** TYPE cont_rec IS (
NAME VARCHAR2(20),
AGE NUMBER(5),
COUNTRY VARCHAR2(30));
CONTESTANT_TABLE IS TABLE OF cont_rec%TYPE INDEX BY BINARY_INTEGER;

**C.** CONTESTANT_TABLE IS TABLE OF CONTESTANT%ROWTYPE;

**D.** CONTESTANT_TABLE IS TABLE OF CONTESTANT%ROWTYPE INDEX BY BINARY_INTEGER;

**53.** Examine the following code block:

```
DECLARE
  CONTESTANT_NAME_TABLE IS TABLE OF
  CONTESTANT.NAME%TYPE INDEX BY BINARY_INTEGER;
  CURSOR CONTESTANT_CSR IS SELECT NAME
    FROM CONTESTANT;
  MYVAL BINARY_INTEGER := 0;
BEGIN
  FOR MY_CONT_REC IN CONTESTANT_CSR LOOP
    CONTESTANT_NAME_TABLE(MYVAL) := MY_CONT_REC.NAME;
    MYVAL := MYVAL + 1;
  END LOOP;
--  HOW MANY ROWS IN TABLE?
END;
```

If you want to find out the number of rows that are in the table, what two methods can you use to do so in the fewest number of program lines possible?

**A.** SELECT COUNT(1) FROM CONTESTANT_NAME_TABLE;

**B.** Value in MYVAL

**C.** CONTESTANT_NAME_TABLE.COUNT

**D.** Use another loop to cycle through the records in CONTESTANT_TABLE

**54.** You are developing a PL/SQL block designed for bulk data operations. When attempting to store table data for multiple rows in a PL/SQL variable, which of the following choices identifies the mechanism best suited for the task?

A. Record

B. Cursor

C. PL/SQL table

D. PL/SQL table of records

55. You declare a cursor as follows: CURSOR c1 IS SELECT * FROM CONTESTANT FOR UPDATE. Which of the following choices correctly describes what happens when this cursor is opened?

   A. Oracle returns an error because the way the records should be updated is not defined.

   B. Oracle retrieves all records in the CONTESTANT table only.

   C. Oracle retrieves all records in the CONTESTANT table into the cursor and locks those rows for update.

   D. Oracle updates all records in the CONTESTANT table as specified in the OPEN statement.

56. You develop a PL/SQL block that will be used in an overall application that records grants for political asylum for Olympic athletes to the country where the games are held. The cursor definition in this block is CURSOR asy_csr IS SELECT NAME FROM CONTESTANT. As you loop through the cursor, you want the ability to update the record back in the table that corresponds to the record in the cursor. Which of the following choices best identifies the way to do so without explicit comparison between the NAME value in the cursor and the NAME value in the table?

   A. UPDATE CONTESTANT SET COUNTRY = 'USA' WHERE CURRENT OF asy_csr;

   B. Redefine the cursor as CURSOR cnt_csr IS SELECT NAME FROM CONTESTANT FOR UPDATE;

   C. UPDATE CONTESTANT SET COUNTRY = 'USA' WHERE NAME = asy_csr.NAME;

   D. You cannot achieve this functionality with PL/SQL.

57. You want to define a cursor that contains a subquery. Which of the following choices best identifies how PL/SQL allows you to handle this situation?

   A. PL/SQL does not allow cursors to contain subqueries.

   B. PL/SQL only allows cursors to contain subqueries resolving to inline views.

**C.** PL/SQL only allows cursors to contain subqueries resolving to a set of comparison values for a WHERE clause.

**D.** PL/SQL allows cursors to contain the same types of subqueries permitted in any SQL query.

58. You develop a PL/SQL program with several blocks three layers deep. PROC_A calls PROC_B, which in turn calls PROC_C. Which of the following choices correctly identifies how Oracle will propagate the error in order to find an exception handler that will resolve an exception being raised in the innermost block?

    **A.** PROC_B, PROC_A, PROC_C

    **B.** PROC_C, PROC_B, PROC_A

    **C.** PROC_A, PROC_B, PROC_C

    **D.** Exception is propagated directly to the user level

59. You are developing PL/SQL process flow into your program. The command used to open a CURSOR FOR loop is which of the following keywords?

    **A.** OPEN

    **B.** FETCH

    **C.** PARSE

    **D.** None, CURSOR FOR loops handle cursor opening implicitly.

60. You are determining the appropriate program flow for your PL/SQL application. Which of the following statements are true about WHILE loops?

    **A.** Explicit EXIT statements are required in WHILE loops.

    **B.** Counter variables are required in WHILE loops.

    **C.** An IF-THEN statement is needed to signal when a WHILE loop should end.

    **D.** All EXIT conditions for WHILE loops are handled in the EXIT WHEN clause.

# Answers to Practice Exam 1

**1.** A. SELECT NAME, JERSEY_NO WHERE JERSEY_NO = 6;

**Explanation** SQL statements in Oracle must have a FROM clause. A SQL statement can lack a WHERE clause, in which case all data in the table will be returned. However, if the statement does not have a FROM clause, Oracle will not know what table to retrieve data from. Recall that a special table called DUAL assists in situations where you don't want to retrieve data from a table, but instead want only to manipulate expressions. **(Topic 2.2)**

**2.** D. CURSOR FOR LOOP

**Explanation** Any time you see a PL/SQL block where the cursor is opened and manipulated manually, you can revise the code into a CURSOR FOR loop to take advantage of Oracle automatically managing many aspects of cursor manipulation for you. The other choices simply rewrite the existing structure, and may save a line or two of coding: But, the CURSOR FOR loop will tremendously reduce your coding burden in this situation. **(Topic 22.3)**

**3.** B. OTHERS

**Explanation** A special exception called OTHERS exists in PL/SQL that will handle all unhandled exceptions captured at that level of processing. Although Oracle will raise the ZERO_DIVIDE exception automatically whenever you attempt to divide a number by zero, coding an exception handler for ZERO_DIVIDE only defines what happens when ZERO_DIVIDE is raised. It does not, for example, handle situations where another exception gets raised, as OTHERS does. The NO_DATA_FOUND and TOO_MANY_ ROWS exceptions are raised when no data or too much data is returned by an implicit or explicit cursor, respectively. **(Topic 24.4)**

**4.** C. RAISE_APPLICATION_ERROR

**Explanation** The RAISE_APPLICATION_ERROR function allows Oracle to return a user-defined error message when an exception condition is raised. The PRAGMA EXCEPTION_INIT keywords (of which PRAGMA is a subset) indicates a compiler directive where you tell Oracle you want to associate an internal error with an exception name of your own devises. The OTHERS exception is a catchall for processing exceptions that would otherwise escape unhandled. Finally, the

EXCEPTION keyword is used to denote the exceptions section of your code block. **(Topic 24.6)**

**5.** A.   Issuing an UPDATE statement

**Explanation**   The only choice that does not end a transaction is the one that continues the transaction, namely issuing another UPDATE statement. A COMMIT tells Oracle to save your data changes and end the transaction, while a ROLLBACK tells Oracle to discard your data changes and end the transaction. Closing SQL*Plus or otherwise ending the session is usually treated as an implicit COMMIT and ends your transaction as well. **(Topic 10.3)**

**6.** B.   COMMIT

**Explanation**   In order to save any change you make in Oracle, you will use the COMMIT command. The SAVEPOINT command merely identifies a logical breakpoint in your transaction that you can use to break up complex units of work. The ROLLBACK command discards every change you made since the last COMMIT. Finally, the SET TRANSACTION command will set up the transaction to be read-only against the Oracle database. **(Topic 10.5)**

**7.** D.   USER_CONS_COLUMNS

**Explanation**   The USER_CONS_COLUMNS dictionary view shows you all the columns in tables belonging to that user that are part of indexes used to enforce constraints. USER_INDEXES is incorrect because that view only displays information about the index itself, not the columns in the index. USER_TAB_COLUMNS displays all the columns in all tables owned by that user. Finally, USER_COLUMNS is not an actual view in the Oracle database. **(Topic 14.2)**

**8.** A.   Unique

**Explanation**   Only unique and primary-key constraints require Oracle to generate an index that supports or enforces the uniqueness of the column values. Foreign keys do not require this sort of index. Check constraints also do not require an index. Finally, NOT NULL constraints do not require an index either. **(Topic 12.1)**

**9.** D.   The view

**Explanation**   When you drop a table with CASCADE CONSTRAINTS option, Oracle removes all associated indexes, triggers, and constraints that reference that table from other tables. Oracle does not remove the views that use that table, however—you must do that manually with the DROP VIEW statement. **(Topic 11.5)**

**10.** D.  MONTHS_BETWEEN

**Explanation**  Each of the choices accepts as input a DATE datatype and returns a DATE datatype—with one exception. The MONTHS_BETWEEN function returns a number indicating how many months there are between two dates you give it. This number will be displayed with numbers to the right of the decimal point, which you can round off if you like. All the rest of the choices return a DATE value in one form or another. **(Topic 4.2)**

**11.** C.  ORDER BY sqrt(1);

**Explanation**  Although the ORDER BY clause allows you to refer to the column you want order determined either by the column name or by the number representing the column order in the SELECT clause of the SELECT statement, you cannot perform any sort of numeric function on that number. Both the ASC and DESC keywords are valid for the ORDER BY clause, indicating ascending order (default) and descending order, respectively. **(Topic 3.2)**

**12.** B.  Table with one column and one row used in various operations

**Explanation**  The DUAL table is a special table in Oracle used to satisfy the requirement of a FROM clause in your SQL statements. It contains one column and one row of data. It is not a dictionary view; rather, it is an actual table. Thus, you should understand why the answer is what it is in this question. As a side note, you would use the DUAL table in arithmetic expressions and would not actually pull real data from the database. Finally, you should never insert data into the DUAL table under any circumstance. **(Topic 2.1)**

**13.** A.  ACTIVE

**Explanation**  The DECODE function is used as a "case" statement, where Oracle will nest through the value in the column identified in the first parameter (in this case ACCTNO). If that value equals the second parameter, then the third parameter is returned. If that value equals the fourth parameter, the fifth parameter will be returned, and so on. If the value equals no parameter, the default value provided in the last parameter (in this case ACTIVE) is returned. TRANSFER would be returned if ACCTNO=590395, SEIZED would be returned if ACCTNO=654321, and CLOSED would be returned if ACCTNO=123456. **(Topic 4.1)**

**14.** **C.** INSERT INTO BANK_ACCT (ACCTNO, NAME) VALUES (&VAR1, '&VAR2');

**Explanation** In order to have statement reusability where you can enter a value on the fly, you must use lexical references as runtime variables. These references are preceded with an ampersand (**&**) character, as in the correct answer. Though you can use nested subqueries in your INSERT statements, this has the effect of inserting multiple rows at once without requiring input from the user. **(Topic 9.1)**

**15.** **B.** 28-APR-07

**Explanation** On this question, you really have to put your thinking cap on. ADD_MONTHS adds a specified number of months indicated by the second parameter to the value in the first parameter. 120 months is 10 years, so if you add 10 to the year in the date given you should come up with 28-APR-07, which is the correct answer.

**TIP**
*Beware of having too much of your time sucked up by this sort of "brain teaser" question.*

**(Topic 4.2)**

**16.** **D.** MONDAY JUNE 26, 2037: 10:30PM

**Explanation** The first statement in this question alters the date format shown in your SQL*Plus session, while the second statement returns the current date and time in that specific format. In this case, your format is the day of the week, followed by the month of the year, the date, the year, and the time in AM/PM format. This being the case, the correct answer is MONDAY JUNE 26, 2037: 10:30PM. **(Topic 9.2)**

**17.** **B.** WHERE A.C = 5 AND A.C = B.C (+);

**Explanation** The correct choice illustrates your use of Oracle's outer join function. The question indicates you want to see data in table A, no matter whether there is corresponding data in table B or not. Thus, you place the outer join operation next to the reference to the C column in table B. If the outer join operation is removed (it looks like a (+)), Oracle will only return data from table A for which there are corresponding records in table B. If the outer join operator is used for both tables, then you will get a syntax error. If you omit the join operator comparing values from table A to table B, Oracle will return a Cartesian product of the data you requested from A with all the data from table B. **(Topic 5.2)**

Chapter 1:   OCP Exam 1: Introduction to SQL and PL/SQL   **53**

**18. B.** All values in the referenced column in the parent table must be present in the referencing column in the child.

**Explanation** Referential integrity is from child to parent, not vice versa. The parent table can have many values that are not present in child records, but the child record must correspond to something in the parent. Thus, the correct answer is all values in the referenced column in the parent table must be present in the referencing column in the child. **(Topic 12.1)**

**19. B.** SQRT

**Explanation** All the choices indicate GROUP BY functions, except for the SQRT function, which is a single-row function acting on each value in each column row, one at a time or individually. AVG processes data from multiple rows in a column and produces one result, the average value for all of them. COUNT processes all values in a column or columns and counts the number of row values in that column or columns. The STDDEV function takes all values in a column of rows and determines the standard deviation for that set of values. **(Topic 6.1)**

**20. C.** NVL returns NULL if the first value is not equal to the second.

**Explanation** The only statement in this question that is not true is NVL returns NULL if the first value is not equal to the second. NVL is specifically designed to avoid returning NULL for a column, by substituting another value that you pass as the second parameter. All other statements made in these choices are true about NVL—it handles many different datatypes, and both values passed must be the same datatype. **(Topic 4.1)**

**21. A.** Records

**Explanation** %ROWTYPE is a special keyword in PL/SQL that allows you to define a record that conforms to the datatypes for rows in a particular table, as in EMP%ROWTYPE for a set of datatypes in a row from the EMP table. Although that row may contain columns of VARCHAR2 or NUMBER datatype, a record datatype is a more accurate way to describe this feature. However, because PLS_INTEGER data cannot be stored in Oracle tables, you will never see this datatype in a %ROWTYPE record. **(Topic 21.2)**

**22. B.** 418

**Explanation** The key here is being able to distinguish between CURRVAL and NEXTVAL. Only NEXTVAL will actually change the sequence value. CURRVAL only selects the current value, so you can factor out the four people who have issued statements requesting CURRVAL and pay attention only to those users requesting

NEXTVAL. There are two of those, so the sequence, which started at 394, has been incremented twice by 12. 394 + 12 + 12 = 418. **(Topic 15.2)**

    **23.** B.   The high-water mark was not reset.

**Explanation**   The SELECT COUNT(*) statement takes a long time because Oracle had to inspect the table in its entirety in order to derive the rowcount, even though the table was empty. To avoid this situation on large tables, use the TRUNCATE statement rather than DELETE. TRUNCATE resets the high-water mark on your table, thus reducing the time it takes Oracle to perform SELECT COUNT(*) operations. **(Topic 11.5)**

    **24.** B.   CREATE OR REPLACE VIEW

**Explanation**   The column definitions for a view can only be changed by re-creating the view with the CREATE OR REPLACE VIEW statement. The ALTER VIEW command is used only to recompile a view, while INSERT INTO VIEW is not a valid SQL statement. Although CREATE VIEW will technically work, you must first drop the view you want to re-create, which requires two statements, not one. CREATE OR REPLACE VIEW is the most accurately correct choice offered. **(Topic 13.2)**

    **25.** A.   A join statement without a WHERE clause

**Explanation**   Cartesian products are the result of SELECT statements that contain malformed WHERE clauses. SUM and AVG operations are group functions and do not produce Cartesian products. Selecting data from the DUAL table will not produce a Cartesian product because only one table is involved—and a table with only one row at that! **(Topic 5.1)**

    **26.** B.   Creating an appropriate LOGIN.SQL file

**Explanation**   SQL*Plus shows its roots in UNIX systems through the LOGIN.SQL file. This file is used to specify settings used in your session. LOGIN.SQL runs automatically after you log in to Oracle. SQL*Plus in Windows environments does not have a Preferences menu, eliminating that choice. You shouldn't attempt to use the ALTER TABLE or ALTER USER statements for this purpose, either. **(Topic 9.5)**

    **27.** D.   WITH CHECK OPTION

**Explanation**   The appropriate clause is WITH CHECK OPTION. You can add this clause to a CREATE VIEW statement so that the view will not allow you to add rows to the underlying table that cannot then be selected in the VIEW. The WITH ADMIN/GRANT OPTION clauses are used to assign administrative ability to users along with granting them a privilege. The WITH SECURITY OPTION is a work of fiction—it does not exist in Oracle. **(Topic 13.3)**

**28. D. INTEGER**

**Explanation** Although you can declare variables in PL/SQL blocks using the INTEGER datatype, you cannot store INTEGER datatype data in Oracle tables. All other datatypes shown, namely NUMBER, RAW, and DATE, can all be stored in the Oracle database, as well as being used as datatypes for PL/SQL variables. **(Topic 11.3)**

**29. B. TO_CHAR**

**Explanation** TO_CHAR is used to convert DATE values, numbers, and other things into text strings. The CONVERT operation is used to convert a text string from one character set to another, while the TO_NUMBER operation converts numeric text to true numbers. The TO_DATE function is used to convert a properly formatted text string into a DATE value. **(Topic 4.3)**

**30. C. Use the SET LONG statement.**

**Explanation** The SET LONG command allows you to increase the buffer size SQL*Plus will use to retrieve LONG data values. This statement is used because the view text is stored in a LONG column in the appropriate dictionary view. The dictionary view itself does not need to be increased, nor can you somehow solve this problem with the ALTER USER statement. Finally, the NLS_DATE_FORMAT option is used for date formatting, not LONG columns. **(Topic 9.2)**

**31. B. All records**

**Explanation** Since the UPDATE statement does not contain a WHERE clause, the change will be made to every record in the table. There is no way to accurately update only the first or last record in the table. No records will be updated if there is something wrong with the UPDATE statement, such as a column being referenced incorrectly. **(Topic 10.1)**

**32.** A. TOO_MANY_ROWS

**Explanation** The answer to this question is TOO_MANY_ROWS, an Oracle predefined exception that gets raised automatically in the situation described in the question. The OTHERS exception is a catchall that handles any exception that would otherwise go unhandled at this level of execution. ZERO_DIVIDE is raised automatically whenever you attempt to divide by 0. Finally, NO_DATA_FOUND is the conceptual opposite of the correct answer. **(Topic 24.3)**

**33.** B. ALTER TABLE

**Explanation** The ALTER TABLE statement allows you to easily add columns after the table is created, with minimal impact to your system. Unlike views, you do not use the OR REPLACE keyword for this effort, thus creating a powerful distracter for the user who is more familiar with views than with underlying tables. The CREATE TABLE could be used for the task, but you would first need to issue the DROP TABLE statement to get rid of the initial table. **(Topic 11.4)**

**34.** B. Foreign-key

**Explanation** Foreign-key relationships require that you grant REFERENCES privileges on a table to the user creating the foreign-key relationship from their table to yours. There is no particular special privilege that must be granted to create unique, check, or NOT NULL constraints other than CREATE TABLE. **(Topic 16.3)**

**35.** C. The statement fails due to primary-key constraint.

**Explanation** It should be obvious that the statement fails, the real question here is why. The reason is because of the primary-key constraint on UPC_CODE. As soon as you try to add a duplicate record, the table will reject the addition. Although the view has WITH CHECK OPTION specified, this is not the reason the addition fails. It would be the reason an INSERT fails if you attempt to add a record for a day other than today, however. **(Topic 13.4)**

**36.** D. LIKE

**Explanation** In the situation where you want to use wildcards, Oracle offers the LIKE comparison operator. This operator allows you to search for text strings like the one you're looking for. The IN operator specifies a set of values to which the comparison value can be equal to one of, while EXISTS allows you to use a subquery as a lookup validity test for some piece of information. BETWEEN specifies a range comparison, such as BETWEEN 1 AND 5. **(Topic 3.1)**

**37.** A.  Use DEFINE to capture value

**Explanation**  The DEFINE command can be used to identify a variable and assign it a value for use throughout a script running in SQL*Plus. This is useful when executing a number of SQL statements in batch. Although the ACCEPT command can perform the same function, the key factor that makes this the wrong answer is mention of no user interaction in the question. Hardcoded values will work, but they make the script almost completely not reusable. Finally, although lexical references using ampersand (**&**) followed by a label will allow you statement reusability, your users will have to keep entering values every time a statement containing the lexical reference is processed. **(Topic 9.4)**

**38.** A.  WHERE EMP.EMPID = 39284 AND EMP.EMPID = EXPNS.EMPID;

**Explanation**  Since you only want data from either table where there is a match in the other, you are performing a regular join or "equijoin" operation. In Oracle, you would not use the outer join (**+**) operator for this purpose. This eliminates all the choices where an outer join operator is displayed. **(Topic 5.1)**

**39.** A.  DATE variables

**Explanation**  %TYPE can be used to declare a variable as the same datatype as a table column, as in EMPLOYEE.LASTNAME%TYPE for the LASTNAME column of the EMPLOYEE table. All other datatypes offered as choices are valid datatypes in PL/SQL, but not in Oracle tables, so you could not use the %TYPE keyword to reference these datatypes in your code. Of the choices given, only DATE variables can be used as column datatypes in Oracle. **(Topic 19.2)**

**40.** C.  4104930504

**Explanation**  The only record that will not be present from the choices given is 4104930504, because UPC code #402392340 does not exist at the time this statement is issued. It was already changed to 50393950, and thus the 4104930504 update fails when you issue it. As an aside, this question is really tricky because in order to get the answer right you have to read the question for a long time, and that wastes time when you're taking the OCP exams.

**Note**
*This question will take up an enormous amount of time if you're not careful.* **(Topic 10.5)**

**41.** A. DROP VIEW

**Explanation** When a table is dropped, Oracle eliminates all related database objects, such as triggers, constraints, and indexes—except for views. Views are actually considered separate objects, and although the view will not function properly after you drop the underlying table, Oracle will keep the view around after the table is dropped. **(Topic 13.5)**

**42.** C. 4

**Explanation** The general rule of thumb here is that, if you have *n* tables you want to join, four in this case, you will generally need *n*-1 comparison operations in your WHERE clause joined together by AND, three in this case. In addition, recall from the question that you want to restrict return data further based on values in the first table. Thus, your WHERE clause would have four conditions, and may look something like the following block:

```
WHERE
A.COLUMN1 = 5             AND
A.COLUMN1 = B.COLUMN1     AND
B.COLUMN2 = C.COLUMN2     AND
C.COLUMN3 = D.COLUMN3
```

**(Topic 5.1)**

**43.** B. %TYPE variables

**Explanation** You would use the %TYPE keyword to assign dynamically the datatype of a variable according to the datatype in a column of a table. %ROWTYPE is used for declaring variable records according to all columns in a table, so it is almost, but not quite, correct. VARCHAR2 variables might be the result of using %TYPE, but remember, you didn't actually know what the datatype of the variable you were declaring was—only that it was the same for a particular column of a table. Finally, you will never wind up with a FLOAT variable, because Oracle does not allow FLOAT variables to be used as datatypes in table columns. **(Topic 19.2)**

**44.** A. Password authentication and granting privileges

**Explanation** Although in order to get database access you need to create user privileges, the two real components of Oracle's security model are password authentication and granting privileges. When a user is created, the user will still not be able to connect to Oracle unless they are granted a privilege (CREATE SESSION), and even when they connect they still cannot see anything unless someone gives them permission to via the GRANT command. **(Topic 16.1)**

Chapter 1: OCP Exam 1: Introduction to SQL and PL/SQL **59**

**45.** C. SPOOL

**Explanation** The SPOOL command makes SQL*Plus write an output file containing all information transacted in the session, from the time you turn spooling on and identify the output file to the time you either turn spooling off or end the session. PROMPT causes SQL*Plus to prompt you to enter data using a specialized request message of your own devising, while ECHO causes an error because it is not a valid command in SQL*Plus. Finally, the DEFINE command is used for variable definition and variable assignment in SQL*Plus scripts. **(Topic 2.3)**

**46.** A. DECLARATION and EXCEPTION only.

**Explanation** The DECLARATION section of your code block must contain the PRAGMA keyword, a compiler directive used to associate named exceptions with internal Oracle errors. The exception handler must contain an exception handler for the named exception. The only area that does not require coding is the execution section of your code block, because Oracle will automatically raise your named exception whenever the internal error occurs in code execution. **(Topic 24.1)**

**47.** B. SELECT A.STUDENT_ID, A.LOCATION, B.LOCATION FROM TEST_SCORE A, TEST_SCORE B WHERE A.STUDENT_ID = B.STUDENT_ID AND A.LOCATION <> B.LOCATION AND TRUNC(A.TEST_DATE)+30 >= TRUNC(B.TEST_DATE) AND TRUNC(A.TEST_DATE)-30 <= TRUNC(B.TEST_DATE);

**Explanation** This question is probably the hardest on the exam. Even if you have a bit of SQL experience, this question will take you a while. When taking OCP, the last thing you need is time-waster questions to throw you off. **(Topic 5.3)**

**48.** C. select * from EMPLOYEE where empid = (select empid from invoice where invoice_no = 4399485);

**Explanation** If you can use a subquery, you should do so. There is only one choice that displays a subquery, so that one must be the answer. All the other choices depend on the empid being provided, not the invoice number. **(Topic 7.1)**

**49.** A. To put returned data into sorted order

**Explanation** The HAVING clause is best used to include or exclude certain data groups, not to return data in sort order. The ORDER BY clause handles that task. **(Topic 6.4)**

**50.** D. Roles

**Explanation** Roles allow you to group privileges together into one object and grant the privileges to the user at one time. There are no privileges related to indexes other than the privilege to access the associated table. Tables and sequences both require privileges to be granted to a user or role, they do not simplify the act of privilege management in any way. **(Topic 16.2)**

**51.** A. ALTER USER

**Explanation** The ALTER USER statement with the IDENTIFIED BY clause is used to change a user's password. ALTER ROLE is used for modifying the actual role object, and affects users insofar as the user has been granted the role. Of the remaining choices, although user SNOW may be able to execute those statements depending on what privileges he is granted, none of these privileges will handle what the question requires. **(Topic 16.1)**

**52.** C. User SNOW would need a synonym for table EMP.

**Explanation** User SNOW needs a synonym in order to refer to a table he doesn't own without prefixing that reference with a schema owner. Without privileges, SNOW would not see the data, even with privileges or roles with the appropriate privileges granted. If there is no synonym, SNOW still has to prefix references to EMP with REED, as in REED.EMP. Tables don't have passwords, databases do, so that choice is patently incorrect. **(Topic 15.4)**

**53.** C. Whenever the COMMIT command is issued

**Explanation** In PL/SQL, data changes are committed using the COMMIT command, and will only take place when that command is issued. Oracle will not automatically commit data changes when the PL/SQL block ends, eliminating that choice. Only if a COMMIT command is present after each individual update will the change be committed. Finally, if you are the creator of the block, when you disconnect from Oracle has nothing to do with another user making changes to data with your code. **(Topic 19.4)**

**54.** C. Explicit cursors with a CURSOR FOR loop

**Explanation** Explicit cursors with a CURSOR FOR loop is the way to go for this situation. You would first need to write an explicit cursor so that you could work with each row individually, which eliminates all the implicit cursor choices. There is no way to "write" an implicit cursor, as implicit cursors are handled by the Oracle RDBMS in a way that is transparent to the user. However, the second part of the question is how you will move through each row of output. Here, you need a loop more than you need cursor attributes. **(Topic 22.1)**

**55.** D.   Passing empid values as parameters to the cursor

**Explanation**   You would reduce the number of cursors declared by having a single cursor that accepted a value for EMPID as a parameter. Although you might use the cursor in a CURSOR FOR loop, you wouldn't rely on that feature to reduce the overall number of cursors in your database. The variable declaration keyword %ROWTYPE helps you reduce the amount of work you need to do to set up a record variable, but does nothing to reduce the number of cursors you declare. Finally, %NOTFOUND is an implicit cursor attribute that again has nothing to do with how many cursors you have to declare in your code block. **(Topic 23.1)**

**56.** D.   Oracle returns an error

**Explanation**   In this situation, you cannot use the ORDER BY clause in a subquery. Oracle will return an error. Thus, no data will be returned from any table, so all other choices are wrong. **(Topic 7.4)**

**57.** D.   No special syntax is required.

**Explanation**   No special syntax is required to place SQL statements into your PL/SQL block. The **/\* \*/** markers are used for commenting out portions of your code, while EXEC SQL and colons are required only when embedding SQL statements into Pro*C programs, a topic not covered by this exam. **(Topic 19.3)**

**58.** B.   SELECT to_char(nvl(sqrt(59483), '0')) FROM DUAL;

**Explanation**   The "select to_char(nvl(sqrt(59483), '0')) from dual;" statement is a valid statement. The "select nvl(sqrt(59483)) from dual;" statement does not pass enough parameters to the nvl( ) function. The "select TO_CHAR(nvl(sqrt(59483), 'VALID')) from dual;" statement breaks the rule in nvl( ) that states that both parameters passed into the function must be the same datatype. The "select (to_char(nvl(sqrt(59483), '0')) from dual;" statement is missing a matching closing parenthesis after '0'. **(Topic 4.2)**

**59. C.** column PLAY_TABLE heading "My Plays and Authors"

**Explanation** The heading clause to the column command in SQL*Plus acts in the same way as a column alias does in SQL—it modifies the output of the query to use a heading of your design. Despite its similarity, however, the heading clause is not the same as an alias in SQL. Thus, both the choice identifying the ALIAS clause and the choice using the AS keyword are both incorrect. The choice containing the FORMAT clause should be easy to eliminate. **(Topic 9.2)**

**60. C.** The SELECT will receive NO ROWS SELECTED.

**Explanation** Although the query will succeed (translation—you won't receive an error), you must beware of the distracter in choice B. In reality, choice C is the better answer because it more accurately identifies what really will occur when you issue this statement. This view will behave as any SELECT statement would when you list criteria in the WHERE clause that no data satisfies, by returning NO ROWS SELECTED. This is not an error condition, but you wouldn't call it a successful search for data, either, making both those choices incorrect. Finally, SELECT statements never add data to a table. **(Topic 13.3)**

# Answers to Practice Exam 2

**1.** C.

```
DECLARE
   CURSOR My_Employees IS
      SELECT name, title FROM employee;
BEGIN
   FOR csr_rec IN My_Employees LOOP
      INSERT INTO MY_EMPS (MY_EMPNAME, MY_EMPTITLE)
      VALUES (csr_rec.name, csr_rec.title);
   END LOOP;
END;
```

**Explanation** If you understand the nature of a CURSOR FOR loop, you should be able to easily identify the correct answer. Otherwise, you should skip this question and come back to it because you will wind up wasting a lot of time reading the code for each choice—time better spent answering other easier questions. For your information, a CURSOR FOR loop does three things for you. It declares the fetch variable (csr_rec in the code block) implicitly. It also handles the exit condition automatically. Finally, it takes care of opening and closing the cursor without requiring you to code explicit OPEN and CLOSE commands. **(Topic 22.3)**

**2.** C. Use the SET LONG statement.

**Explanation** The SET LONG command allows you to increase the buffer size SQL*Plus will use to retrieve LONG data values. This statement is used because the trigger text is stored in a LONG column in the appropriate dictionary view. The dictionary view itself does not need to be increased, nor can you somehow solve this problem with the ALTER USER statement. Finally, the NLS_DATE_FORMAT option is used for date formatting, not LONG columns. **(Topic 13.1)**

**3.** D. GROUP BY COW_NAME;

**Explanation** The problem with this statement is that not enough leading columns from the query are referred to in the GROUP BY clause. As a result, you will receive the ORA-00979 (not a GROUP BY expression) error. The correct GROUP BY clause would read "GROUP BY FARM_NAME, COW_NAME;". All other areas of the statement are syntactically and semantically correct. **(Topic 6.3)**

**4.** E. Anonymous blocks

**Explanation** All PL/SQL blocks are blocks that Oracle can store within the database, except for anonymous blocks. These are compiled and run when you submit them to Oracle, and then eventually discarded. There is little opportunity for you to reuse the code unless you store the code as a text file and rerun it in your session. **(Topic 17.1)**

**5.** B. MOD(CARTON, FILL_STATUS)

**Explanation** The line containing reference to the MOD( ) operation is the one containing the error. Because this is a single-row function, it cannot be used as the GROUP BY expression in a SQL statement containing the GROUP BY expression. The rest of the statement is correct. If you substituted a grouping expression like SUM, AVG, or COUNT, you would have a correct statement. **(Topic 6.2)**

**6.** B. SELECT A.LASTNAME, B.DEPT_NO FROM EMP A, (SELECT EMPID, DEPT_NO FROM DEPT) B WHERE A.EMPID = B.EMPID;

**Explanation** An inline view is an undeclared view consisting only of a parenthetical select statement in a FROM clause. This subquery is then treated like a view in other areas of the main query. While choices A and C involve use of subqueries, only the use of a subquery in the FROM clause of a SELECT statement constitutes an inline view. Choice D is not really a subquery at all, but rather a way to get SQL*Plus to write a SELECT statement for every line of output from the query. **(Topic 8.3)**

**7.** C. L

**Explanation** The square root of 40 is a fraction between 6 and 7, which rounds up to 7 according to the algorithm behind the ceil( ) function. This means that the VAR2 = '7' flag in the ELSIF will resolve to true. Thus, VAR2 is set to 'L', and then written to the database with the INSERT statement at the end. Be careful not to waste time on reviewing all the intricacies of the PL/SQL block provided. **(Topic 20.2)**

**8.** D. VAR1 := VAR2 + 3049;

**Explanation** The main problem with this block of PL/SQL code has to do with the VAR1 := VAR2 + 3049 statement. This is because VAR1 cannot be assigned a value in this code block because the variable is defined as a constant. VAR2 NUMBER := 0; is a proper variable declaration. The INTO VAR2 clause is appropriate in a PL/SQL fetch statement. Finally, the WHERE NAME = 'LEWIS';

clause is well constructed. All other lines of code in the block not identified as choices are syntactically and semantically correct. **(Topic 17.4)**

**9.** A.   CREATE FUNCTION FOO (VAR1 IN VARCHAR2) IS

**Explanation**   There is no definition of return value datatype in this code block, making the function declaration line the correct answer. Although it may seem that the IF-THEN statement in the third line of the code block is incorrect because you are comparing a VARCHAR2 variable to the number "6", in reality Oracle handles this situation just fine because there is an implicit type conversion occurring in the background. Finally, the SELECT, INTO, FROM, and WHERE clauses of the fetch statement are all constructed correctly. **(Topic 17.2)**

**10.** D.   DROP TABLE

**Explanation**   This is not an easy question. To rid your table of an index associated with a constraint, you will need to do something to the table or constraint, not to the index. The ALTER TABLE DROP CONSTRAINT works for indexes associated with unique constraints, and the ALTER TABLE DROP PRIMARY KEY statement works for indexes associated with primary keys. Dropping the table removes all associated database objects, including indexes. However, simply dropping the index with the DROP INDEX statement is not possible. **(Topic 15.3)**

**11.** B.   Values must be part of a fixed set defined by CREATE or ALTER TABLE

**Explanation**   A check constraint may only use fixed expressions defined when you create or alter the table with the constraint definition. The reserved words like SYSDATE and USER, or values from a lookup table are not permitted, making those answers incorrect. Finally, NULL values in a column are constrained by NOT NULL constraints, a relatively unsophisticated form of check constraints. **(Topic 12.2)**

**12.** C.   Table FOOBAR has no primary key, and therefore no index on MOO.

**Explanation**   Because table FOOBAR has no primary key, you cannot obtain data from it rapidly the way you could if the MOO column was set up as the primary key, and thus indexed. So, although Oracle not using the primary key is technically true, the more accurate answer is that the table had no primary key to use, and therefore no index on MOO. There are no views involved, and the table didn't get dropped. **(Topic 11.2)**

**13.** D. USER_INDEXES, indexes with the same name as the constraint

**Explanation** Since an associated index is generated automatically by Oracle, you will look in the USER_INDEXES view to find the associated object. And, since Oracle uses the name of the constraint in order to name the index created with that constraint, you will look for indexes that have the name EMP_PK_01. There is little correlation between tables and sequences, other than sequences can be used to populate the columns of a table. The USER_TABLES view will offer little value either, since only the EMP table will appear in it, and you are not looking for another table with the same name. **(Topic 10.1)**

**14.** B. To improve performance on columns with few unique values

**Explanation** Bitmap indexes are primarily designed to improve performance on searches that involve column data that is static and has few unique values. The ideal example of this is whether a person is male or female—it usually doesn't change, and these are the only two choices. All other choices referring to table columns in this question identify when it is appropriate to use B-tree indexes, the other main type of index available in Oracle. Also, understand that indexes do not improve performance on sequences. **(Topic 15.1)**

**15.** D. A loop exit condition must be defined.

**Explanation** No loop exit condition is defined for this code block. You don't need an exception handler in this code block for it to execute properly, and since it is anonymous, you don't need execute permission on it, eliminating those answers. Finally, you don't have enough information to determine if the user cannot insert onto the table, because you haven't been able to compile it yet. **(Topic 20.3)**

**16.** D. Nothing, Oracle raises this as an exception automatically.

**Explanation** Oracle raises an exception automatically when an attempt to SELECT data INTO a fetch variable fails. However, to handle that exception, you would use the NO_DATA_FOUND exception, not ROWTYPE_MISMATCH, making that choice incorrect. You also do not need to include any implicit cursor variable for Oracle to detect this situation, making those other choices including implicit cursor attributes like %FOUND or %NOTFOUND incorrect as well. **(Topic 19.5)**

**17.** **A.** insert into EMPLOYEE values (59694,'HARRIS', NULL);

**Explanation** This choice is acceptable because the positional criteria for not specifying column order is met by the data in the VALUES clause. When you would like to specify that no data be inserted into a particular column, one method of doing so is to insert a NULL. Choice B is incorrect because not all columns in the table have values identified. When using positional references to populate column data, there must be values present for every column in the table. Otherwise, the columns that will be populated should be named explicitly. Choice C is incorrect because when a column is named for data insert in the INSERT INTO clause, then a value must definitely be specified in the VALUES clause. Choice D is incorrect because using the multiple row INSERT option with a SELECT statement is not appropriate in this situation. **(Topic 10.2)**

**18.** **D.** WHERE C.COW_NAME = 'BESS' AND C.CARTON_NUM = C1.CARTON_NUM;

**Explanation** Two components are required in your WHERE clause—you need a join clause and something that only pulls records from COW_MILK for BESS. The right answer is WHERE C.COW_NAME = 'BESS' AND C.CARTON_NUM = C1.CARTON_NUM. Another choice is similar to this one, but since it uses the "not equal" or <> clause for getting information only for BESS, it is not the choice you want. The other two choices are incomplete, and therefore wrong. **(Topic 5.1)**

**19.** **D.** The INSERTs contain duplicate data due to the reset sequence.

**Explanation** The correct answer is that the INSERTs contain duplicate data due to the reset sequence. When you drop and re-create the sequence from its original code, you reset the start value for that sequence. Subsequent INSERT statements will then attempt to add rows where the value in the primary key is duplicated information. There is no information about read-only status in the question, so you should assume that is not the answer. Dropping a sequence does nothing to a table's primary key—there is no relationship between the two. Finally, although it is true that any cached sequence values that existed when the sequence was dropped are now unusable, this point has little relevance to the question at hand. **(Topic 15.2)**

**20.** **B.** EXISTS

**Explanation** Only when using the EXISTS statement must you use a correlated subquery. Although you can use a subquery with your use of IN, you are not required to do so because you can specify a set of values instead. The BETWEEN keyword indicates a range of values and does not allow use of a subquery. The

LIKE keyword is used for wildcard comparisons and also does not allow use of a subquery. **(Topic 7.2)**

**21.** D. ABS

**Explanation** All functions except for ABS will give you a result of 4093 when you pass them 4093.505. ABS returns the absolute value of the number you pass into the function. ROUND can do it if you also pass in a second parameter defining the precision to which you want to round the function, while TRUNC will do it with only 4093.505 as input. FLOOR does it too, because it is the logical opposite of the CEIL function. **(Topic 4.2)**

**22.** B. Use ACCEPT to capture name value for each run

**Explanation** The ACCEPT command is the best way to handle the situation. Although you could use DEFINE to assign a value to a variable used throughout the script, only ACCEPT allows you to dynamically enter a value for that variable. Lexical substitutions identified with the **&** character will only work for the current statement, meaning that the same value assigned in one statement will not be used in the next statement unless you reenter it. **(Topic 9.1)**

**23.** B. TRUNCATE

**Explanation** Once a TRUNCATE operation is complete, that's it—the change is made and saved. This is because TRUNCATE is not a DML operation that can be performed as part of a transaction. If you want to get the data back after truncating, you have to recover it. For any other operation listed as a choice in this question, such as INSERT, UPDATE, and DELETE statements, Oracle allows you to discard the changes using the ROLLBACK command. **(Topic 11.5)**

**24.** A. SAVEPOINT

**Explanation** SAVEPOINT operations simply act as logical breakpoints in a transaction. They do not cause Oracle to save or discard data, merely act as a breakpoint with which you can perform partial transaction rollbacks later. All other commands, namely SET TRANSACTION and COMMIT, indicate the beginning of a new transaction. Creating a new session with Oracle implicitly begins a transaction as well. **(Topic 10.5)**

Chapter 1:  OCP Exam 1: Introduction to SQL and PL/SQL    **69**

**25.** B.  A FROM clause

**Explanation**   No SQL statement can survive without a FROM clause. For this reason, Oracle provides you with the DUAL table, so that you can perform arithmetic operations on expressions and not on table data while still satisfying this syntactic construct. Since this statement already has a SELECT clause, you don't need to add another. The WHERE clause is optional, but since the statement already has one, you don't need to add another. Finally, your SQL statement does not require an ORDER BY clause. **(Topic 2.2)**

**26.** D.  Values from a cursor cannot be referenced directly.

**Explanation**   The problem lies in the line reading ...VALUES (UPC_CODE_CRSR);. You cannot reference the cursor directly in this way because a cursor is merely an address in memory. Instead, you have to reference the values as they are fetched into a variable. The cursor looping mechanism itself is fine and does not need to be rewritten. The exception handler does not need to be defined for the PL/SQL block, either. Finally, since this is an anonymous block, there is no concept of "having permission" to execute it—if you submit it, you can execute it. **(Topic 22.1)**

**27.** C.  Code a WHEN OTHERS exception handler in PROC_A.

**Explanation**   The OTHERS exception handler in PROC_A will prevent exception propagation to the user level if no exception handler exists in PROC_B. Remember, Oracle always raises its own exceptions. If that exception is not handled locally, it is propagated to the next level up, where either there must be an explicit exception handler or the WHEN OTHERS handler. **(Topic 18.3)**

**28.** B.  DECLARATION, EXECUTION, and EXCEPTION

**Explanation**   The exception you define is a user-defined exception. You must include support for this type of exception in the declarative, execution, and exception section of the PL/SQL block. Support for an Oracle predefined exception needs only to be included in the exception handler, whereas if you wanted to associate an internal error with a named exception, you would code support for it in the declaration and exception section of your code block. **(Topic 24.1)**

**29.** A.  SET TRANSACTION

**Explanation**   The SET TRANSACTION command is used to define the transaction state to be read-only. ROLLBACK and COMMIT statements are used to end the transaction, while the SAVEPOINT command denotes logical breakpoints for the transaction. **(Topic 10.5)**

**30.** C. Bitmap index

**Explanation** Bitmap indexes work well in situations where the data in the column is static. In this case, the column contains gender information, which will rarely if ever change. The number of distinct possible values is limited to only two as well. Thus, this column is a bad candidate for B-tree indexes of any sort, but perfect for bitmap indexes. Remember, B-tree indexes work well for columns with high cardinality or number of distinct values corresponding to the overall number of entries in the column. **(Topic 15.1)**

**31.** A. Optional, one-to-many

**Explanation** This question describes the notation you should use on your logical data model, and the appropriate answer is optional and one-to-many. This is because the relationship described between invoices and invoice items is optional, given that invoices may have no invoice items. The second part of the notation is the ordinality of the relationship. In this case, one invoice can have many items. **(Topic 12.1)**

**32.** D. ACTIVE

**Explanation** The DECODE function acts as a case statement. The first parameter indicates the column whose values you want decoded. If the value in the column equals parameter 2, then DECODE returns parameter 3. If the value in the column equals parameter 4, DECODE returns parameter 5, and so on. If the value in the column doesn't equal any of the other parameters specified, then DECODE returns the default value specified as the last parameter. Thus, since the column value is something not specified for any of the parameters, the returned value is the default, ACTIVE. **(Topic 4.3)**

**33.** B. Tablespaces

**Explanation** A tablespace, the logical object used for storing database objects like tables and indexes, maps most directly to a datafile because tablespaces can have one or many datafiles. Although segments and extents are stored in datafiles, the mapping is much closer between tablespace and datafile because both are storage containers. Finally, although both containers are comprised of Oracle blocks, the concept of Oracle blocks has less meaning at the filesystem level, where the datafile to the OS will look just like any other file in the host system. **(Topic 1.1)**

    **34.** B, D and E.   RDBMS defines how to obtain data for you, RDBMS allows flexibility in changing data relationships, *and* RDBMS is able to model relationship other than master-detail.

**Explanation**   A relational database differs from hierarchical databases like IMS in many ways. First, the RDBMS handles data access methods implicitly within the engine, shielding users from defining how to access data physically on the machine (i.e., "open this file, search for this text string," etc.)—hierarchical systems like IMS require that you define methods to traverse the master-detail relationships to obtain information. Both hierarchical databases and RDBMS systems can store data in master-detail fashion, which eliminates one choice. Also, because hierarchical databases require that you store all data in master-detail format and define the methods used to access the data, hierarchical databases are less flexible than RDBMS systems when it comes to changing the way data relates to other data. Finally, RDBMS systems can model data in relationships other than master-detail. **(Topic 1.2)**

    **35.** B.   Ease of integrating programs written in different languages

**Explanation**   Developers typically don't use PL/SQL if they need to integrate programs written in different languages as part of one application. Although later versions of Oracle allow integration with C using EXTPROC, integrating with other languages like COBOL, ADA, and FORTRAN generally makes better use of the Oracle precompilers. However, a developer might choose to use PL/SQL if it is important to have easy access to SQL, the ability to handle cursors, or the ability to handle error situations without necessarily having to code an explicit conditional operation for every type of error encountered. **(Topic 1.3)**

    **36.** D.   WHERE COL_A IN (SELECT NUM FROM TAB_OF_NUMS)

**Explanation**   The WHERE clause in choice D is an excellent example of the definition of a subquery, which is the example being asked for in the question. Choice A is not a comparison operation between a column and a set of values, as there is only one value being compared. Choice B is a comparison of a column to a set of values, but the set is static and defined at the time the query is issued. Choice C is a range comparison operation, a variant on choice B, and also therefore wrong. Only choice D allows Oracle to dynamically generate the list of values to which COL_A will be compared. **(Topic 7.2)**

**37.** D. SELECT NAME FROM CONTESTANT WHERE COUNTRY IN (SELECT COUNTRY FROM MEDALS WHERE NUM_GOLD + NUM_SILVER + NUM_BRONZE > 10)

**Explanation** The SELECT NAME FROM CONTESTANT WHERE COUNTRY IN (SELECT COUNTRY FROM MEDALS WHERE NUM_GOLD + NUM_SILVER + NUM_BRONZE > 10) query is correct because it contains the subquery that correctly returns a subset of countries that have contestants who won 10 or more medals of any type. Choice A is incorrect because it contains a join operation, not a subquery. Choice B is simply a rewrite of choice A to use a multiple-row subquery, but does not go far enough to restrict return data. Choice C is a single-row subquery that does essentially the same thing as choice B. **(Topic 7.3)**

**38.** C. Multiple-column subquery, the youngest contestant from all countries

**Explanation** Since the main query compares against the results of two columns returned in the subquery, this is a multiple-column subquery that will return the youngest contestant from every country in the table. This multiple-column subquery is also a multiple-row subquery, but since the defining factor is the fact that two columns are present, you should focus more on that fact than on the rows being returned. This fact eliminates choices A and B. The subquery does return multiple rows, however. You should also be sensitive to the fact that the main query must use an IN clause, not the equals sign (=), making choice D incorrect as well. **(Topic 8.1)**

**39.** C. BERTRAND

**Explanation** If you guessed SOO, guess again. The correct answer is BERTRAND because the subquery operation specified by the IN clause ignores NULL values implicitly. Thus, because SOO has no country defined, that row is not selected as part of the subquery. So, as a result, BERTRAND shows up as having the youngest age for anyone in the results of this query. Choices C and D will appear in the result set as well, but since they are both older than BERTRAND, they cannot be the youngest contestant. **(Topic 8.2)**

**40.** B. TABLE

**Explanation** The object being referred to is a table. A table has many columns, each of which is functionally dependent on the key column. Choice A is incorrect because a cursor is simply the result of a query, which may or may not have been against a table, and does not require any kind of storage in a segment. A sequence is a number generator in Oracle that, again, does not require storage in a segment other than a dictionary segment, making choice C incorrect. Finally, a view is similar to a table in that it contains many columns, each of which is functionally dependent on the key. However, views contain no data needing to be stored in a segment, so choice D is wrong as well. **(Topic 11.1)**

**41. B.** Executable

**Explanation** The executable section of a PL/SQL block is where the main operation of the block is written. Thus, any conditional operation such as the one referred to by the question would be written in the executable section of the PL/SQL block. The declaration section is used to declare variables, eliminating choice A. The exception section is where exception handlers are defined for error management, eliminating choice D as well. **(Topic 17.2)**

**42. A.** The variable is declared incorrectly.

**Explanation** Variables must be declared in the declaration section of a code block, making choice A the correct answer. The looping mechanism is set up correctly, eliminating choice B. The INSERT statement is correct as well, eliminating choice C. Finally, the loop needn't be closed in an exception handler. It can be closed in the executable section as well. It is simply important that the cursor be closed somewhere. This fact pattern eliminates choice D. **(Topic 17.3)**

**43. D.** Using the START command

**Explanation** The START command in SQL*Plus is designed for executing the contents of a file. This file may or may not contain any of the other methods listed as choices. Thus, choice D is the correct answer. The EXECUTE command is definitely a way to execute PL/SQL blocks in SQL*Plus, as it is possible to execute PL/SQL blocks from within other PL/SQL blocks. These facts eliminate choices A and B. Finally, you can execute PL/SQL blocks from within SELECT statements so long as the PL/SQL block being executed is a function. **(Topic 17.5)**

**44. A and D.** VAR_1 CONSTANT NUMBER(3) :=96; *and* VAR_1 NUMBER(3) INITIAL 96;

**Explanation** Declaring variables with initial values in Oracle PL/SQL is accomplished either by assigning a value to the variable at the time of declaration with the assignment operator (:=) or the DECLARE keyword. If you do not use either of these methods, your initial value declaration will not be correct. Choice A identifies the correct way to declare a constant, but unfortunately, once declared you cannot assign another value to it. The INITIAL keyword is used in storage declarations for database objects, not as part of the PL/SQL command syntax. **(Topic 17.5)**

**45.** C.  Execution section

**Explanation**  Only the execution section, as denoted by the BEGIN and END keywords, is required in order for the PL/SQL block to compile. The declaration section is not required, but if it does appear, it must appear before the execution section. Thus, choice A is incorrect. The exception section is also not required, and can appear either at the end of the execution section or at any point within the execution section. Thus, choice B is incorrect. Finally, the "parameter passing" section or named PL/SQL block declaration section is not required because anonymous blocks are permitted in Oracle, thus making choice D incorrect as well. **(Topic 18.1)**

**46.** C.  The nested block must be defined after variables used in the main block.

**Explanation**  In PL/SQL, the rule about nested blocks is that the sub-block must be defined after the variables, cursors, and constants defined for use in the main block. Thus, choice C is correct. You can have named subprograms in anonymous blocks in PL/SQL, thus meaning that choice A is incorrect. There is no requirement in PL/SQL that variables passed to other blocks must have the same name as the parameter defined in the sub-block. In fact, there are compelling reasons not to do so. Thus, choice B is incorrect. The DEFAULT keyword is used as an alternative to the assignment operator in PL/SQL for giving a declared variable an initial value, thus making choice D incorrect as well. **(Topic 18.3)**

**47.** A.  Package constants in the local procedure

**Explanation**  You would not use synonyms to identify package constants in the local procedure. Nor would you need to—these constants would be available in the local procedure without any scoping difficulties. Choices B, C, and D all identify exactly the types of situations where synonyms are useful. These situations include reference to stand-alone procedures and tables in distributed databases, or reference to procedures and tables in the same database that are owned by different users. **(Topic 18.5)**

**48.** D.  GOTO

**Explanation**  Of the control structures given, only the GOTO command allows you to jump to a different portion of the PL/SQL block unconditionally. Even the IF TRUE statement, which always executes the block of code contained in the IF-THEN (and thus, an IF-THEN-ELSE) structure, is not correct because it does not allow you to jump to a completely different section of code without running any kind of test. For this reason, choices A and C are incorrect. Finally, choice B is incorrect because a LOOP statement simply iterates through a block of code for as many times as specified by the looping construct. **(Topic 20.1)**

**49.** D.   NULL

**Explanation**   Because there is no row in the table where the country is Japan, the SELECT statement returned no value. Thus, the length of VAR1 will be NULL. Anything evaluated in conjunction with NULL becomes NULL as well, and thus VAR2 is assigned when the length of VAR1 plus 55 is executed. Thus, choice D is the correct answer. **(Topic 20.4)**

**50.** A.   The label is not followed by an executable statement.

**Explanation**   All labels in PL/SQL statements must be unique within their scope and must also precede an executable statement. In this case, the label precedes an END LOOP clause, which is not an executable statement unto itself. Instead, the END LOOP clause is part of the overall iteration construct used to define the loop. Thus, you must have an executable statement following the label and before the END LOOP clause. For your information, the NULL keyword can be used in this context following the label, as NULL by itself followed by a semicolon actually constitutes an executable statement. **(Topic 20.5)**

**51.** B.
```
TYPE cont_rec IS (
NAME VARCHAR2(20),
AGE NUMBER(5),
COUNTRY VARCHAR2(30));
CONTESTANT_RECORD cont_rec;
```

**Explanation**   The correct answer, shown as choice B, is correct because the question asks you to define a user-defined record. This simply means you have to first define the elements of this record using the TYPE declaration command, then define a variable as that type. Choice A simply has you declaring stand-alone variables for each of the elements in the record, which will work correctly but is not a user-defined record. Choice C is a representation of how to define a record using the %ROWTYPE attribute, which is the most efficient way to define this record, but is not a user-defined record unto itself. Finally, choice D identifies an invalid command syntax. **(Topic 21.1)**

**52.** D. `CONTESTANT_TABLE IS TABLE OF CONTESTANT%ROWTYPE INDEX BY BINARY_INTEGER;`

**Explanation** To declare a PL/SQL table of records where each record corresponds to a particular table in the Oracle database, you can use the %ROWTYPE attribute in the table declaration itself, thus making choice D correct. Choice A is incorrect because you cannot define a PL/SQL table of records using native datatypes in the form of a multidimensional array as the syntax in that choice's command would suggest. Choice B is also incorrect because the use of the %TYPE attribute gives only one column datatype, thus making the PL/SQL table a one-dimensional table. Furthermore, the manner in which the type declaration is constructed is incorrect in that choice as well. Finally, choice C is missing the all-important indexing mechanism required in your PL/SQL table of record, making that choice incorrect as well **(Topic 21.4)**

**53.** B and C. Value in MYVAL *and* CONTESTANT_NAME_TABLE.COUNT

**Explanation** After exiting the cursor FOR loop, the value in the MYVAL variable will represent the number of records in the PL/SQL table, so referencing that variable is one quick way to get the number of rows in the PL/SQL table. Another is to use the COUNT attribute, available on every PL/SQL table. While you can develop another FOR loop to count the number of rows in the PL/SQL table, as indicated by choice D, this would require several additional lines of code. This is not as efficient as choices B or C, so choice D is wrong. Finally, you cannot reference a PL/SQL table using group functions in SQL the way you can in an Oracle database table. **(Topic 21.3)**

**54.** D. PL/SQL table of records

**Explanation** When dealing with bulk data operations, if you want to use a PL/SQL variable to hold data from multiple table rows, your best bet is a PL/SQL table of records. This is because each record can act as a row of data, while the PL/SQL table indexing mechanism allows you to store each row as an element of an array. In essence, you store and treat the table data as a two-dimensional array. Choice A is incorrect because only a single row of data can be stored in a record. Choice B is incorrect because even though the cursor object can be used to refer to an entire table's worth of information, the cursor itself is merely an address in memory of an executed SQL statement, not an actual variable. Choice C is incorrect because a PL/SQL table is only a one-dimensional array. So, only tables with single columns could be stored in it. **(Topic 21.5)**

**55. C.** Oracle retrieves all records in the CONTESTANT table into the cursor and locks those rows for update.

**Explanation** The FOR UPDATE clause allows you to simultaneously collect one or several rows from a table and place a lock on those rows in the table for change during the code block. The change will not be made until you issue an UPDATE statement, however, making choice D incorrect. Because Oracle does not try to update the statement, choice A is incorrect, too. It is important to remember that the FOR UPDATE clause also locks rows from the original table, or else the cursor would simply select all the data and choice B would be correct. **(Topic 23.2)**

**56. A.** UPDATE CONTESTANT SET COUNTRY = 'USA' WHERE CURRENT OF asy_csr;

**Explanation** The WHERE CURRENT OF clause allows you to reference back to the original table record corresponding to this cursor record without explicitly defining a WHERE clause to do so in the UPDATE statement. Thus, you achieve the same functionality in choice A as you would get with choice C, but since choice C is attempting to reference the actual cursor value rather than the variable into which that cursor record's values were fetched, choice C is actually invalid and is therefore incorrect. Choice B is also incorrect because the FOR UPDATE clause only locks the records for update, it doesn't actually change any records at all. Finally, because choice A is the correct answer, choice D is inherently incorrect. **(Topic 23.3)**

**57. D.** PL/SQL allows cursors to contain the same types of subqueries permitted in any SQL query.

**Explanation** Any subquery permitted in a SQL SELECT statement is also fair game for a cursor. Thus, choices B and C both identify types of subqueries permitted in cursors. But because both statements are correct, neither choice by itself is the complete answer, so both choices are wrong. Choice A is also wrong inherently. **(Topic 23.4)**

**58. B.** PROC_C, PROC_B, PROC_A

**Explanation** PL/SQL first looks at the exception section in the current code block to find a handler for the exception being raised. If none is found, Oracle goes to the procedure caller's exception section to find a handler. This process continues either until an exception handler is identified or until the error is returned to the user level. However, Oracle will not return an error to the user level automatically in any situation—it will always attempt to identify an exception handler first. **(Topic 24.5)**

**59.** D.  None, CURSOR FOR loops handle cursor opening implicitly.

**Explanation**  The CURSOR FOR loops handle, among other things, the opening, parsing, and executing of named cursors. No other LOOP construct gives you the implicit support granted by a CURSOR FOR loop, so be sure you know how to construct these powerful looping mechanisms both for OCP and for your development efforts. **(Topic 22.3)**

**60.** D.  All EXIT conditions for WHILE loops are handled in the EXIT WHEN clause.

**Explanation**  There is no need for an EXIT statement in a WHILE loop, since the exiting condition is defined in the WHILE statement, eliminating choice A. Choice B is also wrong because you don't specifically need to use a counter in a WHILE loop the way you do in a FOR loop. Finally, choice C is incorrect because even though the EXIT condition for a WHILE loop evaluates to a Boolean value (for example, `exit when (this_condition_is_true)`, the mechanism to handle the exit does not require an explicit IF-THEN statement. **(Topic 20.3)**

# CHAPTER 2

## OCP Exam 2: Database Administration

OCP Exam 2 in the Oracle DBA track covers concepts and practices around routine Oracle database administration. To pass this exam, you need to demonstrate an understanding of the features available in Oracle for administering your database objects and the overall database itself. In more recent editions of OCP Exam 2, the focus has included understanding the use of Oracle utilities for administrative purposes, such as IMPORT and EXPORT, in addition to use of SQL*Loader. In addition, you should also be sure you understand the use of NLS for language control.

## OCP Exam 2 Topic Areas

The following topic areas are covered in OCP Exam 2. Note that these concepts are taken directly from the Oracle OCP Candidate Guide for OCP Exam 2, and are current as of the publication of this book. The topics and subtopics are as follows:

1. Oracle Architectural Components
    1.1. List the structures involved in connecting a user to the Oracle server
    1.2. List the stages in processing a query
    1.3. List the stages in processing a DML statement
    1.4. List the stages in processing COMMITs
2. Using Administrative Tools
    2.1. Use the Server Manager line mode
    2.2. Identify administration applications supplied with the Oracle Enterprise Manager
    2.3. Use Oracle Enterprise Manager components
3. Managing an Oracle Instance
    3.1. Set up operating system and password file authentication
    3.2. Create the parameter file
    3.3. Start an instance and open the database
    3.4. Close a database and shut down an instance
    3.5. Get and set parameter values
    3.6. Manage sessions
    3.7. Monitor ALERT and trace files

4. Creating a Database
    4.1. Prepare the operating system
    4.2. Prepare the parameter file
    4.3. Create the database
5. Data Dictionary Views and Standard Packages
    5.1. Construct the data dictionary views
    5.2. Use the data dictionary
    5.3. Prepare the PL/SQL environment using the administrative scripts
    5.4. Administer stored procedures and packages
6. Maintaining the Control File
    6.1. Examine the uses of the control file
    6.2. Examine the contents of the control file
    6.3. Obtain the control file information
    6.4. Multiplex the control file
7. Maintaining Redo Log Files
    7.1. Explain the use of the online redo log file
    7.2. Obtain log and archive information
    7.3. Control log switches and checkpoints
    7.4. Multiplex and maintain online redo log files
    7.5. Plan online redo log files
    7.6. Troubleshoot common redo log file problems
8. Managing Tablespaces and Datafiles
    8.1. Describe the logical structure of the database
    8.2. Create tablespaces
    8.3. Change the size of tablespaces using different methods
    8.4. Change the status and storage settings of tablespaces
    8.5. Relocate tablespaces
    8.6. Prepare necessary tablespaces

9. Storage Structures and Relationships
    9.1. List the different segment types and their uses
    9.2. Control the use of extents by segments
    9.3. State the use of block space utilization parameters by objects
    9.4. Obtain information about storage structures from the data dictionary
    9.5. Locate the segments by considering fragmentation and lifespans
10. Managing Rollback Segments
    10.1. Plan the number and size of rollback segments
    10.2. Create rollback segments using appropriate storage settings
    10.3. Maintain rollback segments
    10.4. Obtain rollback segment information from the data dictionary
    10.5. Troubleshoot rollback segment problems
11. Managing Temporary Segments
    11.1. Distinguish the different types of temporary segments
    11.2. Allocate space for temporary segments within a database
    11.3. Obtain temporary segment information for a database or instance
12. Managing Tables
    12.1. Distinguish between different Oracle datatypes
    12.2. Create tables using appropriate storage settings
    12.3. Control the space used by tables
    12.4. Analyze tables to check integrity and migration
    12.5. Retrieve information about tables from the data dictionary
    12.6. Convert between different formats of ROWID
13. Managing Indexes
    13.1. List the different types of indexes and their uses
    13.2. Create B-tree and bitmap indexes
    13.3. Reorganize indexes
    13.4. Drop indexes
    13.5. Get index information from the data dictionary

14. Maintaining Data Integrity
    - 14.1. Implement data integrity constraints and triggers
    - 14.2. Maintain integrity constraints and triggers
    - 14.3. Obtain constraint and trigger information from the data dictionary
15. Using Clusters and Index-Organized Tables
    - 15.1. Create and maintain clusters
    - 15.2. Use index-organized tables
    - 15.3. Retrieve information about clusters and tables from the data dictionary
16. Loading and Reorganizing Data
    - 16.1. Load data using direct-load INSERT
    - 16.2. Load data into Oracle tables using SQL*Loader conventional and direct paths
    - 16.3. Reorganize data using EXPORT and IMPORT
17. Managing Users
    - 17.1. Create new database users
    - 17.2. Alter and drop existing database users
    - 17.3. Monitor information about existing users
18. Managing Profiles
    - 18.1. Create and assign user profiles to users
    - 18.2. Control use of resources and profiles
    - 18.3. Alter and drop profiles
    - 18.4. Administer passwords using profiles
    - 18.5. Obtain information about profiles, assigned limits, and password management
19. Managing Privileges
    - 19.1. Identify system and object privileges
    - 19.2. Grant and revoke privileges
    - 19.3. Control operating system or password file authentication

20. Managing Roles
    20.1. Create and modify roles
    20.2. Control availability of roles
    20.3. Remove roles
    20.4. Use predefined roles
    20.5. Display role information from the data dictionary
21. Auditing
    21.1. Differentiate between database auditing and value-based auditing
    21.2. Use database auditing
    21.3. View enabled auditing options
    21.4. Retrieve and maintain auditing information
22. Using National Language Support
    22.1. Choose a character set and national character set for a database
    22.2. Specify the language-dependent behavior using initialization parameters, environment variables, and the ALTER SESSION command
    22.3. Use the different types of NLS parameters
    22.4. Explain the influence on language-dependent application behavior
    22.5. Obtain information about NLS usage

# Practice Exam 1

1. Automatic archiving of redo information is enabled, and all redo logs are found on the same disk resource. Which background processes may conflict with one another's operation?

   A. SMON and LGWR

   B. ARCH and RECO

   C. PMON and DBWR

   D. ARCH and LGWR

2. You are adding redo logs to the Oracle database. Creating a new redo log adds information to which of the following Oracle resources?

   A. Shared pool

   B. Control file

   C. SGA

   D. PGA

3. You need to find where the data dictionary tables are stored in your Oracle database. The tables that store information about the Oracle database—such as table names, users, and online rollback segments—are found in which of the following tablespaces?

   A. SYSTEM

   B. TEMP

   C. RBS

   D. INDEX

4. You are performing the steps that will create your Oracle data dictionary. The objects in the Oracle data dictionary are part of which of the following schemas?

   A. SYSTEM

   B. SYS

   C. PUBLIC

   D. SCOTT

5. As the DBA, you are attempting to limit users' misuse of Oracle's ability to use host machine resources. Which of the following features of the Oracle database is useful for this purpose?

   A. Rollback segments

   B. Roles

   C. Profiles

   D. Parameter files

6. You are creating some new rollback segments to handle transaction processing. Which of the following storage parameters is not permitted in your rollback segment STORAGE clause?

   A. PCTINCREASE

   B. INITIAL

   C. NEXT

   D. INITRANS

7. You have identified a table in the database that is experiencing severe row chaining. Which of the following choices best identifies a way to correct the problem?

   A. Increase PCTUSED

   B. Increase PCTFREE

   C. Increase PCTINCREASE

   D. Increase NEXT

8. Which of the following choices best identifies an Oracle feature allowing you to save multiple online copies of redo information on several disks to prevent problems with media failure?

   A. Multiplexing

   B. Archiving

   C. Redoing

   D. Logging

9. The DBA is about to perform some administrative tasks. Specifying the OPTIMAL parameter has which of the following appropriate uses?

   A. Limiting concurrent users

   B. Limiting concurrent transactions

   C. Limiting growth of rollback segments

   D. Limiting growth of tables

10. Auditing is in use on the Oracle database. Database audit information is stored in which of the following tables?

    A. SYS.DBA_AUDIT_STATEMENT

    B. SYS.AUD$

    C. SYS.DBA_AUDIT_TRAIL

    D. SYS.DBA_PRIV_AUDIT_OPTS

    E. SYS.OBJ$

11. You have a database with thousands of tables and users. Managing complex databases with many objects and users is best handled with which of the following access methods?

    A. Granting privileges to profiles directly

    B. Granting privileges to users directly

    C. Use of profiles

    D. Granting privileges to roles directly

12. The DBA has identified a need for clustering on the database. After creating the index cluster, which of the following tasks must be complete before the DBA can proceed with populating tables in a cluster with data?

    A. Cluster key index must be created

    B. Table index must be created

    C. Table high-water mark must be reset

    D. SET TRANSACTION USE ROLLBACK SEGMENT statement must be issued

13. You are attempting to increase the checkpoint interval on your database. Each of the following choices will affect the duration and/or frequency of checkpoints, except one. Which is it?

    A. Size of redo logs

    B. Number of datafiles

    C. LOG_CHECKPOINT_INTERVAL

    D. LOG_CHECKPOINT_TIMEOUT

14. As the result of configuring an area of the Oracle database, the Oracle RDBMS has been spending more time managing the space utilization of blocks on a high transaction volume OLTP system. Which of the following choices identifies a potential cause for this behavior?

    A. High PCTFREE

    B. High PCTUSED

    C. Low PCTFREE

    D. Low PCTUSED

15. You intend to prevent excessive host machine processing by user SPANKY on the database. Which of the following choices indicates the step you must take in order for this to be possible in the current instance?

    A. Issue GRANT LIMITER TO SPANKY, where LIMITER is a profile

    B. Issue GRANT LIMITER TO SPANKY, where LIMITER is a role

    C. Issue ALTER USER SPANKY PROFILE LIMITER, where LIMITER is a profile

    D. Issue ALTER USER SPANKY PROFILE LIMITER, where LIMITER is a role

16. Your application issues the following statement regularly.
    ```
    SELECT * FROM BANK_ACCT
    WHERE ACCT_BALANCE BETWEEN 1000 AND 100000;
    ```
    Which of the following database objects would be inappropriate for use with this statement?

    A. Materialized views

    B. Indexes

    C. Index-organized tables

    D. Hash clusters

17. You have 60 rollback segments in your database, for which TRANSACTIONS_PER_ ROLLBACK_SEGMENT is set to 49 and TRANSACTIONS is set to 1000. During periods of heavy usage, about how many rollback segments will be actively used by Oracle?

    A. 50

    B. 60

    C. 20

    D. 30

18. The DBA needs to reorganize a tablespace. Which of the following privileges will be used in order to log into Oracle while the database is open, but not available to other users?

    A. CREATE SESSION

    B. RESTRICTED SESSION

    C. CONNECT

    D. MOUNT

19. You are trying to alter the initial segment size given to a table. Which of the following keywords would be used as part of this process?

    A. DROP TABLE

    B. ALTER TABLE

    C. RESIZE

    D. COALESCE

20. You are in the process of creating users in the database. Which of the following clauses in a CREATE USER statement prevents a user's disk sorts from conflicting with dictionary objects?

    A. IDENTIFIED BY

    B. TEMPORARY TABLESPACE

    C. DEFAULT TABLESPACE

    D. DEFAULT ROLE

21. In order to allow remote administration of users and tablespaces on an Oracle database, which of the following types of files must exist in the database?

    A. Password file

    B. Initialization file

    C. Datafile

    D. Control file

    E. Nothing, SYSDBA privileges are not required for these actions.

22. All of the following choices identify a component of Oracle's redo architecture, except one. Which of the following is not a direct component of Oracle's redo mechanism when the database is in ARCHIVELOG mode?

    A. DBW0

    B. Redo log buffer

    C. LGWR

    D. Online redo log

    E. CKPT

    F. Archive redo logs

23. You are preparing to perform a data load into Oracle. In which of the following locations can parameters for the SQL*Loader execution not be located?

    A. Command line

    B. Control file

    C. Datafile

    D. Parameter file

24. Examine the following statement:
    ```
    CREATE TABLE SPANKY.EMPLOYEE
    (empid         NUMBER(10),
    lastname      VARCHAR2(25),
    firstname     VARCHAR2(25),
    salary        NUMBER(10,4),
    ```

```
CONSTRAINT      pk_employee_01
PRIMARY KEY     (empid))
TABLESPACE orgdbdata
PCTFREE    20   PCTUSED    50
INITRANS   1    MAXTRANS   255
NOCACHE         LOGGING
INITIAL 100K    NEXT  150K
MINEXTENTS 4    MAXEXTENTS 300
PCTINCREASE 20 );
```

**What is wrong with this statement?**

**A.** The primary key is declared improperly.

**B.** Both the index and data from the table must be stored in the same tablespace.

**C.** The statement will not succeed because a NOT NULL constraint is needed on the EMPID column.

**D.** The statement will succeed, but no data will be inserted.

**E.** The STORAGE clause is improperly defined.

25. User ANN has INSERT privilege on the EMP table WITH GRANT OPTION. ANN grants the INSERT privilege to SIMON. What is the most immediate effect of the DBA revoking ANN's privilege?

    **A.** ANN's records will be removed from table EMP.

    **B.** ANN will continue to have the ability to add records to EMP.

    **C.** SIMON will not be able to add records to the EMP table anymore.

    **D.** DBA's ability to add records to EMP will be revoked.

26. You have a table and you are trying to determine appropriate PCTFREE and PCTUSED values for it. The initial INSERT of new data into the table will leave most of its large columns NULL, to be filled in later by subsequent UPDATE. Records are never removed. What is the appropriate value combination for PCTFREE and PCTUSED?

    **A.** PCTUSED = 99, PCTFREE = 1

    **B.** PCTUSED = 40, PCTFREE = 30

    **C.** PCTUSED = 40, PCTFREE = 10

    **D.** PCTUSED = 80, PCTFREE = 10

27. You are configuring your index to be stored in a tablespace. Which of the following storage parameters are not appropriate for indexes?

    A. OPTIMAL

    B. INITIAL

    C. PCTINCREASE

    D. NEXT

28. You need to manage some configuration for new and existing users. Which of the following clauses are available in ALTER USER statements but not in CREATE USER statements?

    A. IDENTIFIED BY

    B. TEMPORARY TABLESPACE

    C. PROFILE

    D. DEFAULT ROLE

    E. ACCOUNT LOCK

    F. PASSWORD EXPIRE

29. You are developing a disk space allocation plan given the list of database objects in your system. Which of the following database objects in Oracle do not permit STORAGE assignment?

    A. Sequences

    B. Indexes

    C. Tables

    D. Rollback segments

    E. Tablespaces

30. When you arrive at work in the morning, you have messages from several users complaining that they have received the following error when they tried logging into Oracle with their new userid and password:

    ```
    Error accessing PRODUCT_USER_PROFILE
    Warning:  Product user profile information not loaded!
    ```

    What do you need to do in order to solve the problem?

**A.** Run PUPBLD.SQL as SYSTEM

**B.** Do a SHUTDOWN ABORT

**C.** Drop and re-create the users

**D.** Drop and re-create the database

31. **During regular database operation, which background process will take smaller blocks of free space in a tablespace and move things around to make bigger pieces of free space?**

    **A.** DBW0

    **B.** LGWR

    **C.** ARCH

    **D.** SMON

    **E.** PMON

32. **You are designing the physical database layout on your host machine. What is the relationship between tablespaces and datafiles in the Oracle database?**

    **A.** One tablespace has only one datafile.

    **B.** Many tablespaces can share one datafile.

    **C.** One tablespace can have many datafiles.

    **D.** One datafile can contain many tablespaces.

33. **In order to set resource cost high on CPU time, and low on the overall time a user spends connected to Oracle, which of the following would be appropriate?**

    **A.** Increase value of COMPOSITE_LIMIT

    **B.** Increase value on CPU_PER_SESSION, decrease value on CONNECT_TIME

    **C.** Decrease value on CPU_PER_SESSION, increase value on LOGICAL_READS_PER_SESSION

    **D.** Set PRIVATE_SGA to UNLIMITED

34. You are attempting to take the ORGRBS01 tablespace offline, and receive the following error: ORA-01546 - cannot take tablespace offline. What might be causing the problem?

    A. A table has too many extents allocated to it.

    B. Your INIT.ORA file is unavailable.

    C. An uncommitted transaction is still in progress.

    D. The online redo log is being archived.

35. You are analyzing how Oracle processes user statements. SQL and PL/SQL parse information is stored in which of the following database memory areas?

    A. Library cache

    B. Row cache

    C. Dictionary cache

    D. Large area

    E. Buffer cache

36. Information in the buffer cache is saved back to disk in each of the following situations except one. In which situation does this not occur?

    A. When a time-out occurs

    B. When a log switch occurs

    C. When the shared pool is flushed

    D. When a checkpoint occurs

37. You want to set up password management on your Oracle database. Which of the following choices indicates what you should do to view an example for setting up a password management function?

    A. Set RESOURCE_LIMIT to TRUE

    B. Run UTLPWMG.SQL

    C. Drop the DEFAULT profile

    D. Run CATPROC.SQL

**38.** Inspect the following transcript from user ATHENA's session:

```
SQL> create table obobobo (bobobo varchar2(3))
  2>    tablespace rman;
create table obobobo (bobobo varchar2(3))
*
ERROR at line 1:
ORA-01536: space quota exceeded for tablespace 'RMAN'
```

**Where can the DBA look to find out information to solve this problem?**

**A.** Looking in the DBA_TS_QUOTAS dictionary view

**B.** Looking in the DBA_USERS view

**C.** Looking in the DBA_TAB_COLUMNS view

**D.** Looking in the DBA_TABLESPACES view

**39.** The DBA issues the following statement:

```
CREATE USER DBADMIN
IDENTIFIED BY DBADMIN;
```

**What profile will user DBADMIN have?**

**A.** DEFAULT

**B.** None

**C.** CONNECT

**D.** DBA

**40.** You have OEM 2.0 set up on your machine for management of an Oracle8 database, and you want to determine the number of tablespaces available on your host system. Which tool would you use?

**A.** Schema Manager

**B.** Tablespace Manager

**C.** Security Manager

**D.** Recovery Manager

41. You have several profiles in your database, each with various values set to make users stay on the database for various periods of time. Where would you look to find information about the appropriate profile to assign a user who should connect for only very short periods of time?

    A. DBA_USERS

    B. DBA_PROFILES

    C. RESOURCE_COST

    D. RESOURCE_LIMIT

42. You are about to run an INSERT statement that will load 2,000,000 rows into the EMP_BKP table. Which of the following choices identify an INSERT statement that will do so using the direct path?

    A. INSERT /*+DIRECT */ INTO EMP_BKP (SELECT * FROM EMP);

    B. INSERT /*+APPEND */ INTO EMP_BKP (SELECT * FROM EMP);

    C. INSERT INTO EMP_BKP NOLOGGING (SELECT * FROM EMP);

    D. INSERT statements do not have a direct path option.

43. You have finished creating your new database and have run scripts to create the data dictionary views. Which of the following choices identify what you need to do next to create Oracle-supplied packages?

    A. CATPROC.SQL

    B. CATALOG.SQL

    C. UTLPWDMG.SQL

    D. UTLLOCKT.SQL

44. You are trying to strengthen security on your database. Which of the following Oracle resources support password-authenticated security over and above the abilities a user might be granted in accessing an application?

    A. Profiles

    B. Tables

    C. Rollback segments

    D. Roles

**45.** A query of the appropriate views yields the following output:

```
NAME                         EXTENTS
------------------------     -------
SYSTEM                             8
RB0                               17
RB1                               22
CTXROL                           444
```

If extents for each rollback segment are all 1MB, how would you go about decreasing the number of extents allocated to CTXROL?

**A.** Issue ALTER ROLLBACK SEGMENT CTXROL NEXT 2M;

**B.** Issue ALTER ROLLBACK SEGMENT CTXROL SHRINK;

**C.** Issue ALTER ROLLBACK SEGMENT CTXROL STORAGE (OPTIMAL 10M);

**D.** Drop and re-create the rollback segment.

**46.** Another DBA has set up auditing to be in place on your database. Which of the following choices indicates where you could look to find out what the enabled auditing options were for your database?

**A.** ALL_DEF_AUDIT_OPTS

**B.** DBA_AUDIT_TRAIL

**C.** AUD$

**D.** DBA_AUDIT_SESSION

**47.** A disk crashes that contains the only copies of all four of your online redo log files. How would you alter your Oracle database to prevent this from causing much damage in the future?

**A.** Change the CONTROL_FILES parameter in the INIT.ORA file

**B.** Use the ALTER DATABASE ADD LOGFILE GROUP 5;

**C.** Create multiple members for each of your four groups and place them on different disks

**D.** Set LOG_BLOCK_CHECKSUM in the INIT.ORA file

48. A table has a primary key that has been disabled. Upon reenabling it, the DBA discovers that users have entered duplicate records into the table. Which of the following database objects might play a role in rectifying the situation?

    A. EXCEPTIONS

    B. DBA_TABLES

    C. USER_TAB_COLUMNS

    D. AUD$

49. After creating a new user for your Oracle database, a user still complains he or she cannot log in because of insufficient privileges errors. Which of the following actions should you take?

    A. Grant CREATE TABLE privileges to the user

    B. Reset the user's password

    C. Grant the CONNECT role to the user

    D. Unlock the user's account

50. On an Oracle server installation, which of the following reorganizations of your indexes would be appropriate in order to improve performance of queries on tables containing all words in the dictionary starting with the letter 'S'?

    A. Convert your B-tree index to a bitmap index

    B. Convert your bitmap index to a B-tree index

    C. Convert your B-tree index to a reverse-key index

    D. Convert your reverse-key index to a B-tree index

51. You have a business rule that requires you to perform a lookup according to the following criteria. If the incoming column value starts with A, that means it is a code applying to the "A" subsidiary of a large corporation and you must perform a lookup against a table in that subsidiary's schema. If the incoming value is B, that means it is a code applying to the "B" subsidiary of a large corporation and you must perform a lookup against a different table in another schema. What Oracle structure would you use for data integrity on this business rule?

A. CHECK constraint

B. Foreign key

C. INSERT trigger

D. Stored procedure

**52.** You plan to store large blocks of text in your table. You want the column to be large enough to store about ten sentences. The column must also be fixed width. Which of the following datatypes are most appropriate?

A. CLOB

B. LONG

C. VARCHAR2

D. CHAR

**53.** You have enabled an audit in your database using the following statement:

```
AUDIT UPDATE, DELETE
ON spanky.cat_toys
BY ACCESS
WHENEVER NOT SUCCESSFUL;
```

**Which choice best explains how Oracle will audit data?**

A. Successful INSERT statements on CAT_TOYS performed by SPANKY will be recorded.

B. Unsuccessful UPDATE and DELETE statements performed by any user on CAT_TOYS will be recorded.

C. Unsuccessful UPDATE and DELETE statements performed by user ACCESS on CAT_TOYS will be recorded.

D. Unsuccessful UPDATE and DELETE statements performed by SPANKY on any table will be recorded.

**54.** The primary key of the EMP table has three columns, EMPID, LASTNAME, and FIRSTNAME. You issue the following SELECT statement:

```
SELECT * FROM EMP WHERE LASTNAME = 'HARRIS' AND FIRSTNAME = 'BILLI'
AND EMPID = '5069493';
```

Where would you look to see if this query will use the index associated with the primary key?

- A. DBA_IND_COLUMNS
- B. DBA_TAB_COLUMNS
- C. DBA_INDEXES
- D. DBA_CLU_COLUMNS

55. You are importing data from an EXPORT dump file that belonged to a different user than you would like to own the objects after the import is complete. Which of the following parameters would you use to perform this task?

- A. INCTYPE
- B. DIRECT
- C. TOUSER
- D. IGNORE

56. You issue the following statement:

```
DROP PROFILE LTD_PROGRAMMER;
```

The LTD_PROGRAMMER profile was granted to several users on the Oracle database. What happens to those users?

- A. The users who had the LTD_PROGRAMMER profile can no longer log in to Oracle.
- B. The users who had the LTD_PROGRAMMER profile now have the DEFAULT profile.
- C. The users who had the LTD_PROGRAMMER profile now have no profile.
- D. Nothing. You cannot drop a profile that has been granted to users.

57. You want to reduce the number of extents a segment will allocate as part of table growth. Each of the following choices indicates an action that will do so, except one. Which is it?

- A. Running EXPORT with the COMPRESS parameter set to Y
- B. Increasing the value set for PCTUSED on the table
- C. Increasing the value set for PCTINCREASE on the table
- D. Increasing the value set for NEXT on the table

58. You are planning which segments to place in which tablespaces. Which of the following segment types usually have the lowest turnover in the Oracle database?

    A. Rollback segments

    B. Table segments

    C. Temporary segments

    D. System segments

59. You issue the SHUTDOWN command at 3 P.M. on a Friday. Two hours later, the database is still in the process of shutting down. Which of the following options did you most likely use in order to shut down the database?

    A. SHUTDOWN ABORT

    B. SHUTDOWN IMMEDIATE

    C. SHUTDOWN TRANSACTIONAL

    D. SHUTDOWN NORMAL

60. The user is selecting data from the Oracle database. Which of the following processes handles obtaining data from Oracle for that user?

    A. The user process obtains information on its own.

    B. The DBW0 process obtains information for the user.

    C. The server process obtains information for the user.

    D. The listener process obtains information for the user.

# Practice Exam 2

1. **If the DBA wants to find information about how often transactions are wrapping transaction information between multiple rollback segment extents, where would the DBA look to find that information?**

   A. DBA_ROLLBACK_SEGS

   B. V$ROLLSTAT

   C. V$ROLLNAME

   D. DBA_SEGMENTS

2. **You issue the following statement within Oracle: CREATE TABLESPACE MY_TBLSPC DATAFILE '/oracle/dbf/mytblspc01.dbf' SIZE 10M ONLINE;—where will Oracle obtain storage settings for this tablespace?**

   A. Nowhere. Tablespaces don't need storage settings.

   B. From Oracle default storage settings.

   C. From storage settings of the first object created in the tablespace.

   D. From storage settings set for the SYSTEM tablespace.

3. **The result of SELECT COUNT(*) FROM DBA_TABLES WHERE TABLESPACE_NAME = 'MY_TBLSPC' is listed as follows:**

   ```
   COUNT(*)
   ----------------
   150
   ```

   You then issue the DROP TABLESPACE MY_TBLSPC command. What happens next?

   A. The DROP TABLESPACE command succeeds.

   B. The DROP TABLESPACE command fails because you didn't include the CASCADE CONSTRAINTS option.

   C. The DROP TABLESPACE command fails because you didn't include the INCLUDING CONTENTS option.

   D. You cannot drop a tablespace after creating it.

4. **After starting Server Manager in line mode, you issue the SHUTDOWN IMMEDIATE command. What most likely will happen next?**

   A. The database shuts down.

   B. The database does not shut down because users have to disconnect.

C. Server Manager returns an error saying you need to connect to Oracle first.

D. Nothing happens. Server Manager is not a line mode tool.

5. You need to view the initialization parameter settings for your Oracle database. Which of the following choices does not identify a method you can use to obtain values set for your initialization parameters?

   A. Issue SELECT * FROM DBA_PARAMETERS; from SQL*Plus

   B. Issue SELECT * FROM V$PARAMETER; from SQL*Plus

   C. Issue SHOW PARAMETERS from Server Manager

   D. Use OEM Instance Manager

6. You need to kill a user session in Oracle. Which of the following views contain the information you need to perform this operation?

   A. V$SESSTAT

   B. V$PARAMETER

   C. DBA_USERS

   D. V$SESSION

7. You issue the following statement in Oracle:
```
CREATE UNIQUE BITMAP INDEX employee_lastname_indx_01
ON employee (lastname ASC)
TABLESPACE ORGDBIDX
PCTFREE 12
INITRANS 2 MAXTRANS 255
LOGGING
NOSORT
STORAGE ( INITIAL 900K
NEXT 1800K
MINEXTENTS 1
MAXEXTENTS 200
PCTINCREASE 0 );
```
   What is wrong with this statement?

   A. You cannot use the NOSORT keyword in creating an index.

   B. Bitmap indexes cannot be unique.

   C. The TABLESPACE clause must be omitted.

   D. You should omit the ASC keyword.

8. You manage database access privileges with roles where possible. You have granted the SELECT_MY_TABLE role to another role, called EMP_DEVELOPER. To view information about other roles that may be granted to EMP_DEVELOPER, which of the following dictionary views are appropriate?

    A. DBA_ROLE_PRIVS

    B. DBA_TAB_PRIVS

    C. USER_SYS_PRIVS

    D. ROLE_ROLE_PRIVS

9. Your current session displays date information in the following format: 10-FEB-1999:10:15AM. Which of the following statements most likely produced this result?

    A. ALTER SESSION SET NLS_DATE_FORMAT = 'DD-MON-YYYY:HH:MIAM';

    B. ALTER SESSION SET NLS_DATE_FORMAT = 'DD-MON-YY:HH24:MI';

    C. ALTER SESSION SET NLS_DATE_FORMAT = 'DD-MON-YY:HH:MIAM';

    D. ALTER SESSION SET NLS_DATE_FORMAT = 'DD-MON-YYYY:HH24:MI';

10. You need to set up auditing in an order entry and product shipment application so that when the ORDER_STATUS column in the ORDERS table changes to 'SHIPPED', a record is placed in a special table associated with a part of the application that gives sales representatives a daily list of customers to call on a follow-up to make sure the customer is satisfied with the order. Which of the following choices represents the best way to perform this auditing?

    A. Statement auditing

    B. Object auditing

    C. Audit by access

    D. Value-based auditing

11. You are in the process of granting several permissions to a role. Which of the following privileges is not a system privilege?

    A. ANALYZE ANY

    B. INDEX

C. CREATE ROLLBACK SEGMENT

D. CREATE SYNONYM

12. When sizing temporary tablespaces, you should try where possible to make the default INITIAL storage setting for the temporary tablespace a multiple of which of the following initialization parameters?

    A. LOG_BUFFER

    B. DB_BLOCK_BUFFERS

    C. SORT_AREA_SIZE

    D. SHARED_POOL_SIZE

13. You want to query a table that you know is part of a cluster. To determine what other tables are part of that cluster, what dictionary view would be useful?

    A. DBA_OBJECTS

    B. DBA_CLUSTERS

    C. DBA_TABLES

    D. DBA_CLU_TABLES

14. When you issue the COMMIT statement in your session, which of the following things will not occur?

    A. Acquired row or table locks are released.

    B. Cached data is saved immediately to disk.

    C. Acquired rollback segment locks are released.

    D. Redo entry generated for committed transaction.

15. You are processing an UPDATE statement. At what point in SQL statement processing is the data change actually made to block buffers?

    A. When the cursor is opened

    B. When the statement is parsed

    C. When data is fetched from the cursor

    D. When the statement is executed

16. You are defining storage for various segment types in the Oracle database. Which of the following is not a valid type of segment in Oracle?

    A. Data segment

    B. Rollback segment

    C. Temporary segment

    D. Sequence segment

17. You need to identify the remaining free space in a tablespace. From which of the following views would you get this information most easily?

    A. DBA_TABLESPACES

    B. DBA_FREE_SPACE

    C. V$TABLESPACE

    D. DBA_EXTENTS

18. If you wanted to find the name and location of your control files, you could find that information in each of the following locations, except one. Which is it?

    A. V$CONTROLFILE_RECORD_SECTION

    B. V$CONTROLFILE

    C. V$PARAMETER

    D. INIT.ORA file

19. You are planning the storage requirements for your database. Which of the following is an effect of maintaining a high PCTFREE for a table?

    A. Oracle will manage filling data blocks with new records more actively.

    B. Oracle will manage filling data blocks with new records less actively.

    C. Oracle will leave more space free in data blocks for existing records.

    D. Oracle will leave less space free in data blocks for existing records.

20. The DBA has a table created with the following statement:

    ```
    CREATE TABLE EMPL
    (EMPID NUMBER(10),
    LASTNAME VARCHAR2(40),
    RESUME LONG RAW);
    ```

The DBA attempts to issue the following statement:
```
ALTER TABLE EMPL
ADD ( PERF_APPRAISE LONG);
```

**What happens?**

**A.** The statement succeeds.

**B.** The statement succeeds, but column is added as VARCHAR2.

**C.** The statement fails.

**D.** The statement adds a disabled constraint.

21. **The following statement is issued on the database:**
```
AUDIT DELETE
ON SYS.AUD$
BY ACCESS;
```

**What will Oracle audit?**

**A.** Delete activity on SYS.AUD$ by anyone

**B.** Insert activity on SYS.AUD$ by the DBA

**C.** Delete activity on ACCESS by SYS

**D.** Delete activity on ACCESS by AUD$

22. **User ANN has INSERT privilege on the EMP table. What is the most immediate effect of the DBA revoking ANN's privilege?**

**A.** ANN's records will be removed from the database.

**B.** ANN will not have the ability to create tables.

**C.** ANN will not be able to access the database anymore.

**D.** Users to which ANN granted INSERT privileges will not be able to INSERT.

23. **The EMP table has just acquired its fourth extent, giving it a total of 8.625MB of total space allocation. Which of the following choices identifies its storage parameters?**

**A.** INITIAL=2MB, NEXT=2MB, PCTINCREASE=25

**B.** INITIAL=2MB, NEXT=3MB, PCTINCREASE=50

**C.** INITIAL=1MB, NEXT=2MB, PCTINCREASE=25

**D.** INITIAL=2MB, NEXT=2MB, PCTINCREASE=50

24. If you wished to make it so that every user in Oracle could have only one connection to the database at a time, which of the following choices identifies how you would do it?

   A. Set LICENSE_MAX_SESSIONS = 1 in INIT.ORA

   B. Set SESSIONS_PER_USER in the DEFAULT profile to 1

   C. Set IDLE_TIME in the default profile to 1

   D. Set SESSIONS_PER_USER = 2 in INIT.ORA

25. Records from the data dictionary information are stored in which of the following database memory areas?

   A. Library cache

   B. Row cache

   C. Session UGA

   D. Buffer cache

26. Which of the following choices correctly describes the difference between a data load via the conventional path and the direct path?

   A. One runs faster than the other.

   B. A conventional path data load bypasses most of the Oracle RDBMS, while a direct path data load is a high-speed version of the SQL INSERT.

   C. A direct path data load bypasses most of the Oracle RDBMS, while a conventional path data load is a high-speed version of the SQL INSERT.

   D. The conventional path runs when the CONVENTIONAL command-line parameter is set to TRUE.

27. The location of indexes in a database and the size of those indexes is information that can be found in which of the following dictionary views?

   A. DBA_TS_QUOTAS

   B. DBA_OBJECTS

   C. DBA_SEGMENTS

   D. DBA_INDEXES

28. Into which file do records rejected by Oracle due to primary-key constraint violations get placed by SQL*Loader?

    A. Datafile

    B. Discard file

    C. Log file

    D. Bad file

29. You have a long-running process you want to assign to a specific rollback segment brought online for that express purpose. What statement can be used for this task?

    A. ALTER DATABASE

    B. SET TRANSACTION

    C. ALTER ROLLBACK SEGMENT

    D. ALTER TABLE

30. In a situation where no multiplexing of redo logs takes place, what happens when Oracle cannot read data from the online redo log group for archiving?

    A. Nothing.

    B. Oracle will automatically switch redo logs when detected.

    C. Oracle eventually won't allow new records to be added to the database.

    D. The instance crashes.

31. If the DBA suspects that unauthorized users are attempting to access Oracle by guessing other people's passwords, what may he or she do to discover if this is the case?

    A. AUDIT SESSION BY ACCESS WHENEVER NOT SUCCESSFUL

    B. AUDIT SESSION BY ACCESS WHENEVER SUCCESSFUL

    C. AUDIT SESSION BY NELSON WHENEVER SUCCESSFUL

    D. AUDIT LOGIN BY ACCESS WHENEVER NOT SUCCESSFUL

32. All of the following will alter the number of checkpoints that occur in one hour on the database, except one. Which is it?

    A. Decreasing tablespace size

    B. Decreasing size of redo log members

    C. Setting LOG_CHECKPOINT_INTERVAL greater than the size of the redo log file

    D. Setting LOG_CHECKPOINT_TIMEOUT to zero

33. You are defining profile areas on your Oracle database. Which of the following profile areas can be used to control the resource usage for the other four?

    A. LOGICAL_READS_PER_SESSION

    B. CONNECT_TIME

    C. COMPOSITE_LIMIT

    D. CPU_PER_SESSION

    E. PRIVATE_SGA

34. User ANN has CREATE ANY TABLE privilege with administrative abilities on that privilege. Which of the following statements show how to revoke the administrative component from ANN without limiting her overall ability to create tables?

    A. REVOKE ADMIN OPTION FROM CREATE ANY TABLE;

    B. REVOKE ADMIN OPTION FROM CREATE ANY TABLE; then GRANT CREATE ANY TABLE TO ANN;

    C. REVOKE CREATE ANY TABLE FROM ANN; then GRANT CREATE ANY TABLE TO ANN;

    D. REVOKE CREATE ANY TABLE FROM ANN WITH ADMIN OPTION; then GRANT CREATE ANY TABLE TO ANN;

35. The DBA is defining a default role for users. Which of the following is not an acceptable method for defining a default role?

    A. ALTER USER DEFAULT ROLE ALL;

    B. ALTER USER DEFAULT ROLE ALL EXCEPT ROLE_1;

**C.** ALTER USER DEFAULT ROLE NONE;

**D.** ALTER USER DEFAULT ROLE NONE EXCEPT ROLE_1;

36. **You issue the following statement from Server Manager: STARTUP MOUNT. Where does Oracle obtain values for starting the instance?**

    **A.** From your INIT.ORA file

    **B.** From Oracle default values

    **C.** From the default settings for the tablespace

    **D.** From the default settings in your redo log file

37. **You are analyzing the components of the redo log mechanisms in your Oracle database. Which of the following purposes does the CKPT process serve?**

    **A.** Writes dirty buffers to disk

    **B.** Writes current redo log number to datafile headers

    **C.** Writes redo log information to disk

    **D.** Read information into memory for users

38. **You are creating your rollback segments. Which of the following choices represents the approach that most closely mirrors common guidelines used for sizing your rollback segment extents?**

    **A.** Use PCTINCREASE 50

    **B.** Make the NEXT extent 20% larger than the INITIAL

    **C.** Make the NEXT extent 20% smaller than the INITIAL

    **D.** All extents should be the same size

39. **You are architecting the database to be used in a production OLTP environment. Which of the following choices best illustrates why you should multiplex online redo logs?**

    **A.** To take advantage of the increase in storage space

    **B.** To avoid degraded redo log performance

    **C.** To reduce dependency on the redo log buffer

    **D.** To prevent users from waiting if a redo log member cannot be archived

40. Which of the following options enables Oracle to calculate the approximate location of a row without doing a single disk read?

    A. INITIAL

    B. HASHKEYS

    C. PCTINCREASE

    D. Reverse-key index

41. You are configuring some new profiles for your database. Which of the following is not an area that you can specify a resource profile limit on?

    A. LOGICAL_READS_PER_SESSION

    B. CONNECT_TIME

    C. LOGICAL_WRITES_PER_SESSION

    D. IDLE_TIME

42. You are developing a control file for use with SQL*Loader. Which of the following is not an option for loading data via SQL*Loader?

    A. TRUNCATE

    B. REPLACE

    C. APPEND

    D. UPDATE

43. You are attempting to clear an unarchived redo log file. In order to manually enact a log switch, which of the following statements is appropriate?

    A. ALTER DATABASE

    B. ALTER SYSTEM

    C. ALTER USER

    D. ALTER REDO LOG

44. Which of the following clauses are available in ALTER USER statements but not in CREATE USER statements?

- A. IDENTIFIED BY
- B. TEMPORARY TABLESPACE
- C. PROFILE
- D. DEFAULT ROLE

45. Which of the following choices lists an ALTER USER option that can be executed by the user herself or himself?

    - A. DEFAULT TABLESPACE
    - B. IDENTIFIED BY
    - C. TEMPORARY TABLESPACE
    - D. PROFILE

46. In order to set a limit on the combined resource usage for users, which of the following statements would be appropriate?

    - A. ALTER PROFILE DEFAULT LIMIT COMPOSITE_LIMIT 3500;
    - B. RESOURCE_COST=TRUE
    - C. Set CPU_PER_SESSION = 100 in DEFAULT profile
    - D. Set LICENSE_MAX_SESSIONS = 1 in INIT.ORA

47. To allocate another role to a user, which command is most appropriate?

    - A. ALTER USER
    - B. ALTER DATABASE
    - C. ALTER SYSTEM
    - D. GRANT

48. Which of the following operations does not require Oracle to store information in a rollback segment as part of the transaction?

    - A. INSERT
    - B. SELECT
    - C. UPDATE
    - D. DELETE

49. You have enabled dedicated servers to be used on your Oracle database system. Session information when dedicated servers are being used is stored where in the Oracle database?

   A. In the PGA

   B. In the shared pool

   C. In the buffer cache

   D. In the redo log buffer

   E. Large area

50. You are modifying your database schema. Which of the following table changes will not be permitted unless you drop and re-create the table from scratch?

   A. Altering a column datatype

   B. Getting rid of a column

   C. Increasing the width of a VARCHAR2 column

   D. Adding a DATE column

51. Which of the following clauses in a CREATE USER statement restricts the number of tables a user can add to a tablespace?

   A. QUOTA ON

   B. DEFAULT TABLESPACE

   C. PROFILE

   D. IDENTIFIED BY

52. You have a block space utilization identified by the following values: PCTFREE 25, PCTUSED 30. Which of the following choices best describes the block management on your database?

   A. Little free space left for UPDATEs, and space left free by DELETEs actively filled in by Oracle

   B. Little free space left for UPDATEs, and space left free by DELETEs not actively filled in by Oracle

**C.** Much free space left for UPDATEs, and space left free by DELETEs actively filled in by Oracle

**D.** Much free space left for UPDATEs, and space left free by DELETEs not actively filled in by Oracle

53. You are defining the path a user process takes to get information out of the Oracle database. Which of the following purposes does the process labeled D009 serve?

   **A.** Writes dirty buffers to disk

   **B.** Writes current redo log number to datafile headers

   **C.** Dispatches user process access to a shared server

   **D.** Writes redo log entries to disk

54. You are considering using the MTS architecture on the Oracle database. Session information when shared servers are being used is stored where in the Oracle database?

   **A.** In the PGA

   **B.** In the shared pool

   **C.** In the buffer cache

   **D.** In the redo log buffer

   **E.** Large area

55. The DBA executes the following statement:
    ```
    CREATE OR REPLACE VIEW MY_VW AS
    SELECT EMPID, LASTNAME, FIRSTNAME,
    TO_CHAR(SALARY) AS SALARY FROM EMP;
    ```

    If the SALARY column in the EMP table is datatype NUMBER(10), what will the datatype of the SALARY column be in MY_VW?

   **A.** ROWID

   **B.** NUMBER

   **C.** DATE

   **D.** VARCHAR2

**56.** You have defined your national language on the Oracle database to be English, and the text data in some tables contains German characters. In order to ensure that you can list this text data in ascending alphabetical order according to German syntax, while still ensuring the language on the database is English, which of the following parameters could be set?

   **A.** NLS_DATE_FORMAT

   **B.** NLS_RULE

   **C.** NLS_TERRITORY

   **D.** NLS_SORT

**57.** When choosing a character set and national character set, which of the following factors should not enter into consideration?

   **A.** Your character set must either be US7ASCII or a superset of it.

   **B.** Your national character set and character set should be closely related where possible.

   **C.** You can use variable-length multibyte character sets as both character sets on your database.

   **D.** Oracle supports only English-like languages as its character set for entering SQL and PL/SQL commands.

**58.** You are working for the UN as an Oracle DBA. You maintain databases in multiple countries in multiple languages. To determine the date conventions for a database in a particular country, you might use which of the following database views?

   **A.** V$NLS_PARAMETERS

   **B.** NLS_DATE_FORMAT

   **C.** DBA_DATES

   **D.** V$NLS_VALID_VALUES

**59.** You are running Oracle in America in support of a financial analysis project for the government of Egypt. In order to produce reports that display money amounts as Egyptian pounds, rather than dollars, which of the following initialization parameters would be useful?

A. NLS_SORT

B. NLS_CURRENCY

C. NLS_LANG

D. NLS_DATE_FORMAT

60. You are trying to find the ALERT file on a host machine for a database you have never administered before. Which of the following initialization parameters is used to identify the location of the ALERT file?

A. BACKGROUND_DUMP_DEST

B. USER_DUMP_DEST

C. LOG_ARCHIVE_DEST

D. CORE_DUMP_DEST

# Answers to Practice Exam 1

**1. D.** ARCH and LGWR

**Explanation** The ARCH and LGWR processes may have a tendency to conflict with one another when log switches occur because both processes will attempt to access the same disk resources at the same times during this operation. SMON and LGWR is incorrect because SMON handles instance recovery and tablespace coalescence, and since datafiles and redo log files won't usually be on the same disk, there is little overlap between the two functions. **(Topic 7.6)**

**2. B.** Control file

**Explanation** Creating a new redo log on your Oracle database adds information to the control file. The shared pool is incorrect because information is added to that resource when SQL or PL/SQL statements are issued by users against Oracle. The SGA is a superset of the shared pool, thus being wrong as well. A program global area (PGA) is a memory region containing data and control information for a single process. **(Topic 6.2)**

**3. A.** SYSTEM

**Explanation** Using standard tablespace naming conventions, the SYSTEM tablespace contains all Oracle data dictionary objects. TEMP is incorrect because it identifies the temporary tablespace, which is designed to hold temporary segments for disk sorts. RBS is also incorrect because that tablespace is designed to store rollback segments. Finally, the INDEX tablespace is incorrect because that nomenclature is used to identify the tablespace that holds indexes. **(Topic 5.1)**

**4. B.** SYS

**Explanation** Objects in the Oracle data dictionary are part of the SYS schema. Although the SYSTEM user owns some important database objects, the dictionary views and their underlying tables are not one of them, making that choice incorrect. The PUBLIC user is more of an alias for granting access for various things to many users, not so much a user in and of itself, thus making that choice incorrect as well. Finally, user SCOTT is commonly found in training Oracle databases, but its existence is by no means guaranteed—nor will it ever own objects as critical as the data dictionary. **(Topic 5.1)**

**5.** C. Profiles

**Explanation** Profiles are appropriately used for the purpose of limiting a user's ability to manipulate host machine resources, making it the correct answer. Rollback segments allow transaction-level read consistency, but do not limit usage of the host machine in any substantial way, thus making this choice incorrect. Roles limit the user's ability to perform actions based on the privileges granted to those roles, but since the user may need a certain type of access and may be able to properly handle that access using appropriate methods, this choice is incorrect because you have no accurate way to limit resource usage using roles. Finally, parameter files such as INIT.ORA may contain settings that limit resource usage, perhaps through limiting the number of users that may connect at any one time, but this answer is incorrect because INIT.ORA parameters will do little to restrict user's misuse of host machine resources once connected. **(Topic 18.2)**

**6.** A. PCTINCREASE

**Explanation** You may never set a percentage increase for a rollback segment. Because rollback segments have the potential to grow out of control, this feature is designed to prevent problems where the segments allocated for a rollback segment are growing wildly out of control as well. The INITIAL and NEXT parameters must be specified so that the rollback segment will have some substance, so these choices are incorrect. The INITRANS parameter may be specified as well, so this choice is also incorrect. **(Topic 10.2)**

**7.** B. Increase PCTFREE

**Explanation** Actually, although PCTFREE isn't the complete solution, it will reduce chaining for future records added to the table. PCTUSED is not a component in the solution because that parameter simply reduces the frequency a data block will spend on a free list. Changing the value set for PCTINCREASE or NEXT may decrease the number of extents a table will allocate if that table is growing fast, but this parametric change does little to nothing about chaining at the block level, making both those answers incomplete and incorrect. **(Topic 12.3)**

**8.** A. Multiplexing

**Explanation** The term "multiplexing" is the correct answer because that term refers to having online copies (as opposed to archives) of redo logs. These logs are then spread across several disks to reduce I/O bottlenecks. Archiving is incorrect because this choice means that the copy of the redo log information made will not be available online. Neither redoing nor logging accurately describe what the question asks for, either. **(Topic 7.4)**

**9. C.** Limiting growth of rollback segments

**Explanation** OPTIMAL is an option set for rollback segments that helps to regulate or limit their growth. To limit concurrent users and/or concurrent transactions, you would set INIT.ORA parameters like LICENSE_MAX_USERS or USER_PROCESSES, thus making that choice incorrect. Finally, if you wanted to limit the growth of tables, you might use parameters like NEXT or PCTINCREASE, not OPTIMAL. **(Topic 10.1)**

**10. B.** SYS.AUD$

**Explanation** The AUD$ table contains all audit information Oracle records using that feature. Although some of the other choices identify views you can use to view the audit trail records, you must remember that a view is not a table and that a table actually stores data while views only provide a means for seeing the data in some specialized way. **(Topic 21.4)**

**11. D.** Granting privileges to roles directly

**Explanation** The choice mentioning use of roles is the correct answer. You would first grant the privileges to roles, and then give the roles to users. Profiles are not used for granting or revoking privileges or access; they are used instead for limiting host machine processing, making those two choices incorrect. Also, granting users privileges directly is the support nightmare you are trying to avoid. **(Topic 20.1)**

**12. A.** Cluster key index must be created

**Explanation** You must create a cluster key index for the cluster in order to populate clusters with data. You can create the tables without the cluster key index, which mimics the effect of resetting (or setting the first time) a table's high-water mark, which means that choice is incorrect. Table indexes do not need to be created in order to populate a clustered table with data. Finally, though the transaction where you insert data into the clustered table most likely will use a rollback segment, you never need to explicitly assign a rollback segment to the transaction, making that choice incorrect. **(Topic 15.1)**

**13. B.** Number of datafiles

**Explanation** The size of redo logs can have an effect on checkpoint intervals, because larger redo logs usually mean less frequent log switches. Fewer log switches mean fewer checkpoints. The number of datafiles will affect the duration of a checkpoint, because although the CKPT process has to write checkpoint sequence information to each datafile header (and more datafiles means more headers), this is not a time-consuming activity and happens in parallel with other activities occurring during a checkpoint. Finally, the two INIT.ORA parameters identified in this question have a direct correlation on the frequency of checkpoints. **(Topic 7.3)**

14. B. High PCTUSED

**Explanation** A high setting for PCTUSED will make Oracle fill data blocks with new records when comparatively fewer records are deleted from the block. In contrast, a low setting for PCTUSED causes Oracle to fill data blocks only after many records have been deleted from the block. PCTUSED identifies the threshold for Oracle to return a block to a free list for addition of new records. Lowering PCTUSED will make Oracle manage its block space utilization less actively, while PCTFREE simply indicates how much space should be left over for updates that make records grow. **(Topic 9.3)**

15. D. Issue ALTER USER SPANKY PROFILE LIMITER, where LIMITER is a role

**Explanation** The correct method for limiting Oracle's use of the host machine on SPANKY's behalf is with a profile, not a role, eliminating half the choices right there. The next aspect to consider is how to properly assign a profile to a user. This is accomplished with an ALTER USER statement, not a GRANT, making the choice indicating a GRANT statement where LIMITER is a profile incorrect. **(Topic 18.1)**

16. D. Hash clusters

**Explanation** Range operations do not perform well when the data is stored in a cluster. Though it is more efficient in general to use comparison operations instead of range operations, normal tables will work fine with range operations, making that choice incorrect. Indexes can process range operations just fine as well, making that choice incorrect. So can index-organized tables, which again makes that choice incorrect. **(Topic 15.1)**

17. C. 20

**Explanation** Recall that the number of rollback segments used in Oracle is a product of TRANSACTIONS divided by TRANSACTIONS_PER_ROLLBACK_SEGMENT. In this case, 1000/49 = about 20. **(Topic 10.1)**

**18. B. RESTRICTED SESSION**

**Explanation** The DBA needs the RESTRICTED SESSION privilege to make the database open but not available for users. The DBA could simply revoke the CREATE SESSION privilege from all users and simply leave the database open, but this task may require issuing several REVOKE commands, followed by the same number of GRANTs later. It's easier simply to use RESTRICTED SESSION. The CONNECT role is similar to CREATE SESSION in that CREATE SESSION is granted to CONNECT, which is then often granted to users. There is no such thing as a MOUNT privilege. **(Topic 19.1)**

**19. A. DROP TABLE**

**Explanation** You cannot alter or resize the initial extent on your table using the ALTER TABLE command; making that choice incorrect. Nor can you use the RESIZE or COALESCE keywords, as these are used as part of tablespace operations. Your only alternative is to drop and re-create the table using different storage settings. **(Topic 12.4)**

**20. B. TEMPORARY TABLESPACE**

**Explanation** By assigning a TEMPORARY TABLESPACE other than SYSTEM, the DBA reduces the possibility that a user will interfere with the overall operation of the Oracle database when disk sorts are performed by users. The IDENTIFIED BY clause is incorrect because that is where the password is assigned, not disk usage. The DEFAULT TABLESPACE is also incorrect even though that clause is used to define disk usage, because the disk usage is for creating permanent objects, not temporary ones. Finally, the DEFAULT ROLE clause is only available in ALTER USER statements, not CREATE USER statements, and is used to change the permissions available to the user. **(Topic 17.1)**

**21. E. Nothing, SYSDBA privileges are not required for these actions.**

**Explanation** The correct answer is nothing. Since the DBA does not plan to use remote administration for startup, shutdown, backup, or recovery, there is no need for a password file. Instead, the DBA can simply connect in normal mode using the SYS or other privileged account to create and administer users and tablespaces. **(Topic 3.1)**

**22.** A. DBW0

**Explanation** DBW0, though affected by the transaction logging mechanism—particularly during log switches and checkpoints—is not an actual part of Oracle's transaction logging mechanism. The redo log buffer, LGWR, CKPT, and archive/online redo logs are all part of the operation of Oracle's transaction logging mechanism. **(Topic 7.1)**

**23.** C. Datafile

**Explanation** You will not be able to find SQL*Loader runtime parameter definitions in the datafile unless the data you are loading is in the control file, in which case it is still considered part of the control file. Other than that, you can find the parameter settings in the command line, control file, and parameter file. **(Topic 16.2)**

**24.** E. The STORAGE clause is improperly defined.

**Explanation** The correct answer to this question is that the STORAGE clause is improperly defined. Instead of simply naming the different storage parameters loose in the statement, you must bundle them into a STORAGE clause, which is denoted with the STORAGE keyword and set inside parentheses. The primary key is declared properly, so there are no problems on that end. You never need to put index and table data in the same tablespace, and in fact there are compelling reasons not to do so, making that choice wrong as well. Finally, you do not need to define a separate NOT NULL constraint on the EMPID column because the primary-key index will handle it for you. For reasons of a malformed STORAGE clause, the CREATE table statement will not succeed, making that choice incorrect as well. **(Topic 12.2)**

**25.** C. SIMON will not be able to add records to the EMP table anymore.

**Explanation** When object privileges given WITH GRANT OPTION are revoked from a user who has given them to other users, Oracle cascades the revocation. So, not only will ANN lose the ability to add records to EMP (making the choice stating she can continue to add records to EMP incorrect), SIMON loses the ability as well, making that the correct answer. The DBA herself does not lose the ability to add records to EMP, because she is the person revoking privileges. ANN's records will stay in the EMP table, even though she cannot add new ones either, making that choice incorrect as well. **(Topic 19.2)**

**26.** B.  PCTUSED = 40, PCTFREE = 30

**Explanation**  The choice where PCTUSED is 99 and PCTFREE is 1 should be discarded immediately, because you should never set the space allocation options in a way that adding the two produces 100 as a result. Since rows are never removed, you can set PCTUSED relatively low. This leaves you with the two choices where PCTUSED is 40. Next, consider row growth. The rows in this table are going to grow substantially, which means you need a higher PCTFREE than just 10 percent. Remember, the largest columns are going to be NULL on initial insert and then populated later. To avoid row migration, you are best off choosing PCTUSED = 40, PCTFREE = 30. **(Topic 12.2)**

**27.** A.  OPTIMAL

**Explanation**  The OPTIMAL storage clause is used primarily for storing rollback segments in Oracle. You do not use it for any other database object. All the rest, namely INITIAL, PCTINCREASE, and NEXT, are valid for use. **(Topic 13.1)**

**28.** D.  DEFAULT ROLE

**Explanation**  You do not use the DEFAULT ROLE clause in CREATE USER statements. It is part of the ALTER USER syntax because when a user is created, the user doesn't have any roles granted to it yet. IDENTIFIED BY is for password definition, and is part of the CREATE USER statement. TEMPORARY TABLESPACE keeps the user's disk sorts out of the SYSTEM tablespace, and is part of the CREATE USER statement. PROFILE, ACCOUNT LOCK, and PASSWORD EXPIRE are all aspects of a robust CREATE USER statement, and therefore all these other choices are incorrect. **(Topic 17.2)**

**29.** A.  Sequences

**Explanation**  Sequences do not use storage parameters, and although they are database objects, they are not stored in tablespaces per se. A sequence is merely a structure that generates a number according to a set of rules. These numbers are not stored as data in Oracle; only the definition for generating the number is stored in the data dictionary. The rest of the objects, including tablespaces, allow a storage clause, though for tablespaces that storage clause acts as default settings for objects created in that tablespace that don't have a storage clause of their own. **(Topic 8.4)**

**30.** A.  Run PUPBLD.SQL as SYSTEM

**Explanation**   In this situation, Oracle needs user profile information to be generated for the users. In the error output for this message, Oracle will instruct you what is needed to resolve the issue, which is to run PUPBLD.SQL to build the product user profile information. You do not need to shut down the database with the ABORT option—moreover, you shouldn't, because that will require a database recovery. Nor will dropping and re-creating the users help—they will get the same error 10 minutes later when they try logging on again. Finally, you shouldn't waste your time dropping and re-creating the database. **(Topic 5.1)**

**31.** D.  SMON

**Explanation**   SMON coalesces free space in a tablespace on a regular basis, as well as managing instance recovery after instance failure. You will learn more about instance recovery in Exam 3. LGWR is wrong because that process simply handles writing log information from memory to disk. ARCH handles copying online redo logs to archive destinations and is also wrong. DBWO is incorrect because it only performs writes of data blocks from buffer cache to disk, and PMON is wrong because it handles process recovery—something you will not cover until OCP Exam 3. **(Topic 8.1)**

**32.** C.  One tablespace can have many datafiles.

**Explanation**   A tablespace is a collection of one or more datafiles residing on your host machine that Oracle treats as one logical area for storing data. This fact eliminates the choice that says one tablespace, one datafile. Also, the two other choices basically state the same thing—that one datafile can contain many tablespaces—and this is just not true. **(Topic 8.1)**

**33.** B.  Increase value on CPU_PER_SESSION, decrease value on CONNECT_TIME

**Explanation**   The correct answer is increase value on CPU_PER_SESSION, decrease value on CONNECT_TIME. This makes resource costs for CPU time higher, and connection time lower. The COMPOSITE_LIMIT increase is too imprecise—remember, one of the resource costs is increasing, while the other is decreasing. Increasing COMPOSITE_LIMIT will only increase a user's ability to use host system resources. PRIVATE_SGA has nothing to do with CPU time or connection time, and therefore is incorrect. **(Topic 18.2)**

**34.** C. An uncommitted transaction is still in progress.

**Explanation** The first thing to look at in this situation is the tablespace name: ORGRBS01. Oracle recommends having different tablespaces for different purposes. A tablespace containing the string "RBS" or "ROLLBACK" will most likely contain rollback segments. And, if one of the rollback segments is online and in use (indicated by a session having a lock on it), you will get the ORA-01546 error when you try to take the tablespace offline. A tablespace containing overextended tables can be taken offline, so that answer is incorrect. The INIT.ORA file being unavailable has no impact on taking a tablespace offline, but might interfere with restarting your Oracle database. And although in some situations you might see performance degradation because of an online redo log being archived, this will not interfere with taking a tablespace offline. **(Topic 10.5)**

**35.** A. Library cache

**Explanation** The library cache, sometimes referred to as the shared SQL area, stores parse and execution plan information for SQL and PL/SQL statements running on your database. The row and dictionary caches are one in the same, and store data dictionary information for quick retrieval, and thus are incorrect. The large pool allocation heap is used in multithreaded server systems for session memory, by parallel execution for message buffers, and by backup processes for disk I/O buffers. Finally, the buffer cache stores data blocks for quicker retrieval by server processes, and is also incorrect. **(Topic 1.1)**

**36.** C. When the shared pool is flushed

**Explanation** The data in the buffer cache will not be saved to disk when you flush the shared pool. You flush the shared pool with the ALTER SYSTEM FLUSH SHARED_POOL command. Items in the buffer cache are saved to disk when a time-out occurs and when a checkpoint occurs. Since a checkpoint happens every log switch, buffer cache information is saved to disk when a log switch occurs, too. **(Topic 7.1)**

**37.** B. Run UTLPWMG.SQL

**Explanation** Running UTLPWMG.SQL is the first step you must accomplish before being able to set up password management on your Oracle database. Unlike other areas of resource limitation, you do not need to set the RESOURCE_LIMIT parameter to TRUE, making that choice incorrect. Nor should you drop the DEFAULT profile beforehand. Creating a password verification function is optional, because Oracle provides you with one in the software release. **(Topic 18.4)**

**38.** A. Looking in the DBA_TS_QUOTAS dictionary view

**Explanation** The DBA_TS_QUOTAS view contains quota information for users and tablespaces. This is the DBA's best bet in identifying what ATHENA's limits are, and how they could be set differently. DBA_USERS only identifies default and temporary tablespaces for ATHENA, which isn't useful because the CREATE TABLE statement identifies its own tablespace storage. DBA_TAB_COLUMNS won't even have information about this table or anything related to tablespace quotas, because it lists the columns in every table on the database. The DBA_TABLESPACES choice is a good distracter. To avoid choosing the wrong answer, you need to be sure you are familiar with the use of dictionary views like this one. **(Topic 17.3)**

**39.** A. DEFAULT

**Explanation** All users are assigned the DEFAULT profile if none is identified in the CREATE USER statement. CONNECT and DBA are both roles, so those choices are incorrect. And although there is no PROFILE clause in this statement, it would be incorrect to assume that no profile gets assigned to the user because of it. **(Topic 17.1)**

**40.** B. Tablespace Manager

**Explanation** The correct answer is Tablespace Manager. Although database objects are part of schemas and stored in tablespaces, you would not use Schema Manager unless you actually wanted to manipulate the objects themselves (as opposed to the tablespaces). Security Manager is for user privilege and role management, thus being incorrect, and Recovery Manager is for backup and recovery on your database, making that an incorrect choice as well. **(Topic 2.1)**

**41.** B. DBA_PROFILES

**Explanation** DBA_PROFILES is the dictionary view where you can find information about profiles and the resource settings associated with them. The DBA_USERS view is incorrect because it only identifies what profile is assigned to a user. RESOURCE_COST is incorrect because it only identifies the relative cost assigned to those resources that can be lumped together using resource costing. RESOURCE_LIMIT is incorrect because it is not a view—it is an initialization parameter that must be set in order to use profiles. **(Topic 18.5)**

**42. B.** INSERT /*+APPEND */ INTO EMP_BKP (SELECT * FROM EMP);

**Explanation** Probably the biggest distractor on this question is the choice stating there is no direct path for INSERT statements. Though not commonly used, hints do exist, and have been around for a long time. You need to understand them in order to pass OCP Exam 2. The correct hint in this case is /*+APPEND */. /*+DIRECT */ is not a real hint. You could use the NOLOGGING option for your INSERT statement in Oracle, but this will not cause the INSERT statement to take the direct path. **(Topic 16.1)**

**43. A.** CATPROC.SQL

**Explanation** The CATPROC.SQL script must be run after running CATALOG.SQL to create your Oracle-supplied packages. UTLPWDMG.SQL is a script you run later to add password management, while UTLLOCKT.SQL is a script you also run later to detect whether there are lock-wait events on your database. **(Topic 5.3)**

**44. D.** Roles

**Explanation** Roles permit you to configure password authentication to limit the use of the privileges they bestow. This is accomplished with the IDENTIFIED BY clause—the same as in the CREATE or ALTER USER statements. Profiles don't require passwords, nor do tables or rollback segments, unless you count the password you supplied to log in to the database. **(Topic 20.2)**

**45. B.** Issue ALTER ROLLBACK SEGMENT CTXROL SHRINK;

**Explanation** The SHRINK keyword used in an ALTER ROLLBACK SEGMENT command will cause the rollback segment to shrink in size, deallocating all the extra extents. Resizing the NEXT extent is the wrong way to go because all extents in a rollback segment should be the same size, so that answer is incorrect. You don't need to drop and re-create the rollback segment for this task, making that choice also incorrect. Finally, you could alter the setting for OPTIMAL, but this won't necessarily do much for you with regard to actually changing the allocation for the rollback segment. **(Topic 10.3)**

**46. A.** ALL_DEF_AUDIT_OPTS

**Explanation** The ALL_DEF_AUDIT_OPTS dictionary view shows you the options in place for auditing on the database. DBA_AUDIT_TRAIL is incorrect because that view actually shows you the results of the audit, as does DBA_AUDIT_SESSION.

The AUD$ table is the underlying table for all views like DBA_AUDIT_TRAIL and DBA_AUDIT_SESSION, making that choice incorrect as well. **(Topic 21.3)**

**47.** C.   Create multiple members for each of your four groups and place them on different disks

**Explanation**   To solve this problem, you must create multiple members for each of your four groups and place them on different disks. The INIT.ORA file has nothing whatsoever to do with multiplexing online redo logs, so you can eliminate those choices. Finally, although adding groups improves some situations, you are not looking for more redo logs—you are looking for more members in each log. **(Topic 7.4)**

**48.** A.   EXCEPTIONS

**Explanation**   The EXCEPTIONS table can be used by the DBA to identify ROWIDs for rows with duplicate primary keys. The DBA_TABLES view is not going to help, because you don't need to know the table, tablespace, or storage information to enable or fix a primary key. USER_TAB_COLUMNS is also of limited value. Finally, AUD$ is no good because that's where audit records are stored. You might be able to find the folks who did it, but that isn't going to solve the problem. **(Topic 14.1)**

**49.** C.   Grant the CONNECT role to the user

**Explanation**   The appropriate resolution is to somehow allow the user to create a session with Oracle. This is done in two ways, either by granting CREATE SESSION privileges or by granting the CONNECT role, which has the CREATE SESSION privilege granted to it. Unlocking the user's account won't help because they haven't even gotten to the point where they can successfully connect yet, while resetting the user's password and granting CREATE TABLE privileges are both incorrect for roughly the same reason. **(Topic 20.4)**

**50.** C.   Convert your B-tree index to a reverse-key index

**Explanation**   Oracle recommends using reverse-key indexes in situations where the leading significant figures of a number or characters in a string are not unique enough to provide the lead-in differentiation required for making an index perform better. If the reverse-key index choices had not been present, the B-tree index choices would have been more correct—making for strong distractors. Any conversion between bitmap and B-tree indexes is unnecessary and detrimental because bitmap and B-tree indexes improve query performance in exactly opposite situations. **(Topic 13.3)**

**51.** C. INSERT trigger

**Explanation** The INSERT trigger would work best in this situation. This is because the constraint requires lookups against different tables for different value classifications. This complexity is more than any declarative integrity constraint in the Oracle database could handle, making triggers the logical choice. And, while you can obtain the functionality you need with PL/SQL, a stored procedure alone won't have the intelligence required to run every time data is added to the table. **(Topic 14.1)**

**52.** D. CHAR

**Explanation** The CHAR datatype is the most appropriate for this given situation because you want to store data in a fixed-width column. That means the column will contain extra blanks to the full, declared size of the column. VARCHAR2, CLOB, and LONG do not allow you to do this, because they are variable-width column datatypes. Also, ten sentences of text is probably not more than 2,000 characters, the limit for CHAR datatypes in Oracle8. **(Topic 12.1)**

**53.** B. Unsuccessful UPDATE and DELETE statements performed by any user on CAT_TOYS will be recorded.

**Explanation** The correct answer is unsuccessful UPDATE and DELETE statements performed by any user on CAT_TOYS will be recorded. Auditing data change activities BY ACCESS causes Oracle to write one record for each audited statement; in comparison to this, BY SESSION causes Oracle to write a single record for all SQL statements of the same type issued in the same session. The WHENEVER NOT SUCCESSFUL clause means only unsuccessful statements will be recorded. Finally, only the CAT_TOYS table will be audited. **(Topic 21.1)**

**54.** A. DBA_IND_COLUMNS

**Explanation** You would look in the DBA_IND_COLUMNS to see what the column order for the primary-key index was. The DBA_TAB_COLUMNS will only tell you what columns are in the table. The DBA_INDEXES table will give you structural information about the index, but not its contents. The DBA_CLU_COLUMNS view will only obtain information about clustered columns. **(Topic 14.2)**

**55.** C. TOUSER

**Explanation** The correct answer is TOUSER. The INCTYPE parameter identifies the type of incremental import you plan to perform, while IGNORE is designed so that you can import row data for tables that already exist in the database without seeing all the errors produced when Oracle attempts to re-create the table. Finally, DIRECT is not a parameter you can use with IMPORT. **(Topic 16.3)**

**56.** D.   Nothing. You cannot drop a profile that has been granted to users.

**Explanation**   The correct answer is nothing. You cannot drop a profile that has been granted to users without specifying the CASCADE option. That option is missing from the statement you issued, so nothing happens. Had you included the CASCADE option, users who had the LTD_PROGRAMMER profile might now have the DEFAULT profile, so watch out for distractors like that one. Otherwise, all other statements are incorrect. **(Topic 18.3)**

**57.** B.   Increasing the value set for PCTUSED on the table

**Explanation**   You can increase the values set for PCTINCREASE and NEXT using the ALTER TABLE statement to reduce the number of extents a segment will allocate as part of table growth. If you wanted, you could reorganize the table using EXPORT with the COMPRESS option. But, you couldn't use PCTUSED to perform this task. **(Topic 9.2)**

**58.** D.   System segments

**Explanation**   SYSTEM object segments typically have the lowest turnover of all database segments in Oracle. This is because SYSTEM tables are never dropped and re-created, or truncated (AUD$ table notwithstanding). Rollback segments frequently allocate and deallocate extents, as do temporary segments. User-defined tables usually have more volatility than SYSTEM-owned objects. **(Topic 9.5)**

**59.** D.   SHUTDOWN NORMAL

**Explanation**   You most likely used the SHUTDOWN NORMAL option to turn off the Oracle database. SHUTDOWN NORMAL will not end existing sessions; instead, it will wait for users to finish their work and disconnect, but it will not allow others to log in after the SHUTDOWN command is issued. SHUTDOWN IMMEDIATE would have forced user transactions to roll back and disconnected them at the time the statement was issued, while SHUTDOWN ABORT would simply end database operation, terminating all uncommitted transactions in progress. SHUTDOWN TRANSACTIONAL is a new option that allows users already connected to complete their current transaction, but after that disconnecting them in order to speed database shutdown. **(Topic 3.4)**

**60.** C. The server process obtains information for the user.

**Explanation** Information is obtained for user processes by means of the server process. DBW0 is incorrect because that process writes data to disk, not from disk into memory. The user process certainly doesn't do this work on its own, and the listener process doesn't actually obtain data from disk for the user either. **(Topic 1.2)**

# Answers to Practice Exam 2

**1.** B.  V$ROLLSTAT

**Explanation** The V$ROLLSTAT view contains information about various rollback segment performance statistics, including the frequency of wraps. DBA_ROLLBACK_SEGS isn't used for this purpose because the only dynamic information the dictionary view contains about rollback segments is whether they are online or offline. V$ROLLNAME only contains the name and rollback segment number for all rollback segments in Oracle. Finally, DBA_SEGMENTS gives information about individual segments in the rollback segment, but no dynamic performance information. **(Topic 10.4)**

**2.** B.  From Oracle default storage settings.

**Explanation** Oracle comes configured with default storage settings for tablespaces predefined, making that the correct answer. These settings vary from operating system to operating system. Although you do not need to set up default tablespace storage settings when you create the tablespace, it is recommended that you do so. Furthermore, to say that default settings come from nowhere is inaccurate—they come from Oracle default settings. **(Topic 8.2)**

**3.** C.  The DROP TABLESPACE command fails because you didn't include the INCLUDING CONTENTS option.

**Explanation** In this situation, the DROP TABLESPACE command fails because you didn't include the INCLUDING CONTENTS option. To drop the tablespace, you must issue DROP TABLESPACE BY_TBLSPC INCLUDING CONTENTS. There may be some problem with cascading constraints, but you don't have enough information to declare this the correct answer, so it's wrong. Obviously, the DROP TABLESPACE command does not succeed. Finally, you must certainly drop a tablespace after creating it. **(Topic 8.2)**

**4.** C.  Server Manager returns an error saying you need to connect to Oracle first.

**Explanation** After starting Server Manager and before you start doing anything substantial with it, you must connect to Oracle as a privileged user. If you don't connect as a privileged user but try performing privileged activities anyway, Server Manager returns errors. The database will not shut down until after you issue SHUTDOWN IMMEDIATE while connected to Oracle, but once issued, Oracle will disconnect users forcibly and also roll back their transactions. Finally, Server Manager most certainly is a command-line mode tool. **(Topic 2.1)**

**5. A.** Issue SELECT * FROM DBA_PARAMETERS; from SQL*Plus

**Explanation** The SELECT * FROM DBA_PARAMETERS statement yields nothing because DBA_PARAMETERS is not a valid dictionary view in Oracle. The V$PARAMETER view is appropriate for this purpose, as is the SHOW PARAMETERS command in Server Manager. Finally, Instance Manager will show you initialization parameters in a GUI display. **(Topic 3.5)**

**6. D.** V$SESSION

**Explanation** The V$SESSION view contains information about all users connected to Oracle. You will need to obtain the SID and SERIAL# for the session in order to forcibly disconnect the session from Oracle. The V$SESSTAT view contains session statistics and their values, but not information about specific users connected to Oracle. V$PARAMETER contains the parameters set when the instance started. DBA_USERS is a view that gives you information about each user's configuration, such as default and temporary tablespace information, but you would never use DBA_USERS to find information to kill a session. **(Topic 3.6)**

**7. B.** Bitmap indexes cannot be unique.

**Explanation** When you issue this statement, Oracle will give you a syntax error, stating it was looking for the INDEX keyword after UNIQUE instead of the BITMAP keyword. Thus, you cannot create bitmap indexes as unique indexes. You certainly can use the NOSORT, TABLESPACE, and ASC keywords in this statement, and in this statement they are all used correctly. But, the UNIQUE BITMAP bit makes it invalid, and Oracle will give you an error. **(Topic 13.2)**

**8. D.** ROLE_ROLE_PRIVS

**Explanation** ROLE_ROLE_PRIVS is the correct answer because it displays all the roles and the roles granted to the roles. DBA_ROLE_PRIVS shows only users that have roles granted to them. DBA_TAB_PRIVS shows the users with object privileges granted to them. The USER_SYS_PRIVS view shows only those system privileges granted to you, the user connected to Oracle. **(Topic 20.5)**

**9. A.** ALTER SESSION SET NLS_DATE_FORMAT = 'DD-MON-YYYY:HH:MIAM';

**Explanation** Since all the statements are roughly the same, you must look carefully at the syntax in order to know what the correct answer is. The proper date format is 'DD-MON-YYYY:HH:MIAM', which obtains you the result 10-FEB-1999:10:15AM.

DD-MON-YY:HH24:MI gives you a result of 10-FEB-99:10:15, so it is incorrect, while DD-MON-YY:HH:MIAM gives you 10-FEB-99:10:15AM, which is also incorrect. Finally, DD-MON-YYYY:HH24:MI gives you a result of 10-MON-1999:10:15, which is still incorrect. **(Topic 22.2)**

**10.** D. Value-based auditing

**Explanation** Value-based auditing best describes this situation. Statement auditing is not right because you don't want to audit every statement—only those that change a particular column to a particular value. Triggers will work best for this situation. You don't want to audit every access on the ORDERS table, either, so object auditing is out. Finally, many different users might have the ability to change order status in several different phases of the order entry and shipment process, so audit by access isn't necessarily appropriate. Value-based auditing is auditing done by triggers or programmatically to detect when specific values change to specific other values. **(Topic 21.1)**

**11.** B. INDEX

**Explanation** Of the privileges mentioned, only the INDEX privilege is an object privilege. The rest are system privileges. One way to ensure that you understand the difference between system and object privileges is to remember that object privileges give access to objects, while system privileges let you create objects. In this case, however, even this basic principle of Oracle privileges is violated in concept because even though the INDEX privilege lets you create indexes off of tables, it is still an object privilege. Thus, the best way to distinguish object privileges from system privileges is simply to memorize the object privileges (there are less than a dozen of them) and simply assume everything else is a system privilege. **(Topic 19.1)**

**12.** C. SORT_AREA_SIZE

**Explanation** Your INITIAL default storage setting for the temporary tablespace should be some multiple of SORT_AREA_SIZE because this ensures a relationship between the area in memory used for sorts and the utilization of disk space for that purpose when you run out of space in memory. LOG_BUFFER is the size of the redo log buffer and has little to do with disk sorts. DB_BLOCK_BUFFERS is the number of buffers that constitutes the buffer cache, and again there is little relationship between the buffer cache and disk sorts. Finally, SHARED_POOL_SIZE is exactly that—the size of the shared pool—which, again, has little to do with disk sorts. **(Topic 11.2)**

**13.** C. DBA_TABLES

**Explanation** The DBA_TABLES view will tell you the name of the cluster that the table belongs to, so that you can query for tables that belong to the cluster. DBA_OBJECTS will not give you this information. Neither will DBA_CLUSTERS, which instead gives you configuration and storage information for the cluster. Finally, DBA_CLU_TABLES is a fictitious spin-off on DBA_CLU_COLUMNS, a real dictionary view. **(Topic 15.3)**

**14.** B. Cached data is saved immediately to disk.

**Explanation** Oracle divorces transaction activity from disk I/O by having a database writer process handle writing changes to disk. This activity doesn't necessarily happen immediately, and completion of the commit doesn't depend on it happening. All the other activities, such as releasing locks on tables, rows, or rollback segments, does happen, however, and a COMMIT statement generates a redo entry. **(Topic 1.4)**

**15.** D. When the statement is executed

**Explanation** Data changes are made at the time Oracle actually executes the statement. Opening and parsing the statement all occur before the statement is executed, so the data change hasn't occurred yet. UPDATE statements do not have data to fetch from a cursor the way SELECT statements do, so there is no fetch activity in a DML statement like an UPDATE. **(Topic 1.3)**

**16.** D. Sequence segment

**Explanation** Sequences are not physically stored in a tablespace as database objects. Rather, their definition is stored in the data dictionary and in memory, and called upon when values from the sequence are required. All the other choices identify valid types of segments in Oracle. **(Topic 9.1)**

**17.** B. DBA_FREE_SPACE

**Explanation** If you only wanted to know how much of a particular tablespace was free, you would use the DBA_FREE_SPACE view. DBA_TABLESPACES and DBA_EXTENTS will tell you the total allocation for the tablespace and the total amount of space allocated for objects in that tablespace, respectively, and although you could calculate the free space from those two amounts, it is far easier to simply select the appropriate value from DBA_FREE_SPACE. V$TABLESPACE will only give you the tablespace name and number for the tablespace on the database. **(Topic 9.4)**

18. A. V$CONTROLFILE_RECORD_SECTION

**Explanation** Information about the name and location of your control files can be found in the two database views V$CONTROLFILE and V$PARAMETER, and in the INIT.ORA file. However, the V$CONTROLFILE_RECORD_SECTION will not tell you your control file locations. **(Topic 6.3)**

19. C. Oracle will leave more space free in data blocks for existing records.

**Explanation** By keeping PCTFREE high, Oracle will leave more space free in database blocks for existing records to grow via later UPDATEs. PCTUSED is the storage option that dictates how Oracle manages filling data blocks on tables more or less actively, so those choices should be easily eliminated. **(Topic 9.3)**

20. C. The statement fails.

**Explanation** The ALTER TABLE statement will fail because you cannot have more than one column in an Oracle table with a LONG datatype. You can, however, have multiple LOB type columns in the same table in Oracle8 and Oracle8*i*. Oracle is not programmed to create the LONG column for you using a different datatype. **(Topic 12.1)**

21. A. Delete activity on SYS.AUD$ by anyone

**Explanation** This audit statement will monitor anyone deleting data from the AUD$ table owned by SYS. Auditing data change activities BY ACCESS causes Oracle to write one record for each audited statement; in comparison to this, BY SESSION causes Oracle to write a single record for all SQL statements of the same type issued in the same session. The ON keyword indicates the database object, which in this case is AUD$ owned by SYS. The DELETE keyword indicates the type of activity Oracle should monitor, eliminating the choice referring to an INSERT statement. **(Topic 21.2)**

**22.** D.  Users to which ANN granted INSERT privileges will not be able to INSERT.

**Explanation**  Though it doesn't say whether or not ANN had the GRANT OPTION on this object privilege, the choice stating that users to which ANN granted INSERT privileges will not be able to INSERT is the only thing that truly happens when the DBA revokes INSERT privileges from ANN. So long as the DBA didn't revoke ANN's CREATE SESSION privilege (nothing in the question points to this conclusion), ANN can still connect. Records for a user are never removed when an object privilege is revoked, either. Finally, nothing in the question pointed to the conclusion that ANN was ever able to create tables, so discard that choice as well. **(Topic 19.2)**

**23.** C.  INITIAL=1MB, NEXT=2MB, PCTINCREASE=25

**Explanation**  This question will make you use your scratch paper, but beware—it may suck up a lot of your time too if you're not careful! You will probably want to simply devise a quick formula and plug in values. The formula is INITIAL + NEXT + (NEXT * (1 + PCTINCREASE)) + (NEXT * (1 + PCTINCREASE) * (1 + PCTINCREASE)). 2+2+(2*1.25) + (2*1.25*1.25) = 9.625, so the INITIAL=2MB, NEXT=2MB, PCTINCREASE=25 choice is out. Simply looking at the values for choice INITIAL=2MB, NEXT=3MB, PCTINCREASE=50 should tell you that two of them are greater than the previous choice explained, so this one must be out as well. You are looking for the choice that has smaller values than the first choice discussed, and there is only one: INITIAL=1MB, NEXT=2MB, PCTINCREASE=25. Plugging in the numbers gives you 1+2+(2*1.25) + (2*1.25*1.25), or 8.625, so that choice is the right answer. **(Topic 12.2)**

**24.** B.  Set SESSIONS_PER_USER in the DEFAULT profile to 1

**Explanation**  The best way to handle the job the question indicates is to make an adjustment to the user profile, not the INIT.ORA file, eliminating two choices right there. After that, it's simply a matter of choosing the profile limit that looks the best. In this case, SESSIONS_PER_USER looks more like something that would limit user sessions in Oracle, more so than IDLE_TIME would. **(Topic 18.3)**

**25.** B.  Row cache

**Explanation**  Data dictionary records are kept in a memory area of the shared pool. This is to improve overall performance of the Oracle database by keeping frequently accessed areas of the dictionary in memory. The library cache is where SQL statement parse trees are stored, not dictionary information. The session UGA will contain no dictionary information, and thus, choice C is incorrect. The buffer cache stores recently used information from SQL statements that didn't use the data dictionary. **(Topic 5.2)**

**26.** C.  A direct path data load bypasses most of the Oracle RDBMS, while a conventional path data load is a high-speed version of the SQL INSERT.

**Explanation**  The most accurate description of why these two paths differ is that the direct path data load bypasses most of the Oracle RDBMS, while a conventional path data load is a high-speed version of the SQL INSERT. Simply saying one is faster than the other doesn't really get to the heart of the matter, while the other statements are technically invalid. **(Topic 16.2)**

**27.** C.  DBA_SEGMENTS

**Explanation**  DBA_SEGMENTS is the most useful view for the purpose of finding the location of indexes in a tablespace or datafile, and the amount of space used by those indexes. DBA_TS_QUOTAS will give you information about how much space a user's objects can use in a tablespace, but that's about it. DBA_OBJECTS will tell you when the object was created, but not how big it is. DBA_INDEXES will give you information about storage configuration, but not actual storage allocation. **(Topic 13.5)**

**28.** D.  Bad file

**Explanation**  The bad file is where SQL*Loader puts records that couldn't be loaded into the database because of constraints, datatype inconsistencies, or similar problems. The datafile is where information to load comes from. The discard file also contains records that weren't loaded, but the SQL*Loader control file contains the test criteria for discarding records, not the database itself. Finally, the log file merely tells you how the load went. **(Topic 16.2)**

**29.** B.  SET TRANSACTION

**Explanation**  The SET TRANSACTION statement is used to assign transactions to specific rollback segments. Though not typically recommended, this can be a useful technique, particularly if you have one or two long-running batch processes and specific large rollback segments that are usually offline but brought online to handle this specific need. ALTER DATABASE will not assign a transaction to a rollback segment, nor will ALTER TABLE, so those choices are wrong. Finally, you must avoid the obvious distractor in ALTER ROLLBACK SEGMENT—the question clearly indicates that the rollback segment is *already* online. **(Topic 10.3)**

**30.** C. Oracle eventually won't allow new records to be added to the database.

**Explanation** In this situation, Oracle eventually won't allow new records to be added to the database, and the entire database will go into a prolonged wait state until the redo log is cleared. So, something will happen, and Oracle will not switch to a new redo log automatically. But, the instance does not crash, either—it simply freezes, and won't allow changes to be made or new users to connect. **(Topic 7.5)**

**31.** A. AUDIT SESSION BY ACCESS WHENEVER NOT SUCCESSFUL

**Explanation** The appropriate statement is AUDIT SESSION BY ACCESS WHENEVER NOT SUCCESSFUL. SESSION refers to CREATE SESSION or logon activity. Auditing data change activities BY ACCESS causes Oracle to write one record for each audited statement; in comparison to this, BY SESSION causes Oracle to write a single record for all SQL statements of the same type issued in the same session. You only want users recorded who attempt to log in but fail, so that eliminates all the statements containing WHENEVER SUCCESSFUL. **(Topic 21.2)**

**32.** A. Decreasing tablespace size

**Explanation** All choices affect the number of checkpoints on the database, except for decreasing tablespace size. Smaller redo logs cause log switches to occur more frequently, making for more frequent checkpoints. Setting LOG_CHECKPOINT_TIMEOUT to zero makes checkpoints happen less frequently, as does setting LOG_CHECKPOINT_INTERVAL greater than the size of the redo log file. However, checkpoints have nothing to do with the size of your database's tablespaces. **(Topic 7.3)**

**33.** C. COMPOSITE_LIMIT

**Explanation** In this question, you must read the choices carefully, and understand what is being asked. The real question here is whether you understand resource costs and composite limits. Each of the choices other than COMPOSITE_LIMIT can be rolled up into COMPOSITE_LIMIT with the use of resource costing. Only the resources available for profiles can be included as part of a composite limit. **(Topic 18.2)**

**34.** C. REVOKE CREATE ANY TABLE FROM ANN; then GRANT CREATE ANY TABLE TO ANN;

**Explanation** In a REVOKE command, you don't refer to the ADMIN OPTION at all. However, when you revoke a privilege that was granted with administrative capability, the entire privilege along with administrative capability is removed. As such, you must grant the privilege back to the user without administrative privileges in order for the user to continue using the privilege. **(Topic 19.2)**

**35.** D. ALTER USER DEFAULT ROLE NONE EXCEPT ROLE_1;

**Explanation** You may use the EXCEPT keyword in your ALTER USER DEFAULT ROLE command, but only if the ALL keyword is also used. The NONE keyword in this command must be used by itself, which makes the choice that says ALTER USER DEFAULT ROLE NONE EXCEPT ROLE_1; a bad statement, and thus the correct answer. **(Topic 20.2)**

**36.** A. From your INIT.ORA file

**Explanation** Oracle will always prefer to use your INIT.ORA file to determine startup settings. You can get away without specifying the absolute path of your INIT.ORA file for the PFILE parameter if you have a copy of the INIT.ORA file for this database stored in the DBS directory under $ORACLE_HOME in UNIX (DATABASE directory in NT). If no INIT.ORA file is found and if a location is not specified using PFILE, then Oracle will not mount or open your database, but will use some internal default settings to start an idle instance. Tablespace default settings have no function in database startup, nor is anything regarding initialization parameters read from the redo log file. **(Topic 3.3)**

**37.** B. Writes current redo log number to datafile headers

**Explanation** The CKPT process handles two things in Oracle: it signals to DBWR that dirty buffers must be written to disk, and it also writes log sequence numbers to datafile headers and the control file. It does not, however, write dirty buffers to disk—DBWR does that. It also doesn't write redo log information to disk, only LGWR does that. Finally, it does not read data from disk into memory for user processes—the server process performs this task. **(Topic 7.1)**

**38.** D. All extents should be the same size

**Explanation** To be fair, there are many schools of thought on sizing rollback segments. However, a prevalent school is that extents should be the same size. Choice A is incorrect because PCTINCREASE is not a valid storage clause on the CREATE ROLLBACK SEGMENT command. Choices B and C are also logically flawed, considering the prevalence of sizing rollback segment extents to be the same. **(Topic 10.1)**

**39.** D. To prevent users from waiting if a redo log member cannot be archived

**Explanation** The choice identifying the reason for multiplexing redo logs to prevent users from waiting if a redo log member cannot be archived is probably the best answer. You do not have enough information to tell if there is an increase in storage space on your host machine; besides, multiplexing is also supposed to prevent I/O bottlenecks between the ARCH and LGWR processes—which improves redo log performance, not degrades it. However, in some cases—such as when two redo log members are on the same disk—you might see some performance degradation associated with double-writes to disk. Finally, there will always be a dependency on the redo log buffer, because users write their redo entries there instead of directly to disk. **(Topic 7.1)**

**40.** B. HASHKEYS

**Explanation** The HASHKEYS keyword indicates that you are using hash clusters, which are often able to calculate the address on disk of your data and read it into memory with as little as one disk read. The PCTINCREASE and INITIAL keywords indicate storage options available for most database objects. These have nothing at all to do with the question. Finally, though reverse-key indexes can improve performance on queries by permitting table access by ROWID, at least one disk read will be required in order to load the index block into memory in order to find the appropriate key value/ROWID combination. **(Topic 15.1)**

**41.** C. LOGICAL_WRITES_PER_SESSION

**Explanation** Each of the following choices indicates an appropriate resource profile, except for LOGICAL_WRITES_PER_SESSION. LOGICAL_READS_PER_SESSION is the number of reads to the buffer cache that are permitted in the session before Oracle must terminate. CONNECT_TIME defines a hard time-out for connections to the database before Oracle closes the session. IDLE_TIME is another time-out that defines how long a session can be connected while doing no work. All these keywords indicate settings within a resource profile. So, since LOGICAL_WRITES_PER_SESSION is not a real resource profile setting, that choice is the correct answer. **(Topic 18.2)**

**42.** D. UPDATE

**Explanation** The goal in this question is to update existing data records during a data load. One example of where this might occur is when records are fed into a system where it is possible that the record already exists but may have been changed. All of the choices in the question indicate ways you can load data into tables using SQL*Loader, except for UPDATE. You cannot change existing records using SQL*Loader, only load new ones into an existing table. If you want to create a process that will update existing records or add ones that don't exist in the table, you will need to use PL/SQL in conjunction with the UTL_FILE Oracle-supplied package, or utilize an Oracle precompiler to do so programmatically outside the database. **(Topic 16.2)**

**43.** B. ALTER SYSTEM

**Explanation** The ALTER SYSTEM SWITCH LOGFILE statement is used to manually switch a log file. ALTER DATABASE is not used, nor is ALTER USER, nor is ALTER REDO LOG, which incidentally isn't even a real SQL statement. **(Topic 7.3)**

**44.** D. DEFAULT ROLE

**Explanation** You cannot use the DEFAULT ROLE clause in the CREATE USER statement, because no roles have been granted to the user yet. This is an interesting little fact to keep in mind about the CREATE USER statement that may find its way onto your OCP exam. Other than that, assigning a TEMPORARY TABLESPACE, password with IDENTIFIED BY, or a user profile, are all fair game. **(Topic 17.2)**

**45.** B. IDENTIFIED BY

**Explanation** Of the choices given, only the IDENTIFIED BY clause indicates a clause that can be issued in the ALTER USER statement by the users themselves. All the rest are managed by the DBA. This is, of course, true in the absence of the user being granted the ALTER ANY USER system privilege, but there is no indication in the question that should cause you to believe that the user has the ALTER ANY USER privilege. **(Topic 17.2)**

**46.** A. ALTER PROFILE DEFAULT LIMIT COMPOSITE_LIMIT 3500;

**Explanation** To perform the action indicated in the question, you would use the ALTER PROFILE DEFAULT LIMIT COMPOSITE_LIMIT 3500; statement. RESOURCE_COST is not an appropriate INIT.ORA parameter; instead, you would use RESOURCE_LIMITS. You wouldn't in fact need to make a change to a licensing parameter in the INIT.ORA file at all. Finally, changing a resource limit for the profile doesn't alter its cost or its composite limit. **(Topic 18.3)**

**47.** D. GRANT

**Explanation** Giving a role to a user is the same process as giving a privilege to a user—and it is handled with the same command, GRANT. ALTER USER may be used to switch the default role later, but not until the role is actually granted. Since we are only working with one user, there is no need for a system- or database-wide alteration. **(Topic 20.2)**

**48.** B. SELECT

**Explanation** Since rollback segments are allocated for all transactional statements, all the DML statements will force the user to acquire a rollback segment. However, no rollback segment gets allocated when the SELECT statement is issued, making that the correct answer. **(Topic 10.3)**

**49.** A. In the PGA

**Explanation** When dedicated servers are in use, session information is stored in the PGA for the session. If MTS was in place, then the shared pool would have been the correct answer. Session information is never stored in the buffer cache or redo log buffer. **(Topic 1.1)**

**50.** B. Getting rid of a column

**Explanation** You only need to drop and re-create the table if you want to remove a column from that table. You can do some altering of datatypes, such as increasing the width of a VARCHAR2 column or converting a VARCHAR2 column to a CHAR column, without having to drop the table, and you can add columns to a table without dropping the table. **(Topic 12.1)**

**TIP**
*The limitation against removing columns from tables was removed in Oracle8i.*

**51.** A. QUOTA ON

**Explanation** The QUOTA clause in a CREATE USER statement will limit the amount of space the user can allocate in a tablespace with his or her own tables. It will not, however, impose consistent limits on the amount of data a user can add to his or her own or another user's tables, usually. DEFAULT TABLESPACE, PROFILE, and IDENTIFIED BY have nothing to do with tablespace space allocation. **(Topic 17.2)**

**52. D.** Much free space left for UPDATEs, and space left free by DELETEs not actively filled in by Oracle

**Explanation** A high PCTFREE value (25 is fairly high) will leave much free space for UPDATEs to increase the size of each row, while a low value for PCTUSED (30 is low) means that space left free by table DELETE operations will not return the block to a free list quickly. Little free space left for UPDATEs, and space left free by DELETEs actively filled in by Oracle means that PCTUSED is high (60–70) and PCTFREE is low (5–10). Little free space left for UPDATEs, and space left free by DELETEs not actively filled in by Oracle means that PCTFREE is low (5–10) and PCTUSED is low (20–30). Much free space left for UPDATEs, and space left free by DELETEs actively filled in by Oracle means that PCTFREE is high (20–30) and PCTUSED is high (60–70). **(Topic 9.3)**

**53. C.** Dispatches user process access to a shared server

**Explanation** DNNN, where NNN is a three-digit number (009 in this case), indicates a dispatcher process, which is a process that runs in the MTS or multithreaded server environment, making that choice the correct answer. DBWR writes dirty buffers to disk, making that choice incorrect, while CKPT writes the current redo log number to datafile headers during checkpoints and log switches, making that choice incorrect. The LGWR process writes redo log entries to disk. **(Topic 1.1)**

**54. B.** In the shared pool

**Explanation** When MTS is in use, session information is stored in the shared pool. Only when dedicated servers are being used will Oracle store session information in the PGA, making that choice incorrect. Session information is never stored in the buffer cache, redo log buffer, or large area. **(Topic 1.1)**

**55. D.** VARCHAR2

**Explanation** Views adopt the datatype of the columns from the base tables they select from, as long as there are no data conversion functions present in the view. In this case, the underlying column is a number, but there is also a TO_CHAR operation on that column, making the resulting datatype in the view a VARCHAR2. **(Topic 12.1)**

**56. D. NLS_SORT**

**Explanation** The NLS_SORT parameter allows you to define overriding sort order according to a language other than the national language set for the database. NLS_DATE_FORMAT is no use here, because that simply identifies the date format. NLS_RULE is an invalid national language set variable. One potential distractor in this situation is the NLS_LANG variable, which is used to define the language set the database will use. NLS_LANG consists of *language_territory.charset* and therefore it implicitly can influence the sorting, while NLS_TERRITORY helps Oracle identify the peculiarities of the geographical location the database runs in. **(Topic 22.4)**

**57. C. You can use variable-length multibyte character sets as both character sets on your database.**

**Explanation** You can NOT use variable-length multibyte character sets as both character sets on your database, so the choice stating you can shouldn't enter into consideration when choosing a character set and national character set for your database. Other than that, you should consider making your character set US7ASCII or a superset of it (although the national character set can be whatever you choose), your national character set and character set should be closely related where possible, and Oracle supports only English-like languages as its character set for entering SQL and PL/SQL commands. **(Topic 22.1)**

**58. A. V$NLS_PARAMETERS**

**Explanation** The view you might use for this purpose is V$NLS_PARAMETERS. NLS_DATE_FORMAT is actually an initialization parameter, not a view, so you should be able to eliminate that one immediately as a choice. DBA_DATES is not a real view, so you should be able to eliminate that choice as well. This leaves you with V$NLS_VALID_VALUES. You should investigate the database views supporting language specifications before taking OCP Exam 2. **(Topic 22.5)**

**59. B. NLS_CURRENCY**

**Explanation** The NLS_CURRENCY parameter could be set in your database to indicate the currency symbol is not $. NLS_SORT allows you to alter the default sort order in support of other languages. NLS_LANG is the parameter that indicates to Oracle the national language for this database, while NLS_DATE_FORMAT is used to indicate the date display characteristics. **(Topic 22.3)**

**60.** A. BACKGROUND_DUMP_DEST

**Explanation** You can find your ALERT file in the directory specified by the BACKGROUND_DUMP_DEST initialization parameter because the ALERT file is similar in behavior to a background process trace file that tracks—only it tracks system-wide events, not just events occurring for one background process. USER_DUMP_DEST is used to identify the location for user trace files from user sessions. LOG_ARCHIVE_DEST is used to identify where Oracle places archived redo logs. CORE_DUMP_DEST is where Oracle places core dump files from a failed process. **(Topic 3.7)**

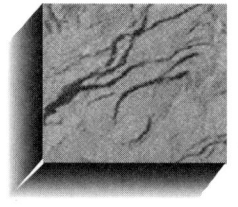

# CHAPTER 3

OCP Exam 3:
Backup and
Recovery Workshop

OCP Exam 3 in the Oracle DBA track covers concepts and practices around Oracle database backup and recovery. To pass this exam, you need to demonstrate an understanding of the features available in Oracle for backing up your databases for recovery purposes. You will also need to demonstrate an understanding of the methods available in Oracle for database recovery. In more recent editions of OCP Exam 3, the focus has been on backup and recovery methods surrounding Oracle's ARCHIVELOG mode. In addition, Oracle8 and Oracle8*i* have a new tool called RMAN that replaces EBU for backup and recovery that you will also need to understand.

## OCP Exam 3 Topic Areas

The following topic areas are covered in OCP Exam 3. Note that these concepts are taken directly from the Oracle OCP Candidate Guide for OCP Exam 3, and are current as of the publication of this book. The topics and subtopics are as follows:

1. Backup and Recovery Considerations

    1.1. Define business, operational, and technical requirements for a backup and recovery strategy

    1.2. Identify the components of a disaster recovery plan

    1.3. Discuss the importance of testing a backup and recovery strategy

2. Oracle Recovery Structures and Processes

    2.1. Identify Oracle processes, file structures, and memory components as they pertain to backup and recovery

    2.2. Observe the importance of checkpoints, redo logs, and archives

    2.3. Identify the process of synchronizing files during a checkpoint

    2.4. Multiplex control files and redo logs

3. Oracle Backup and Recovery Configuration

    3.1. Identify recovery implications of operating in NOARCHIVELOG mode

    3.2. Describe the differences between ARCHIVELOG and NOARCHIVELOG mode

    3.3. Configure a database for ARCHIVELOG mode and automatic archiving

### Chapter 3: OCP Exam 3: Backup and Recovery Workshop

      **3.4.** Use INIT.ORA parameters to duplex archive log files

**4.** Oracle Recovery Manager Overview

      **4.1.** Determine when to use RMAN

      **4.2.** List uses of Backup Manager

      **4.3.** Identify the advantages of RMAN with and without a recovery catalog

      **4.4.** Create a recovery catalog

      **4.5.** Connect to Recovery Manager

**5.** Oracle Recovery Catalog Maintenance

      **5.1.** Use Recovery Manager to register, resync, and reset a database

      **5.2.** Maintain the recovery catalog using change, delete, and catalog commands

      **5.3.** Query the recovery catalog to generate reports and lists

      **5.4.** Create and execute scripts to perform backup and recovery operations

      **5.5.** Create, store, and run scripts

**6.** Physical Backups without Oracle Recovery Manager

      **6.1.** Perform database backups using operating system commands

      **6.2.** Describe the recovery implications of closed and open backups

      **6.3.** Perform closed and open database backups

      **6.4.** Identify the backup implications of the LOGGING and NOLOGGING modes

      **6.5.** Identify different types of control file backups

      **6.6.** Discuss backup issues associated with read-only tablespaces

      **6.7.** List data dictionary views useful for backup operations

**7.** Physical Backups Using Oracle Recovery Manager

      **7.1.** Identify types of RMAN backups

      **7.2.** Describe backup concepts using RMAN

      **7.3.** Perform incremental and cumulative backups

      **7.4.** Troubleshoot backup problems

      **7.5.** View information from the data dictionary

8. Types of Failures and Troubleshooting

   8.1. List the types of failure that may occur in an Oracle database environment

   8.2. Describe the structures for instance and media recovery

   8.3. Use the DBVERIFY utility to validate the structure of an Oracle database file

   8.4. Configure checksum operations

   8.5. Use log and trace files to diagnose backup and recovery problems

9. Oracle Recovery without Archiving

   9.1. Note the implications of media failure with a database in NOARCHIVELOG mode

   9.2. Recover a database in NOARCHIVELOG mode after media failure

   9.3. Restore files to a different location if media failure occurs

   9.4. Recover a database in NOARCHIVELOG mode using RMAN

10. Complete Oracle Recovery with Archiving

    10.1. Note the implications of instance failure with an ARCHIVELOG database

    10.2. Describe a complete recovery operation

    10.3. Note the advantages and disadvantages of recovering an ARCHIVELOG database

    10.4. Recover an ARCHIVELOG database using RMAN and Backup Manager

11. Incomplete Oracle Recovery with Archiving

    11.1. Identify the situations to use an incomplete recovery to recover the system

    11.2. Perform an incomplete database recovery

    11.3. Recover after losing current and active logs

    11.4. Use RMAN in an incomplete recovery

    11.5. Work with tablespace point-in-time recovery

12. Oracle EXPORT and IMPORT Utilities

    12.1. Use the EXPORT utility to create a complete logical backup of a database object

    12.2. Use the EXPORT utility to create an incremental backup of a database object

    12.3. Invoke the direct-path method export

    12.4. Use the IMPORT utility to recover a database object

13. Additional Oracle Recovery Issues

    13.1. List methods for minimizing downtime

    13.2. Diagnose and recover from database corruption errors

    13.3. Reconstruct a lost or damaged control file

    13.4. List recovery issues associated with an offline or read-only tablespace

    13.5. Recover from the loss of the recovery catalog

# Practice Exam 1

1. The DBA has decreased LOG_CHECKPOINT_INTERVAL to 6000 and changed LOG_CHECKPOINT_TIMEOUT from 0 to 5. Which of the following choices best identifies the impact these settings will have on the Oracle database?

    **A.** The increased checkpoint frequency will improve recoverability of the instance, but will adversely impact performance.

    **B.** The increased checkpoint frequency will improve recoverability of the instance, and will improve performance.

    **C.** The decreased checkpoint frequency will worsen recoverability of the instance, but will improve performance.

    **D.** The decreased checkpoint frequency will worsen recoverability of the instance, but will adversely affect performance.

2. The DBA is evaluating possible settings for init.ora parameters affecting checkpoint frequency. Which of the following is an effect on an Oracle database running in ARCHIVELOG mode if checkpoints occur rarely? (Choose three)

    **A.** Datafiles do not get synchronized between log switches.

    **B.** The instance is unrecoverable.

    **C.** DBW0 could fall behind in its processing.

    **D.** Opening the database after SHUTDOWN ABORT may take longer.

    **E.** Truncating tables will take a long time.

3. A machine hosting the Oracle database has three separate physical disks (called DISK1, DISK2, and DISK3, respectively) used for storing three online redo logs. Which of the following configurations is best in order to multiplex redo log members across these three separate disks when redo logs are being archived?

    **A.** DISK1: redo01a.dbf, redo01b.dbf; DISK2: redo02a.dbf, redo02b.dbf; DISK3: redo03a.dbf, redo03b.dbf

    **B.** DISK1: redo01a.dbf, redo03b.dbf; DISK2: redo01b.dbf, redo03a.dbf; DISK3: redo02a.dbf, redo02b.dbf

**C.** DISK1: redo01a.dbf, redo03b.dbf; DISK2: redo01b.dbf, redo02a.dbf; DISK3: redo03a.dbf, redo02b.dbf

**D.** DISK1: redo01a.dbf, redo02a.dbf, redo03a.dbf; DISK2: redo01b.dbf, redo02b.dbf, redo03b.dbf; DISK3: redo01c.dbf, redo02c.dbf, redo03c.dbf

4. The DBA is configuring archive multiplexing in an Oracle8 database. Which of the parameters given ensures that every copy of archive redo logs will be written to its destination?

   **A.** LOG_ARCHIVE_DUPLEX_DEST

   **B.** LOG_ARCHIVE_FORMAT

   **C.** LOG_ARCHIVE_MIN_SUCCEED_DEST

   **D.** LOG_ARCHIVE_DEST

5. The DBA is evaluating the use of RMAN in a backup and recovery strategy for Oracle databases. Which of the following are reasons NOT to use RMAN in conjunction with the overall method for backing up and recovering those databases?

   **A.** When backup and recovery is required for Oracle8 or Oracle8*i*

   **B.** When the database consists of large but mostly static datafiles

   **C.** When automation of the backup processing is required

   **D.** When use of a recovery catalog is not feasible

   **E.** When your backup strategy must encompass files other than Oracle database files

6. You are attempting to create a robust backup and recovery strategy using Oracle Enterprise Manager 2.0. Which of the following tools allow you to start and stop the Oracle instance? (Choose two)

   **A.** Storage Manager

   **B.** Backup Manager

   **C.** Data Manager

   **D.** Schema Manager

   **E.** Instance Manager

7. You are creating a recovery catalog for your production database. Which of the following roles must be granted to the recovery catalog owner in order for RMAN to work properly? (Choose two)

    A. RECOVERY_CATALOG_OWNER

    B. EXP_FULL_DATABASE

    C. SYSDBA

    D. EXECUTE_CATALOG_ROLE

8. You are attempting to connect to RMAN on the command line. In order to connect to the production database at the time you start RMAN, which of the following command-line options must be specified at the time of login?

    A. TARGET

    B. MSGLOG

    C. RCVCAT

    D. CMDFILE

9. You are backing up an Oracle database on the UNIX platform while the database is still open. Before issuing the TAR command, which of the following statements should be issued?

    A. SHUTDOWN IMMEDIATE

    B. SHUTDOWN ABORT

    C. ALTER DATABASE DATAFILE BEGIN BACKUP

    D. ALTER TABLESPACE BEGIN BACKUP

10. You are evaluating the complexity of an existing recovery strategy in your organization. Offline backups on NOARCHIVELOG mode databases offer which of the following benefits over offline backups on ARCHIVELOG databases?

    A. Complete recovery to point of failure

    B. Ease of use

    C. Fast restoration of transactions executed after backup

    D. Ideal recoverability for extensive production data

11. The DBA is attempting to back up the Oracle database control file. After issuing the ALTER DATABASE BACKUP CONTROLFILE TO TRACE command, where can the DBA find the backup control file creation materials Oracle created for him or her?

    A. USER_DUMP_DEST

    B. LOG_ARCHIVE_DEST

    C. CORE_DUMP_DEST

    D. BACKGROUND_DUMP_DEST

12. After performing a data load of static data on a tablespace, the DBA performs a backup. If the DBA then sets the tablespace to read-only mode, when is the next time a backup should be taken?

    A. Immediately after placing the tablespace into read-only mode

    B. The next time a data load is performed on the tablespace

    C. The next time the database is put into read-only mode

    D. The next time the DBA shuts down the database

    E. Never. The data will not change.

13. You are trying to determine the status of a database backup. In order to determine the datafiles involved in the backup, which of the following queries are appropriate?

    A. SELECT FILE# FROM V$DATAFILE WHERE STATUS = 'ONLINE'

    B. SELECT FILE# FROM V$BACKUP WHERE STATUS = 'ACTIVE'

    C. SELECT FNAME FROM V$DATAFILE WHERE STATUS = 'ACTIVE'

    D. SELECT FNAME FROM V$BACKUP WHERE STATUS = 'ONLINE'

14. You are generating a script for database backup in RMAN. Which of the following keywords indicates whether or not to back up empty blocks in a datafile or changed blocks?

    A. FILESPERSET

    B. LEVEL

    C. TYPE

    D. CURRENT

15. You are attempting to identify synchronization between files on a mounted database that was just backed up. Which of the following dictionary views may offer assistance in this task?

    A. V$BACKUP_CORRUPTION

    B. V$LOGFILE

    C. V$DATAFILE_HEADER

    D. V$BACKUP

16. An Oracle database ensures detection of the need for database recovery by checking for synchronization using which of the following background processes?

    A. DBW0

    B. LGWR

    C. CKPT

    D. SMON

17. In the event of corruption encountered as the result of performing checksum operations in the Oracle database, which of the following tasks must be executed in order for operation of the database to continue?

    A. Execute the SHUTDOWN ABORT command.

    B. Issue the ALTER DATABASE CLEAR UNARCHIVED LOGFILE GROUP command.

    C. Configure the LOG_BLOCK_CHECKSUM parameter.

    D. Run the DBVERIFY utility.

18. With NOARCHIVELOG enabled on your Oracle database, what files are required in order to execute database recovery?

    A. Datafiles, log files, and control file

    B. Datafiles and archive logs

    C. Datafiles and log files

    D. Datafiles only

19. The DBA is evaluating use of RMAN in conjunction with databases running in NOARCHIVELOG mode. An advantage to recovery of a NOARCHIVELOG database using RMAN includes which of the following choices?

A. Storage of recovery scripts in the recovery catalog

B. Satisfying requirement of tracking archives for the database

C. Ease of use

D. Ability to combine restore and recover database operations into one script

20. In order to minimize risks associated with performing a tablespace point-in-time recovery, each of the following choices identifies the items you should have on hand, except one. Which is it?

A. Only the datafiles comprising the tablespace to be recovered

B. All archive redo logs since the database was backed up

C. A complete backup of the database

D. A recent database export

21. An export of a database is taken with FULL=Y. Later imports performed using this dump file will be able to populate this database with all the following sets of data, except one. Which is it?

A. Objects belonging to a particular user schema

B. Information from the SYSTEM tablespace

C. Contents of the control file

D. A specific list of tables

22. The DBA wants to create an incremental export of the database. The export should contain a rollup of all exports taken since the last full export. Which of the following command-line options would be used to direct EXPORT for this process?

A. INCREMENTAL

B. INCTYPE

C. COMPLETE

D. SYSTEM

23. The DBA is considering generation of export dumps on the direct path. All of the following items can be stored in an export dump generated on the direct path, except two. Which two are they?

A. Bitmap indexes

B. LOBs

C. BFILEs

D. Tables

E. Profiles

24. The DBA is attempting to diagnose database corruption with DBVERIFY. Which of the following command-line options are not associated with the use of this tool? (Choose two)

   A. FILE

   B. BADFILE

   C. LOGFILE

   D. DIRECT

25. After recovering the recovery catalog from a backup control file, the DBA finds that many backup entries in the recovery catalog are no longer present. In order to clear out unverifiable backup items, which of the following commands are appropriate?

   A. RESET

   B. RESYNC

   C. VERIFY

   D. UNCATALOG

26. A backup strategy needs to be formulated for a development environment. The goal is recoverability for changes made daily to database objects and stored procedures, rather than for data. Which of the following configurations is most appropriate?

   A. ARCHIVELOG mode in conjunction with nightly offline backups

   B. NOARCHIVELOG mode in conjunction with nightly offline backups

   C. ARCHIVELOG mode in conjunction with online backups twice daily

   D. NOARCHIVELOG mode in conjunction with weekly exports

27. The DBA is evaluating a disaster recovery plan for a production system. Which two of the following options can be used to address systems where business needs include high availability and fault tolerance of the Oracle database system?

   A. Advanced replication

   B. RMAN

   C. Hot standby database

D. NOARCHIVELOG mode

E. ARCHIVELOG mode

28. **After a session makes a change to a table in the Oracle database, at what point is that change physically written to the database files?**

    A. When the transaction commits

    B. When the user disconnects

    C. When a checkpoint occurs

    D. As soon as the change is made

29. **The Oracle database is experiencing peak transaction volume. In order to reduce I/O bottlenecks created by large amounts of redo write activity, which of the following steps can be taken?**

    A. Increase the size of the rollback segments

    B. Increase the size of the log buffer

    C. Increase the size of the buffer cache

    D. increase the size of the shared pool

30. **To prevent database corruption due to opening a database when a datafile has been restored from backup, the Oracle database employs which of the following methods?**

    A. Synchronizing datafile headers by CKPT

    B. Uncommitted transaction rollback by PMON

    C. Instance recovery by SMON

    D. Distributed transaction recovery with RECO

31. **Currently, there is only one copy of a control file for a production Oracle database. How could the DBA reduce the likelihood that a disk failure would eliminate the only copy of the control file in the Oracle database?**

    A. Copy the control file and issue the ALTER DATABASE statement.

    B. Issue ALTER DATABASE BACKUP CONTROLFILE TO TRACE and restart the instance.

    C. Add another control filename to the INIT.ORA file.

    D. Copy control file to second location and add second name and location to INIT.ORA.

## 162 Oracle8 Certified Professional DBA Practice Exams

32. The DBA is considering operation of a production database in NOARCHIVELOG mode. Data recovery would be supplemented by exports of data taken about every 6 hours. Which of the following choices correctly identifies the recovery implications of this setup?

    A. Recovery to point of failure would be faster because no archive logs would need to be applied.

    B. Recovery to point of failure would be slower because users would have to key in up to 6 hours of lost data.

    C. Recovery to point of failure would be impossible because exports are incompatible with NOARCHIVELOG mode.

    D. Recovery to point of failure would be unnecessary because NOARCHIVELOG mode offers fault tolerance.

33. The DBA has just created a database in NOARCHIVELOG mode. Which of the following two reasons may cause him or her to leave the database in that mode for production operation? (Choose two)

    A. Business requirement for point-in-time database recoveries

    B. Medium transaction volume on the database system between backups

    C. Low transaction volume on the database system between backups

    D. Limited available disk space on the machine hosting Oracle

34. The DBA has configured a production database to run in ARCHIVELOG mode and then gone home for the night. At 3 A.M., the support pager goes off. In investigating the issue, it seems that connected users cannot issue any transactions, and no additional users can connect to the database. What is the problem?

    A. The Oracle instance crashed.

    B. The archiver process is hung.

    C. All online redo logs are full.

    D. The SYSTEM tablespace has been truncated.

35. In archive log multiplexing environments on Oracle8*i* databases, which of the following parameters is used for defining the name of the archive log in the additional destination?

    A. LOG_ARCHIVE_FORMAT

    B. LOG_ARCHIVE_MIN_SUCCEED_DEST

C. LOG_ARCHIVE_DUPLEX_DEST

D. LOG_ARCHIVE_DEST

36. The DBA wants to ensure interoperability for backups between Oracle and third-party backup tools such as Veritas. Which of the following choices identifies the component used for this purpose?

    A. RMAN

    B. MML

    C. DML

    D. OCI

37. The DBA is looking for simpler alternatives for backup and recovery in Oracle8. Rather than defining scripts for backup and recovery processing using the command-line editor, which of the following OEM tools can assist?

    A. Recovery Manager

    B. Backup Manager

    C. Storage Manager

    D. OEM console

38. The DBA is configuring use of RMAN with a recovery catalog. When using a recovery catalog in conjunction with RMAN, where can the actual backup copies of database information be found?

    A. On tape or disk staging area

    B. In the recovery catalog

    C. In the production database

    D. In the Oracle software distribution

39. The DBA is assessing maintenance of recovery catalog creation. Once created, where does the recovery catalog draw much of its information from when maintenance is performed on it?

    A. Production database files

    B. Recovery catalog control file

    C. Production database control file

    D. Archived redo logs

**40.** If connection to the production database is not established from the command line, which of the following choices identifies an appropriate command syntax to issue from within RMAN to establish connection?

   **A.** connect rcvcat scott/tiger@prod

   **B.** connect prod scott/tiger@prod

   **C.** connect target system/manager@prod

   **D.** connect target rman/rman@rcat

**41.** The DBA is configuring RMAN for use as the backup/recovery tool for the Oracle database. After creating the production database and the recovery catalog, which command is used for establishing the baseline information required in the recovery catalog for proper RMAN usage?

   **A.** RESET

   **B.** REGISTER

   **C.** RESYNC

   **D.** REPORT

**42.** The DBA has shut down the database and made copies of all datafiles manually as a benchmark backup for stress testing. Which of the following RMAN commands will make that backup usable in the context of the rest of the contents of the recovery catalog?

   **A.** RESYNC

   **B.** CATALOG

   **C.** REPORT

   **D.** LIST

**43.** The DBA needs to identify available backups for the sys03.dbf datafile belonging to the SYSTEM tablespace. Which of the following commands would be most appropriate for this process?

   **A.** LIST COPY OF TABLESPACE SYSTEM;

   **B.** REPORT NEED BACKUP INCREMENTAL 5 DATABASE;

   **C.** LIST COPY OF DATAFILE '/u03/oradata/prod/sys03.dbf';

   **D.** LIST INCARNATION OF DATABASE PROD;

44. The DBA is developing scripts in RMAN. In order to store but not process commands in a script in RMAN for database backup, which of the following command choices are appropriate?

    A. RUN { ... }

    B. EXECUTE SCRIPT { ... }

    C. CREATE SCRIPT { ... }

    D. ALLOCATE CHANNEL { ... }

45. The DBA is developing a script for backups that will ensure that no block corruption is permitted in a datafile. Which of the following commands is appropriate for that script?

    A. SET MAXCORRUPT 0

    B. SET DBVERIFY ON

    C. SET LOG_BLOCK_CHECKSUM ON

    D. SET ARCHIVELOG DESTINATION '/u03/oradata/prod/arch'

46. The DBA is considering dropping and re-creating indexes using the NOLOGGING option. Which of the following identifies the trade-off a DBA makes in using LOGGING vs. NOLOGGING?

    A. Time vs. money

    B. Speed vs. recoverability

    C. Space on disk vs. space in memory

    D. CPU vs. tape

47. The DBA makes a copy of Oracle database datafiles as part of an attempted backup. Later, the DBA realizes that the instance was running. Which of the following statements is true about the backup?

    A. The backup is completely unusable, under all circumstances.

    B. The backup might be usable, so long as the database was running in ARCHIVELOG mode.

    C. The DBA has taken a reliable NOARCHIVELOG backup of the system.

    D. The datafiles of the backup are unusable, but the control file is.

48. When backing up an ARCHIVELOG database, which of the following choices identifies the factors that would significantly contribute to a rapid recovery time? (Choose three)

    A. Frequency of backups

    B. Number of multiplexed control files

    C. Size of datafiles

    D. I/O speed

    E. Available memory

49. The DBA has just finished making operating system copies of datafiles for the backup. Which of the following choices identifies how the DBA should complete the backup?

    A. Switch online redo logs, back up control file to trace, and take tablespaces out of backup mode

    B. Back up control file to trace, switch online redo logs, save backup control file and redo logs to tape

    C. Take binary copy of control file, take tablespaces out of backup mode, dismount database

    D. Take tablespaces out of backup mode, back up control file to trace, switch online redo logs

50. You issue the ALTER DATABASE BACKUP CONTROLFILE TO TRACE command. Which of the following choices best describes the control file backup that is made by executing this command?

    A. A flat file script used to create the control file

    B. A binary copy of the control file

    C. A flat file copy of the control file

    D. A binary script used to create the control file

51. The DBA doesn't want to be bothered with backing a particular tablespace up anymore, because data never changes. Instead, the tablespace objects need to be available only for query access. Which of the following commands would be used?

    A. ALTER DATABASE BACKUP CONTROLFILE TO TRACE

    B. ALTER TABLESPACE READ ONLY

**C.** ALTER TABLESPACE OFFLINE

**D.** ALTER DATABASE DATAFILE END BACKUP

52. **The DBA issues the following query:**

    ```
    select t.name, substr(d.name,1,40) dfname, d.fuzzy
    from v$tablespace t, v$datafile_header d
    where t.ts# = d.ts#;
    ```

    **Which of the following describes what the output in the FUZZY column will represent?**

    **A.** The number of blocks that are corrupt in the file

    **B.** Whether the file is being backed up

    **C.** Whether AUTOEXTEND has been enabled on that file

    **D.** Whether blocks are being written to the file by DBWR

53. **The strategy pursued in backing up a database using RMAN consists of creating backup datafiles to be stored on disk for later usage. In RMAN terminology, this strategy is better known as which of the following choices?**

    **A.** Backup sets

    **B.** Tags

    **C.** Image copies

    **D.** Incrementals

54. **The DBA is reviewing the alert log for a database and encounters an ORA-00600 error containing numerous codes. This error seems to occur at intervals that coincide with the execution of an important batch process. Which choice best identifies how the DBA should proceed?**

    **A.** Attempt review of all datafiles using DBVERIFY

    **B.** Ensure that the core dump directory is empty and contact Oracle Support

    **C.** Stop running the batch process

    **D.** Remove all background and user trace files and contact Oracle Support

55. **The DBA is planning backup capacity using RMAN. Which of the following choices best describes streaming?**

    **A.** The process by which RMAN communicates with the underlying OS

    **B.** The method used for writing backup sets to tape

**C.** The ability RMAN has to take multiple backups of multiple databases at the same time

**D.** The performance gain added by parallel processing in RMAN

56. The DBA has executed a level 0 backup and a level 1 backup. If the DBA then executes another level 1 backup, what information in the database will be backed up?

   **A.** All changed blocks since the level 1 backup only

   **B.** All changed blocks since the level 2 backup

   **C.** All blocks in the database

   **D.** No changes will be saved

57. While backing up the Oracle database, the machine hosting Oracle loses power unexpectedly. After restarting the machine, what must be done to recover the database?

   **A.** Issue the ALTER DATABASE DATAFILE END BACKUP command and open the database

   **B.** Recover the database using offline backups and open the database using the RESETLOGS option

   **C.** Recover the database using logical exports and open the database

   **D.** Restore the database from the most recent backup, roll forward, and open the database

58. The DBA needs to find information about RMAN backups in the Oracle database. She or he queries the contents of the V$BACKUP_CORRUPTION view to determine specific information. From where does Oracle draw the information found in this view?

   **A.** Control file

   **B.** Recovery catalog

   **C.** SGA

   **D.** RMAN

59. Instance failure has occurred as the result of the DBA tripping over the host machine's power cord. Which of the following steps does Oracle perform first as part of crash recovery on an Oracle database?

   **A.** Server process rolls back uncommitted transactions

   **B.** DBW0 uses redo information to write data to datafiles

- **C.** SMON detects unsynchronization between datafiles
- **D.** The database opens

**60.** **At the command prompt, the DBA executes DBVERIFY using the following command:**

```
dbv blocksize=4096 logfile=dbv.log feedback=0
```

**Which of the following choices best identifies the result of this command?**

- **A.** The execution will corrupt all datafiles.
- **B.** DBVERIFY will detect corruption in all datafiles.
- **C.** DBVERIFY will return an error.
- **D.** DBVERIFY will change all block sizes to 4096.

# Practice Exam 2

1. The DBA wants to verify the integrity of all redo logs before they are archived. Which of the following choices best identifies the way for the DBA to do so?

    A. Set LOG_BLOCK_CHECKSUM to TRUE in INIT.ORA

    B. Run DBVERIFY on every log file

    C. Issue the ALTER DATABASE LOG BLOCK CHECKSUM command

    D. Issue the ALTER DATABASE ARCHIVELOG command

2. The DBA gets a page at 3 A.M. indicating that the Oracle instance has crashed. In the alert log, the DBA finds an ORA-07445 error indicating that an SNP process crashed. Which of the following places might be the next place the DBA could look for more information on this failure?

    A. The V$DATABASE view

    B. Trace files in the BACKGROUND_DUMP_DEST directory

    C. Trace files in the USER_DUMP_DEST directory

    D. Trace files in the CORE_DUMP_DEST directory

3. A database has just experienced media failure where the control file is no longer available. All datafiles are lost. After restoring files from the last backup, which of the following choices best identifies the first step in performing complete recovery when the database is running in ARCHIVELOG mode?

    A. Re-create control file

    B. Use RESETLOGS option to open database

    C. Apply archive logs to restore lost data

    D. Perform roll-forward

    E. Issue ALTER DATABASE RECOVER USING BACKUP CONTROLFILE command

4. Backups occur on an Oracle database at 1:30 A.M. every morning. The DBA comes into work one day to find that data had been loaded into the database incorrectly, causing data corruption. Before the problem can be corrected, a media failure occurs. Which of the following backup

strategies will not support recovery up to a point in time within 60 minutes of when the error occurred in this situation?

**A.** Offline backups with ARCHIVELOG enabled

**B.** Online backups with ARCHIVELOG enabled

**C.** Hourly full database exports

**D.** Offline backups with ARCHIVELOG disabled

5. The database running in NOARCHIVELOG mode experiences media failure. After restoring the datafiles from backup, what is the next step in performing the database recovery?

**A.** Roll forward using archived redo

**B.** Open the database with the RESETLOGS option

**C.** Open the database without the RESETLOGS option

**D.** Delete and re-create the control file to change archiving mode

6. To improve performance of complete media recovery when a disk cannot be replaced immediately, which of the following statements could be used?

**A.** ALTER DATABASE ARCHIVELOG

**B.** ALTER DATABASE DATAFILE OFFLINE DROP

**C.** ALTER DATABASE RENAME FILE

**D.** ALTER TABLESPACE READ ONLY

7. The DBA wants to use RMAN in conjunction with database recovery. Which two of the following choices identify what must take place regarding backups if RMAN is to be used in recovering NOARCHIVELOG databases? (Choose two)

**A.** Control file and datafile backup taken using RMAN

**B.** Backup control file taken manually must be registered, but not datafiles

**C.** Backup control file not registered with recovery catalog

**D.** Neither backup control file nor datafiles need be registered with RMAN

**E.** Control and datafiles registered with the recovery catalog

8. The DBA is considering use of ARCHIVELOG mode as a backup strategy for a database. In which of the following situations would this strategy be inappropriate?

   A. Addressing recovery needs for DSS systems

   B. Addressing recovery needs of OLTP systems

   C. Addressing recovery needs of order entry systems

   D. Addressing recovery needs of volatile databases

9. You are developing a recovery strategy to improve performance. Which of the following choices does not identify an appropriate step for minimizing the drawback associated with the backup strategy?

   A. Leave recent archive logs on disk for ARCHIVELOG database

   B. Take more frequent backups for ARCHIVELOG database

   C. Take less frequent backups for NOARCHIVELOG database

   D. Use daily full and hourly incremental exports for NOARCHIVELOG database

10. After issuing the ALTER DATABASE RECOVER USING BACKUP CONTROLFILE command, which of the following steps is performed during complete recovery of a database?

    A. Restoring datafiles from backup when prompted

    B. Opening database with RESETLOGS option

    C. Roll-forward of data from archive logs

    D. Re-creation of control file from backup

11. You are recovering an ARCHIVELOG database. While restoring files from backup, you realize that one of your backup datafiles was not registered in the recovery catalog. What items are required in order to complete recovery of the database?

    A. An export dump registered with RMAN

    B. All archive logs generated since tablespace was created

    C. A backup control file registered with RMAN

    D. A working installation of Backup Manager to assist

12. The DBA takes a full online backup of the database at 11 A.M. At 3:30 it is discovered that a user inserted bad data after the backup, on which 17,000 other transactions based their processing. To handle this situation in the most straightforward way possible prior to Oracle8*i*, which of the following methods are most effective?

    **A.** IMPORT from an export taken the day before

    **B.** Complete recovery

    **C.** Time-based recovery

    **D.** Tablespace point-in-time recovery

13. The DBA takes a full online backup of the database at 11 A.M. At 3:30 it is discovered that a user inserted bad data after the backup, on which 17,000 other transactions based their processing. To handle this situation, which of the following statements would be used?

    **A.** ALTER DATABASE RECOVER AUTOMATIC UNTIL TIME

    **B.** ALTER DATABASE RECOVER AUTOMATIC UNTIL CANCEL

    **C.** ALTER DATABASE RECOVER AUTOMATIC UNTIL CHANGE

    **D.** ALTER DATABASE RECOVER AUTOMATIC UNTIL CANCEL USING BACKUP CONTROLFILE

14. During normal database operation, a set of disks fails on the host machine. As the result, all online redo logs are lost. Which of the following choices best explains the method needed to handle the recovery after restoring datafiles from an earlier backup and performing roll-forward?

    **A.** ALTER DATABASE OPEN RESETLOGS

    **B.** ALTER DATABASE RECOVER UNTIL CANCEL USING BACKUP CONTROLFILE

    **C.** ALTER DATABASE RECOVER USING BACKUP CONTROLFILE

    **D.** CREATE CONTROLFILE REUSE DATABASE NORESETLOGS

15. Before connecting RMAN to perform complete recovery, the DBA must ensure which of the following steps have occurred?

    **A.** The production database is mounted but not open and the recovery catalog is available.

    **B.** The production database is online and the recovery catalog database is not available.

**C.** The production database and the recovery catalog database are not available.

**D.** Both the production database and the recovery catalog are not available.

16. Several applications all use the same database for production data processing. The DBA has delineated that every application have its own schema and associated tablespace for database objects. A data load fails, containing the tablespace associated with the order entry application, causing that application to have corrupt data. How might the DBA perform recovery for this system?

    **A.** Complete database recovery with database closed

    **B.** Incomplete recovery with database open

    **C.** Incomplete recovery with database closed

    **D.** Tablespace point-in-time recovery with database open

17. A development database is backed up nightly using the EXPORT utility. To improve performance on the export while simultaneously ensuring that all objects are captured, which of the following steps might occur?

    **A.** Set CONSTRAINTS=N

    **B.** Increase value set for BUFFER

    **C.** Set LOG=N

    **D.** Reduce the nonzero value for FEEDBACK

18. In situations where the DBA wants to create a data recovery strategy around the EXPORT utility, which of the following parameters can set up EXPORT to take data saves of only changed row data? (Choose two)

    **A.** FULL

    **B.** TABLES

    **C.** OWNER

    **D.** INCTYPE

19. The DBA wants to run an export. Which of the following choices identifies the situation where EXPORT will not need to interact with the RDBMS other than to connect to retrieve data?

    **A.** OWNER=SYS

    **B.** DIRECT=Y

C. ROWS=Y

D. FULL=Y

20. The DBA migrates a database from a test environment to production. Later, the DBA realizes that the objects in the production database are stored in the DATA tablespace. In order to move all indexes into the INDEX tablespace, which of the following import parameters can be used?

   A. FROMUSER and TOUSER

   B. INDEXFILE

   C. ROWS

   D. INDEXES

21. The DBA is attempting to plan recovery strategy around rapid recovery time. Which of the following choices is not a solution that is appropriate for reducing recovery time?

   A. Using a disk staging area for backups

   B. More frequent backups

   C. More frequent checkpoints

   D. Running the database in NOARCHIVELOG mode

22. During database operation, a user encounters the following error: ORA-1578: Oracle data block corrupted. In order to correct the problem, which two of the following methods can be employed?

   A. Drop and re-create the object

   B. Restore from backup and roll forward using archive redo logs

   C. Run the DBVERIFY command

   D. Change LOG_BLOCK_CHECKSUM to TRUE and restart the database

   E. Use RMAN corruption detection features in database backup

23. The DBA is cloning a production database to the same machine for testing. When reconstructing a control file, which of the following commands allow you to rename your database?

   A. CREATE CONTROLFILE SET DATABASE NORESETLOGS

   B. CREATE CONTROLFILE REUSE DATABASE NORESETLOGS

**C.** CREATE CONTROLFILE SET DATABASE RESETLOGS

**D.** CREATE CONTROLFILE REUSE DATABASE RESETLOGS

24. After restoring the database from backup and re-creating the control file, the DBA discovers that a datafile was missing. The database is now open, and usage has continued. Which of the choices identifies the fastest way to recover, assuming that the data in the missing datafile is unneeded?

   **A.** Issue the ALTER DATABASE DATAFILE OFFLINE DROP command

   **B.** Recover the database without restoring, and open the database with the RESETLOGS option

   **C.** Shut down the database, restore from backup, recover, and open the database

   **D.** Restore the binary control file backup and open the database using the NORESETLOGS option

25. The machine hosting the recovery catalog database is lost in a tornado. In order to recover this information for RMAN, which of the following choices is most accurate?

   **A.** Create a new recovery catalog and proceed as normal

   **B.** Restore the recovery catalog from tape backup

   **C.** Create a new recovery catalog using the CATALOG command

   **D.** Create a new recovery catalog using the RESYNC CATALOG FROM BACKUP CONTROLFILE command

26. The DBA is about to complete an online backup. If the DBA suspects he or she will need to perform recovery later, which of the following dictionary views contains information necessary to assist in defining when the recovery will complete?

   **A.** V$LOG

   **B.** V$BACKUP

   **C.** V$DATAFILE

   **D.** V$CONTROLFILE

27. The DBA notices that all redo logs are showing a status of ACTIVE in the V$ views. Which of the following choices best identifies the reason for this status? (Choose two)

**A.** The database is experiencing intense, long-running transactions.

**B.** The database is undergoing crash recovery.

**C.** The database is undergoing media recovery.

**D.** The database is being backed up.

28. Users are complaining of database availability issues due to recovery required for addressing data corruption issues. Which of the following approaches could be used to remedy the situation?

    **A.** Tuning the backup process for faster complete recovery

    **B.** Running Oracle in NOARCHIVELOG mode

    **C.** Taking frequent exports of the tables experiencing frequent data corruption

    **D.** Offline backups

29. A disk crashes, taking with it the duplexed members of three logfile groups. In order to recover in this situation, which of the following processes are required?

    **A.** Closed recovery from offline backup

    **B.** Re-create the logfile members

    **C.** Tablespace point-in-time recovery

    **D.** Full database import

30. A user experiences statement failure when updating a record on the Oracle database. Which of the following choices identifies appropriate action to be taken by the DBA?

    **A.** Forward the session trace file to the user.

    **B.** Restart the instance.

    **C.** Recover the tablespace containing the record in question.

    **D.** No action on the part of the DBA is required.

31. When a log switch occurs on the Oracle database, which of the following background process handles datafile synchronization?

    **A.** LGWR

    **B.** DBW0

C. CKPT

D. ARCH

32. Which of the following shutdown options requires instance recovery the next time the database is started?

   A. TRANSACTIONAL

   B. ABORT

   C. IMMEDIATE

   D. NORMAL

33. In order to multiplex control files in the Oracle database, which of the following INIT.ORA parameters are used?

   A. LOG_ARCHIVE_DUPLEX_DEST

   B. ROLLBACK_SEGMENTS

   C. CONTROL_FILES

   D. None. Control file multiplexing is set up in the CREATE DATABASE statement.

34. The DBA configures a backup strategy using OS scripts. Later, media failure occurs. The DBA then realizes that certain key datafiles were not backed up. Which of the following choices indicate the best way this problem can be corrected?

   A. Running the database in ARCHIVELOG mode

   B. Testing backup strategy for recoverability

   C. Using a third-party tool for backup management

   D. Using RMAN for backup management

35. The DBA is configuring the backup architecture in an Oracle database. Which of the following choices does not identify a way the DBA can influence the frequency of checkpoints?

   A. LOG_ARCHIVE_START value

   B. LOG_CHECKPOINT_INTERVAL value

   C. Size of online redo logs

   D. LOG_CHECKPOINT_TIMEOUT value

36. The DBA is creating backup strategy in Oracle that will involve both the recovery catalog and logical backups. To do so, which two of the following scripts must be run?

    A. catexp.sql

    B. catrman.sql

    C. catalog.sql

    D. catproc.sql

    E. catrep.sql

37. You are attempting to determine the progress of a backup using RMAN. Which of the following views would be appropriate for calculating this information as a percentage?

    A. V$BACKUP_CORRUPTION

    B. V$SESSION_LONGOPS

    C. V$ARCHIVED_LOG

    D. V$INSTANCE

38. The DBA has performed several incomplete recoveries using RMAN. Now, she or he needs to determine how many have been performed. To determine what version of the database she or he is currently using, which of the following commands is appropriate?

    A. REPORT NEED BACKUP

    B. LIST BACKUPSET

    C. REPORT UNRECOVERABLE

    D. LIST INCARNATION

39. The DBA has just performed an incremental level 2 backup. Which of the following backup types will give her or him a cumulative backup without taking the time to back up all blocks in the datafiles?

    A. Incremental level 3

    B. Full

    C. Cumulative level 3

    D. Cumulative level 1

**40.** The DBA is using RMAN to increase performance by saving all backup information first to a staging area. Later, all information in the staging area will be written to offline media in a first-in, first-out fashion. Which of the following commands are appropriate in RMAN to actually allow RMAN to write the information to the staging area, rather than to offline media?

**A.** ALLOCATE CHANNEL TYPE DISK

**B.** ALLOCATE CHANNEL devicename

**C.** RELEASE CHANNEL

**D.** BACKUP FULL (DATABASE *name*) TO STAGING AREA

**41.** The DBA wants to use archive log multiplexing on an Oracle8*i* database. Which of the following choices indicates how many archive destinations Oracle8*i* will maintain when the setting for ARCHIVELOG mode for an archive destination is set to BEST-EFFORT?

**A.** 1

**B.** 2

**C.** 3

**D.** 4

**42.** You are using RMAN to handle backup and recovery of your Oracle database. Which of the following commands is required in order to keep the recovery catalog information about database recoverability up-to-date?

**A.** REGISTER

**B.** RESET

**C.** REPORT

**D.** RESYNC

**43.** Logical backup strategy consists of full exports on Thursday mornings, cumulative exports on Monday mornings, and incrementals on all other mornings. The database crashes on Tuesday afternoon. After re-creating the database from script, which of the following exports would be imported first?

**A.** Export taken the prior Monday

**B.** Export taken Tuesday

C. Export taken the prior Thursday

D. The database is unrecoverable

44. **The DBA is recovering an Oracle database. Which of the following database recovery strategies improves recovery time by allowing the instance to start with the datafiles containing dirty blocks from uncommitted transactions?**

   A. ARCHIVELOG mode

   B. Faster warmstart

   C. More frequent backups

   D. Starting Oracle with dirty datafiles offline

45. **After re-creating a database control file, the DBA attempts to start the database with files missing. In which of the following situations is this possible?**

   A. When one of three datafiles for a tablespace is missing

   B. When one copy of a multiplexed control file is missing

   C. When one member of a redo log group is missing

   D. When all members of a redo log group are missing

46. **The DBA is about to export the database. When exporting data on the direct path, which of the following parameters will have no meaning?**

   A. USERID

   B. BUFFER

   C. ROWS

   D. CONSTRAINTS

47. **The organization is developing a backup and system recoverability strategy. Which of the following choices identifies an operational requirement for a backup and recoverability strategy?**

   A. Required availability due to business hours

   B. Speed of recovery due to lost earnings

   C. Procedures for rotating tapes in a tape library

   D. Ensuring online backup validity by running in ARCHIVELOG mode

48. The DBA is configuring a high-volume-transaction production OLTP application for recoverability. Which of the choices indicates an area of configuration that is not required for complete recovery to the point of failure in the system?

    A. Large pool

    B. ARCH process

    C. ARCHIVELOG mode

    D. LOG_ARCHIVE_DEST

49. The DBA is setting up Oracle to run in ARCHIVELOG mode. Which of the following initialization parameters need not be configured in order to do so?

    A. LOG_ARCHIVE_DEST

    B. LOG_ARCHIVE_DUPLEX_DEST

    C. LOG_ARCHIVE_FORMAT

    D. LOG_ARCHIVE_START

50. The DBA runs her or his test environment in NOARCHIVELOG mode. Offline backups are taken every night. A disk crashes, rendering her or his database inoperable. Which of the following choices identifies the long-term implications of running Oracle in this way?

    A. Data changes after backup will be recoverable, but database object definitions will not.

    B. Data changes will not be recoverable unless the change was made before the most recent backup.

    C. Most likely, end users will feel little impact because this is not a production system.

    D. The database will be easy to recover.

51. The DBA is attempting to determine when to use RMAN. Which of the following situations is probably the least appropriate for doing so?

    A. Recovery of high-volume transaction systems

    B. Recovery for databases with ARCHIVELOG enabled

    C. Recovery for static DSS systems like data marts

    D. Recovery for databases used for order entry

**Chapter 3: OCP Exam 3: Backup and Recovery Workshop** 183

52. The DBA is using RMAN for database backup and recovery. Once created, which of the following commands can be used for execution of a backup routine in RMAN?

    A. RUN

    B. ALLOCATE CHANNEL

    C. EXECUTE

    D. RESET

53. The DBA is developing scripts to handle backup and recovery. Before copying datafiles in an online backup, which of the following statements must be issued to ensure validity of the backup?

    A. ALTER DATABASE DATAFILE OFFLINE

    B. ALTER TABLESPACE READ ONLY

    C. ALTER SYSTEM ARCHIVE LOG START

    D. ALTER TABLESPACE BEGIN BACKUP

54. When the Oracle database is running in ARCHIVELOG mode, which of the following choices best illustrates the difference between offline and online backups with respect to complete recoverability?

    A. Offline backups are faster to recover from than online backups.

    B. Online backups offer increased availability and system uptime for database backups.

    C. Offline backups offer complete recoverability, whereas online backups do not.

    D. Online backups require use of RMAN for process management, whereas offline backups do not.

55. The DBA is setting up a backup strategy using RMAN. Which of the following statements is not true with respect to generation of backup sets to tape?

    A. Datafile backup sets can utilize streaming, but archive log backup sets cannot.

    B. Archive log backup sets can utilize streaming, but datafile backup sets cannot.

    C. Datafiles cannot be streamed with archive logs in a backup set.

**D.** Neither archive log backup sets nor datafile backup sets support streaming when RMAN is used.

**56.** The following backup script is used in RMAN:

```
RUN { MAXCORRUPT 0
ALLOCATE CHANNEL c1 NAME '/dev/rmt0';
BACKUP FULL FILESPERSET 10 SKIP OFFLINE ( DATABASE FORMAT arch_%S );
RELEASE CHANNEL c1; }
```

Which of the following choices identifies the line in this script that increases the likelihood of a valid backup being available for recovery?

**A.** RUN { MAXCORRUPT 0

**B.** ALLOCATE CHANNEL c1 NAME '/dev/rmt0';

**C.** BACKUP FULL FILESPERSET 10 SKIP OFFLINE ( DATABASE FORMAT arch_%S );

**D.** RELEASE CHANNEL c1; }

**57.** The DBA is considering recovery methods. Which of the following recovery types permit the database to be open during recovery?

**A.** Full database recovery

**B.** Tablespace recovery

**C.** Change-based recovery

**D.** Time-based recovery

**58.** The instance fails on an Oracle database. Which of the following steps must occur after SMON recovers the instance?

**A.** Uncommitted transactions must be rolled back.

**B.** The database must be opened.

**C.** The datafiles must be restored.

**D.** The archive logs must be applied.

**59.** The DBA is determining how to recover the database. She or he knows the SCN for the last known good transaction on the database. Which of the following recovery types should she or he employ?

**A.** Change-based recovery

**B.** Time-based recovery

C. Cancel-based recovery

D. Export-based recovery

60. The DBA has a complete export of all database contents. She or he uses IMPORT to apply all data in the export dump to a database. Database objects were precreated using a separate script. Which of the following choices best identifies how the import will proceed?

A. The import will terminate unsuccessfully.

B. The import will execute successfully with warnings.

C. The import will execute successfully without warnings.

D. The import will execute unsuccessfully with warnings.

# Answers to Practice Exam 1

1. **A.** The increased checkpoint frequency will improve recoverability of the instance, but will adversely impact performance.

**Explanation** Decreasing the value for LOG_CHECKPOINT_INTERVAL and increasing LOG_CHECKPOINT_TIMEOUT to anything above 0 will increase the frequency of checkpoints on the instance, which improves instance recoverability but adversely impacts performance. Thus, all choices stating that checkpoint frequency has reduced are incorrect, and the choice stating that performance will improve is also incorrect. **(Topic 2.2)**

2. **A, C, and D.**

**Explanation** Datafiles are synchronized during checkpoints, so when checkpoints happen only when log switches occur, then datafiles do not get synchronized between log switches. Also, because LGWR signals DBW0 to write dirty buffers to disk during checkpoints, DBW0 could fall behind in its processing if checkpoints happen less frequently. Finally, opening the database after SHUTDOWN ABORT may take longer because Oracle is performing extended crash recovery due to excessive dirty blocks in memory. However, the instance will be recoverable so long as the redo logs are not damaged, and there should not be any impact on truncating tables because the truncate command is DDL, not DML. **(Topic 2.3)**

3. **C.** DISK1: redo01a.dbf, redo03b.dbf; DISK2: redo01b.dbf, redo02a.dbf; DISK3: redo03a.dbf, redo02b.dbf

**Explanation** The correct choice, DISK1: redo01a.dbf, redo03b.dbf; DISK2: redo01b.dbf, redo02a.dbf; DISK3: redo03a.dbf, redo02b.dbf, reflects a design choice where every redo log group's members are located on logically separate disks. Two of the other choices are weakened because at least one of the online redo log groups has all its members on one disk, creating a single point of disk failure. Choice D is an excellent distractor for the following reason: When you issue a commit, LGWR must successfully write data to the log before acknowledging the commit, meaning that asynchronous I/O is bypassed. Multiplexed writes are issued in parallel. The commit is not acknowledged until all log groups complete their write. Assuming the disk access through both controllers (in the case where you have two multiplexed files with two separate controllers) is comparable, both should finish about the same time, and the impact on performance should be minimal. However, the ARCH process creates additional traffic overhead on each and every log switch, which may have a tendency to create a performance bottleneck. **(Topic 2.4)**

**4.** C. LOG_ARCHIVE_MIN_SUCCEED_DEST

**Explanation** The LOG_ARCHIVE_MIN_SUCCEED_DEST parameter ensures that Oracle maintains every archive log destination identified in the INIT.ORA file. LOG_ARCHIVE_DEST and LOG_ARCHIVE_DUPLEX_DEST merely identify two archiving destinations, while the LOG_ARCHIVE_FORMAT is used mainly for identifying the naming convention to be used by ARCH in creating the archive logs. **(Topic 3.4)**

**5.** E. When your backup strategy must encompass files other than Oracle database files

**Explanation** Use of RMAN for backing up the Oracle database is not appropriate when your backup strategy must encompass files other than Oracle database files, or when backup and recovery is required for versions of Oracle prior to Oracle8. Two of the choices identify situations where backing up using RMAN is a good idea, because of features such as incremental backups or lights-out automation using scripts. And, although it's not recommended to run RMAN without a recovery catalog due to diminished functionality, it's not required that you use a recovery catalog with RMAN. **(Topic 4.1)**

**6.** B and E. Backup Manager and Instance Manager

**Explanation** The Backup Manager and Instance Manager tools allow you to start and stop the Oracle database. Data Manager, Schema Manager, and Storage Manager do not. **(Topic 4.2)**

**7.** A and C. RECOVERY_CATALOG_OWNER and SYSDBA

**Explanation** The recovery catalog schema owner needs both the RECOVERY_CATALOG_OWNER role and the SYSDBA role granted to it in order to perform its tasks. The EXP_FULL_DATABASE and EXECUTE_CATALOG_ROLE roles are not necessary to grant directly to the recovery catalog owner, however. **(Topic 4.4)**

**8.** A. TARGET

**Explanation** The TARGET option defines the connect string for your target, or production, database. MSGLOG is used to define a message log file, while RCVCAT defines the connect string for your recovery catalog. CMDFILE identifies a file containing a script RMAN can run to process whatever activities need to be executed. **(Topic 4.5)**

**9.** D. ALTER TABLESPACE BEGIN BACKUP

**Explanation** Before beginning to take the backup of your physical datafiles in Oracle, you must put the database in ARCHIVELOG mode. This is accomplished by the ALTER TABLESPACE BEGIN BACKUP command. Both shutdown choices are incorrect because the idea behind an open database backup is to back up the database while it is available to users—that is, not shut down. **(Topic 6.1)**

**10.** B. Ease of use

**Explanation** Offline backups on NOARCHIVELOG mode databases offer ease of use with respect to database recovery because there really is only one choice—restore the database from backup datafiles. However, this method does not provide complete recovery to the point of database failure, nor does it provide fast restoration of transactions executed after backup. Finally, the use of NOARCHIVELOG mode combined with offline backups is far from ideal for recovery of extensive production data. **(Topic 6.2)**

**11.** A. USER_DUMP_DEST

**Explanation** The script containing the CREATE CONTROLFILE command generated by ALTER DATABASE BACKUP CONTROLFILE TO TRACE is found in the USER_DUMP_DEST directory on the machine hosting the Oracle database. **(Topic 6.5)**

**12.** A. Immediately after placing the tablespace into read-only mode

**Explanation** Since the data in a read-only tablespace will not be changed, the DBA only needs to back up the tablespace once, after placing the tablespace into read-only mode. However, one more backup should be taken so that the read-only status of the tablespace is captured along with the data in the tablespace. Without this second backup, if the DBA has to recover the tablespace, the DBA must also remember to set the tablespace into read-only mode again or else the data will be susceptible to change. **(Topic 6.6)**

**13.** B. SELECT FILE# FROM V$BACKUP WHERE STATUS = 'ACTIVE'

**Explanation** The appropriate dictionary view to query from in this situation is V$BACKUP, not V$DATAFILE, which eliminates half the choices. To narrow down further, you must either know that the appropriate status to look for on this view is ACTIVE or that the FNAME column does not exist in the V$BACKUP view. **(Topic 6.7)**

**14.** B. LEVEL

**Explanation** The LEVEL keyword in RMAN is used for defining the increment level for the backup, which is the closest of all the choices in identifying whether the database backup will back up changed or empty blocks in a datafile. FILESPERSET is used for defining the number of datafiles that are permitted in a backup set, while TYPE indicates whether a channel is type disk or tape. Finally, the CURRENT keyword is used for indicating whether to include the current control file or a backup copy. **(Topic 7.3)**

**15.** C.  V$DATAFILE_HEADER

**Explanation**   The V$DATAFILE_HEADER view contains useful information about sequence numbers listed in datafile headers, the method Oracle uses for identifying synchronization between files on an Oracle database. The V$BACKUP_CORRUPTION view offers little value here, because that view contains only information about name and information in the control file about archived redo logs. Nor does the V$LOGFILE view add much information, because that view focuses on information about your online redo logs. Finally, V$BACKUP adds little value because it only talks about backups in the database. The key trick to avoid here is distraction—the question is about file synchronization and dictionary information, not about backups specifically. **(Topic 7.5)**

**16.** D.  SMON

**Explanation**   The SMON process is tasked with determining the need for, and possibly conducting, instance recovery during database startup. While CKPT handles writing sequence numbers to datafiles for the purpose of synchronization, that process is not the one that checks for synchronization during startup. Nor is DBW0, which only writes dirty buffers to the datafiles. Finally, LGWR may signal CKPT to write sequence numbers to datafile headers during a log switch, but has no role in instance recovery. **(Topic 8.2)**

**17.** B.  Issue the ALTER DATABASE CLEAR UNARCHIVED LOGFILE GROUP command.

**Explanation**   When log block checksumming detects block corruption, the corrupt log must be cleared using the ALTER DATABASE CLEAR UNARCHIVED LOGFILE GROUP command or else database activity will eventually halt. This is because the ARCH process will not archive a redo log if that log is found to be corrupt. There is no need to issue a SHUTDOWN ABORT unless you want to wait for Oracle to perform instance recovery. The DBVERIFY utility is used for detecting corruption on datafiles, not redo logs. **(Topic 8.4)**

**18.** A.  Datafiles, log files, and control file

**Explanation**   In order to recover (or better, restore) a database running in NOARCHIVELOG mode in Oracle, you need to restore all files associated with that database, including datafiles, log files, and control files. However, since the database is running in NOARCHIVELOG mode, there are no archive logs associated with the database. **(Topic 9.2)**

**19.** A. Storage of recovery scripts in the recovery catalog

**Explanation** The primary benefit for using RMAN in conjunction with backup and recovery of NOARCHIVELOG databases is central storage of recovery scripts in the recovery catalog. There is no requirement for tracking database archives in a NOARCHIVELOG database. And, since there are no archives, there is no roll-forward process involved in recovering a NOARCHIVELOG database, eliminating the need for restore and recover operations in the same recovery script. Finally, RMAN somewhat encumbers the process of backups for NOARCHIVELOG databases. **(Topic 9.4)**

**20.** A. Only the datafiles comprising the tablespace to be recovered

**Explanation** In order to perform tablespace point-in-time recovery, you usually need a complete database backup and all archive logs required to roll forward to the point in time you wish to recover the tablespace to. Alternately, if your database export contains the database objects in the tablespace at the point in time you want to recover to, you can use the recent database export to get your recovery. However, you should not attempt a tablespace point-in-time recovery if all you have on hand are the datafiles comprising the tablespace to be recovered, because file synchronization issues on an ARCHIVELOG database will force Oracle to roll forward if you restore only some, but not all, of the datafiles. **(Topic 11.5)**

**21.** C. Contents of the control file

**Explanation** EXPORT can dump all data in every object in every user's schema when FULL=Y, which then allows for later import of objects belonging to a particular user's schema. This form of export also allows for repopulation of information from the SYSTEM tablespace, as well as from a specific list of tables. However, the actual contents of a control file cannot be restored using the EXPORT tool. **(Topic 12.1)**

**22.** B. INCTYPE

**Explanation** The INCTYPE parameter is used to direct EXPORT's processing of incremental backup types. The other choices merely identify possible values for this parameter. **(Topic 12.2)**

**23.** B and C.   LOBs and BFILEs

**Explanation**   Of the objects listed, only LOBs and BFILEs will not be stored in an export dump file in Oracle8*i*. The other objects like bitmap indexes and tables and profiles will definitely be stored in export dump files in Oracle8*i*. **(Topic 12.3)**

**24.** B and D.   BADFILE and DIRECT

**Explanation**   Of the command-line options listed, the only two not associated with DBVERIFY are BADFILE and DIRECT. These two command-line options are associated with SQL*Loader. FILE and LOGFILE will simply not cut it. **(Topic 13.2)**

**25.** D.   UNCATALOG

**Explanation**   The UNCATALOG command is useful for removing recovery catalog items that no longer exist. Other commands with the exception of VERIFY are used for routine recovery catalog maintenance. The VERIFY command does not exist in RMAN language. **(Topic 13.5)**

**26.** B.   NOARCHIVELOG mode in conjunction with nightly offline backups

**Explanation**   In development environments like the one described in the question, the best approach for backup and recovery is nightly offline backups in conjunction with the Oracle database running in NOARCHIVELOG mode. When data recovery is not a requirement, archive redo logs are overkill and unnecessarily consume disk resources that could be used for other things, thus eliminating all choices mentioning ARCHIVELOG mode. Finally, because the goal is to be able to recover changes made daily, backups must be taken daily, not weekly. **(Topic 1.1)**

**27.** A and C.   Advanced replication and hot standby database

**Explanation**   For an all-Oracle solution to issues of fault tolerance or high availability, advanced replication can be used to maintain multiple versions of a database over a LAN or WAN connection. In addition, the hot standby database works well to ensure maximum recoverability in minimal downtime. RMAN, though useful in cataloging database backups, gives no high availability in the event of machine failure. Neither NOARCHIVELOG mode nor ARCHIVELOG mode are meant to address high availability or fault tolerance, though running the database in ARCHIVELOG mode is good for ensuring complete recovery. **(Topic 1.2)**

**28.** C.   When a checkpoint occurs

**Explanation**   Oracle's architecture makes it possible for asynchronous data writes to disk using the DBW0 process. That is to say, when a user changes data in a table, the data change is not written to disk right away. In fact, the disk write has nothing to do with when the user disconnects or commits the transaction at all. Instead, the data is written to disk when a checkpoint occurs. When this happens, LGWR or CKPT signals DBW0 to write dirty buffers to disk. The more frequently checkpoints happen, the shorter an instance recovery will be. **(Topic 2.2)**

**29.** B.  Increase the size of the log buffer

**Explanation**  By increasing the size of the log buffer, you can cache more redo in memory, giving the LGWR process time to catch up with redo log writes during periods of high transaction volumes. No other SGA (both the buffer cache and shared pool are part of the SGA) change will have this effect, nor will any change made to rollback segments. **(Topic 2.1)**

**30.** A.  Synchronizing datafile headers by CKPT

**Explanation**  In order to prevent users from opening a database when a datafile has been restored from backup, Oracle checks sequence numbers for synchronization in datafile headers. Since the sequence numbers won't match in this case, Oracle won't let you open the database, thereby preventing data corruption issues. Uncommitted transaction rollback does not play a part in this process, nor does instance recovery. Finally, only in situations involving distributed databases will the RECO process be utilized. **(Topic 2.3)**

**31.** D.  Copy control file to second location and add second name and location to INIT.ORA.

**Explanation**  To create and maintain a second copy of the control file, first the DBA must shut down the database. Then, copy the control file to a second location, add that location and filename to the CONTROL_FILES INIT.ORA parameter, and restart the instance. The ALTER DATABASE command is useful for multiplexing redo logs, not control files. Finally, remember that backing up the control file to trace gives you only a script for creating the control file, not a maintained copy of that control file. **(Topic 2.4)**

**32.** B.  Recovery to point of failure would be slower because users would have to key in up to 6 hours of lost data.

**Explanation**  Because the backup scenario leaves up to 6 hours of exposure for lost production data, recovery to point of failure would be slower because users would have to key in up to 6 hours of lost data. The bottom line in this situation is, never run a production database in NOARCHIVELOG mode, and never rely on exports to restore production data. Oracle offers more reliable database backup and recoverability than that. **(Topic 3.1)**

**33.** C and D.

**Explanation** If the host machine had limited space, or if the database experienced very little data change between backups, then there would be little need for the database to run in ARCHIVELOG mode. However, the addition of even a medium amount of transaction volume presents a real business need for switching to ARCHIVELOG mode. Also, point-in-time database recovery is not possible with NOARCHIVELOG databases—only recovery to the point of most recent database backup is possible in that scenario. **(Topic 3.2)**

**34.** C. All online redo logs are full.

**Explanation** The cause of this situation is that all online redo logs are full. Be careful of the distractor choice to this question indicating that the ARCH process is hung. Though this could be a cause for all online redo logs being full, another potential cause is that the ARCH process was never started, a fact not mentioned in the question. Since some users are connected, it's a safe bet that the instance is running, and that the SYSTEM tablespace is intact. **(Topic 3.3)**

**35.** A. LOG_ARCHIVE_FORMAT

**Explanation** Although LOG_ARCHIVE_DUPLEX_DEST is used for defining the second destination for archive logs, the LOG_ARCHIVE_FORMAT parameter is still used for defining the naming format for both sets of archive logs. LOG_ARCHIVE_DEST still identifies the original archive log destination directory, while the parameter known as LOG_ARCHIVE_MIN_SUCCEED_DEST identifies whether Oracle must guarantee that both archive log destinations are maintained. **(Topic 3.4)**

**36.** B. MML

**Explanation** MML stands for media management layer, an interoperability software layer that allows RMAN to work directly with several leading backup tools, such as Legato Networker, Veritas Netbackup, IBM ADSM, and others. RMAN itself does not provide this functionality, but will interface directly with the OS-supplied commands for backup to secondary storage media. DML stands for data manipulation language, Oracle's set of commands for changing, adding, or removing data from the database. OCI stands for Oracle Call Interface, a set of specifications for calling RMAN from within a custom application. **(Topic 4.1)**

**37.** B. Backup Manager

**Explanation** The utility you will use as DBA to simplify RMAN processing is Backup Manager. Recovery Manager, or RMAN, is the command-line utility you are looking to avoid in this question. Storage Manager is used primarily for configuring rollback segments and tablespaces on an Oracle database. Finally, you might use the OEM console to access Backup Manager, but the console itself provides little backup functionality save for allowing you to define jobs that automate database backup. **(Topic 4.2)**

**38.** A.   On tape or disk staging area

**Explanation**   Oracle will store the actual datafile and archive log backups on tape or in a disk staging area, or even some other form of offline storage media. Only catalog information about that backup is stored in the recovery catalog, not the actual backup itself. Aside from being impossible, it would create a single point of failure if a backup was stored in the production database. Finally, the Oracle software distribution will not be used for storing your backups. **(Topic 4.3)**

**39.** C.   Production database control file

**Explanation**   The production database control file is the source of much information found in the recovery catalog for that database. The recovery catalog control file will contain information for recovery of the recovery catalog database, but not for the production database. **(Topic 4.4)**

**40.** C.   connect target system/manager@prod

**Explanation**   The connect target system/manager@prod connection string most resembles a proper connection string because it establishes connection to the target production database as a user with DBA capabilities. All connect strings with anything other than "connect target" in them must be eliminated, because they do not connect the user to the target (i.e., production) database. Also, "connect prod" is a syntax error. **(Topic 4.5)**

**41.** B.   REGISTER

**Explanation**   The REGISTER command is used for initial setup of the recovery catalog in conjunction with the production database. The RESET command is equivalent to opening the database with the RESETLOGS option to reset the archive sequence number to 0. In this case, the entire incarnation of the database in RMAN is also reset. RESYNC is used for synchronizing information between the RMAN recovery catalog and the production database on a maintenance basis. Finally, REPORT is used for generating reports about database backup status on the production database. **(Topic 5.1)**

**42.** B.   CATALOG

**Explanation**   The CATALOG command allows DBAs to enter backups taken manually into the recovery catalog for use with RMAN. RESYNC is used for synchronizing information between the RMAN recovery catalog and the production database on a maintenance basis. REPORT is used for generating reports about database backup status on the production database. Finally, LIST is used for showing information about the current status of the database itself. **(Topic 5.2)**

**43.** C. LIST COPY OF DATAFILE '/u03/oradata/prod/sys03.dbf';

**Explanation** Beware of distractors in this question! The best choice is LIST COPY OF DATAFILE '/u03/oradata/prod/sys03.dbf';. However, a close second is LIST COPY OF TABLESPACE SYSTEM;. For this reason, it is important to read all choices carefully and make a decision about the choice that best answers the question. **(Topic 5.3)**

**44.** C. CREATE SCRIPT { ... }

**Explanation** The best command choice for creating but not running a script in RMAN is the CREATE SCRIPT command. This command will store but not process the contents of the RMAN script generated. The RUN command executes command within curly braces, while EXECUTE SCRIPT is improper syntax approximating the RUN command in meaning. Finally, ALLOCATE CHANNEL is a command that might appear inside the curly braces in developing RMAN scripts. **(Topic 5.4)**

**45.** A. SET MAXCORRUPT 0

**Explanation** RMAN emulates the functionality of the DBVERIFY utility and the LOG_BLOCK_CHECKSUM parameter by detecting block corruption when backups are made. However, proper syntax for setup of this feature in an RMAN script is SET MAXCORRUPT 0. **(Topic 5.5)**

**46.** B. Speed vs. recoverability

**Explanation** When deciding whether to use the LOGGING vs. NOLOGGING attributes when creating database objects, the decision is a trade-off between speedy index creation with NOLOGGING (thereby not generating redo for the action) or recoverability by allowing Oracle to generate redo for crash and media recovery. **(Topic 6.4)**

**47.** B. The backup might be usable, so long as the database was running in ARCHIVELOG mode.

**Explanation** This is a tricky scenario-based question. The right thing to do in this situation would be to take the database offline for another backup, or leave the ARCHIVELOG database online with the tablespaces in backup mode to take an online backup. Thus, the implication is that this is not a reliable backup of the system, and it isn't if the database is running in NOARCHIVELOG mode. That said, it should be noted that the backup might be usable if the database was in ARCHIVELOG mode, so long as transaction volumes weren't too high on the database. **(Topic 6.1)**

**48.** A, C, and D.  Frequency of backups, size of datafiles, and I/O speed

**Explanation**  Of the choices given, the speed of a database recovery would be influenced significantly by the frequency of database backups. In addition, the size of the datafiles being restored would proportionally affect the recovery speed. In other words, the larger the datafiles, the longer the restoration from tape. Finally, I/O speed is a factor. On a typical host machine, it takes the most time to perform I/O writes to disk—precisely the operation you will do a lot of when restoring from tape. **(Topic 6.2)**

**49.** D.  Take tablespaces out of backup mode, back up control file to trace, switch online redo logs

**Explanation**  The correct steps for completing this backup are to take the tablespaces out of backup mode, back up the control file to trace, and then switch online redo logs. When those things are finished, you should also be sure to save everything to tape. However, you should also be sure to take the tablespaces out of backup mode before saving everything to tape because the save to tape can be time-consuming, leaving you exposed to database failure during a backup, which is not a good thing. **(Topic 6.3)**

**50.** A.  A flat file script used to create the control file

**Explanation**  The ALTER DATABASE BACKUP CONTROLFILE TO TRACE command creates a flat file (not binary) script that is used for creating the control file. The ALTER DATABASE BACKUP CONTROLFILE TO *'file'* command allows you to create a binary copy of the control file. No flat file copy of the control file can be created in Oracle. **(Topic 6.5)**

**51.** B. ALTER TABLESPACE READ ONLY

**Explanation**  The ALTER TABLESPACE READ ONLY command is used for placing the tablespace into read-only mode, thus permitting query-only access. Beware of the distractor choice displaying ALTER TABLESPACE OFFLINE, because the DBA is actually trying to set up the tablespace for read-only access. Nothing in the question would indicate that a control file backup was necessary. **(Topic 6.6)**

**52.** B.  Whether the file is being backed up

**Explanation**  The FUZZY column in the V$DATAFILE_HEADER view indicates whether the datafile is in the process of being backed up. During this time, the read consistency of data in the backup is in question, hence requiring that all archive logs generated during the backup be saved as part of the backup set. **(Topic 6.7)**

**53.** C.   Image copies

**Explanation**   Image copies are backup datafile copies stored on disk for later usage. Backup sets are sets of backup data stored on tape by RMAN. Beware of the distractor choice, tags. Tags are basically just names for image copies or backup sets. **(Topic 7.1)**

**54.** B.   Ensure that the core dump directory is empty and contact Oracle Support

**Explanation**   ORA-00600 is usually indicative of a serious problem with the Oracle software. In situations where numerous ORA-00600 errors are found in the alert log, the DBA should contact Oracle Support. Because ORA-00600 errors can also be associated with background or server processes crashing, a situation that leaves core dumps in the CORE_DUMP_DEST directory the size of the Oracle SGA, the DBA should remove the core dumps so that file system does not fill. Oracle Support does not typically need core dumps to troubleshoot, but will need background and user trace files, so don't remove the contents of BACKGROUND_DUMP_DEST or USER_DUMP_DEST. Application of DBVERIFY is not typically required in this situation. And, because this batch process is important, you most likely should not stop running it. **(Topic 8.2)**

**55.** B.   The method used for writing backup sets to tape

**Explanation**   In RMAN, backup set streaming is the method used for writing backup sets to tape where blocks from various datafiles may not appear contiguously on the tape stream. The process by which RMAN communicates with the underlying OS is known as allocating channels. RMAN does not have the ability to back up more than one database at a time. Streaming can contribute to a parallel processing gain in RMAN, but only if there are multiple tape drives available during backup for RMAN to stream to. **(Topic 7.2)**

**56.** A.   All changed blocks since the level 1 backup only (not unique, because B could also be correct)

**Explanation**   RMAN allows you to create multilevel incremental backups. Each incremental level is denoted by an integer, for example, 0, 1, 2, etc. A level 0 incremental backup, which is the base for subsequent incremental backups, copies all blocks containing data. When you generate a level *n* incremental backup in which *n* is greater than 0, you back up all blocks changed after the most recent backup at level *n* or lower (the default type of incremental backup, which is called a differential backup). You also back up all blocks changed after the most recent backup at level *n* - 1 or lower (called a cumulative backup). A level 1 backup in this case is an incremental backup. RMAN will only save blocks that changed since the last incremental backup. This process saves a great amount of time and money on tapes for an organization. The other backups mentioned will take more space on tape to back up, and will take additional time as well, because all blocks of a database will need to be saved. **(Topic 7.3)**

**57.** A. Issue the ALTER DATABASE DATAFILE END BACKUP command and open the database

**Explanation** In this situation, the DBA can circumvent recovery by issuing the ALTER DATABASE DATAFILE END BACKUP command for every datafile currently in backup mode, and open the database. There is no need to recover in this situation, either from offline backup, online backup, or exports. **(Topic 7.4)**

**58.** A. Control file

**Explanation** The control file contains much of the information needed by RMAN to support backups and recovery. Good distractors in this question include the recovery catalog choice and the RMAN choice. Though the control file and recovery catalog can both contain information pertinent to RMAN, a V$ table in Oracle will contain information only from the instance in which that view is found. Armed with this knowledge, the SGA might also seem to be a good distractor as well. **(Topic 7.5)**

**59.** C. SMON detects unsynchronization between datafiles

**Explanation** Before any other step takes place during instance recovery, the SMON process first has to detect that instance recovery is necessary by determining whether database files are synchronized. After that, the DBW0 process uses redo information to write data to datafiles, and this is called the roll-forward process. Next, the database opens. Finally, the server processes will roll back uncommitted transactions. **(Topic 8.1)**

**60.** C. DBVERIFY will return an error.

**Explanation** Because the FILE command-line option is required for DBVERIFY, this command will return an error because that option was not provided. There is no default functionality in DBVERIFY stating that if FILE is not specified it should check all datafiles. DBVERIFY does not corrupt datafiles, it detects corruption. Nor does DBVERIFY change block sizes. **(Topic 8.3)**

# Answers to Practice Exam 2

**1.** A.   Set LOG_BLOCK_CHECKSUM to TRUE in INIT.ORA

**Explanation**   To configure Oracle to verify the integrity of every redo log before archiving it, the DBA must set the LOG_BLOCK_CHECKSUM INIT.ORA parameter to TRUE. The DBA would run DBVERIFY only on datafiles, not log files. LOG BLOCK CHECKSUM is not an appropriate command-line option for the ALTER DATABASE command. Finally, the DBA should already have set up archive logging, but this alone does not ensure that your database will be free of block corruption in the log files. **(Topic 8.4)**

**2.** B.   Trace files in the BACKGROUND_DUMP_DEST directory

**Explanation**   SNP processes are the processes that run in the background on an Oracle database that handle both snapshot replication and processes running out of the Oracle job queue. If one crashes, mention is usually made in the alert log. A trace file is written to the BACKGROUND_DUMP_DEST directory where the DBA can go to find out more information about the failure. **(Topic 8.5)**

**3.** A.   Re-create control file

**Explanation**   In this stage of the database recovery, you should re-create your control file using the control file creation script taken during the most recent backup. This way, the sequence numbers for all database files are out of sync, and Oracle will know that recovery is required. Issue the ALTER DATABASE RECOVER USING BACKUP CONTROLFILE statement in order to recover lost data (also known as performing roll-forward) by applying archive logs. When this is complete, you will then use the RESETLOGS option to open the database. **(Topic 10.2)**

**4.** D.   Offline backups with ARCHIVELOG disabled

**Explanation**   The main implication of NOARCHIVELOG mode is that you cannot recover your database to a point in time other than the time you took your backup. With all other backup methodologies described (including the one using exports), you should be able to recover data changes to a point in time within 60 minutes of when the error occurred in this situation. **(Topic 9.1)**

**5. C.** Open the database without the RESETLOGS option

**Explanation** Once you have restored your backup datafiles to overlay the old database, you are done with recovery of the Oracle database running in NOARCHIVELOG mode. RESETLOGS is used only when discarding online redo logs after incomplete recovery running in ARCHIVELOG mode. And, since you are not archiving redo logs in NOARCHIVELOG mode, there is no roll-forward process using archived redo. You needn't delete or re-create the control file to change archiving mode. **(Topic 9.2)**

**6. C.** ALTER DATABASE RENAME FILE

**Explanation** The best statement in this case is ALTER DATABASE RENAME FILE. After physically restoring the files from the disk that could not be restored to an alternate location, you must tell Oracle where to find those files. The ALTER DATABASE ARCHIVELOG statement is useless at this point because media failure has already occurred. Making the tablespace read only will not facilitate complete recovery, either. Finally, although you could get things rolling on recovery by dropping the datafiles from the disk that cannot be recovered right away, you will not achieve complete recovery in the situation **(Topic 9.3)**

**7.** A and E.

**Explanation** In order to use RMAN in conjunction with recovery, the control files and datafiles must all be either taken by RMAN or registered with the recovery catalog. Any backup datafile or control file not taken with RMAN or registered with the recovery catalog cannot be used for recovery in conjunction with RMAN. **(Topic 9.4)**

**8. A.** Addressing recovery needs for DSS systems

**Explanation** DSS stands for decision support system, a type of database containing static or read-only data used for query and report access. This system needn't be supported with ARCHIVELOG mode because there won't likely be much transaction processing on that system. OLTP stands for online transaction processing, a system type characterized by high data transaction volumes. ARCHIVELOG is highly appropriate for that system type, along with order entry systems, which (ideally) have high transaction volumes as well. Finally, a volatile database is the same as a high transaction volume database, so ARCHIVELOG is appropriate for that system type as well. **(Topic 10.1)**

**9. C.** Take less frequent backups for NOARCHIVELOG database

**Explanation** Of all choices given, each identifies a way to improve performance for the associated database type, except for taking less frequent backups for

NOARCHIVELOG databases. This actually increases the time required to recover this type of database. **(Topic 13.1)**

**10.** C. Roll-forward of data from archive logs

**Explanation** The ALTER DATABASE RECOVER USING BACKUP CONTROLFILE statement causes roll-forward of data from archive logs to occur, which is the next step to perform during complete recovery of the database. After that, the database will be opened using the RESETLOGS option. Restoring datafiles from backup happens before recovery, and re-creation of control file from backup happens between restoration and recovery. **(Topic 10.4)**

**11.** B. All archive logs generated since tablespace was created

**Explanation** If you do not have a backup datafile registered with RMAN, you can essentially re-create the datafile from scratch so long as you have all archive logs taken since the time the tablespace was created. You will not need a backup control file registered with RMAN for this situation. And, though an export dump may help in this situation, export dumps are not typically registered with RMAN. Finally, although the Backup Manager program is useful for interacting with RMAN, you can also operate RMAN from the command line. **(Topic 10.4)**

**12.** C. Time-based recovery

**Explanation** Time-based recovery is an incomplete recovery method based on a defined time. Complete recovery would not be sufficient because it would simply restore all the bad data changes made after the backup. Importing from an export dump taken a day before would require the users to rekey lots of lost data. Finally, tablespace point-in-time recovery is probably a little more complex an option than is truly required for this situation. **(Topic 11.1)**

**13.** A. ALTER DATABASE RECOVER AUTOMATIC UNTIL TIME

**Explanation** The ALTER DATABASE RECOVER AUTOMATIC UNTIL TIME statement is used in this situation because you want to execute a time-based incomplete recovery. For cancel-based recovery, you would use ALTER DATABASE RECOVER AUTOMATIC UNTIL CANCEL, though the use of AUTOMATIC would reduce the interaction between Oracle and the DBA in this situation. The ALTER DATABASE RECOVER AUTOMATIC UNTIL CHANGE statement is useful for change-based recovery, where the database is recovered up to a specific committed SCN. Finally, the ALTER DATABASE RECOVER AUTOMATIC UNTIL CANCEL USING BACKUP CONTROLFILE is not appropriate for reasons already covered, but also because there is no mention of recovering the control file in this situation. **(Topic 11.2)**

**14.** **A.** ALTER DATABASE OPEN RESETLOGS

**Explanation** Once roll-forward is performed to the point in time where there are no longer redo logs to support further transaction processing, Oracle needs you to open the database using the RESETLOGS option so that Oracle can regenerate your online redo logs and reset the sequence numbers in datafile headers for synchronization. The ALTER DATABASE RECOVER statement in two of the choices initiates the roll-forward process, which according to the question is already complete. Finally, the CREATE CONTROLFILE command would be issued before rolling forward, so at this point it should already have been issued. **(Topic 11.3)**

**15.** **A.** The production database is mounted but not open and the recovery catalog is available.

**Explanation** Before connecting to RMAN to perform complete recovery, the DBA should ensure that the production database is offline, but mounted, and that the recovery catalog database is online. If the recovery catalog is offline, then no information RMAN needs to perform recovery will be available. **(Topic 11.4)**

**16.** **D.** Tablespace point-in-time recovery with database open

**Explanation** In situations where only one tablespace has experienced a problem, the rest of the database can stay open while the DBA takes the corrupted tablespace offline to perform tablespace point-in-time recovery. The entire database needn't have complete or incomplete recovery because only one tablespace experienced a problem. **(Topic 11.5)**

**17.** **B.** Increase value set for BUFFER

**Explanation** By increasing the value set for BUFFER, the DBA ensures that a larger buffer is used by EXPORT, which improves overall performance by capturing more information in each attempt. By setting CONSTRAINTS to N, the DBA may improve export performance somewhat, but this improvement is offset by the fact that a complete export is not taken. Changing LOG settings will not affect the overall performance of the export, and reducing the nonzero value for FEEDBACK actually reduces performance by requiring EXPORT to provide feedback more frequently. **(Topic 12.1)**

**18.** **A and D.** FULL and INCTYPE

**Explanation** The INCTYPE parameters allow DBAs to take incremental exports of changed rows only for faster data saves between full exports. The FULL parameter sets up EXPORT to save all data in the database. The TABLES parameter allows DBAs to export only named tables to the dump file. The OWNER parameter allows

DBAs to export only those objects that are part of a particular schema in the binary dump. **(Topic 12.2)**

    **19.** B.   DIRECT=Y

**Explanation**   When the direct path export option is used, EXPORT can obtain data directly from datafiles itself, bypassing most steps in the SQL processing mechanism, the relational database management system, or RDBMS. This is when DIRECT=Y. A user export, where OWNER=Y, is a conventional path export. Neither ROWS nor FULL will influence whether EXPORT uses the conventional or direct path for obtaining data. **(Topic 12.3)**

    **20.** B.   INDEXFILE

**Explanation**   The INDEXFILE parameter is useful for situations where you want to generate a script that allows re-creation of all indexes in a database. Oracle will attempt to place objects in a database into the tablespace of the same name as the tablespace in the database the object came from. Thus, if the EMP table is stored in a DATA tablespace on one database, export will attempt to put EMP in the DATA tablespace on the new database. INDEXES is inappropriate because it simply acts as a flag to allow or suppress the capture of indexes to the export dump, while FROMUSER and TOUSER allow for migration of database objects from one schema owner to another. Finally, ROWS acts as a flag to allow or suppress the capture of row data to the export dump. **(Topic 12.4)**

    **21.** D.   Running the database in NOARCHIVELOG mode

**Explanation**   Of the choices given, running your database in NOARCHIVELOG mode is likely to increase recovery time, rather than reduce it. By taking more frequent checkpoints, you reduce the time required for instance recovery, while disk staging areas reduce the time required for restoring datafiles. Finally, more frequent backups mean shorter time spent in recovery and/or less time users must spend rekeying lost entries. **(Topic 13.1)**

    **22.** A and B.   Drop and re-create the object *and* restore from backup and roll forward using archive redo logs

**Explanation**   Once corruption is detected, the most effective method for correcting it is to restore the datafiles from a recent backup and roll forward using archive logs. Using DBVERIFY is an effective way to detect block corruption, but since Oracle has already detected this corruption, there is no need for doing so again. Both the LOG_BLOCK_CHECKSUM and RMAN's block corruption detection features can be useful in ensuring that redo logs do not propagate corruption to your backups, but again, they do not correct corruption once detected. **(Topic 13.2)**

**23.** C. CREATE CONTROLFILE SET DATABASE RESETLOGS

**Explanation** When re-creating the control file to clone a production database to test environments, the SET and RESETLOGS clauses are used in the CREATE CONTROLFILE statement. The REUSE clause is used for taking the existing database name and simply re-creating the control file, while the NORESETLOGS also prevents you from resetting the log sequence number in datafile headers once recovery is complete (i.e., limiting your recovery option to complete recovery). **(Topic 13.3)**

**24.** A. Issue the ALTER DATABASE DATAFILE OFFLINE DROP command

**Explanation** Because the data in the datafile is no longer needed, the DBA can recover most quickly by issuing the ALTER DATABASE DATAFILE OFFLINE DROP command to eliminate all reference to this datafile. Later, the DBA can also drop the associated tablespace. All options indicating restoration or recovery will require more time. **(Topic 13.4)**

**25.** B. Restore the recovery catalog from tape backup

**Explanation** While the RESYNC CATALOG FROM BACKUP CONTROLFILE command is a quick fix for restoring a recovery catalog when a backup is not available, it is less accurate than simply restoring the recovery catalog from tape backup. Likewise, the CATALOG command is simply a way to manually record entries in the recovery catalog, which leaves room for human error. Finally, creating a new recovery catalog without any restoration activity is essentially starting from scratch, which is the least accurate way to recover the recovery catalog. **(Topic 13.5)**

**26.** A. V$LOG

**Explanation** When ready to take tablespaces out of backup mode, the DBA should query the V$LOG table to determine the current sequence number. This way, the DBA will know what archive log was being written when online backup completed. This information is useful in defining the recovery process. **(Topic 6.3)**

**27.** A and B. The database is experiencing intense, long-running transactions *and* the database is undergoing crash recovery.

**Explanation** During periods of intense, long-running transactions (such as that which might be seen in real-time replication databases or long-running batch processes) it is not unusual to see multiple online redo logs with a status of ACTIVE. When a redo log is ACTIVE, it is needed for crash recovery, and possibly in use for that purpose. It may be in use for block recovery. It might or might not be archived. **(Topic 8.2)**

**28.** C. Taking frequent exports of the tables experiencing frequent data corruption

**Explanation** Frequent exports give the DBA added insurance against corruption in specific database objects. Since the database can be open during import, only users needing to access the corrupted data should find the database unavailable. NOARCHIVELOG mode has only one recovery option—closed database restoration and users rekeying data, while even a well-tuned backup process focused on complete recovery will require some downtime for that recovery. **(Topic 12.1)**

**29.** B. Re-create the logfile members

**Explanation** Since only one member of each duplexed logfile group is lost, there is no need for any recovery process, save for re-creating the lost logfile members on either the disk replacement or another drive. **(Topic 11.3)**

**30.** D. No action on the part of the DBA is required.

**Explanation** Statement failure is simply a situation where the user receives an error when he or she issues a SQL statement. No action on the part of the DBA is required. There is no reason to restart or recover the database, and most likely a user session trace file won't even be generated. **(Topic 8.1)**

**31.** C. CKPT

**Explanation** The CKPT process handles writing sequence numbers to datafile headers as part of datafile synchronization during log switches. LGWR tells DBW0 to write dirty buffers to disk during a log switch. DBW0 writes dirty buffers to disk during log switches. ARCH writes the recently filled online redo log to disk after a log switch. **(Topic 2.1)**

**32.** B. ABORT

**Explanation** Shutting down the Oracle database with the ABORT option causes Oracle to require instance recovery the next time the database is started. IMMEDIATE requires no instance recovery because current transactions are rolled back before shutdown. NORMAL requires no instance recovery because all existing users are allowed to finish their work on the database and to disconnect on their own before shutdown. TRANSACTIONAL is a modified shutdown that allows users to commit their current transaction, but otherwise resembles IMMEDIATE shutdown. **(Topic 8.1)**

**33.** C.  CONTROL_FILES

**Explanation**   By adding a new control file name to the CONTROL_FILES parameter, the DBA can multiplex control files on the Oracle database. The INIT.ORA parameter LOG_ARCHIVE_DUPLEX_DEST is used for multiplexing archive redo logs, while ROLLBACK_SEGMENTS states which named rollback segments Oracle should bring online when the database is started. Finally, the CREATE DATABASE statement is not the appropriate place to define control file multiplexing. **(Topic 2.4)**

**34.** B.  Testing backup strategy for recoverability

**Explanation**   The single best way to ensure that the backups being taken will provide complete recovery is to test the backup strategy. This alone is the most important concept to remember in the area of backup setup and deployment. There is not enough specific information in the question to determine whether ARCHIVELOG mode, third-party backup tools, or RMAN would be effective in fixing the problem. Testing the backup strategy in this case would shed more light on how the current strategy was lacking. **(Topic 1.3)**

**35.** A.  LOG_ARCHIVE_START value

**Explanation**   The key to the question is that you must first identify all the choices that identify a way the DBA can influence frequency of checkpoints. These include settings for the LOG_CHECKPOINT_INTERVAL and LOG_CHECKPOINT_TIMEOUT parameters. Also, since the frequency of log switches influences when a checkpoint will occur, changes in the size of online redo logs will influence checkpoint frequency as well. This leaves you with LOG_ARCHIVE_START, which starts the ARCH process when the instance starts, and LOG_BUFFER, which sizes the redo log buffer in the SGA. **(Topic 2.2)**

**36.** A and B.  catexp.sql and catrman.sql

**Explanation**   This question can be a little tricky, especially because one of the scripts is run automatically when you execute catalog.sql. The catexp.sql script will create dictionary objects used for taking exports, the method for logical backups in an Oracle database. Also, catrman.sql will create the database objects required for the recovery catalog. The catalog.sql and catproc.sql scripts create the basic data dictionary objects and Oracle-supplied packages, and though these scripts are required for overall database operation, they are less directly involved in the backup strategies mentioned in the question. Finally, catrep.sql is used for setup of advanced replication. **(Topic 4.4)**

**37.** B.   V$SESSION_LONGOPS

**Explanation**   The information used for calculating backup progress in RMAN is V$SESSION_LONGOPS, using the SOFAR and TOTALWORK columns. V$BACKUP_CORRUPTION is used for finding information in the control file about corrupt datafile backups. V$ARCHIVED_LOG view is used for finding information about archive logs in the database. The V$INSTANCE view is used for determining instance information, such as how long the instance has been running. **(Topic 7.4)**

**38.** D.   LIST INCARNATION

**Explanation**   The LIST INCARNATION command in RMAN is useful for determining what version of the database is in place in production. REPORT NEED BACKUP is a way for determining which datafiles need to be backed up because they haven't been backed up recently. The LIST BACKUPSET command in RMAN is good for determining available backup sets. REPORT UNRECOVERABLE is good for telling you that, if the database crashed right now, which datafiles you would not be able to recover. **(Topic 5.3)**

**39.** C.   Cumulative level 3

**Explanation**   Oracle provides an option to make cumulative incremental backups at level 1 or greater. In a cumulative level *n* backup, RMAN backs up all the blocks used since the most recent backup at level *n* - 1 or lower. For example, in a cumulative level 2 backup, RMAN determines which level 1 backup occurred most recently and copies all blocks changed since that backup. If no level 1 backup is available, RMAN copies all blocks changed since the base level 0 backup. **(Topic 7.3)**

**40.** A.   ALLOCATE CHANNEL TYPE DISK

**Explanation**   The ALLOCATE CHANNEL TYPE DISK command is useful for RMAN to write backup information elsewhere on disk, which is where the backup staging area will most likely be found. When the device is explicitly named in the ALLOCATE CHANNEL command, it is likely that the reason for doing so is to write information to tape. You do not identify a device name in the ALLOCATE CHANNEL command when that device is a disk. RELEASE CHANNEL is the command you use when you are done writing information to disk and want RMAN to close the channel. Finally, the BACKUP command given as a choice is not correct syntax. **(Topic 7.1)**

**41.** A.  1

**Explanation**  This question is tricky, especially if you know Oracle8*i*. Only in that version of the Oracle database or higher, you are able to set up more than two archive destinations. However, in Oracle8, you are only able to duplex archive destinations. Thus, any value greater than 2 in this situation is eliminated straightaway. However, if the archiving mode for one of those destinations is BEST-EFFORT, then the value for LOG_ARCHIVE_MIN_SUCCEED_DEST is 1. **(Topic 3.4)**

**42.** D.  RESYNC

**Explanation**  The RESYNC command is used for keeping information in the recovery catalog current with information about the production database found in the database's control file. The REGISTER command is used for first-time setup of the recovery catalog. The RESET command is used for ending incomplete recovery of a production database using RMAN, and is equivalent to issuing ALTER DATABASE OPEN RESETLOGS. The REPORT command is useful for showing information about the recoverability status of the database. **(Topic 5.1)**

**43.** B.  Export taken Tuesday

**Explanation**  The first step in logical database recovery is to import the contents of the most recent backup with the INCTYPE parameter set to SYSTEM. From there, you will apply the most recent full export taken Thursday, followed by the most recent cumulative export taken Monday, followed by all incrementals taken since Monday. **(Topic 12.4)**

**44.** B.  Faster warmstart

**Explanation**  The faster warmstart feature, also known as fast transaction rollback, allows databases to start before dirty buffers from uncommitted transactions in datafiles that have been rolled back. Later, server processes will implicitly roll back dirty blocks as they are located. **(Topic 13.1)**

**45.** A.  When one of three datafiles for a tablespace is missing

**Explanation**  If a datafile is missing from a tablespace with multiple datafiles, it is possible to start the database after creating the control file. When your database is online, you can find out which datafiles are missing by looking in the V$DATAFILE dictionary view for ones with a name similar to "MISSING0001." To recover from this situation, you will later need to take the tablespace offline. The database cannot start if control files or online redo logs are missing. You will receive errors when you attempt to re-create the control file in these situations. **(Topic 13.1)**

**46.** B. BUFFER

**Explanation** In situations where direct path EXPORT is used, the BUFFER parameter has little meaning because BUFFER defines the size of the data buffer used for capturing data in conventional path EXPORT. All other parameters retain their usual meaning; however, only the USERID parameter is required when actually running EXPORT, so long as you want to use the default settings for ROWS and CONSTRAINTS, which is Y. **(Topic 12.3)**

**47.** C. Procedures for rotating tapes in a tape library

**Explanation** Unlike the other choices, procedures for rotating tapes in a tape library are operational, rather than business or technical requirements. They constitute what those in a data center would consider operational procedures. Required database availability due to business hours or speedy recovery due to lost earnings when the system is offline are business requirements, while ensuring online backup validity by running Oracle in ARCHIVELOG mode is a technical requirement. **(Topic 1.1)**

**48.** A. Large pool

**Explanation** The large pool configured in the Oracle database is the only choice truly not required for high-volume-transaction OLTP environments. The ARCH process is required in order to ensure that there are no extended waits experienced by users due to filled redo logs not being archived. Running Oracle in ARCHIVELOG mode is also a requirement if you want recovery to the point of database failure. Finally, if you are running in ARCHIVELOG mode, you will need to set up an archive destination using the LOG_ARCHIVE_DEST parameter. **(Topic 2.1)**

**49.** B. LOG_ARCHIVE_DUPLEX_DEST

**Explanation** The LOG_ARCHIVE_DUPLEX_DEST parameter is not required for configuring archiving on your Oracle database. However, you also do need to configure the DEST and FORMAT parameters, but don't need to change the default values if you don't want to do so. LOG_ARCHIVE_DEST has a default value that you can change to set up at least one archive log destination setup. The LOG_ARCHIVE_FORMAT parameter can be set so as to have a naming convention in place. Finally, LOG_ARCHIVE_START should be used so that ARCH will be available to handle automatic archiving on your database. **(Topic 3.3)**

**50.** B. Data changes will not be recoverable unless the change was made before the most recent backup.

**Explanation** NOARCHIVELOG mode typically means that data changes are unrecoverable unless the change was made before the most recent backup, or the database is read-only. Beware of some tough distractors in this question. First, it is difficult to say if end users will feel no impact. Perhaps there is a correction to a severe usage problem that users need to test. A crash on the test database could cause serious impact. Also, there is not enough information to say whether the database will be easy to recover. Perhaps developers made several adjustments to the test database after the most recent backup, all of which will now need to be redone. **(Topic 3.1)**

**51.** C.  Recovery for static DSS systems like data marts

**Explanation**  In most cases, RMAN needn't be used for backup or recovery on static databases, and can add levels of complexity that have no value in such systems. This is because certain key functions like incarnation tracking is not possible with NOARCHIVELOG databases. High-volume transaction systems, such as order entry, are likely to be using ARCHIVELOG mode, because of the strong need for high availability and recoverability inherent in use of that mode. Thus, RMAN is a good fit for those types of systems. **(Topic 4.1)**

**52.** A.  RUN

**Explanation**  The RUN command in RMAN is used for execution of existing scripts for backup or recovery. ALLOCATE CHANNEL is a command that might appear in an existing script to allow RMAN to communicate with the operating system to perform key functions. The EXECUTE command is not recognized syntax in RMAN, while RESET is a command used for incomplete recovery in RMAN. **(Topic 5.1)**

**53.** D.  ALTER TABLESPACE BEGIN BACKUP

**Explanation**  The ALTER TABLESPACE BEGIN BACKUP statement is used to begin database backup of each tablespace. In this way, Oracle can ensure that read consistency is maintained even though the datafile copy is being made while actual data in the datafile is undergoing change. Taking the datafile offline is not necessary, nor is it necessary to make the tablespace read-only. Finally, starting the ARCH process is recommended whenever archiving is used, but this is not directly correlated to the actual scripting process of backing up the archivelog database. **(Topic 6.3)**

**54.** B.  Online backups offer increased availability and system uptime for database backups.

**Explanation**  Online backups offer increased availability and system uptime for database backups. Other than that, there is little difference between recovery from offline and online backups when Oracle runs in ARCHIVELOG mode. Both offer complete recoverability to point of failure. And, since both require application of archive logs, there is little difference between the two as far as time required for complete recovery. Finally, online backups do not require the use of RMAN. **(Topic 6.2)**

**55.** C. Datafiles cannot be streamed with archive logs in a backup set.

**Explanation** Datafiles cannot be streamed with archive logs in a backup set. However, archive logs can be streamed in with other archive logs, and datafiles can be streamed with other datafiles in a backup set. Both can be streamed as well. **(Topic 7.2)**

**56.** A. RUN { MAXCORRUPT 0

**Explanation** The line containing reference to the MAXCORRUPT command reduces the likelihood of corruption in datafiles, in turn increasing the chances of a valid backup being available for recovery. **(Topic 8.4)**

**57.** B. Tablespace recovery

**Explanation** With few exceptions, tablespace recovery permits the database to be open, so long as the tablespace being recovered is offline. Incomplete recovery such as change-based or time-based recovery, requires that the database be offline. So does full database recovery. **(Topic 9.1)**

**58.** B. The database must be opened.

**Explanation** After SMON performs instance recovery, the database can be opened. Remember, this is instance recovery, not media recovery. There is no need for datafile restoration or roll-forward using archive logs. Any uncommitted transactions will be rolled back after the database is open due to faster warmstart. **(Topic 10.1)**

**59.** A. Change-based recovery

**Explanation** The best method to employ for recovery in this situation is change-based recovery, because the DBA knows the SCN of the last known good transaction. If the DBA knew approximately what time the last known good transaction occurred, time-based recovery would be most appropriate. If the DBA wanted maximum interaction during recovery, cancel-based recovery would be most appropriate. Finally, if the DBA didn't care about recovery to a point in time other than when an export took place, export-based recovery would work. **(Topic 11.1)**

**60.** B. The import will execute successfully with warnings.

**Explanation** Since no information is given about the value for the IGNORE parameter, you must assume that the default value of N is in place (i.e., IMPORT will not ignore creation errors coming from the database). Thus, the import will execute successfully, but with warnings, since the database objects IMPORT tries to create will already exist in the database. However, these errors will not be enough to cause IMPORT to terminate unsuccessfully. **(Topic 12.4)**

# CHAPTER 4

## OCP Exam 4: Performance Tuning Workshop

CP Exam 4 covers issues related to tuning the Oracle database. To pass this exam, you need to demonstrate an understanding of the features available in Oracle for tuning your databases for performance purposes. You will also need to demonstrate an understanding of the special views available in Oracle for performance tuning. In more recent editions of OCP Exam 4, the focus has been on use of GUI tools like Oracle Enterprise Manager and Oracle Expert as part of the overall tuning process.

# OCP Exam 4 Topic Areas

The following topic areas are tested in OCP Exam 4. These topics are taken from the OCP Candidate Guide published by Oracle and are up-to-date as of this printing. You should download the Candidate Guide for the OCP DBA track before taking this exam to ensure that these topic areas are still current by accessing the Oracle University Web site at **education.oracle.com/certification**. The topics are as follows:

1. Business Requirements and Tuning
    - 1.1. List the different roles associated with the tuning process
    - 1.2. Define the steps associated with the tuning process
    - 1.3. Identify different tuning goals
2. Oracle Alert, Trace Files, and Events
    - 2.1. Identify the location and usefulness of the alert log file
    - 2.2. Identify the location and usefulness of the background and user process trace files
    - 2.3. Retrieve and display wait events
    - 2.4. Set events through OEM to be alerted about predefined situations
3. Utilities and Dynamic Performance Views
    - 3.1. Collect statistics using the dynamic troubleshooting and performance views
    - 3.2. Diagnose statistics using the UTLBSTAT/UTLESTAT output report
    - 3.3. Use appropriate OEM tuning tools
4. Tuning Considerations for Different Applications
    - 4.1. Use the available data access methods to tune the logical design of the database

# Chapter 4: OCP Exam 4: Performance Tuning Workshop 215

- **4.2.** Identify the demands of online transaction processing systems (OLTP)
- **4.3.** Identify the demands of decision support systems (DSS)
- **4.4.** Reconfigure systems on a temporary basis for particular needs

5. SQL Tuning
   - **5.1.** Identify the roles of the DBA in application tuning
   - **5.2.** Use star queries and hash joins to enhance data access operations
   - **5.3.** Use optimizer modes to enhance SQL statement performance
   - **5.4.** Use Oracle tools to diagnose SQL statement performance
   - **5.5.** Track and register module usage for packages, procedures, and triggers
   - **5.6.** Identify alternative SQL statements to enhance performance

6. Generic Operating System Tuning Issues and Oracle
   - **6.1.** List the primary steps for operating system tuning
   - **6.2.** Identify similarities between operating system and database tuning
   - **6.3.** Explain the difference between a process and a thread
   - **6.4.** Describe paging and swapping

7. Tuning the Shared Pool
   - **7.1.** Tune the library cache and the data dictionary cache
   - **7.2.** Measure the shared pool hit percentage
   - **7.3.** Size the shared pool appropriately
   - **7.4.** Pin objects in the shared pool
   - **7.5.** Tune the shared pool reserved space
   - **7.6.** List the UGA and session memory considerations

8. Tuning the Buffer Cache
   - **8.1.** Describe how the buffer cache is managed
   - **8.2.** Calculate the buffer cache hit ratio
   - **8.3.** Examine the impact of adding or removing buffers
   - **8.4.** Create multiple buffer pools
   - **8.5.** Size multiple buffer pools

- **8.6.** Monitor buffer cache usage
- **8.7.** Make appropriate use of table caching
9. Tuning the Redo Log Buffer
    - **9.1.** Determine if processes are waiting for space in the redo log buffer
    - **9.2.** Size the redo log buffer appropriately
    - **9.3.** Reduce redo operations
10. Database Configuration and I/O issues
    - **10.1.** Diagnose inappropriate use of the SYSTEM, RBS, TEMP, DATA, and INDEX tablespaces
    - **10.2.** Detect I/O problems
    - **10.3.** Ensure that files are distributed to minimize I/O contention
    - **10.4.** Use striping where appropriate
    - **10.5.** Tune checkpoints
    - **10.6.** Tune background process I/O
11. Using Oracle Blocks Efficiently
    - **11.1.** Determine an appropriate block size
    - **11.2.** Optimize space usage within blocks
    - **11.3.** Detect and resolve row migration
    - **11.4.** Monitor and tune indexes
    - **11.5.** Appropriately size extents
12. Optimize Sort Operations
    - **12.1.** Identify the SQL operations that require sorts
    - **12.2.** Ensure that sorting is done in memory where possible
    - **12.3.** Use direct writes for large sorts
    - **12.4.** Allocate temporary space appropriately

## Chapter 4: OCP Exam 4: Performance Tuning Workshop

13. Rollback Segment Tuning
    13.1. Use dynamic performance views to check rollback segment performance
    13.2. Reconfigure and monitor rollback segments
    13.3. Define the number and size of rollback segments
    13.4. Allocate rollback segments to specific transactions
14. Monitoring and Detecting Lock Contention
    14.1. Define the levels of Oracle locking
    14.2. List possible causes of lock contention
    14.3. Use Oracle utilities to diagnose lock contention
    14.4. Resolve contention in an emergency
    14.5. Prevent locking problems
    14.6. Recognize Oracle errors arising from deadlocks
15. Latch and Contention Issues
    15.1. Use Oracle tools to diagnose and resolve free list contention
    15.2. Identify specific latch contention situations
    15.3. Diagnose and resolve redo allocation and redo copy latch contention
    15.4. Diagnose and resolve LRU latch contention
16. Tuning with Oracle Expert
    16.1. List the features of Oracle Expert
    16.2. Create a tuning session
    16.3. Gather, view, and edit the input data
    16.4. Analyze the collected data using rules
    16.5. Review tuning recommendations
    16.6. Implement tuning recommendations

## Practice Exam 1

1. You are defining event monitors via Enterprise Manager to detect problems. Which of the following events could be used for detecting whether the cause of a database not being available is the fact that the host machine is offline?

    A. DB UpDown

    B. Node UpDown

    C. Listener UpDown

    D. Tablespace Full

2. Performance on the database has slowed down, causing long delays for users. If the DBA wanted to determine if the cause was related to long-running reports on the Oracle database, which of the following views would he or she use to do so?

    A. V$SYSSTAT

    B. V$SQLAREA

    C. V$SQLTEXT

    D. V$SGASTAT

3. You are attempting to generate the statistics report using Oracle scripts. Which of the following parameters must be set in order to ensure accurate information in that report?

    A. SQL_TRACE

    B. AUDIT_TRAIL

    C. TIMED_STATISTICS

    D. LOG_ARCHIVE_START

4. You are planning to use Oracle Enterprise Manager tools in conjunction with tuning. Which of the following tools are appropriate for determining which users are consuming the highest level of resources with respect to your Oracle database?

    A. Performance Manager

    B. SQL Analyze

C. TopSessions

D. Oracle Expert

5. Your EMPLOYEE table contains a column called STATUS, which contains the status of any particular employee. Only three valid values exist for this column, and the value only changes when an employee is hired, terminated, or retired. To improve performance on queries utilizing the STATUS column, which of the following choices is appropriate?

   A. B-tree Indexes

   B. Bitmap indexes

   C. Hash clusters

   D. Index-organized tables

6. A database characterized by high transaction volume is experiencing performance problems when data is being entered by users. Which of the following choices best identifies a solution to this performance problem?

   A. Reduce the number of indexes on the most active tables.

   B. Tune queries for speedier lookup data access.

   C. Use hash clusters to move associated tables closer together on disk.

   D. Convert B-tree indexes to bitmap indexes.

7. A data warehouse application consisting of a dozen tables is reloaded nightly with new information for analysis. Which of the following choices identifies the best way to manage primary-key constraints for performance?

   A. Primary keys should be in place before data is loaded to enforce business rules.

   B. Primary-key constraints should be maintained by Oracle while data is loaded.

   C. Eliminate primary-key constraints, as they are unnecessary in data warehouses.

   D. Rebuild primary-key constraints after data is loaded for best performance.

8. The DBA needs a methodology for reconfiguring a production database for particular needs. For example, the DBA increases a parameter such as SORT_AREA_RETAINED_SIZE during his or her maintenance work on a DBA maintenance weekend. Which of the following choices describes the most appropriate methodology?

    A. Set up hot standby databases to the production system.

    B. Use and maintain multiple INIT.ORA files.

    C. Clone production to a test environment nightly.

    D. Have scripts on hand to implement snapshot replication quickly.

9. An application developer is attempting to tune the functionality of a particular application module. Which of the following choices best identifies the ideal activities of the DBA in support of this developer's work?

    A. Setup of session tracing and running output through TKPROF

    B. Altering SGA settings to optimize use of real memory

    C. Moving datafiles to improve load balancing

    D. Working with the system engineer to configure a new host system

10. The DBA is attempting to improve performance of join queries involving two or more tables by avoiding the "NOT IN" FILTER operation. Which of the following choices identifies a component of doing so?

    A. HASH_JOIN_ENABLED

    B. ALWAYS_ANTI_JOIN

    C. HASH_AREA_SIZE

    D. HASH_MULTIBLOCK_IO_COUNT

11. The DBA wants to optimize query performance to emphasize high-speed execution of queries involved in batch processing. Which of the following choices best identifies optimizer goals for doing so?

    A. CHOOSE

    B. ALL_ROWS

    C. FIRST_ROWS

    D. RULE

12. You are attempting to tune the performance of a particular module's usage in the Oracle database. Which of the following choices best identifies the step you need not take first in setting up to use AUTOTRACE as part of this exercise?

    A. Run utlxplan.sql.

    B. Run plustrce.sql.

    C. Issue the SET AUTOTRACE ON command in the SQL*Plus session.

    D. Run catrep.sql.

13. The DBA is attempting to track performance of PL/SQL modules in an Oracle environment. SQL*Plus cannot be used. How can the application module be set so that a user session trace file is generated, even without using the ALTER SESSION command?

    A. Through use of the AUTOTRACE utility

    B. With the DBMS_SESSION package

    C. With the DBMS_DDL package

    D. With the DBMS_OUTPUT package

14. The DBA is assisting application developers in tuning the application. One developer uses the following query to obtain data:

    SELECT * FROM BASEBALL_TEAM WHERE TEAM_LOCATION IN (SELECT CITY_NAME FROM TEAM_CITIES);

    Which of the following choices identifies the best alternative from a performance perspective while simultaneously giving the correct result?

    A. SELECT * FROM BASEBALL_TEAM WHERE EXISTS (SELECT CITY_NAME FROM TEAM_CITIES WHERE CITY_NAME = TEAM_LOCATION);

    B. SELECT * FROM BASEBALL_TEAM WHERE TEAM_LOCATION IN (SELECT * FROM TEAM_CITIES);

    C. SELECT TEAM_LOCATION FROM BASEBALL_TEAM WHERE TEAM_LOCATION IN (SELECT CITY_NAME FROM TEAM_CITIES);

    D. SELECT TEAM_LOCATION FROM BASEBALL_TEAM WHERE TEAM_LOCATION = 'LOUISVILLE' OR TEAM_LOCATION = 'SCHRIEVEPORT' OR TEAM_LOCATION = 'LOS ANGELES';

15. The DBA is attempting to tune non-Oracle aspects of database operation. Which of the following choices indicates the best choice location for hardware bottlenecks?

    A. CPU

    B. Network

    C. Memory

    D. I/O

16. The DBA is attempting to tune memory aspects of an Oracle database from the hardware perspective. Which of the following choices best identifies how the DBA may address this task?

    A. Tuning buffer cache utilization

    B. Adjusting the shared pool size

    C. Ensuring the redo allocation latch is not a bottleneck

    D. Ensuring SGA fits in real memory

17. The DBA is monitoring background activities on an Oracle database. Which of the following terms correctly identifies the method in Windows environments loosely akin to processes in UNIX?

    A. Processes

    B. Threads

    C. Dispatchers

    D. Servers

18. The host system is running low on real memory. Which of the following choices best identifies the effect this could have on Oracle performance?

    A. Oracle performance improves because virtual memory handles SGA processing better than real memory.

    B. Oracle performance degrades because real memory handles SGA processing better than virtual memory.

    C. Oracle performance improves because host automatically shuts down processes conflicting with Oracle.

    D. Oracle performance does not change because Oracle dynamically alters its real memory allocation.

19. Pins on the library cache are 4039253, and reloads are 59836. What is the hit ratio for the library cache?

    A. Not enough information provided

    B. 0.985

    C. 67.5

    D. 0.001

20. The sum number of getmisses on dictionary cache information is 303, and the sum number of gets is 204930. What is the hit ratio on the dictionary cache?

    A. Not enough information provided

    B. 676.3

    C. 0.001

    D. 0.998

21. The DBA is attempting to increase SQL statement reuse in the shared pool. Which of the following choices will not further her or his attempts in doing so?

    A. Restricted use of ad hoc queries on the database

    B. Standard methods for authoring SQL in applications

    C. Reduced use of dynamic SQL in applications

    D. Increasing reliance on DBMS_SQL for report generation

22. In order to pin PL/SQL packages in memory, the DBA must run the keep( ) procedure found in which of the following Oracle-supplied packages?

    A. DBMS_DDL

    B. DBMS_SQL

    C. UTL_FILE

    D. DBMS_SHARED_POOL

23. The DBA is attempting to tune shared pool reserved space. Which of the following tools or commands is not one where the DBA would normally obtain this information?

    A. V$PARAMETER

    B. The STARTUP command

**C.** In Instance Manager

**D.** The SHOW PARAMETER command

24. The DBA is attempting to tune session memory size. Where is memory allocated in support of server processing associated with a user session?

   **A.** The machine hosting the database.

   **B.** The client machine.

   **C.** Application server.

   **D.** None. Server processing takes place in the SGA.

25. The DBA is tuning buffer cache operation. Which of the following choices does not identify a time when Oracle will write blocks in the dirty buffer write queue to disk?

   **A.** When a time-out occurs

   **B.** When a log switch occurs

   **C.** When a commit occurs

   **D.** When the buffer cache has no free buffers

26. Output from V$SYSSTAT includes 12380 for physical reads, 874357 for block gets, and 234258 for consistent gets. Which of the following choices identifies the buffer cache hit rate?

   **A.** 0.988

   **B.** 3.732

   **C.** 0.267

   **D.** 0.001

27. The DBA is sizing multiple buffer pools of the SGA. Which of the following choices identifies how many LRU latches are allocated to the buffer cache in this configuration?

   **A.** A fixed number of 5

   **B.** At most one latch for every 50 buffers

   **C.** One latch for each pool

   **D.** At least one latch for every 50 buffers

28. You are sizing the buffer cache for multiple buffer pools. In order to use the appropriate V$ view for viewing multiple buffer pool statistics, which of the following scripts must be run?

    A. catexp.sql

    B. catalog.sql

    C. plustrce.sql

    D. catperf.sql

29. You are monitoring activity against the buffer cache on your database. Which two of the following views are used for this purpose (choose two)?

    A. V$SYSSTAT

    B. V$SESSTAT

    C. V$BUFFER_POOL_STATISTICS

    D. V$ROWCACHE

    E. V$SGA

30. The DBA is attempting to use table caching. Which of the following choices best identifies the point at which cached table data is actually loaded into memory?

    A. When the instance starts

    B. The next time the table is queried in any way

    C. As soon as the ALTER TABLE CACHE command is issued

    D. The next time the table is queried using the TABLE ACCESS FULL operation

31. You are trying to determine whether processes are waiting for space in the log buffer. Which of the following records would you want to see statistical information for?

    A. Redo size

    B. Redo writes

    C. Redo buffer allocation retries

    D. Redo log space requests

**32.** You are sizing the redo log buffer in your Oracle database. Which of the following choices identifies the most important consideration you will face when sizing this memory area?

   **A.** Wasting real memory on Oracle SGA

   **B.** Sizing the SGA out of real memory

   **C.** Processes waiting for log buffer space

   **D.** A good ratio of space to each of Oracle's shared memory areas

**33.** The DBA is attempting to tune redo log operations on an Oracle database. In order to improve performance on the time users wait to write redo data, which of the following choices identifies the steps the DBA should take?

   **A.** Set LOG_SMALL_ENTRY_MAX_SIZE 80

   **B.** Set LOG_SMALL_ENTRY_MAX_SIZE 120

   **C.** Set LOG_SMALL_ENTRY_MAX_SIZE 70

   **D.** Set LOG_SMALL_ENTRY_MAX_SIZE 30

**34.** The DBA has configured the database tablespaces in the following way:

```
DISK 1: Oracle software, TEMP and TOOLS tablespace
DISK 2: DATA, USERS, and INDEX tablespace
DISK 3: Redo logs, control file
DISK 4: RBS tablespace, SYSTEM tablespace
DISK 5: Redo logs, control file
```

   How could the DBA reconfigure this arrangement in a more optimal fashion?

   **A.** Move TEMP tablespace to DISK 3

   **B.** Move INDEX tablespace to DISK 1

   **C.** Move all redo logs to DISK 5

   **D.** Move SYSTEM tablespace to DISK 1

**35.** You are attempting to determine whether tablespaces are being misused. Which of the following queries can be used to determine if the DBA let users create their database objects in the wrong place by leaving those users pointing to the wrong default tablespace?

   **A.** SELECT COUNT(*) FROM DBA_SEGMENTS WHERE SEGMENT_TYPE = 'ROLLBACK' AND TABLESPACE_NAME <> 'RBS';

**B.** SELECT COUNT(*) FROM DBA_TABLES WHERE OWNER NOT IN ('SYS','SYSTEM') AND TABLESPACE_NAME = 'SYSTEM';

**C.** SELECT COUNT(*) FROM DBA_SEGMENTS WHERE SEGMENT_TYPE = 'TABLE' AND TABLESPACE_NAME <> 'DATA';

**D.** SELECT COUNT(*) FROM DBA_OBJECTS WHERE SEGMENT_TYPE = 'TABLE';

**36.** You are attempting to perform load balancing of your Oracle database. Which of the following views is useful for identifying physical reads and writes on disk datafiles, broken out by datafile?

**A.** V$DATAFILE

**B.** V$FILESTAT

**C.** V$SGASTAT

**D.** V$SYSSTAT

**37.** You are attempting to distribute I/O on your Oracle database. Which of the following is a technique that often results in poor performance?

**A.** Redo logs stored in RAID 5 arrays

**B.** Partitioning large tables across multiple disks

**C.** Mirrored datafile copies using hardware mirroring

**D.** Placing datafiles for the same tablespace on multiple disks

**38.** Database design and tuning strategy call for ensuring that instance recovery takes minimal time. The application does not produce big redo log entries. Which of the following choices best identifies how the DBA can ensure this happens?

**A.** Set LOG_CHECKPOINT_TIMEOUT to 0.

**B.** Increase the size of online redo logs.

**C.** Set LOG_CHECKPOINT_INTERVAL to 5000.

**D.** Decrease the size of online redo logs.

**39.** When tuning background processes in Oracle8*i*, which of the following steps is not typically required for optimizing LGWR performance?

**A.** Setting CHECKPOINT_PROCESS to TRUE

**B.** Multiplexing redo logs

C. Ensuring the archive destination does not contain online redo logs

D. Using more redo logs on high volume OLTP systems

40. The DBA is configuring a database with DB_BLOCK_SIZE of 4K. Which of the following system types will this block size typically work best with?

   A. Online transaction processing

   B. Data mart

   C. Full-text search databases

   D. Decision support system

41. Your OLTP application has several tables that are frequently updated in the course of the day, populating several null columns with data. To avoid chaining, which of the following combinations are most appropriate for a database in this situation?

   A. DB_BLOCK_SIZE = 2048; PCTFFREE 20

   B. DB_BLOCK_SIZE = 8192; PCTFFREE 5

   C. DB_BLOCK_SIZE = 4096; PCTFFREE 10

   D. DB_BLOCK_SIZE = 8192; PCTFFREE 20

42. Application developers are concerned about row migration on the database. Assuming the DBA does not want to build her or his own table, before running the appropriate command, which of the following scripts should be run by the DBA?

   A. plustrce.sql

   B. utldtree.sql

   C. utlchain.sql

   D. catperf.sql

43. The composite key for table SOFTWARE_SALES contains columns PRODUCT, VERSION, and CITY, in positions 1, 2 and 3, respectively. Which of the following queries is tuned to properly search for data in the database?

   A. SELECT * FROM SOFTWARE_SALES WHERE PRODUCT = 'OCP PREP' AND CITY = 'TOLEDO';

   B. SELECT * FROM SOFTWARE_SALES WHERE CITY = 'TOKYO' AND VERSION = 4.1;

C. SELECT * FROM SOFTWARE_SALES WHERE VERSION = 4.1 AND CITY = 'TOKYO';

D. SELECT * FROM SOFTWARE_SALES WHERE VERSION = 4.1;

44. You are trying to determine whether a statement will require a sort or not. Which of the following SQL statements will require that the RDBMS perform a sort?

   A. SELECT EMPID, LASTNAME FROM EMP UNION SELECT SSN, LASTNAME FROM PEOPLE;

   B. SELECT * FROM CATTLE_RANCHERS WHERE OWNER = 'MILLIE';

   C. UPDATE CATTLE_RANCHERS SET RANCH_NAME = 'CIRCLE_K';

   D. INSERT INTO EMP (EMPID, LASTNAME) VALUES (1234567,'FRANKIE');

45. You are attempting to properly determine how large the initial extent should be for a table. Which of the following choices best identifies a procedure that may aid in the task?

   A. Size of row * number of rows in table

   B. Tablespace size / number of tables in data model

   C. Number of tables / size of each row

   D. Number of tables * number of rows

46. SORT_AREA_SIZE is 65536 on an Oracle database. If ten users issue SQL statements requiring sorts on a small amount of data, which of the following choices best identifies how much space in memory will be used, and whether or not the sort will happen in memory?

   A. 64K for sort area total, disk sorts will be used

   B. 640K for sort area total, memory sorts will be used

   C. 64K for sort area, memory sorts will be used

   D. 2M for sort area, memory sorts will be used

47. A data warehouse application DBA is attempting to tune disk sorts. Which of the following choices best identifies a way to assist the DBA in doing so on an Oracle8 database?

   A. SORT_DIRECT_WRITES=TRUE

   B. SORT_AREA_SIZE=2048

C. NEXT=20K for TEMP tablespace default storage

D. ALTER USER TEMPORARY TABLESPACE

48. **SORT_AREA_SIZE is set to 131072. Which of the following choices best identifies a way to tune tablespaces in order to maximize performance of disk sorts?**

    A. Set NEXT on SYSTEM to 512K

    B. Set NEXT on TEMP to 512K

    C. Set NEXT on DATA to 512K

    D. Set NEXT on INDEX to 512K

49. **You are attempting to monitor rollback segment performance. Which of the following methods could be used to determine if a rollback segment was recently used in support of a long-running transaction?**

    A. V$WAITSTAT

    B. V$SYSSTAT

    C. V$ROLLSTAT

    D. DBA_ROLLBACK_SEGS

50. **In monitoring the database rollback segments on the MINX database, you discover that RBS02 is stretched past the size of 2M, which you believe is appropriate for overall database activity. Which two of the following commands will have the effect of reducing the size of the rollback segment (choose two)?**

    A. ALTER ROLLBACK SEGMENT RBS02 OFFLINE;

    B. ALTER ROLLBACK SEGMENT RBS02 STORAGE (NEXT 2048);

    C. ALTER ROLLBACK SEGMENT RBS02 STORAGE (PCTINCREASE 20);

    D. ALTER ROLLBACK SEGMENT RBS02 SHRINK;

    E. ALTER ROLLBACK SEGMENT RBS02 STORAGE (OPTIMAL 2M);

51. **The Oracle instance is running in standard mode. Only one instance has the database mounted and opened. Which of the following choices correctly identifies how many rollback segments will be online at startup?**

    A. None. Rollback segments are brought online manually when the instance starts.

    B. Determined by TRANSACTIONS/OPEN_CURSORS.

**C.** All will be online, except for SYSTEM rollback segment.

**D.** Rollback segments named in INIT.ORA will be online.

52. **Which of the following statements best describes the method Oracle uses to allocate rollback segments to transactions?**

    **A.** Each transaction is assigned to a rollback segment in a round-robin manner unless a specific rollback segment is requested.

    **B.** Each transaction is assigned to the same rollback segment until that segment fills, and then the next rollback segment is used.

    **C.** Transactions must identify a rollback segment for Oracle to assign them to, or else Oracle does not assign a rollback segment.

    **D.** Rollback segments are assigned to transactions in progress only if changes to data are made.

53. **Two separate transactions issue LOCK TABLE EMP IN SHARE MODE to request a SHARE lock on the EMP table. The second transaction issues an UPDATE statement that affects several rows. The first transaction then issues an UPDATE statement that affects several rows. Ten percent of the total number of rows being changed are affected by both transactions. Which of the following statements best describes how Oracle handles this situation?**

    **A.** The first transaction that acquired the SHARE lock will be able to complete its transaction while the other waits.

    **B.** The first transaction that acquired the SHARE lock will be able to make all its changes, and the second transaction will only make 90 percent of its changes until the first transaction completes.

    **C.** Both transactions can change data, but neither transaction will complete until the other relinquishes its lock.

    **D.** Neither transaction can change data, but either transaction can complete until the other relinquishes its lock.

54. **The application developer is trying to determine the cause of a performance issue involving locks and contention. Which of the following situations could likely be contributing to an issue with lock contention?**

    **A.** Default locking used for UPDATE statements

    **B.** Lack of use of COMMIT statements

    **C.** Frequent use of LOCK TABLE commands

    **D.** Transaction processing commands found where expected

**55.** The DBA needs to detect lock contention on the Oracle database. Which of the following tools comes standard with the Oracle8*i* Server license?

   **A.** Lock Manager

   **B.** UTLLOCKT

   **C.** Performance Manager

   **D.** TopSessions

**56.** The DBA has just killed a user session. Which three of the following choices identify an event that will happen next?

   **A.** SMON will recover the instance.

   **B.** PMON rolls back the active transaction.

   **C.** The user is disconnected.

   **D.** Locks held by the killed session are released.

   **E.** Committed data from the killed session is removed.

   **F.** The killed user's account is locked.

**57.** The DBA is attempting to institute measures that will prevent locking problems on existing applications. Which of the following is a good means for doing so?

   **A.** Killing offending user transactions

   **B.** Monitoring for waiting sessions using Lock Manager

   **C.** Thorough application code reviews

   **D.** Discouraging future development using the LOCK TABLE command

**58.** A deadlock has just occurred on the database. Where might the DBA look to determine more information?

   **A.** The audit trail

   **B.** DBW0 dump file

   **C.** LGWR trace file

   **D.** alert log

**59.** The DBA is attempting to determine whether free-list contention is a problem on the database. When using the V$SYSTEM_EVENT view in doing so, which of the following choices best identifies the statistic the DBA
would look for?

   **A.** Free list

   **B.** Buffer busy waits

   **C.** Undo header waits

   **D.** Undo segment waits

**60.** The DBA is about to begin performance tuning. Before tuning memory structures in the Oracle database, in which of the following areas should the DBA examine tuning?

   **A.** Disk I/O bottlenecks

   **B.** SQL statements

   **C.** Latches and locks

   **D.** Dispatchers and shared servers

# Practice Exam 2

1. You are attempting to retrieve and display wait events for your entire Oracle database. Which of the following dictionary views can assist in your doing so?

    A. V$SYSSTAT

    B. V$SYSTEM_EVENT

    C. V$SESSTAT

    D. V$SESSION_EVENT

2. The PMON background process crashes, causing the Oracle instance to fail. After calling Oracle Support, they request that you provide the arguments to the ORA-00600 error that occurred before the database crashed. In which of the following places would you find this information?

    A. USER_DUMP_DEST

    B. LOG_ARCHIVE_DEST

    C. BACKGROUND_DUMP_DEST

    D. CORE_DUMP_DEST

3. After analyzing database behavior, the DBA realizes that the overall cause of performance problems is that log switches happen too frequently on the Oracle database. Which of the following database components are likely to have assisted her or him in this determination?

    A. The alert log

    B. V$DATAFILE

    C. The audit trail

    D. AUTOTRACE

4. The DBA is attempting to work with users to tune a report that runs on the Oracle database. Which of the following choices identifies a tuning goal that is appropriate for this situation?

    A. Improving I/O performance for the database

    B. Increasing SGA allocation

    C. Adding an index to a table to improve query performance

    D. Adding CPUs to the host machine

5. Tuning a database application is in progress on an Oracle database. Which of the following steps will be executed only after more focused efforts for tuning a specific application using the Oracle database have failed?

   A. Memory usage analysis

   B. Acquiring more disk controllers

   C. SQL statement tuning

   D. Upgrading the machine hosting the Oracle database

6. The organization is defining roles in the tuning process. Which group of people will likely need to be involved in making decisions about hardware acquisitions within the overall organizational picture for improving performance of an application?

   A. Managers

   B. Users

   C. DBAs

   D. Developers

7. Once Oracle Expert has completed its analysis and you have completed your review of its recommendation, which of the following tabs would you use to begin implementation of those recommendations in the Oracle Expert tool?

   A. Scope

   B. View/Edit

   C. Scripts

   D. Recommendations

8. The DBA is planning to run Oracle Expert to tune the database. Which of the following choices identifies the step that must be accomplished before defining data classes that will be collected?

   A. Analyze collected data using rules.

   B. Implement recommendations.

   C. Define tuning session scope.

   D. Review recommendations.

9. The DBA is using Oracle Expert for the first time. Which of the following choices identifies the step that must be conducted before a tuning session must be created?

    A. Create the Oracle Expert repository.

    B. Connect to the Oracle Expert repository.

    C. Set the tuning scope.

    D. Analyze the statistics.

10. The DBA is attempting to use Oracle Expert. Which of the following choices identifies the OEM component that must be installed in order to make Oracle Expert available for use?

    A. Diagnostics Pack

    B. Standard Management Pack

    C. Change Management Pack

    D. Tuning Pack

11. The DBA has just issued the following query:

    ```
    SELECT P.PID, N.NAME, (L.MISSES/L.GETS)*100
    FROM V$PROCESS P, V$LATCHNAME N, V$LATCH L
    WHERE P.LATCHWAIT IS NOT NULL
    AND P.LATCHWAIT = L.ADDR
    AND L.LATCH# = N.LATCH#
    AND N.NAME = 'cache buffers lru chain';
    ```

    Which of the following choices identifies the object this DBA is trying to detect latch contention on?

    A. Log buffer

    B. Buffer cache

    C. Shared pool

    D. Large pool

12. The DBA has altered settings for LOG_SMALL_ENTRY_MAX_SIZE and LOG_SIMULTANEOUS_COPIES. Which of the following latch types is the DBA attempting to resolve contention for?

    A. LIBRARY CACHE

    B. REDO ALLOCATION

C. AQ STATISTICS

D. DONE QUEUE

13. **The DBA is attempting to identify specific situations in which latch contention may exist. In which of the following situations are latches not used to govern access to an object?**

    A. Writing parse trees to the shared pool

    B. Writing redo to the log buffer

    C. Writing active buffers to the buffer cache

    D. Writing data changes to a table in active transactions

14. **Developers are attempting to reduce the amount of lock contention experienced in a Forms application. Which of the following choices is not a recommendation the DBA might make in supporting this activity?**

    A. Use the minimum level of locking required to execute data changes.

    B. Issue LOCK TABLE IN EXCLUSIVE MODE commands frequently.

    C. Utilize the SELECT FOR UPDATE statement frequently.

    D. Defer to the locking level used by Oracle for UPDATE statements.

15. **The DBA wants to use the UTLLOCKT utility in Oracle. Which of the following scripts must be run prior to its use?**

    A. catblock.sql

    B. utllockt.sql

    C. catexp.sql

    D. catrman.sql

16. **Two users are waiting for a resource to become free in Oracle. Which of the following commands must be issued in order to free that resource?**

    A. LOCK TABLE

    B. SAVEPOINT

    C. COMMIT

    D. ROW SHARE

17. The DBA is monitoring usage of a rollback segment with OPTIMAL set to 1M. Assuming NEXT is set to 50K, which of the following choices indicates the point at which the rollback segment will shrink, and the view the DBA should use to monitor this activity?

   A. 10, V$ROLLNAME

   B. 15, V$ROLLSTAT

   C. 25, V$SYSSTAT

   D. 30, V$ROLLSTAT

18. The DBA has set SORT_AREA_SIZE to 65536. Given an 8K block size, which of the following choices indicates the best default storage setting for NEXT on the TEMP tablespace?

   A. 125K

   B. 180K

   C. 256K

   D. 500K

19. The DBA is attempting to improve performance by limiting database sorts. Based on this criterion, which of the following choices indicates a database operation the DBA should attempt to minimize?

   A. SELECT statements using a WHERE clause

   B. UPDATE statements

   C. CREATE INDEX statements

   D. DELETE statements

20. The DBA is managing an Oracle database with DB_BLOCK_SIZE set to 16384. Aside from space reserved for header information, which of the following choices identifies the best default storage setting for NEXT to ensure maximum space allocation for extents in a tablespace 128MB in size?

   A. 64K

   B. 128K

   C. 16K

   D. 32K

**21.** The DBA issues the following query:

```
SELECT NAME, VALUE FROM V$SYSSTAT WHERE NAME IN
('table scans (short tables)', 'table scans (long tables)',
'table scan rows gotten', 'table fetch by rowid');
```

**What is the DBA attempting to do?**

**A.** Measure buffer cache hit performance.

**B.** Measure index usage and performance.

**C.** Measure table usage and size.

**D.** Measure shared pool hit performance.

**22.** The DBA is considering use of striping on an Oracle database. In which of the following situations is hardware striping across an array of disks potentially damaging to performance?

**A.** DATA tablespace datafiles

**B.** INDEX tablespace datafiles

**C.** Redo logs

**D.** Control files

**23.** You are attempting to determine whether there is a problem with I/O on the Oracle database. Which of the following views are useful for this purpose?

**A.** V$WAITSTAT

**B.** V$IOSTAT

**C.** V$SYSSTAT

**D.** V$FILESTAT

**24.** You are monitoring the performance of your buffer cache pools. Which of the following views can be used to calculate hit statistics on the multiple buffer pools in your Oracle buffer cache?

**A.** V$SYSSTAT

**B.** V$BUFFER_POOL_STATISTICS

**C.** V$SGASTAT

**D.** V$MULTIPLE_BUFFER_POOL

25. After creating multiple buffer pools in your Oracle database, which of the following choices best identifies how to switch a table laced into the right buffer pool?

    A. Setting the BUFFER_POOL_KEEP parameter

    B. Setting the BUFFER_POOL_RECYCLE parameter

    C. With the ALTER TABLE statement

    D. With the ALTER SYSTEM statement

26. The DBA is attempting to calculate the buffer cache hit ratio. Which of the following choices identifies the view most suited for assisting in this purpose?

    A. V$SGASTAT

    B. V$SYSSTAT

    C. V$SESSTAT

    D. V$WAITSTAT

27. The DBA is configuring memory settings for the buffer cache. Which of the following choices best identifies the algorithm Oracle uses to purge buffers read in to find data information, and the mechanism used to manage access to that memory area, when a full table scan is being performed?

    A. First-in-first-out, latches

    B. Last-in-first-out, locks

    C. Least-recently used, locks

    D. Least-recently used, latches

28. The DBA wants to tune session memory and UGA allocation. Which two of the following views are used for determining required memory allocations for this area (choose two)?

    A. V$SESSTAT

    B. V$SYSSTAT

    C. V$STATNAME

    D. V$SHARED_POOL_RESERVED

    E. V$SGASTAT

29. Users of a custom application written using server-side PL/SQL packages experience errors when they attempt to run their application. The errors indicate there is not enough room to load the package into memory. Which two of the following settings may be used to help (choose two)?

    A. SHARED_POOL_SIZE

    B. SHARED_POOL_RESERVED_SIZE

    C. V$SHARED_POOL_RESERVED

    D. SHARED_POOL_RESERVED_MIN_ALLOC

    E. DB_BLOCK_BUFFERS

30. The DBA is attempting to tune the shared pool. Which three of the following choices identify views that assist in determining whether the shared pool is too large or small (choose three)?

    A. V$SYSSTAT

    B. V$LIBRARYCACHE

    C. V$ROWCACHE

    D. V$DICTCACHE

    E. V$SGASTAT

31. The DBA is comparing background operations in Oracle on Windows and UNIX platforms. Which of the following choices best compares the operations of processes to threads?

    A. Multiple threads require their own memory allocations, while multiple processes can share the same memory allocation.

    B. Different processes and threads can run concurrently on different processors.

    C. Each thread in the Oracle process will use a private memory area.

    D. Multiple processes in UNIX are treated as the same thread.

32. The DBA is participating in work to tune the Oracle database's underlying host system. Which of the following choices best identifies the similarity between Oracle database tuning and operating system tuning?

    A. Sizing the TEMP tablespace versus sizing swap space

    B. Adding more CPU to handle Oracle versus adding more CPU to handle other processes

**C.** Setting process prioritization higher for certain Oracle processes than for other non-Oracle processes

**D.** Ensuring the SGA fits into real memory

33. The DBA is working with a systems engineer to ensure appropriate host configuration of an Oracle database. Which of the following choices best identifies a primary step for OS tuning that the DBA will need to take?

    **A.** Sizing SGA to fit into real memory

    **B.** Optimizing default extent settings in the TEMP tablespace

    **C.** Sizing Oracle blocks as a multiple of OS blocks

    **D.** Specifying hardware cache for disk controllers

34. The DBA is configuring for high-performance SQL queries in data warehouse applications. Which of the following RDBMS execution steps is used for obtaining data from multiple tables in the execution plan generated for a star query?

    **A.** NESTED LOOPS

    **B.** MERGE JOIN

    **C.** INDEX UNIQUE SCAN

    **D.** FILTER

35. The DBA is working with OEM tools to tune the database running in Windows. Which of the following choices identifies the tool provided for OEM in this capacity, along with the appropriate software pack?

    **A.** AUTOTRACE in Change Management Pack

    **B.** Storage Manager in Tuning Pack

    **C.** Performance Monitor in Diagnostics Pack

    **D.** Performance Monitor in Tuning Pack

36. The DBA needs to identify system-wide wait information for the Oracle database. Which of the following locations stores data regarding the amount of time Oracle waits for user processes to reply via Net8?

    **A.** Oracle Enterprise Manager console

    **B.** V$SESSION_WAIT

    **C.** DBA_WAITERS

    **D.** PLAN_TABLE

**37.** The user issues the ALTER SESSION SET SQL_TRACE = TRUE. In which of the following locations will information be produced supporting the use of this command?

   **A.** SYS.AUD$

   **B.** USER_DUMP_DEST

   **C.** BACKGROUND_DUMP_DEST

   **D.** SQL_TRACE_DEST

**38.** The DBA is attempting to identify the frequency of log switches on the database. Which of the following files and locations may be useful for her or him to do so?

   **A.** The session trace files in USER_DUMP_DEST

   **B.** The date stamps on core dumps in CORE_DUMP_DEST

   **C.** The INIT.ORA file in ORACLE_HOME/dbs

   **D.** The ALERT log in BACKGROUND_DUMP_DEST

**39.** The DBA is recommending tuning methods to users of a custom application. Which of the following choices best identifies a recommendation that has the greatest potential for improving performance with the most limited scope?

   **A.** Upgrading from an existing machine with four processors to a new one with eight

   **B.** Increasing the SGA settings for the Oracle database

   **C.** Downloading a new patch for the Oracle Server

   **D.** Changing the WHERE clause of a specific SQL statement to utilize an index

**40.** The IT department at a large auto manufacturer is experiencing problems with performance on a custom billing application. Which of the following tasks identifies the best individual and concept area to begin the tuning process?

   **A.** The business analyst refining the billing process

   **B.** The application developer analyzing the code

   **C.** The DBA reorganizing the tablespaces

   **D.** The systems engineer reconfiguring the RAID array

41. You are about to attempt to detect whether row migration is the source of a performance problem on your database. Which of the following choices identifies what you will do first?

    A. Look at the contents of report.txt.

    B. Use the ANALYZE command.

    C. Increase the value of PCTFREE.

    D. Decrease the value of PCTUSED.

42. In your initialization file, you have TRANSACTIONS set to 150 and the parameter TRANSACTIONS_PER_ROLLBACK_SEGMENT set to 1,000. If, after database startup, your database has 15 rollback segments, and 12 of them are online, how many rollback segments will Oracle tend to use on your database?

    A. 7

    B. 10

    C. 12

    D. 15

43. You are determining appropriate space usage for your application, an OLTP system where data is highly volatile. Keeping a high PCTFREE for that system has which of the following effects?

    A. Keeps the data blocks filled to capacity with table or index data

    B. Works well for both OLTP and decision support systems

    C. Maximizes performance on the database buffer cache

    D. Reduces the possibility of row chaining and data migration

44. You test an application's SQL statements in a session using TKPROF and find that the total blocks read from disk total is 40,394. You then assign the tables referenced by this application to the recycle pool. When rerunning TKPROF, you find that your total blocks read from disk is now 50,345. How should you tune your database (choose two)?

    A. Increase your keep pool.

    B. Increase your buffer cache.

C. Decrease your recycle pool.

D. Assign the tables referenced by the application to the default pool.

E. Increase your library cache.

F. Issue the ANALYZE TABLE COMPUTE STATISTICS command.

45. You have assigned three tables to the keep pool. How should you determine the appropriate size for your keep pool?

    A. Based on the size of your shared pool

    B. Based on the number of blocks in the table only

    C. Based on the number of blocks in the table plus blocks in associated indexes

    D. Based on the number of blocks in associated indexes only

46. The DBA is evaluating an increase in the size of the buffer cache. Statistics returned from the appropriate view show the following information:

    ```
    RANGE               HITS
    --------------------------
    0-100               45039
    101-200             9002
    201-300             901
    301-400             602
    401-500             120
    ```

    Based on this information, which of the following choices identifies the best number of buffers to add to the buffer cache?

    A. 100

    B. 200

    C. 300

    D. 400

    E. 500

47. After configuring MTS, the DBA notices a severe decline in the hit ratios of both the dictionary and library cache. Assuming no other INIT.ORA changes were made, which of the following may be the cause?

    A. The SGA has been sized out of real memory.

    B. There are not enough LRU latches active on the system.

C. The shared server processes have been given a lower priority than LGWR.

D. Session information is now being stored in the shared pool.

48. You have decided that, to improve performance on your database, you must keep a small lookup table called LOOKUP_VALUES in memory. Which of the following statements will cause Oracle to load data from that table into memory?

    A. alter table LOOKUP_VALUES cache;

    B. alter table LOOKUP_VALUES storage (buffer_pool keep);

    C. select * from LOOKUP_VALUES;

    D. alter table LOOKUP_VALUES storage (buffer_pool recycle);

49. In order to improve the hit ratio on your library cache, you will want to configure Oracle in such a way that which of the following statistics decreases?

    A. Reloads

    B. Physical reads

    C. Gets

    D. Getmisses

50. By setting the LOG_SMALL_ENTRY_MAX_SIZE from 120 to 40, which of the following things will most likely happen?

    A. Buffer cache hit ratio will decrease.

    B. User processes will wait less time for log buffer space.

    C. Paging and swapping will increase.

    D. Oracle will crash.

51. You have just issued a query on the V$CURRENT_BUCKET view. Which of the following activities are you most likely engaged in?

    A. Increasing the size of the buffer cache

    B. Increasing the size of the shared pool

C. Tuning file system I/O

D. Adding real memory to your host machine

52. You are developing an administrative script to assist in pinning an object in the shared pool that Oracle is currently unable to load into shared memory. Which of the following statements should not be used in that script?

    A. SHUTDOWN IMMEDIATE

    B. DBMS_SHARED_POOL.keep( )

    C. DBMS_SHARED_POOL.sizes( )

    D. SHUTDOWN ABORT

    E. startup open

    F. alter system flush SHARED_POOL;

53. You are developing a script that automates the calculation of all actual hit statistics for your database. Which of the following views would be not be referenced at all in that script?

    A. V$LIBRARYCACHE

    B. V$ROWCACHE

    C. V$RECENT_BUCKET

    D. V$SYSSTAT

54. An application has experienced poor performance due to frequent parse tree reloads over the past several hours. To address the problem, the DBA is considering the following approaches. Which of these approaches should the DBA discard immediately?

    A. Adopting standards for uniform SQL statement development

    B. Increasing the value set for SHARED_POOL_SIZE

    C. Increasing the value set for DB_BLOCK_BUFFERS

    D. Setting CURSOR_SPACE_FOR_TIME to FALSE

55. The DBA is about to begin performance tuning. Queries on the appropriate view indicate the problem has to do with SGA sizing. Which of the following items will she or he most likely not tune?

    A. File system or hardware cache usage

    B. Library cache pin and reload usage

    C. Row cache gets and getmisses usage

    D. Buffer cache and multiple buffer pool usage

56. You are considering an increase to the number of buffers in the buffer cache. Which of the following views will contain appropriate statistics for determining the right number of buffers to add, if any?

    A. V$SYSSTAT

    B. V$RECENT_BUCKET

    C. V$CURRENT_BUCKET

    D. V$BUFFER_POOL_STATISTICS

57. You determine that 35 users, on average, experience contention when concurrently attempting to add data to one table. In order to correct the problem, you have to change which of the following areas?

    A. Latches

    B. Free lists

    C. Redo log buffer

    D. LOG_SMALL_ENTRY_MAX_SIZE

58. The DBA is attempting to tune SQL statement performance. SQL operations listed as output from EXPLAIN PLAN can be interpreted from the following query in which of the following ways?

    ```
    SELECT LPAD(' ',2*level) || operation || ' '
    || options || ' ' || object_name AS query_plan
    ```

```
FROM plan_table
WHERE statement_id = 'your_statement_id'
CONNECT BY PRIOR ID = parent_id
and statement_id = 'your_statement_id'
 7 START WITH ID=1;
```

    **A.** Executed from top to bottom, from outside in

    **B.** Executed from bottom to top, from outside in

    **C.** Executed from top to bottom, from inside out

    **D.** Executed from bottom to top, from inside out

**59.** The DBA is locating the V$INSTANCE view in Oracle. Dynamic performance views in the Oracle instance such as this one are owned by which of the following users?

    **A.** SYSTEM

    **B.** Sysdba

    **C.** Osdba

    **D.** SYS

**60.** You are tuning application SQL statements on table EMP, which has one index on column EMPID, declared as VARCHAR2(20). Which of the following SQL statements has an execution plan that will not use the index?

    **A.** SELECT EMPID from EMP WHERE EMPID = '604';

    **B.** SELECT nvl(EMPID,0) from EMP WHERE EMPID = '604';

    **C.** SELECT ROWID from EMP WHERE EMPID like '604';

    **D.** SELECT * from EMP WHERE EMPID = 604;

# Answers to Practice Exam I

**1.** B.  Node UpDown

**Explanation**  The Node UpDown event is probably the most accurate way to determine whether database unavailability is due to the machine being offline. DB UpDown tells you whether the database went down, but without an associated event informing you about the host machine status, you will not know whether the machine went down because of the host or because of some other reason. Likewise, Listener UpDown gives listener process status but not node status. Finally, the Tablespace Full event has no relation to availability. **(Topic 2.4)**

**2.** B.  V$SQLAREA

**Explanation**  Reports are based on queries, so the DBA is really looking for information on the queries being run on the database and their associated performance statistics. The V$SQLAREA view contains statistics associated with current SQL statements running on the database and a partial listing of the actual SQL text. V$SQLTEXT is a good distractor because it shows you the SQL statements running in the database in their entirety, but it is wrong because V$SQLTEXT does not show statistics associated with particular statements. V$SYSSTAT is used for system-wide statistics collection and review, while V$SGASTAT contains detailed information about the SGA. **(Topic 3.1)**

**3.** C.  TIMED_STATISTICS

**Explanation**  In order for UTLBSTAT/UTLESTAT to be accurate when generating output for report.txt, the TIMED_STATISTICS parameter must be set to TRUE. This way, performance timing statistics will be generated in support of many of the activities this performance routine actually accomplishes. The SQL_TRACE (enables system- or session-wide tracing to occur on the database) parameter needn't be set, nor does the AUDIT_TRAIL (turns on database auditing) parameter. Finally, the LOG_ARCHIVE_START parameter tells Oracle whether to start the ARCH background process, used for archiving logs automatically when log switches occur. **(Topic 3.2)**

**4.** C.  TopSessions

**Explanation**  The TopSessions utility gives you specific information about the resource consumption of the top sessions hitting your Oracle database. While the SQL Analyze tool is used for analyzing SQL statements to improve performance, it is intended more for development or enhancement of SQL code, not for tuning live sessions. Oracle Expert gives comprehensive information about performance tuning, but requires a lot of time to generate recommendations, whereas usually you will want only a snapshot of database use when determining the database top sessions. Finally, Performance Manager is useful for monitoring overall resource usage for the database, but lacks the ability to pinpoint resource usage to a particular session. **(Topic 3.3)**

    **5.** **B.**   Bitmap indexes

**Explanation**   Bitmap indexes are often used for improving query performance on columns containing low cardinality, mostly static data. B-tree indexes do little to improve performance in this situation. Hash clusters could be useful if this situation included table joins between EMPLOYEE and other tables. Finally, index-organized tables work best when queries are performed on a primary-key value used for organizing the table, which STATUS almost surely is not. **(Topic 4.1)**

    **6.** **A.**   Reduce the number of indexes on the most active tables.

**Explanation**   The best approach for maximizing performance on table updates in OLTP systems is to minimize the number of indexes on tables most frequently updated or inserted. This is because every index added to a table increases processing overhead for DML statements against that table. Since the performance issue in question is DML access, not queries, tuning queries is not appropriate for this situation. Because OLTP applications are typically characterized by high-volume data changes, hash clusters are inappropriate because those database objects are used more for static systems such as data warehouses for high-performance query access. Finally, converting B-tree indexes to bitmap indexes is yet another example of how to tune query access on static data, not on how to tune data change activities on OLTP systems. **(Topic 4.2)**

    **7.** **D.**   Rebuild primary-key constraints after data is loaded for best performance.

**Explanation**   When managing indexes associated with primary-key constraints for performance, rebuild primary-key constraints after data is loaded for best performance. Maintaining the index associated with a primary key while data is being loaded reduces the performance of the data load, usually by a factor greater than the time it would take to load data without the key enabled plus the time it takes to rebuild the index. To minimize risk associated with loading duplicate records into the primary-key column, ensure the data is unique before loading data into the table by verifying its origin. Primary-key constraints are usually still required in data warehouses, if only to provide indexing required to improve query performance on reports. **(Topic 4.3)**

**8.** B. Use and maintain multiple INIT.ORA files

**Explanation** By far, the simplest way to reconfigure a production database based on short-term, reoccurring business needs is to maintain two or more INIT.ORA files that configure the database in the way you need the database reconfigured. The choice describing use of a standby database outlines a good strategy for fast recoverability. The choice involving a clone of production to test and scripts for implementing snapshot replication are both good for creating a test environment, but test environments don't always best serve the needs of DBA maintenance weekends, though they are great for testing application developer needs. **(Topic 4.4)**

**9.** A. Setup of session tracing and running output through TKPROF

**Explanation** Of the choices given, setup of session tracing and running session output files through TKPROF is the best way the DBA can support an application developer in his or her task of tuning a particular application module. The choice of altering SGA settings might assist, but since the tuning effort is focused on one module of an application, rather than all modules or applications hitting that database, the DBA is performing tasks too broad in scope. This is the same reason why load balancing is not correct, and also why upgrading to a new host system is not a good solution either. **(Topic 5.1)**

**10.** B. ALWAYS_ANTI_JOIN

**Explanation** All parameters identified as choices except for ALWAYS_ANTI_JOIN are used for setup of hash join operations, which are performance-enhancing alternatives to the FILTER operation for joining output from JOIN queries. **(Topic 5.2)**

**11.** B. ALL_ROWS

**Explanation** By setting the optimizer goal to ALL_ROWS, the DBA enhances performance of the RDBMS optimizer to return all rows of data requested in the most expedient manner possible, thereby increasing overall throughput of batch processes. FIRST_ROWS is useful for optimizing return of the first set of rows for a user query when the user is sitting right there, waiting for the output. Neither CHOOSE nor RULE are optimizer goals; rather, they are optimizer modes—the first indicating cost-based and the second indicating rule-based optimization. **(Topic 5.3)**

**12.** D. Run catrep.sql.

**Explanation** Running catrep.sql before using AUTOTRACE has no role in the functionality of this feature. Instead, this script is used to set up advanced replication between instances. The catrep.sql script is used for setting up snapshot replication, and has little if any role in the use of AUTOTRACE. Before setting up to use AUTOTRACE in the session, you should first ensure that PLAN_TABLE exists and is available to the user running AUTOTRACE. This is accomplished by running the utlxplan.sql script. The plustrce.sql script is used for setting up other objects required for using AUTOTRACE, but should be run only after PLAN_TABLE has been created. Finally, once the other steps are executed, you will issue the SET AUTOTRACE ON command in your session. **(Topic 5.4)**

13. B. With the DBMS_SESSION package

**Explanation** Of the choices given, the most appropriate method for setting up to generate user session trace files is to include calls the set_sql_trace_in_session( ) procedure found in DBMS_SESSION. The AUTOTRACE utility is used from within SQL*Plus, which as the question indicates, cannot be used. The DBMS_DDL package contains procedures that allow for change of database object setup, not session environment. Finally, DBMS_OUTPUT could be tailored for usage in this situation, but would require more work than simply using DBMS_SESSION. **(Topic 5.5)**

14. A. SELECT * FROM BASEBALL_TEAM WHERE EXISTS (SELECT CITY_NAME FROM TEAM_CITIES WHERE CITY_NAME = TEAM_LOCATION);

**Explanation** The SELECT * FROM BASEBALL_TEAM WHERE EXISTS (SELECT CITY_NAME FROM TEAM_CITIES WHERE CITY_NAME = TEAM_LOCATION) query is correct because its use of EXISTS instead of IN enhances performance while still returning the correct result. Two of the other queries that continue use of IN are essentially restatements of the query in the question, while the query using a multiple condition OR in the WHERE clause will not necessarily return the correct result. After all, we have no idea whether the cities named are the only ones in the TEAM_CITIES table. **(Topic 5.6)**

15. A. CPU

**Explanation** The best location for hardware bottlenecks when it comes to database tuning is at the CPU. Network bottlenecks are bad because they mislead administrators into thinking that performance on the machine is optimal in poor performance situations. Memory bottlenecks are also a problem because they cause processors to be underutilized during peak performance periods. The same condition is true for I/O bottlenecks, which cause the CPUs to be idle during periods of waiting for I/O activities to complete. In general, all other bottlenecks will cause CPU to be underutilized. The bottom line with respect to hardware is that the only performance limitation in an application is the speed at which the CPUs can process instructions. **(Topic 6.1)**

**16.** D.  Ensuring SGA fits in real memory

**Explanation**  Of the choices given, ensuring the SGA fits into real memory is the best step a DBA can take when tuning memory utilization from the hardware perspective. When the SGA does not fit into real memory, the database performance suffers overall. The two choices indicating how to alter the size of the SGA are potential distractors because they show how to reduce SGA size to fit into real memory. In reality, two other conditions can be changed for SGA to fit into real memory: 1) add more real memory; or 2) limit the memory usage of server and non-Oracle processes permitted to connect to Oracle. Since the host machine will also need space to run server processes, the DBA can increase the likelihood of SGA fitting into real memory by using MTS and/or limiting use of the host machine for non-Oracle processes. **(Topic 6.2)**

**17.** B.  Threads

**Explanation**  Threads are used in Windows environments within the Oracle.exe process to allow that process to execute background tasks. Separate processes are still used in Windows for MTS operation, such as dispatchers and servers. **(Topic 6.3)**

**18.** B.  Oracle performance degrades because real memory handles SGA processing better than virtual memory.

**Explanation**  Oracle performance degrades because real memory handles SGA processing better than virtual memory. If Oracle is forced into virtual memory, the host will immediately spend a lot more time paging information into and out of real memory to support user requests for data in this situation. **(Topic 6.4)**

**19.** B.  0.985

**Explanation**  Based on the calculation (PINS-RELOADS) / PINS, the hit ratio is 0.985. Beware the distractors that are essentially incorrect calculations of the hit ratio, such as PINS / RELOADS, and RELOADS / PINS. **(Topic 7.2)**

**20.** D.  0.998

**Explanation**  Based on the formula (HITS-MISSES) / HITS, the hit rate on the dictionary cache with these statistics is 0.998, or close to 100 percent. Be careful of distractors that are based on incorrect formulas for calculating hit statistics. **(Topic 7.2)**

**21.** D.  Increasing reliance on DBMS_SQL for report generation

**Explanation**  The use of the DBMS_SQL package increases use of dynamic SQL, which reduces the potential for reuse of SQL. This is because dynamic SQL must be generated on the fly every time it is used. Other choices identify ways to restrict the amount of unique SQL statements issued against the database, thus increasing the potential for statement reuse. **(Topic 7.3)**

**22.** D. DBMS_SHARED_POOL

**Explanation** The DBMS_SHARED_POOL package contains procedures such as keep( ), which is used for pinning PL/SQL packages in the shared pool of the SGA. DBMS_DDL contains procedures allowing users to generate tables and other DDL operations normally not permitted in PL/SQL. DBMS_SQL is used for dynamic SQL generation in the Oracle database prior to Oracle8*i*. Finally, UTL_FILE is used for reading and writing flat files on the host machine from within PL/SQL in the Oracle database. **(Topic 7.4)**

**23.** B. The STARTUP command

**Explanation** Although Oracle generally shows the memory allocation to various areas of the SGA at startup, none of these statistics (not even fixed SGA size) indicates exactly what the shared pool reserved size is set to be. V$PARAMETER will show you the value for this initialization parameter, however. So will Instance Manager. Server Manager shows you this parameter value when you use the SHOW command. **(Topic 7.5)**

**24.** A. The machine hosting the database

**Explanation** The session UGA is stored in the machine hosting the Oracle database, in a memory area outside the Oracle SGA. The client machine may store run-time session information, but does not store information associated with the shared or dedicated servers attached to the Oracle database supporting user processing. The application server only stores this information in *n*-tier environments, and there is not enough information to support this choice. **(Topic 7.6)**

**25.** C. When a commit occurs

**Explanation** Purging the contents of the buffer cache dirty buffer write queue has no association with regular transaction processing. Rather, by disassociating transaction processing from dirty block writes, Oracle frees users from being I/O dependent in write activities. DBW0 writes the dirty buffers to disk when time-outs occur every three seconds, when a log switch occurs, and when the buffer cache is full. **(Topic 8.1)**

**26.** A. 0.988

**Explanation** According to the formula 1 – *(physical reads / (block gets + consistent gets)*, the buffer cache hit rate is 0.988. If you arrived at any other answer, you may have miscalculated. Be sure you understand the formula for buffer cache hit rate both for the OCP exam and for your work tuning an Oracle database. **(Topic 8.2)**

**27.  B.**   At most one latch for every 50 buffers

**Explanation**   The buffer cache should have at most one latch for every 50 buffers in the buffer cache. Any more than that creates inefficiencies in the way the buffer cache is being managed. The number is not fixed, but rather is variable, according to the value set for DB_BLOCK_LRU_LATCHES at database startup. **(Topic 8.4)**

**28.  D.**   catperf.sql

**Explanation**   The catperf.sql script is run to generate the V$BUFFER_POOL_STATISTICS view, used for viewing multiple buffer pool statistics for performance purposes. The catexp.sql script is used for generating objects appropriate for exporting and importing data. Catalog.sql is a good distractor, simply because so much of the Oracle data dictionary is created using that script. Finally, plustrce.sql is used for setup of the AUTOTRACE utility. **(Topic 8.5)**

**29.  A and C.**   V$SYSSTAT and V$BUFFER_POOL_STATISTICS

**Explanation**   The V$SYSSTAT view contains statistics used for calculating the buffer cache hit ratio, while V$BUFFER_POOL_STATISTICS is used for determining the performance of multiple buffer pools. V$SESSTAT contains performance statistics associated with each live session connected to the database, while V$ROWCACHE is used for determining hit ratios on the dictionary or row cache. V$SGA contains summary performance information about the Oracle SGA, not about performance in the buffer cache in particular. **(Topic 8.6)**

**30.  D.**   The next time the table is queried using the TABLE ACCESS FULL operation

**Explanation**   After issuing the ALTER TABLE CACHE statement, Oracle will load table data into the buffer cache the next time a query on that table results in a TABLE ACCESS FULL operation, according to the same principles it would use if the table blocks were loaded into memory as part of a more efficient operation. The data is not loaded at instance startup, nor is the data cached as soon as the ALTER TABLE CACHE statement is issued. The choice indicating the next time the table is queried in any way is a good distractor, but remember—only when table data is loaded using the full table scan algorithm are the blocks purged almost immediately after being loaded. **(Topic 8.7)**

**31.** C. Redo buffer allocation retries

**Explanation** In the V$SYSSTAT view, you would want to see the statistics associated with redo buffer allocation retries in order to determine whether users were waiting for space in the log buffer. Be careful of a good distractor: redo log space requests tells you the overall number of requests for space in the log buffer, but gives no indication of how many of those requests Oracle turned away. **(Topic 9.1)**

**32.** B. Sizing the SGA out of real memory

**Explanation** By far, the worst thing you can do performance-wise on an Oracle database with respect to shared memory is to size the SGA out of real memory. The performance hit the database will experience in this situation will be far worse, on average, than a performance problem caused by processes waiting for log buffer space. There is no rule about ensuring a good ratio to each area of the Oracle SGA. Finally, if you have real memory to spare, you shouldn't worry about wasting it on the SGA, although there are better places to allocate it within the SGA. **(Topic 9.2)**

**33.** D. Set LOG_SMALL_ENTRY_MAX_SIZE 30

**Explanation** The optimal tuning method for setting up the redo buffer INIT.ORA parameters is for both the parameters identified to be the same value. This permits Oracle to prebuild larger redo entries at the same cutoff applied to the size a redo entry must be in order to get written while the process holds the redo copy latch instead of the redo allocation latch. Thus, two choices are eliminated. From there, you need to know that the lower the LOG_SMALL_ENTRY_MAX_SIZE is set to, the shorter the period of time any user process will be allowed to hold the redo allocation latch. Thus, set the LOG_SMALL_ENTRY_MAX_SIZE parameter to 30. **(Topic 9.3)**

**34.** B. Move INDEX tablespace to DISK 1

**Explanation** With only five separate I/O locations at your disposal, configuring an Oracle database becomes a question of balanced trade-offs. In this scenario, the biggest performance impact with respect to the entire system will definitely be having the DATA and INDEX tablespaces in the same location. While SYSTEM and RBS on the same disk could pose a threat to performance initially, eventually all the information the database needs gets read into the row cache, leaving DATA and INDEX to fight it out long term. Thus, the INDEX tablespace should be moved to DISK 1, where it will remain relatively undisturbed by Oracle software, disrupted only occasionally by the errant disk sort. TOOLS and USERS tablespaces are red herrings—typically, these are the least-used tablespaces in your system. **(Topic 10.3)**

**35.** B. SELECT COUNT(*) FROM DBA_TABLES WHERE OWNER NOT IN ('SYS','SYSTEM') AND TABLESPACE_NAME = 'SYSTEM';

**Explanation** This question basically asks how you would figure out if users put their tables into the SYSTEM tablespace because the DBA forgot to point the users to another default tablespace. SELECT COUNT(*) FROM DBA_TABLES WHERE OWNER NOT IN ('SYS','SYSTEM') AND TABLESPACE_NAME = 'SYSTEM' handles that task. The two queries on DBA_SEGMENTS are great distractors—both are well formed and useful for identifying misuse of tablespaces other than SYSTEM. Careful reading of the question will help you avoid traps like this one. **(Topic 10.1)**

**36.** B. V$FILESTAT

**Explanation** The V$FILESTAT view contains statistics about datafile physical reads and writes. The V$DATAFILE view is a good distractor because you will most likely join the information in V$FILESTAT with V$DATAFILE in order to associate the statistics in V$FILESTAT with the appropriate filenames. However, the V$FILESTAT view contains the actual statistics. V$SYSSTAT is also a good distractor because it contains so many other statistics. **(Topic 10.2)**

**37.** A. Redo logs stored in RAID 5 arrays

**Explanation** Generally speaking, the worst performer out of the choices given is having your redo logs running out of RAID 5, particularly on OLTP systems. This is because Oracle writes redo logs sequentially, while RAID 5 is optimized more for scattered writes. **(Topic 10.4)**

**38.** D. Decrease the size of online redo logs.

**Explanation** Without a better frame of reference, it's hard to determine whether the settings for either LOG_CHECKPOINT_INTERVAL are useful, though setting LOG_CHECKPOINT_TIMEOUT to 0 is not helpful because it effectively eliminates any time-out-based checkpoints that may otherwise happen on the database. Thus, you are left with one of the choices indicating sizing the redo logs. By decreasing the size of redo logs, you effectively increase the number of checkpoints by increasing the number of log switches (assuming constant transaction rates), and more frequent checkpoints make instance recovery take less time. Thus, decrease the size of online redo logs. **(Topic 10.5)**

**39.** A. Setting CHECKPOINT_PROCESS to TRUE

**Explanation** The CHECKPOINT_PROCESS was eliminated in Oracle8 and Oracle 8*i*, in favor of simply running the CKPT process all the time. Thus, you will not usually need to set CHECKPOINT_PROCESS to TRUE. All other choices given will improve LGWR performance, and should be considered in the event that LGWR performance proves to be a problem. **(Topic 10.5)**

**40.** A.   Online transaction processing

**Explanation**   An 8K block size is typically the most optimal block size for online transaction processing systems on most platforms. This is because order entry systems typically have smaller amounts of data per record and usually require more free space per row in order to grow later. Data marts and other DSS systems, on the other hand, need more room in each block to store either larger records or more of them for fast searches and reporting. Full-text search databases also contain large blocks of text data, and may experience serious problems with chaining if the block size is set too low. **(Topic 11.1)**

**41.** D.   DB_BLOCK_SIZE = 8192; PCTFFREE 20

**Explanation**   When chaining is a performance issue or concern, the best route to take is one involving larger data blocks and higher value for PCTFREE. Thus, an 8K block size and 20 percent free space in each block is probably the best way to go. Remember, 20 percent of 8K is lots more room to grow than 20 percent of 2K. **(Topic 11.2)**

**42.** C.   utlchain.sql

**Explanation**   The utlchain.sql script is used in this situation because it creates the CHAINED_ROWS table, used in the ANALYZE TABLE LIST CHAINED_ROWS command. The plustrce.sql script is used for setting up the AUTOTRACE feature of SQL*Plus, while utldtree.sql is used for determining object/program dependency trees within applications. The catperf.sql script is used for setup of buffer pool statistics monitoring. **(Topic 11.3)**

**43.** A.   SELECT * FROM SOFTWARE_SALES WHERE PRODUCT = 'OCP PREP' AND CITY = 'TOLEDO';

**Explanation**   The SELECT * FROM SOFTWARE_SALES WHERE PRODUCT = 'OCP PREP' AND CITY = 'TOLEDO' query containing WHERE PRODUCT = 'OCP PREP' AND CITY = 'TOLEDO' will best utilize the primary-key index on the table. Each of the other queries will not perform well because they do not utilize leading columns in the primary-key index. **(Topic 11.4)**

**44.** A.  SELECT EMPID, LASTNAME FROM EMP UNION SELECT SSN, LASTNAME FROM PEOPLE;

**Explanation**   The UNION query will require a sort operation. Other queries that require sorts are those that use the ORDER BY or GROUP BY clause, the COUNT operation, and CREATE INDEX statements. These aren't only ones that use sorts, just some common ones. The other query and the DML statements do not cause the RDBMS to perform a sort. **(Topic 12.1)**

**45.** A.  Size of row * number of rows in table

**Explanation**   The best way to size initial extents for a table is to multiply the size of each row in the table by the number of rows in the table. This way, all the contents of the table fit into the initial extent. This reduces fragmentation and improves performance by keeping all data in a table in close proximity on disk. **(Topic 11.5)**

**46.** B.  640K for sort area total, memory sorts will be used

**Explanation**   Each user connected to Oracle allocates a sort area the size of SORT_AREA_SIZE in the shared pool. Thus, the total amount of sort area for these ten users is 640K, given 64K sort size per user. Also, since only a small amount of data is being sorted for each user, the sort most likely happens in memory. **(Topic 12.2)**

**47.** A.  SORT_DIRECT_WRITES=TRUE

**Explanation**   Since direct writes for disk sorts can improve overall performance of those operations, the SORT_DIRECT_WRITES set to TRUE is the best way to go. Setting SORT_AREA_SIZE as low as 2048 will simply force more disk sorts to occur, which could detract from overall performance if disk sorts are not tuned right. Also, the NEXT default storage setting for the TEMP tablespace is a good thing to set in tandem with the value for SORT_AREA_SIZE, so there's no way to tell if this choice is a good one or not. Finally, though it's important to ensure that all users use a tablespace other than SYSTEM for sorting, this is not a way to actually tune disk sorts. **(Topic 12.3)**

**48.** B.  Set NEXT on TEMP to 512K

**Explanation**   Only a designated tablespace for temporary segments should ever be used for storing sort data. In this tablespace, the NEXT default storage option can be set to a multiple of SORT_AREA_SIZE, in this case 512K. Note that on certain platforms, Oracle will begin writing temporary data to non-TEMP tablespaces if the sort operations being performed fill the TEMP tablespace. Thus, it is often useful to have multiple TEMP tablespaces if you have many users who performing large sorting operations. **(Topic 12.4)**

Chapter 4: OCP Exam 4: Performance Tuning Workshop  **261**

**49.** C. V$ROLLSTAT

**Explanation** The V$ROLLSTAT view in Oracle gives information of the space allocated to every rollback segment in the database, along with whether the rollback segment is online or offline. The V$WAITSTAT view gives wait information for allocating rollback segments, which can indicate that you need to add segments. V$SYSSTAT can aid in calculating the overall wait statistics for rollback segments as well. DBA_ROLLBACK_SEGS gives general information about the rollback segments in your database. You could use Storage Manager in Oracle Enterprise Manager as well. **(Topic 13.1)**

**50.** D and E.  ALTER ROLLBACK SEGMENT RBS02 SHRINK; and ALTER ROLLBACK SEGMENT RBS02 STORAGE (OPTIMAL 2M);

**Explanation** Either by manually shrinking the rollback segment, or by using the OPTIMAL setting, the DBA can ensure that the rollback segments that are stretched out of shape will eventually return to an acceptable size. The NEXT and PCTINCREASE clauses do not have that effect (in fact, PCTINCREASE is not permitted on rollback segments). Nor does simply taking the rollback segment offline have the effect of reducing the size of the rollback segment. **(Topic 13.2)**

**51.** D.  Rollback segments named in INIT.ORA will be online.

**Explanation** Any rollback segment named in the ROLLBACK_SEGMENTS INIT.ORA parameter values will be online. The formula involving both the transaction parameters is only used when Oracle Parallel Server is active. You know that OPS is not in place because the question states that only one instance has the database mounted and opened. The point about rollback segments being brought online manually is accurate, except that it does not take into account the fact that Oracle will always attempt to bring rollback segments online if the ROLLBACK_SEGMENTS parameter or if the transactions parameters are in place. Finally, the SYSTEM rollback segment is ALWAYS brought online, even if no other rollback segments are. **(Topic 13.3)**

**52.** A.  Each transaction is assigned to a rollback segment in a round-robin manner unless a specific rollback segment is requested.

**Explanation** Oracle uses a round-robin algorithm to assign transactions to rollback segments, unless a specific segment is named by the transaction. It is not required that a transaction identify a rollback segment to use. If none is assigned, Oracle picks one automatically. Transactions are not all assigned to the same rollback segment—this causes performance bottlenecks. Unless the SET TRANSACTION READ ONLY command is used, each transaction will be treated as a read/write transaction, and once you make the first change in your transaction, Oracle assigns the transaction to a rollback segment—even if only query access is required! **(Topic 13.4)**

    **53. D.**  Neither transaction can change data, but either transaction can complete until the other relinquishes its lock.

**Explanation**    This question is very tricky, because it requires that you understand exactly what SHARE locks do, which is not an easy task unless you have tested the behavior of SHARE locks on an application. The question itself also has more information than you really need. In this situation, each of the transactions will be able to acquire share locks on the table at the same time; however, neither transaction will be able to change data in the table until the other transaction ends. However, each transaction can complete without the other transaction relinquishing the SHARE lock simply by committing or rolling back. **(Topic 14.1)**

    **54. B.**  Lack of use of commit statements

**Explanation**    The best choice for this question clearly is lack of using commit statements. Commits end old transactions that are holding locks and start new ones. The use of default locking levels for updates is a good way to avoid problems with locking. On the other hand, frequent use of LOCK TABLE commands could indicate that higher levels of locking could be in use—a potential cause for contention. However, this choice is really a distractor, for you are not told exactly what level of locking is in use here. Finally, if transaction-processing commands are found where expected, then chances are contention would be reduced or eliminated. **(Topic 14.2)**

    **55. B.**  UTLLOCKT

**Explanation**    Of the choices given, only one utility—UTLLOCKT—comes standard with the Oracle8*i* Server license. Although the software listed in other choices (which are all part of Oracle Enterprise Manager) is easy to obtain on CD-ROM, they are all subject to additional licensing for OEM software packs. **(Topic 14.3)**

    **56. B, C, and D.**  PMON rolls back the active transaction, the user is disconnected, and locks held by the killed session are released.

**Explanation**    When the DBA marks a session for kill, the user is disconnected, PMON rolls back that user's active transaction, and all associated locks are released. However, no instance recovery is required or performed as the result of killing a session, nor is the user's account locked. Finally, if the user being killed has committed data to the database prior to the kill, that data stays in the database. **(Topic 14.4)**

**57.** C. Thorough application code reviews

**Explanation** Of the choices given, only the use of thorough application code reviews has the possibility of preventing locking problems on existing applications. By killing offensive user transactions, or monitoring for waiting sessions using Lock Manager, the DBA succeeds only in being able to react quickly when there is a problem. To prevent the problem in future applications, the DBA can discourage use of LOCK TABLE, but this will succeed in efforts involving new applications only, not existing ones. **(Topic 14.5)**

**58.** D. alert log

**Explanation** When deadlocks occur, Oracle writes an associated message to the ALERT log, and to the user trace file for the session in which the deadlock occurred. No message gets written to any background process trace file, nor does information about this occurrence get written to the audit trail. **(Topic 14.6)**

**59.** B. Buffer busy waits

**Explanation** When using V$SYSTEM_EVENT to detect free-list contention, the DBA would look for the statistic associated with buffer busy waits. The free-list choice is a good distractor because that's the statistic you would look for if trying to detect free-list contention when using V$WAITSTAT. All other choices refer to detection of rollback segment contention. **(Topic 15.1)**

**60.** B. SQL statements

**Explanation** SQL statements are the first area the DBA should tune on the database, before memory structures. This is because you have more direct control over the impact a change might make. Disk I/O bottlenecks are tuned after memory usage, according to the common tuning methodology offered by Oracle as the basis for OCP. Both latches/locks and dispatchers/shared servers need not necessarily be tuned prior to tuning memory usage, whereas SQL tuning is definitely the first place to start from the DBA perspective. **(Topic 1.2)**

# Answers to Practice Exam 2

**1. B.** V$SYSTEM_EVENT

**Explanation** The V$SYSTEM_EVENT view contains system-wide wait statistics for the operation of your Oracle database. V$SYSSTAT shows system-wide statistics for performance, while V$SESSTAT shows statistics for all current sessions on the Oracle database. V$SESSION_EVENT shows wait statistics on the Oracle database. **(Topic 2.3)**

**2. C.** BACKGROUND_DUMP_DEST

**Explanation** The BACKGROUND_DUMP_DEST location on the host machine will contain trace files written when the PMON process crashed. Within one of those trace files, the DBA should find the parameters returned along with the ORA-00600 error. LOG_ARCHIVE_DEST is the location to which archive logs are saved, while USER_DUMP_DEST is the location to which user process trace files are saved. CORE_DUMP_DEST is where core dumps containing data from the Oracle SGA are saved. **(Topic 2.2)**

**3. A.** The alert log

**Explanation** The alert log is written with timestamp and log sequence information every time a log switch is performed. Thus, the alert log can be useful in identifying situations in which log switches happen too frequently or slowly. V$DATAFILE is used in situations involving management of tablespaces and datafiles. The audit trail is used for monitoring overall usage activity on the database. AUTOTRACE is used for monitoring the activities of a particular session or sessions on the Oracle database. **(Topic 2.1)**

**4. C.** Adding an index to a table to improve query performance

**Explanation** Of the choices given, the choice that appropriately limits scope in this tuning situation is adding an index to a table to improve query performance. The other choices, like improving I/O, increasing SGA, or adding CPUs, might each improve overall database performance, but are inappropriate for the situation in question until more focused tuning efforts prove ineffective. **(Topic 1.3)**

**5. A.** Memory usage analysis

**Explanation** Of the choices given, memory usage analysis is the correct answer. SQL statement tuning is the step that has already been executed according to the situation context identified in the question. The other two choices identify a hardware purchase of some sort. This is usually something that should be put off until careful analysis has been performed in order to isolate the problem to its exact cause, thereby minimizing the cost outlay required for purchasing machinery that may or may not work. **(Topic 1.2)**

**6.** A. Managers

**Explanation** Organizational management is usually the group of people involved in deciding whether or not to execute a purchase of additional hardware to solve a problem with performance. While DBAs, and developers, to a smaller extent, might stand behind that choice as one way to improve performance in a hurry, management will have the budgetary wherewithal to execute the decision. Users may be involved in testing any change to decide whether the problem was solved as the result of a particular activity. **(Topic 1.1)**

**7.** C. Scripts

**Explanation** The Scripts tab will enable you to access scripts Oracle Expert generates automatically for implementation of its recommendations. View/Edit is for determining statistics that will be collected, while Scope is for defining Oracle Expert tuning scope. Finally, Recommendations is where you can review all areas Oracle Expert wants to suggest changes in tuning your Oracle database. **(Topic 16.6)**

**8.** C. Define tuning session scope.

**Explanation** Before defining data classes to be collected, the DBA must define the scope of the tuning session. After defining session tuning scope, the DBA will run Oracle Expert to analyze collected data, review its recommendations, and implement those recommendations. **(Topic 16.3)**

**9.** A. Create the Oracle Expert repository.

**Explanation** The first step to be performed in any situation where the DBA is using Oracle Expert for the first time is to create the Oracle Expert repository in a database. After that repository is created, the DBA can connect to it in order to create the tuning session. Once the tuning session is created, the DBA will then execute steps like setting tuning scope and analyzing statistics. **(Topic 16.2)**

**10.** D. Tuning Pack

**Explanation** Oracle Expert does not come with the standard Management Pack of Oracle Enterprise Manager. Instead, you must install the Tuning Pack. The

Diagnostics Pack comes with several tools that are used for problem monitoring and database diagnostics. The Change Management Pack is used for software version control in that Oracle development environment. **(Topic 16.1)**

**11.** B.   Buffer cache

**Explanation**   In this query, the DBA is trying to detect contention for LRU latches, which regulate access to the buffer cache. Redo allocation and copy latches regulate access to the log buffer, making that choice incorrect. Shared pool latches regulate access to that memory area, making that choice incorrect. Finally, the large memory latch is used for regulating access to the large pool, making that choice incorrect. **(Topic 15.4)**

**12.** B.   REDO ALLOCATION

**Explanation**   In the situation described in the question, the DBA is attempting to resolve contention for the redo allocation latch. This latch is used for regulating which server process can write redo information to the log buffer at any given time. The library cache latch is used for regulating access to the library cache for writing statement parse information, while the AQ statistics latch is used in advanced queuing. Finally, the done queue latch is used by shared servers to write information to the done queue for user processes to pick up information about completed operations. **(Topic 15.3)**

**13.** D.   Writing data changes to a table in active transactions

**Explanation**   When writing data changes to a table in an active transaction, Oracle locks are used to govern access to the object, not latches. In other situations identified involving access to SGA components, latches are used for control and regulation. **(Topic 15.2)**

**14.** B.   Issue LOCK TABLE IN EXCLUSIVE MODE commands frequently.

**Explanation**   The LOCK TABLE IN EXCLUSIVE MODE command grants the user the highest level of locking available on a database object, and therefore should be avoided at all costs. By allocating this level of lock, the user thereby prevents any other user from acquiring any write access to the object until the user commits. Other choices, such as use of minimum level of locking, the SELECT FOR UPDATE statement, and letting Oracle lock objects automatically when using the UPDATE command, all should have the effect of reducing the amount of lock contention experienced on the database. **(Topic 14.5)**

**15.** A.  catblock.sql

**Explanation**   The catblock.sql script must be written prior to running the UTLLOCKT script in Oracle, due to the need for objects generated by running that script. The utllockt.sql script is the one actually doing the work of the UTLLOCKT utility, making that choice incorrect. The catexp.sql script is run prior to exporting data from Oracle, which UTLLOCKT does not depend on. Finally, catrman.sql is run prior to using RMAN, again something that UTLLOCKT does not depend on. **(Topic 14.3)**

**16.** C.  COMMIT

**Explanation**   The COMMIT command must be issued by the user holding the lock in order for the next user to allocate the resource. LOCK TABLE is the statement used to acquire locks, not release them, so that choice is not correct. SAVEPOINT does not actually release locks—it merely defines a unit of completion within a transaction. ROW SHARE is a type of lock, not a specific activity associated with acquiring or releasing a lock. **(Topic 14.2)**

**17.** D.  30, V$ROLLSTAT

**Explanation**   Oracle will shrink the rollback segment when it exceeds 1M in size. Since each extent is sized to be 50K, this means that the rollback segment will shrink after allocating more than 20 extents. Thus, all choices indicating less than 20 extents are incorrect. To narrow down further, you have to know that V$ROLLSTAT (not V$SYSSTAT) is used for monitoring rollback segment usage. Thus, the 30, V$ROLLSTAT choice is the correct answer. **(Topic 13.2)**

**18.** C.  256K

**Explanation**   NEXT extent size in a TEMP tablespace should always be a multiple of SORT_AREA_SIZE to maximize performance of disk sort writes. Thus, 256K is the best answer because it is the only choice that is a multiple of 64K, the value for SORT_AREA_SIZE. **(Topic 12.4)**

**19.** C.  CREATE INDEX statements

**Explanation**   This question tests your knowledge of which SQL operations require sorts. In this case, the only choice given that requires a sort is the CREATE INDEX statement. The choice indicating SELECT statements with a WHERE clause is a good distractor, but there really is not enough information in the choice to indicate whether the operation definitely will or won't require a sort. DML statements such as UPDATE or DELETE typically don't require sorts. **(Topic 12.1)**

**20.** B. 128K

**Explanation** This question is a serious distractor from overall execution of the 30/60 rule, which tells you that you shouldn't waste time on questions that can't be solved quickly. After all, you can always mark a tough question and come back. The answer to this question lies not in being able to calculate which of these extent sizes fit into 128MB evenly, but in knowing that any extent sized smaller than 5 blocks will be rounded up to 5 blocks in the Oracle database. Thus, all extents sized less than 80K will be rounded up to 80K, because 16K * 5 = 80K. **(Topic 11.5)**

**21.** B. Measure index usage and performance.

**Explanation** The query in this question measures index usage and performance by determining how many table scans are happening on long tables versus table data fetched by ROWID. The choice indicating buffer cache performance could be a good distractor, simply because data for measuring buffer cache hit ratio comes from V$SYSSTAT. The other choices, however, should be easy to filter out if you've studied the technical content of OCP. **(Topic 11.4)**

**22.** C. Redo logs

**Explanation** Typically, overall database performance suffers in situations where Oracle redo logs are striped across an array of disks, such as in RAID5 situations. This is because redo logs are written sequentially, while RAID5 supports scattered reads and writes with higher performance, such as the read and write patterns seen in the DATA and INDEX tablespaces. Finally, since control files are read and written fairly infrequently, they rarely pose a threat to overall database performance. **(Topic 10.4)**

**23.** D. V$FILESTAT

**Explanation** The V$FILESTAT view is used for detecting I/O statistics for each file on the Oracle database. The V$WAITSTAT and V$IOSTAT views are good distractors because they seem right, but in reality only an experienced DBA would realize they don't exist in Oracle. Finally, V$SYSSTAT is used more for overall system-wide performance statistics. **(Topic 10.2)**

**24.** B. V$BUFFER_POOL_STATISTICS

**Explanation** This question contains two big distractors: V$SYSSTAT, which is used for calculating overall buffer cache hit ratios, and V$MULTIPLE_BUFFER_POOL, which is a made-up view that uses words from the question to fool you into thinking the choice is correct. The other choice, V$SGASTAT, is just plain wrong. **(Topic 8.6)**

**25.** C.  With the ALTER TABLE statement

**Explanation**  Tables are placed into multiple buffer pools in your Oracle database by issuing the ALTER TABLE statement with the BUFFER_POOL option set in the STORAGE clause. BUFFER_POOL_KEEP and BUFFER_POOL_RECYCLE are both parameters that size the multiple buffer pools. The ALTER SYSTEM command plays no role in this process. **(Topic 8.4)**

**26.** B.  V$SYSSTAT

**Explanation**  The V$SYSSTAT view contains all statistics necessary for determining the buffer cache hit ratio. V$SGASTAT can be useful for determining wait rates on the buffer cache, but wait ratios and hit ratios are not exactly the same thing. In addition, the V$SESSTAT view is not correct because that view determines session statistics, not database system statistics. Finally, though V$WAITSTAT is an actual view in the Oracle database, it is not used in this situation. **(Topic 8.2)**

**27.** A.  First-in-first-out, latches

**Explanation**  The buffer cache purge mechanism is usually referred to as the least-recently used algorithm, thus eliminating all the other algorithmic choices. In addition, you must know that latches (not locks) regulate access to Oracle internal structures such as the buffer cache. However, in this special case, you're really being asked to identify what happens in the special case of how space in the buffer cache is managed during full table scan operations. In this case, Oracle eliminates the buffers almost immediately after reading them into memory in a FIFO fashion, to prevent the buffer cache from being inundated with useless new information and degrading performance for other queries and DML. This is a classic trick question example. **(Topic 8.1)**

**28.** A and C.  V$SESSTAT and V$STATNAME

**Explanation**  The V$SESSTAT view is useful for obtaining values for session and UGA memory allocations, while the V$STATNAME view is useful for associating the output of a query on V$SESSTAT with a meaningful label. V$SYSSTAT does not contain this information because this information is not associated with the Oracle SGA, but rather with shared or dedicated server processes running on the host machine. Nor does this information show up in V$SGASTAT for the same reason. Finally, the V$SHARED_POOL_RESERVED view is also not appropriate because of the emphasis on SGA statistics that view has. **(Topic 7.6)**

**29. B and D.** SHARED_POOL_RESERVED_SIZE and SHARED_POOL_RESERVED_MIN_ALLOC

**Explanation** The SHARED_POOL_RESERVED_SIZE and SHARED_POOL_RESERVED_MIN_ALLOC INIT.ORA parameters can be used for ensuring that there is enough space reserved in the shared pool for large PL/SQL blocks. V$SHARED_POOL_RESERVED is useful for tuning shared pool reserve list configuration. Finally, DB_BLOCK_BUFFERS adds no value to this situation because this parameter is used for sizing the buffer cache, not the shared pool. **(Topic 7.5)**

**30. B, C, and E.** V$LIBRARYCACHE, V$ROWCACHE, and V$SGASTAT

**Explanation** The V$LIBRARYCACHE and V$ROWCACHE views are used for determining the shared pool hit percentage. The V$SGASTAT view is used for determining whether the shared pool is too large, and consistently has large amounts of free space over time. The V$SYSSTAT view is incorrect because that view is used for sizing the buffer cache, while the V$DICTCACHE is a distractor choice meant to confuse you from choosing V$ROWCACHE, based on the fact that the dictionary cache and row cache are the same thing. **(Topic 7.2)**

**31. B.** Different processes and threads can run concurrently on different processors.

**Explanation** The trickiness of each choice in this question identifies an underlying theme in OCP exams—the questions often can be hard to understand. In this case, you have to read each choice carefully, and identify the only one that is a true statement about processes and threads—that different processes and different threads in the same process can run concurrently on different processors. However, since various Oracle background activities are run as threads of the same Oracle process in Windows, they all share the same memory allocation for that process. Thus, the two choices that state in different ways that threads essentially acquire private or separate memory allocations are incorrect. Also, multiple processes in UNIX are definitely not treated as the same thread. **(Topic 6.3)**

**32. A.** Sizing the TEMP tablespace versus sizing swap space

**Explanation** Probably the best similarity comparison to be drawn between Oracle and operating system tuning is how the TEMP tablespace is sized versus sizing OS swap space, because both items serve similar purposes. The TEMP tablespace is used for overflow when Oracle runs out of sort area space in real memory, while OS swap space is used for overflow when processes run out of real memory. Adding more CPUs for Oracle or non-Oracle processing on a host machine is essentially the same task—an OS tuning task. Thus, no real comparison between Oracle and the

OS tuning can be drawn. Similarly, changing process prioritization is an OS tuning task regardless of the processes being prioritized. Finally, ensuring that the SGA fits into real memory is squarely a DBA task—not much OS tuning here. **(Topic 6.2)**

**33.** D. Specifying hardware cache for disk controllers

**Explanation** While some of these choices indicate areas where lines between Oracle database tuning and OS tuning get blurry, only the choice identifying specification of hardware cache for disk controllers is truly an area of true OS tuning that a DBA will want to participate in. While the SGA certainly should be sized to fit in real memory, this is an Oracle database tuning step rather than an OS tuning step (as opposed to selecting SDRAM over SIMM or DIMM memory, which is an OS-centric decision). Optimizing extent allocation again is a DBA decision. Finally, Oracle block sizes are almost invariably a multiple of underlying OS block sizes—Oracle usually doesn't permit oddly sized blocks. **(Topic 6.1)**

**34.** A. NESTED LOOPS

**Explanation** The NESTED LOOPS operation is used in joining data from multiple tables in the execution plan generated for resolving a star query. While MERGE JOIN is another method used for joining data in execution plans, the ideal star query will have Oracle using NESTED LOOPS instead for better performance. A FILTER operation is used for searching data returned from a full table scan, which ideally would not be used in a star query. **(Topic 5.2)**

**35.** D. Performance Monitor in Tuning Pack

**Explanation** Though seemingly trite, more and more OCP questions have focused on understanding the Oracle suite of products for database management. In this case, the Performance Monitor that comes with the OEM Tuning Pack can be used for performance tuning on the Oracle database. AUTOTRACE comes built into the Oracle Server, while Storage Manager assists with tablespace and other storage configuration. **(Topic 3.3)**

**36.** B. V$SESSION_WAIT

**Explanation** The V$SESSION_WAIT view shows wait statistics for all current sessions on the Oracle database. The DBA_WAITERS view has appeared in some versions of Oracle showing information about the user sessions currently waiting for locks held by other sessions. The Enterprise Manager console gives little if any information about the wait statistics for an Oracle database. Finally, PLAN_TABLE is used for storing statement execution plans when the EXPLAIN PLAN command is used. **(Topic 2.3)**

**37.** B. USER_DUMP_DEST

**Explanation** When session tracing is enabled, the DBA can find session trace files in the USER_DUMP_DEST directory on the machine hosting the Oracle database. SYS.AUD$ contains audit trail records, which is not used in this scenario. The BACKGROUND_DUMP_ DEST directory is where all background process trace files can be found in Oracle. Finally, beware of the distractor choice in SQL_TRACE_DEST—it repeats information from the question in order to distract you. In reality, there is no such location on your Oracle database. **(Topic 2.2)**

**38.** D. The ALERT log in BACKGROUND_DUMP_DEST

**Explanation** The ALERT log in BACKGROUND_DUMP_DEST contains date stamp and timestamp information for every log switch that occurs on a live Oracle database. Session trace files do not contain information about log switches, unless the session is for the SYS or SYSTEM user and contains the ALTER SYSTEM ARCHIVE LOG SWITCH statement. Even then, you don't get information about automatic log switches. The INIT.ORA file only contains values for startup parameters. Finally, core dumps in general are of no value. **(Topic 2.1)**

**39.** D. Changing the WHERE clause of a specific SQL statement to utilize an index

**Explanation** Although substantial hardware upgrades generally have strong potential for improving performance of a database application, they also have very wide scope and are very costly. On the other hand, tuning SQL statements to use indexes has substantial performance benefits, and usually requires less than one hour of time to implement. SGA changes and applying database patches also have more significant scope, with questionable performance benefits. **(Topic 1.3)**

**40.** B. The application developer analyzing the code

**Explanation** Typically, the best place to start with performance tuning on an Oracle database is with the application developer and tuning the code. While a tablespace reorganization may solve the problem, typically the biggest performance increases are seen when developers think about how to optimize their code. Also, DBA and system engineer activities usually require a good deal of work to implement. Finally, refining the billing process most likely will require a substantial rewrite of the application, which takes a long time. **(Topic 1.1)**

**41.** B. Use the ANALYZE command.

**Explanation** The ANALYZE command is used to determine what rows are chained and/or migrated in the table being analyzed. You would use report.txt for overall performance-tuning purposes after running UTLBSTAT and UTLESTAT, eliminating that choice. Although you would increase the value set for PCTFREE to resolve migration and chaining issues you would increase the value set for PCTFREE, this is not the method you would take for detecting the problem. The PCTFREE option plays no role in chaining and row migration **(Topic 11.3)**

**42.** A.  7

**Explanation**  Even when you are not using Oracle Parallel Server, the TRANSACTIONS and TRANSACTIONS_PER_ROLLBACK_SEGMENT parameters have some role in determining how effectively Oracle distributes transactions between available rollback segments. So, 1,000 / 150 equals approximately 7. Be careful of seeing the same number in the question and in the answer, as is the case with two choices in this question. **(Topic 13.3)**

**43.** D.  Reduces the possibility of row chaining and data migration

**Explanation**  High PCTFREE means that much space will be left empty in each data block, which reduces the possibility of row chaining and data migration. This doesn't keep the block filled to capacity, and works well for OLTP systems, but not for decision support systems that attempt to maximize their storage capacity. A high PCTFREE has little bearing on effective use of the database buffer cache; if anything, it reduces performance because fewer rows are stored per buffer in the buffer cache. **(Topic 11.2)**

**44.** C and D.  Decrease your recycle pool, and assign the tables referenced by the application to the default pool.

**Explanation**  Use of the recycle pool in this situation actually increases disk read activities, thereby worsening performance, because buffers are being eliminated before SQL statements or transactions complete. Thus, you should assign the tables referenced back to the default pool where they won't be eliminated, and you should decrease the size of your recycle pool. **(Topic 8.5)**

**45.** C.  Based on the number of blocks in the table plus blocks in associated indexes

**Explanation**  When sizing the keep pool, ensure that there is enough room for the entire table plus all associated indexes. If one or the other is omitted, then you may size the keep pool too small and lose blocks, resulting in I/O operations later to read either table or index data back into memory. You wouldn't base the size of the keep pool on anything from your shared pool. **(Topic 8.5)**

**46.** B. 200

**Explanation** It would not be wise to add more than 200 buffers to the buffer cache because then with that number you will enjoy 54,041 more hits in your buffer cache. In contrast, only 1,623 more hits are added by adding 300–500 buffers, or about a 3 percent improvement over adding the first 200 buffers. You would see better value by simply adding the 200 buffers, and making the rest of the real memory available to some other SGA resource, such as the shared pool. **(Topic 8.3)**

**47.** D. Session information is now being stored in the shared pool.

**Explanation** When the multithreaded server architecture is used, Oracle keeps session UGA information in the shared pool, which decreases the amount of space available for other items, such as the library and dictionary cache. Thus, you have your loss of performance. Since no other INIT.ORA parameters have changed, there is no basis for the SGA being sized out of real memory. Also, you don't really have enough information to judge whether CPU scheduling is the real issue. Finally, the problem lies in the shared pool, not the buffer cache or redo log buffer, making choices that refer to those other SGA components incorrect. **(Topic 7.1)**

**48.** C. select * from LOOKUP_VALUES;

**Explanation** Buffers are only loaded into the buffer cache when users select data from objects, not when DDL statements, such as ALTER TABLE, are made. Although choices B and D both enable Oracle to place the LOOKUP_VALUES table into different multiple buffer pools, these statements don't actually cause Oracle to do so at the time the ALTER TABLE statement is issued. The same condition applies to ALTER TABLE LOOKUP_VALUES cache, even though issuing that statement forces Oracle to make blocks from that table persist in the buffer cache. **(Topic 8.7)**

**49.** A. Reloads

**Explanation** By decreasing reloads, you will improve the overall hit ratio and performance on your library cache. Although pins is also a measurement of the library cache, simply increasing pins won't necessarily improve or worsen the overall hit ratio for the library cache. Physical reads, consistent gets, and db block gets are all measurements of buffer cache performance. Gets and getmisses are measurements of the dictionary cache hit ratio and performance. **(Topic 7.1)**

**50.** B. User processes will wait less time for log buffer space.

**Explanation** Setting the LOG_SMALL_ENTRY_MAX_SIZE parameter to a lower value most likely has an effect on the amount of time user processes wait for space in that buffer. Choices A and F refer to the buffer cache, an area of memory not affected by these parameters, so these choices are wrong. The LOG_SMALL_ENTRY_ MAX_SIZE parameter does not, in fact, resize any areas of the SGA, so there shouldn't be any effect on paging and swapping, nor will Oracle crash—eliminating those choices. The number of redo allocation latches is fixed at 1, making that choice also incorrect. **(Topic 9.3)**

**51.** A. Increasing the size of the buffer cache

**Explanation** Given that V$CURRENT_BUCKET is used to estimate the effects of reducing the size of the buffer cache, not increasing it, you are probably trying to determine how to decrease the size of the buffer cache in order to allocate space to another area of the SGA. You wouldn't be tuning I/O, because I/O-tuning improvements are not made by resizing SGA. Nor is it likely that you are adding real memory, for if you were, you might consider an increase to the buffer cache instead. Finally, you have no information indicating that you are porting to Parallel Server in this situation. **(Topic 8.3)**

**52.** D. SHUTDOWN ABORT

**Explanation** You never want to abort database operation unless you are prepared to accept an instance recovery the next time you start the database. You can both determine what objects are in the shared pool and pin an object in that pool using the functions identified as choices from the DBMS_SHARED_POOL package. Now, because Oracle is currently unable to load the object into shared memory, you need to either flush the shared pool using the statement ALTER TABLE FLUSH SHARED_POOL or SHUTDOWN (using any option besides SHUTDOWN ABORT) to save time) and restart the database. **(Topic 7.4)**

**53.** C. V$RECENT_BUCKET

**Explanation** You must generate current and actual hit ratios in the script. These statistics don't come from V$RECENT_BUCKET or V$LATCH. Recall that shared-pool hit ratios are calculated from V$LIBRARYCACHE and V$ROWCACHE views, while buffer cache hit ratios can be calculated from both V$SYSSTAT and V$BUFFER_POOL_STATISTICS views. **(Topic 3.1)**

**54.** C. Increasing the value set for DB_BLOCK_BUFFERS

**Explanation** Reload statistics are a measurement of the shared pool's size, while DB_BLOCK_BUFFERS is designed to affect the buffer cache. If too many reloads occur, your shared pool may be too small or else execution plans in the shared pool are not being retained long enough. You can improve reload statistics by increasing the size of your shared pool, setting CURSOR_SPACE_FOR_TIME to TRUE, or adopting standards for SQL statement development, allowing Oracle to reuse more execution plans. **(Topic 7.3)**

**55.** A.   File system or hardware cache usage

**Explanation**   If the problem has to do with memory allocation, then tuning I/O won't help, thus making the choice identifying I/O file system and/or hardware cache usage your answer. All other choices identify methods for tuning memory, which would address the need identified in the question. **(Topic 6.4)**

**56.** B. V$RECENT_BUCKET

**Explanation**   If you are trying to determine the appropriate increase of buffers to the buffer cache, you should enable use of the V$RECENT_BUCKET view. Although the statistics put into that view come from V$SYSSTAT, it is difficult to extrapolate the appropriate statistics yourself. V$CURRENT_BUCKET is incorrect because this view helps to determine whether to decrease the size of the buffer cache, not increase it. Finally, the V$BUFFER_POOL_STATISTICS view is used to determine multiple buffer pool hit ratios, and should be discarded mainly for the same reason as V$SYSSTAT. **(Topic 8.3)**

**57.** B.   Free lists

**Explanation**   Free lists help to govern access to data blocks associated with an object for data changes, such as updates to existing rows. Since the problem stated in the question is that concurrent users are contending with one another to make changes, the answer is to increase the number of free lists on that object. Changing aspects of redo log handling is incorrect. The problem also has little to do with any of the latches you have studied thus far. **(Topic 15.1)**

**58.** C.   Executed from top to bottom, from inside out

**Explanation**   When the execution plan is pulled from the PLAN_TABLE using the script Oracle provides, the user must read the results from top to bottom, with output from inner operations feeding as input into outer operations. **(Topic 5.4)**

**59.** D.   SYS

**Explanation**   The SYS (a.k.a. INTERNAL) user is the SYSDBA name equivalence to the SYS database user, owner of all V$ dynamic performance views in the Oracle database. SYSTEM can access the performance views, but does not own the views. Beware of a distractor in this question—SYSDBA and OSDBA are privileges granted on the database to the DBA that allow access to the views, not actual users on the database. Note that this question is highly tricky. **(Topic 3.1)**

**60.** D. SELECT * from EMP WHERE EMPID = 604;

**Explanation** In the SELECT * from EMP WHERE EMPID = 604 query, Oracle uses an implicit datatype conversion from VARCHAR2 to NUMBER that prevents the RDBMS from using the index on the EMPID column. All queries use the index on EMPID because of how the WHERE clauses are constructed. The use of functions in the SELECT clause will not cause Oracle not to use the index, either. Beware of the query selecting NVL(EMPID,0) from the EMP table—it's a good distractor because functions cause Oracle not to use indexes. However, this is true only when the function appears in the WHERE clause, not in the SELECT clause! **(Topic 5.6)**

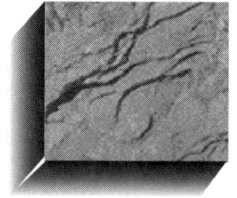

# CHAPTER 5

## OCP Exam 5: Network Administration

OCP Exam 5 covers issues related to networking the Oracle database. To pass this exam, you need to demonstrate an understanding of the features available in Oracle Net8 for connecting client Oracle processes to the database server. You will also need to demonstrate an understanding of the special features available in Oracle Net8 for performance tuning. In more recent editions of OCP Exam 5, the focus has been on use of GUI tools like Net8 Assistant and on the advanced security option.

## OCP Exam 5 Topic Areas

The following topic areas are tested in OCP Exam 5. These topics are taken from the OCP Candidate Guide published by Oracle and are up-to-date as of this printing. You should download the Candidate Guide for the OCP DBA track before taking this exam to ensure that these topic areas are still current by accessing the Oracle University Web site at **education.oracle.com/certification**. The topics are as follows:

1. Overview
    - 1.1 Identify networking business trends and problems
    - 1.2 Describe Oracle's networking solutions
2. Basic Net8 Architecture
    - 2.1 Define the procedure by which Net8 establishes a server connection
    - 2.2 Identify the key components of Net8 architecture and their interaction
3. Basic Net8 Server-Side Configuration
    - 3.1 Configure the listener using Net8 Assistant
    - 3.2 Start the Net8 listener using Listener Control utility (LSNRCTL)
    - 3.3 Stop the Net8 listener using LSNRCTL
    - 3.4 Identify additional LSNRCTL commands
4. Basic Net8 Client-Side Configuration
    - 4.1 Establish a connection from the Net8 client side using the host-naming method
    - 4.2 Configure Net8 client side files and connect using the local-naming method
    - 4.3 Use Net8 Assistant to define preferences on the client side

# Chapter 5: OCP Exam 5: Network Administration

5. Usage and Configuration of Oracle Names
    - 5.1 Configure centralized naming using Net8 Assistant
    - 5.2 Store the network configuration on the local file system
    - 5.3 Store the network configuration in a region database
    - 5.4 Start and stop the names server using Names Control
6. Usage and Configuration of Oracle Intelligent Agent for OEM
    - 6.1 Define the purpose of the Oracle Intelligent Agent
    - 6.2 Start and stop the Oracle Intelligent Agent using the Listener Control utility
    - 6.3 Identify the configuration files used to define the Intelligent Agent
7. Usage and Configuration of the Multithreaded Server
    - 7.1 Identify the components of the multithreaded server (MTS)
    - 7.2 Configure dispatchers using INIT.ORA
    - 7.3 Configure shared servers using INIT.ORA
    - 7.4 Specify the listener address for multithreaded server
    - 7.5 Setup connection pooling using multithreaded server
8. Usage and Configuration of Connection Manager
    - 8.1 Identify the capabilities of Connection Manager
    - 8.2 Configure connection concentration
    - 8.3 Enable network access control
    - 8.4 Configure multiprotocol functionality
9. Troubleshoot the Network Environment
    - 9.1 Set logging and tracing parameters
    - 9.2 Analyze and troubleshoot network problems using log and trace files
    - 9.3 Format trace files using Trace Assistant
10. Security in the Network Environment
    - 10.1 Identify the network security risks during data transmission
    - 10.2 Identify security features in Oracle networking products
    - 10.3 Identify features in the advanced security option
    - 10.4 Configure components of the advanced security option

# Practice Exam 1

1. You need to decide how to configure your Oracle network. Which of the following choices best identifies the method you would use if you wanted application logic and business rules stored on an application running on user desktops?

   A. Mainframe

   B. Client/server

   C. Internet computing

   D. N-tier computing

2. You are attempting to simplify name resolution of Oracle databases within your organization. Which of the following tools are available for this purpose under Net8?

   A. Connection Manager

   B. Net8 Assistant

   C. Oracle Names

   D. Transparent Network Substrate

3. You install Oracle for both client and server. The default configuration order for name resolution using keywords ONAMES, HOSTNAME, and TNSNAMES is maintained. Which of the following choices identifies where Oracle will prefer to look first in order to resolve a database connection?

   A. tnsnames.ora

   B. Host naming

   C. Oracle Names

   D. Net8 Assistant

4. A user issues a SQL query within SQL*Plus. At which OSI layer in the process of resolving that query will Oracle perform any implicit type conversion, such as from number to character?

   A. Application layer

   B. Presentation layer

C. Network layer

D. Session layer

5. You are using Net8 Assistant to configure a listener on the database. Which of the following choices identifies the area within Net8 Assistant where you will define the databases the listener tunes in for connections to?

   A. Database Services

   B. Listening Locations

   C. General Parameters

   D. Other Services

6. You would like to force authentication on listener startup and shutdown to protect uptime. Which of the following commands can be used within LSNRCTL in order to define the password for the listener control session so that you can start up the listener?

   A. set

   B. show

   C. start

   D. change_password

7. You start a Net8 listener on your machine hosting the Oracle database, then notice that the database you were expecting to see the listener serving is not listed. Which of the following areas would you need to change in the appropriate file in order to resolve the issue?

   A. ADDRESS

   B. SID_DESC

   C. SID_LIST

   D. DESCRIPTION_LIST

8. You issue the following command on the machine hosting the Oracle database: lsnrctl services. What is the meaning of the output lsnrctl returns to the command line when this command is run? (Choose two)

   A. Network protocols the listener serves

   B. Connection concentration configured for this listener

C. Connection pooling configured for this listener

D. Service names the listener serves

9. You have multiple listeners on the same single machine hosting Oracle, one for each of the five databases running on that machine. Which of the following choices identifies a way you can manage startup of all listeners?

   A. start

   B. set current_listener *name*

   C. show password

   D. start *name*

10. You are attempting to use host naming on your Oracle database. Which of the following choices identifies what condition must be met for host naming to work (choose two)?

    A. Oracle Names must be used.

    B. There must be two or more databases running on the host.

    C. The alias name defined on the machine name and global database name match.

    D. The listener must be running on TCP/IP.

11. You are using local naming to resolve connect strings to connect descriptors. Which of the following files contain the mapping of elements required for hostname resolution on an Oracle client?

    A. tnsnames.ora

    B. listener.ora

    C. sqlnet.ora

    D. namesini.ora

12. In Net8 Assistant, you configure a trace log for the client side to store information about Net8 tracing. Net8 Assistant stores this configuration information in which of the following files?

    A. sqlnet.ora

    B. listener.ora

    C. tnsnames.ora

    D. net8asst.ora

13. After starting the Oracle Names server, which of the following steps is necessary in order to get clients on the Oracle network to use the Names server for Oracle name resolution?

   A. Nothing. Oracle Names will be detected automatically.

   B. The location of the names server must be defined using tnsnames.ora.

   C. The name resolution precedence order must be changed in listener.ora.

   D. Name resolution order must be changed using Net8 Assistant.

14. You are using local file system storage for Oracle Names. The definition for the TCP port on which the Names server is listening on is defined in can be found in which of the following files?

   A. tnsnames.ora

   B. listener.ora

   C. sdns.ora

   D. snmp_ro.ora

15. You are configuring your Intelligent Agent to run under Oracle. In which of the following files would you make modifications if you wanted the agent to modify an Oracle Names server automatically every time a new database was added to a host machine?

   A. snmp.ora

   B. snmp_ro.ora

   C. snmp_rw.ora

   D. listener.ora

16. You are storing your network configuration information in a region database. In which of the following locations would you find scripts to generate the region database?

   A. rdbms/admin

   B. network/admin

   C. names/admin

   D. network/names

17. You need to shut down the Names server. Which of the following choices identify a means for doing so? (Choose two)

    A. LSNRCTL

    B. NAMESCTL

    C. Net8 Assistant

    D. SVRMGRL

18. You wish to start your Intelligent Agent in Oracle. Which of the following choices identifies the tool you can use to do so?

    A. NAMESCTL

    B. LSNRCTL

    C. Net8 Assistant

    D. AGNTCTRL

19. You are using Intelligent Agent on your Oracle database. Which of the following choices identifies a task that the Intelligent Agent is not designed to handle?

    A. Propagation of messages to the OEM console

    B. Event detection for database management

    C. Propagation of new databases to Oracle Names

    D. Restoration of Names data in event of host system failure

20. You are storing Names information in a region database. Which of the following choices does not identify a table used by Oracle Names for storing region data?

    A. NMO_MASTER

    B. ONRS_SERIAL

    C. ONRS_CONFIG

    D. NMO_NAMES

21. You are configuring your Intelligent Agent in Oracle. Which of the following parameter prefixes are used in the appropriate configuration file to indicate agent settings that affect the agent's integration with Oracle Names?

    A. snmp

    B. nmi

**C.** ora

**D.** dbsnmp

22. After the Intelligent Agent is started, which of the following commands can be issued from the operating system command prompt to shut the agent down?

    **A.** stop

    **B.** dbsnmp_stop

    **C.** LSNRCTL

    **D.** NAMESCTL

23. You are using Intelligent Agent for Oracle. Which of the following choices does not identify a feature the Intelligent Agent provides in conjunction with detecting problems in your database?

    **A.** Failover between hardware nodes

    **B.** Restarting failed instances

    **C.** Extending filled segments

    **D.** Rerunning failed batch jobs

24. You are using multithreaded server for your Oracle database. Once a shared server has completed execution of a user process' data request, which of the following choices identifies where the shared server places data requested by users after statement execution?

    **A.** PGA

    **B.** SGA

    **C.** Request queue

    **D.** Response queue

25. When using MTS on Oracle, which of the following initialization parameters must be set in order to let the Net8 listener connect users to shared servers?

    **A.** MTS_DISPATCHERS

    **B.** MTS_SERVICE

    **C.** MTS_SERVERS

    **D.** MTS_MAX_SERVERS

26. When using MTS on Oracle8, which of the following initialization parameters must be set in order to identify a particular instance to its Net8 dispatchers?

    A. MTS_DISPATCHERS

    B. MTS_SERVICE

    C. MTS_SERVERS

    D. MTS_MAX_DISPATCHERS

27. Your MTS database has been running at peak transaction volume for several hours as users rush to meet a deadline. Then, slowly, users leave for the day. At what point will Oracle begin to downsize servers due to the decrease in server traffic?

    A. Never. Once a server is spawned, it cannot be shut down.

    B. When the Oracle is restarted.

    C. Immediately as users log off.

    D. After the server has sat idle for a while.

28. You are configuring listener address information for an MTS database using Oracle8. The listener port used by Net8 for MTS databases is specified by which of the following parameters?

    A. MTS_LISTENER_ADDRESS

    B. LISTENER

    C. ADDRESS_LIST

    D. ADDRESS

29. Which of the following options to MTS configuration allows Oracle to use a time-out mechanism to temporarily release transport connections that have been idle, making the physical connections available for incoming clients while the logical session with the previous idle connection is still being maintained?

    A. ADDRESS

    B. DISPATCH

C. POOL

D. PROTOCOL

30. You are configuring Net8 on your Oracle network. Which of the following choices identifies the Net8 feature that replaced multiprotocol interchange from SQL*Net version 2?

    A. Connection Manager

    B. Connection Concentration

    C. Connection Pooling

    D. Connection Exchange

31. You set the MULTIPLEX option to "on" in the INIT.ORA file for your MTS_DISPATCHERS parameter. Which of the following options identifies the Net8 feature you configured?

    A. Connection Manager

    B. Connection Concentration

    C. Connection Pooling

    D. Connection Exchange

32. You are configuring the MULTIPLEX option for your INIT.ORA file. Which of the following choices identifies the configuration option that sets this feature to work in the direction of client to server, but not from server to client?

    A. BOTH

    B. IN

    C. OUT

    D. YES

33. You are configuring concentration for your Oracle network client. Which of the following settings in the appropriate file is required in order for concentration to work properly?

    A. MULTIPLEX

    B. SOURCE_ROUTE

    C. DESCRIPTION

    D. ADDRESS

34. You wish to configure network access control on your Oracle network. Which of the following choice combinations identifies both the parameter you need to configure and the file in which you need to configure it?

    A. NAC_START, listener.ora

    B. CMAN, sqlnet.ora

    C. CMAN_RULES, cman.ora

    D. SOURCE_ROUTE, tnsnames.ora

35. You are using the default configuration for multiprotocol functionality in your Oracle network. Which of the following choices identifies the default TCP/IP port used by Connection Manager to listen on for this feature?

    A. 1492

    B. 1521

    C. 1575

    D. 1610

36. You are configuring network access control in your Oracle database. Which of the following choices indicates a rule setting you must mark in order to identify the database to which you want your users connecting?

    A. srv

    B. src

    C. dst

    D. act

37. You have finished configuring your Connection Manager rules for network access control. Which of the following choices identifies the next step you must execute?

    A. Configure connection concentration for clients.

    B. Configure the database listener.

    C. Set up Oracle Names.

    D. Restart the Oracle listener.

**38.** You are defining CMAN_RULES for your Oracle network. Which of the following choices identifies the machine hosting the client that the rule applies to?

   **A.** src

   **B.** dst

   **C.** srv

   **D.** act

**39.** You are reviewing activities of the Connection Manager gateway application. Which of the following choices identifies a log file you might review in order to identify a problem that has occurred with the gateway?

   **A.** cmgw.log

   **B.** cman.log

   **C.** cmadm.log

   **D.** sqlnet.log

**40.** You want to change the directory into which log files are written on your system. Which of the following choices identify the Net8 component for which you may not make this type of change?

   **A.** Listener

   **B.** Connection Manager administrator

   **C.** Oracle Names

   **D.** Connection Manager

**41.** You are setting up multiprotocol functionality in Net8. Which of the following parameters is used for setup of this feature in the appropriate configuration file?

   **A.** CMAN

   **B.** CMAN_RULES

   **C.** CMAN_PROFILE

   **D.** LISTENER

42. You are setting up multiprotocol functionality in Net8. Which of the following choices best describes the process for doing so?

    A. Add a new address to the cman.ora file.

    B. Add a new address to the listener file.

    C. Add a new database service to Oracle Names.

    D. Add a new connect string to tnsnames.ora.

43. You are defining access rules in network access control. Which of the following values is set when you want to prevent a named client from making connection to the database on the server identified?

    A. act=no

    B. act=false

    C. act=reject

    D. act=0

44. You are defining network access rules. The following definition appears in your appropriate configuration file:(rule=(SRC=FLUFFY) (DST= RFRGRTOR) (SRV=FOOD)(ACT=REJECT)). What happens under this rule setting?

    A. All network connections to RFRGRTOR will be denied.

    B. Fluffy's access to the food database on RFRGRTOR is accepted.

    C. Fluffy's access to the food database on RFRGRTOR is rejected.

    D. Fluffy can access only the food database on RFRGRTOR.

45. You are configuring listener tracing in the Oracle listener. Which of the following trace levels is the highest level of tracing available for this purpose?

    A. OFF

    B. USER

    C. ADMIN

    D. SUPPORT

46. You are configuring tracing levels for the Connection Manager. Which of the following parameters are used for doing so?

    A. TRACE_LEVEL_LISTENER

    B. LOG_LEVEL

C. NAMES.TRACE_LEVEL

D. TRACE_LEVEL_SERVER

**47.** You have altered trace settings for your listener. At what time will the new settings take effect?

   A. As soon as you save the file

   B. As soon as you restart the instance

   C. As soon as you restart the listener

   D. As soon as you alter the file

**48.** You would like to format the output of a trace file for easier review. Which of the following utilities in Net8 is available for the purpose?

   A. DBVERIFY

   B. NET8ASST

   C. TRCASST

   D. TKPROF

**49.** You wish to configure encryption and checksums in Net8. Which of the following choices identify the appropriate file in which to do so?

   A. listener.ora

   B. cman.ora

   C. tnsnames.ora

   D. sqlnet.ora

**50.** You are setting the cryptographic key for Net8 advanced security option. Which of the following parameter settings can be used for doing so?

   A. CRYPTO_SEED

   B. CRYPTO_CHECKSUM_TYPES_SERVER

   C. ENCRYPTION_TYPES_SERVER

   D. CRYPTO_CHECKSUM_SERVER

# Practice Exam 2

1. You are analyzing project requirements in order to develop the appropriate Oracle networking implementation. Which two of the following choices do not indicate a benefit of a client/server system (choose two)?

    A. Ease of application use

    B. Low distribution cost

    C. Use of client machine processing power

    D. Scalability

    E. Centralized code management

2. A design diagram for one application system shows several different nodes acting as servers. This "*n*-tier" implementation is most likely a model for which of the following types of architectures?

    A. Client/server

    B. Uniprocessor

    C. Internet computing

    D. Mainframe

3. Net8's ability to manage connectivity between client and server through a uniform interface, independently of the underlying network protocol used to manage a network, is provided by which of the following components?

    A. Oracle Call Interface

    B. Transparent Network Substrate

    C. Oracle Processing Interface

    D. Network Interface

    E. Oracle Protocol Adapter

4. An Oracle Forms application has just issued a SELECT statement to the Oracle database. Which of the following components will be handled on the server within the RDBMS, rather than by Net8?

    A. Two-Task Common

    B. Transparent Network Substrate

**C.** Network Interface

**D.** Oracle Protocol Adapter

**E.** Oracle Call Interface

5. **You are explaining the benefits of Net8 to a project manager as part of the rationale for converting corporate IT to an Oracle platform. Which of the following choices best describes the role of Oracle Connection Manager?**

   **A.** Centralizes management of naming services

   **B.** Offers independence from standard networking protocols

   **C.** Provides the ability to handle connections to one Oracle server from multiple networks

   **D.** Implements high overall network scalability

   **E.** Allows interconnectivity with external naming services

6. **After establishing that a host exists using connect-descriptor information, Net8 encounters an error attempting to locate the Oracle database with SID information given. Which of the following choices identifies the stage of processing where the connection failed?**

   **A.** Host-name resolution

   **B.** Password authentication

   **C.** Connect-string lookup

   **D.** Listener-availability check

   **E.** Oracle SID resolution

7. **Prespawned servers are being used on Oracle to manage user process requests. After Net8 establishes a connection, which of the following processes will connect users to a prespawned server?**

   **A.** Listener

   **B.** Dispatcher

   **C.** Assistant

   **D.** DBWR

8. The Network Routing component of Net8 handles routing data from client to server across a network. Which of the following OSI layers represents where this component resides in the Net8 architecture?

   A. Physical

   B. Link

   C. Network

   D. Transport

   E. Session

9. Your attempt to shut down a running Net8 listener in batch results in an error. Which of the following commands would result in successful completion of the shutdown operation?

   A. LSNRCTL START, followed by LSNRCTL SERVICES

   B. LSNRCTL, followed by SERVICES

   C. LSNRCTL, followed by SET PASSWORD, followed by STOP

   D. LSNRCTL SET PASSWORD, followed by LSNRCTL STOP

   E. LSNRCTL, followed by STOP, followed by CHANGE_PASSWORD

10. You want to define a nondefault trace directory for your Net8 listener process. Using Net8 Assistant, in which of the following areas would you make the necessary changes?

    A. General Parameters

    B. Listening Locations

    C. Database Services

    D. Other Services

11. Your only listener on the host system is called SPACEMAN. You defined the name for the Net8 listener in which of the following areas?

    A. tnsnames.ora

    B. sqlnet.ora

    C. listener.ora

    D. snmp.ora

**12.** Issuing LSNRCTL START from the command line indicates you are running the utility in which of the following modes?

   **A.** Interactive

   **B.** Batch

   **C.** Read-only

   **D.** Write-protected

**13.** Your attempt to shut down the listener is met with "protocol adapter error" and "no listener" messages. This is most likely due to which of the following causes?

   **A.** The listener is running in protected mode.

   **B.** You didn't supply a password for this privileged operation.

   **C.** The version of LSNRCTL you are using is incompatible with the listener.

   **D.** The listener you attempted to stop isn't running.

**14.** You use LSNRCTL to issue a command that allows you to determine how many connections have been refused by the listener on every protocol the listener tunes in to. Which of the following commands is the one you issued?

   **A.** HELP

   **B.** SERVICES

   **C.** RELOAD

   **D.** SPAWN

   **E.** STATUS

**15.** Net8 host-naming services makes several assumptions about your network environment. Which of the following choices is *not* an assumption Net8 host-naming services makes?

   **A.** Your network protocol is TCP/IP.

   **B.** Your listener is listing to port 1521.

   **C.** Your database is using dedicated servers.

   **D.** Your machine name matches the global database name.

16. You are using local naming in your Oracle network. Which of the following contains connection information for databases available to your client?

    A. tnsnames.ora

    B. sqlnet.ora

    C. listener.ora

    D. Net8 Assistant

17. Your database is configured to run multithreaded server. The database experienced a heavy transaction load an hour ago, but is now idle. Which of the following parameters most likely identifies how many server processes are running?

    A. PROCESSES

    B. OPEN_CURSORS

    C. MTS_MAX_SERVERS

    D. MTS_SERVERS

18. Your TNSNAMES file contains an alias, called DB01, which connects you to a database running on a node called DB01. Another DBA adds a new database on a host machine, the SID for which is DB01, and the listener is configured to register automatically with Oracle Names. The default order of host-naming resolution preference is still in place. When you attempt to connect to Oracle using the DB01 connect string, what database do you connect to, and why?

    A. The database on node DB01, because Oracle attempts host-naming resolution first by default

    B. The database on node DB01, because Oracle attempts local-naming resolution first by default

    C. The database whose SID is DB01, because Oracle attempts centralized-naming resolution first by default

    D. The database whose SID is DB01, because Oracle attempts external-naming resolution first by default

Chapter 5: OCP Exam 5: Network Administration **299**

19. You are determining how you plan to store naming information for your Oracle Names servers. Which of the following choices does not describe a feature of regional database repository usage for this purpose?

    **A.** Increased Names server fault tolerance

    **B.** Higher scalability when subnetworks are configured

    **C.** Best for Oracle networks consisting of workgroup configurations

    **D.** Reduced effort for Net8 circulating new Oracle service names

20. You are attempting to define the location of your Names server on the Oracle network. To do so, which of the following tools would you use?

    **A.** Net8 Assistant

    **B.** LSNRCTL

    **C.** Oracle Expert

    **D.** Oracle Enterprise Manager

21. You are looking for the port on the host machine where the Names server is listening. Which of the following files contains that information?

    **A.** listener.ora

    **B.** tnsnames.ora

    **C.** snmp.ora

    **D.** names.ora

22. You are configuring your repository to store naming information within the Oracle database. After creating a user that the Names server will use to connect to the repository, which of the following steps should you undertake?

    **A.** Run the namesini.sql script.

    **B.** Make appropriate changes in the Database tab interface of Net8 Assistant.

    **C.** Click the Optional button to define how Oracle Names refreshes the repository.

    **D.** Edit the names.ora file to define the repository location.

23. You want to start the Oracle Names server. Which of the following tools enable you to perform this task? (Choose two)

    A. Oracle Enterprise Manager

    B. NAMESCTL

    C. LSNRCTL

    D. Net8 Assistant

    E. Instance Manager

    F. Server Manager

24. You are attempting to add a new service manually to your Oracle network using the NAMESCTL utility. Which of the following commands will assist you in this purpose?

    A. REGISTER

    B. REORDER_NS

    C. VERSION

    D. LOG_STATS

    E. SET

25. You want to change the name of the trace file used by your Names server. Which of the following commands will enable you to do so?

    A. REORDER_NS

    B. RELOAD

    C. SET

    D. SHOW

    E. VERSION

    F. REGISTER

26. You are designing your database administrative configuration for your Oracle network to simplify the management effort. Intelligent Agent would assist in which of the following ways? (Choose three)

    A. Increasing system scalability

    B. Identifying events occurring on the database

- C. Allowing you to stop and restart your Oracle database remotely
- D. Allowing you to take backups of your database remotely
- E. Managing SNMP on your database host

27. You need to shut down Intelligent Agent. Which of the following utilities will assist you in doing so?
    - A. Oracle Enterprise Manager
    - B. NAMESCTL
    - C. LSNRCTL
    - D. Net8 Assistant
    - E. Instance Manager
    - F. Server Manager

28. Which of the following processes participate in the multithreaded server architecture? (Choose three)
    - A. Listeners
    - B. Dedicated servers
    - C. Dispatchers
    - D. Database writers
    - E. Names servers
    - F. Shared servers

29. Your dispatcher is configured with the following information:

    MTS_DISPATCHERS=(protocol=NMP)(dispatchers=4)
    MTS_DISPATCHERS=(protocol=TCP)(dispatchers=2)

    If MTS_MAX_DISPATCHERS is set to 8, and you still need to configure the DECnet protocol, what is the maximum number of dispatchers you can set up for that protocol?
    - A. 1
    - B. 2
    - C. 3
    - D. 4

30. You are determining how many shared servers to configure for your multithreaded server architecture on your Oracle OLTP database application. You usually have about 500 concurrent users at any given time. How many shared servers would you be inclined to use initially to test improvements in performance?

    A. 8

    B. 50

    C. 200

    D. 250

31. You are planning to use connection pooling on your Oracle database. Which of the following INIT.ORA parameters would you use to configure this feature?

    A. MTS_MAX_SERVERS

    B. MTS_SERVERS

    C. MTS_LISTENERS

    D. MTS_DISPATCHERS

32. You want to enhance scalability for your application through the use of connection concentration. Which of the following parameters will be modified for that purpose?

    A. MTS_SERVERS

    B. MTS_LISTENER_ADDRESS

    C. MTS_DISPATCHERS

    D. MTS_MAX_SERVERS

33. You are using Connection Manager in your networking configuration. Which of the following is not a component of that tool?

    A. CMNS

    B. CMCTL

    C. CMADM

    D. CMGW

34. You issue the STATUS ADM command from within the Connection Manager control utility. Which of the following descriptions best identifies the result of this command?

   A. Returns statistics for all Connection Manager components

   B. Returns statistics for Connection Manager administrative utility only

   C. Returns status of all Connection Manager components

   D. Returns status of Connection Manager administrative utility only

35. You are configuring connection concentration on your application using the appropriate parameter. Which of the following options for that parameter are appropriate for this purpose?

   A. PROTOCOL

   B. MULTIPLEX

   C. CONCENTRATE

   D. PARTIAL

36. Multiprotocol interchange can be configured as long as Net8 listeners are tuned in to a certain number of network protocols. Which of the following choices indicates a number of protocols that is not acceptable for multiprotocol interchange?

   A. 1

   B. 2

   C. 3

   D. 4

37. You want to enable network access control on your network environment. Which of the following configuration files correctly identifies the file where you would configure network-access control?

   A. listener.ora

   B. sqlnet.ora

   C. INIT.ORA

   D. cman.ora

**E.** names.ora

**F.** access.ora

38. You are about to begin setup for tracing network activity. Which of the following settings would be appropriate if you planned to process your trace file later using Trace Assistant?

   **A.** OFF

   **B.** USER

   **C.** ADMIN

   **D.** SUPPORT

39. Your users report the following network error message to you: ORA-12224: No Listener. To correct the problem, which of the following utilities might you use if you have already set up the listener on your host machine?

   **A.** Net8 Assistant

   **B.** LSNRCTL

   **C.** NAMESCTL

   **D.** CMCTL

40. An excerpt of the contents of a trace file is listed as follows:

```
(c770) nsprecv: packet dump
(c770) nsprecv: 00 72 00 00 06 00 00 00  |.r......|
(c770) nsprecv: 00 00 04 00 00 00 00 F5  |........|
(c770) nsprecv: 03 00 00 00 00 02 00 00  |........|
(c770) nsprecv: 00 18 00 00 00 00 21 00  |......!.|
(c770) nsprecv: 00 00 00 00 00 00 00 00  |........|
(c770) nsprecv: 00 00 00 00 00 00 00 00  |........|
(c770) nsprecv: 00 00 00 00 31 00 00 01  |....1...|
(c770) nsprecv: 00 00 00 36 4F 52 41 2D  |...6ORA-|
(c770) nsprecv: 30 31 30 31 33 3A 20 75  |01013: u|
(c770) nsprecv: 73 65 72 20 72 65 71 75  |ser requ|
(c770) nsprecv: 65 73 74 65 64 20 63 61  |ested ca|
(c770) nsprecv: 6E 63 65 6C 20 6F 66 20  |ncel of |
(c770) nsprecv: 63 75 72 72 65 6E 74 20  |current |
(c770) nsprecv: 6F 70 65 72 61 74 69 6F  |operatio|
(c770) nsprecv: 6E 0A 00 00 00 00 00 00  |n.......|
(c770) nsprecv: normal exit
```

What Net8 network layer component produced this output?

**A.** Two-Task Common

**B.** Network Interface

**C.** Network Session

**D.** Network Transport

**E.** Network Authentication

41. The output from Trace Assistant displays statistical information from your trace file for the session activity only. Which of the following command-line options were most likely used?

**A.** -oq -e

**B.** -e

**C.** -odt -e0 -s

**D.** -s

**E.** None, Trace Assistant shows statistical information only by default

42. You are attempting to design the architecture for your Oracle network. Which of the following choices does not describe a feature of the Oracle advanced security option?

**A.** Uses LDAP for authentication

**B.** Uses Identix for authentication

**C.** Uses Kerberos for authentication

**D.** Uses SecurID for authentication

43. The following parameters are found in the appropriate configuration file:

    ENCRYPTION_CLIENT = requested
    ENCRYPTION_SERVER = required
    ENCRYPTION_TYPE_CLIENT = (RC4_128, DES_40, DES)
    ENCRYPTION_TYPE_SERVER = (RC4_40, RC4_56, DES_40)

Which of the following choices correctly describes how encryption will be used between the client and server?

**A.** RC4_128 encryption will be used.

**B.** RC4_56 encryption will be used.

**C.** RC4_40 encryption will be used.

**D.** DES encryption will be used.

**E.** DES_40 encryption will be used

**F.** No encryption will be used.

44. You are configuring the mode of authentication used in the Advanced Networking Option. Which of the following files will be modified for this purpose?

   **A.** listener.ora

   **B.** sqlnet.ora

   **C.** INIT.ORA

   **D.** cman.ora

   **E.** names.ora

   **F.** access.ora

45. You are configuring the mode of authentication used in the advanced security option. Which of the following parameters will be modified for this purpose?

   **A.** ENCRYPTION_CLIENT

   **B.** ENCRYPTION_SERVER

   **C.** AUTHENTICATION_SERVICES

   **D.** ENCRYPTION_TYPE_CLIENT

   **E.** ENCRYPTION_TYPE_SERVER

   **F.** CRYPTO_SEED

46. You want to use the Cryptography Toolkit feature in Net8. Which of the following scripts must be run to generate the Oracle-supplied packages associated with this product?

   **A.** catproc.sql

   **B.** catalog.sql

   **C.** catoctk.sql

   **D.** catexp.sql

47. You are managing an Oracle network of clients and servers. Which of the following choices identifies the method used by default for transporting messages between Oracle clients and servers on a TCP/IP network?

    A. DES_40

    B. RSA 128-bit

    C. RSA_40

    D. Plain text

48. You are running Oracle in MTS mode. Which of the following files will contain the definition of where the listener is tuned in for Oracle database connections?

    A. sqlnet.ora

    B. INIT.ORA

    C. listener.ora

    D. tnsnames.ora

49. You are configuring your Intelligent Agent on the Oracle database. Which of the following files will contain specific references to the Intelligent Agent ifile in order to define certain parameters used by Intelligent Agent for startup and operation?

    A. snmp_ro.ora

    B. snmp_rw.ora

    C. snmp.ora

    D. listener.ora

50. After spawning a new dedicated server, what does the Net8 listener do to connect a user process to the Oracle database?

    A. Assigns the user process to a dispatcher

    B. Returns a memory address where the dedicated server can be found

    C. Assigns the user process to the shared server

    D. Queues messages for the user process at defined intervals

# Answers to Practice Exam 1

**1. B.** Client/server

**Explanation** Client/server computing is the architectural paradigm in which all application intelligence, business rules, and so on are stored as client software running on a user's desktop. Choice B is therefore correct. Under mainframe computing, all information about an application, be it business rules, data, or user interface, is stored on the centralized mainframe machine. Thus, choice A is incorrect. Both choices C and D indicate an *n*-tier application design, while choice C refers to the currently most popular *n*-tier application design, in which the front end is a Web browser. Both are wrong, because usually under *n*-tier architectures, the business application logic and business rules are stored on a middle tier or the database layer. **(Topic 1.1)**

**2. C.** Oracle Names

**Explanation** Oracle Names offers DBAs the ability to configure and manage database name resolution via a centralized repository or connection string mappings to connect descriptors. Thus, the tnsnames.ora file is not necessary when Oracle Names is in place, and management overhead of new databases coming online from a client naming perspective is reduced. The Transparent Network Substrate is still in place in Net8 because Oracle uses its own protocol for Oracle clients to communicate with servers that is independent of the network over which connectivity between machines is established, thus making choice D incorrect. Choice A is also incorrect because Connection Manager is a feature of Net8 that adds scalability to the overall Oracle network. Choice B is incorrect because Net8 Assistant is used for managing Net8 components, whether local or server naming is used. **(Topic 1.2)**

**3. B.** Host naming

**Explanation** Oracle prefers host naming by default in order to resolve connect strings to connect descriptors. In order for host naming to work, the Oracle database must be named the same thing as the machine hosting the Oracle database is named. If there is any discrepancy, then Oracle will look next in the tnsnames.ora file for name resolution. This fact makes choice A incorrect. Only if host naming and local naming via tnsnames.ora fail will Oracle attempt to locate an Oracle Names server on your network for naming resolution. Thus, choice C is incorrect. Finally, Net8 Assistant is used for configuration of Net8 for client and server, not for actual connect string resolution, making choice D incorrect. **(Topic 2.1)**

**4.** B. Presentation layer

**Explanation** Within the presentation layer of the OSI model, Oracle's two-task common (TTC) process performs implicit type conversions such as the one indicated in the question. Thus, choice B is the answer. The application layer is within the application itself. In this case, SQL*Plus is the application, and this application is fairly thin in that it only serves as a command line into which SQL commands can be entered. So, choice A is wrong. The session layer allows Oracle clients and servers to communicate basic messages back and forth to one another. At this point, no datatype conversion takes place, as the session layer is a basic messaging layer, so choice C is incorrect. Finally, choice D is incorrect because the network layer is the transparent network substrate, where all meaningful Oracle networking activities are executed. **(Topic 2.2)**

**5.** A. Database Services

**Explanation** The Database Services location, brought up within Net8 Assistant by clicking on the pull-down menu in the upper-right side of the interface, is where Oracle databases that will be served by this listener are identified to the listener. Choice B is incorrect because Listening Locations is where the port or other host-specific place the listener will tune into for connections is defined. Choice C is incorrect because General Parameters is where basic information about trace file locations, authentication, and other listener-wide configuration information is placed. Finally, choice D is incorrect because Other Services is where you might define other non-database services (such as EXTPROC) that the listener might serve. **(Topic 3.1)**

**6.** A. set

**Explanation** The set command, as in set password, is used for configuring password authentication for listener startup and shutdown within the LSNRCTL session (however, only in the case where if you did set up a password). This feature can be useful for ensuring database uptime. To view a password that has already been set, you can issue the show command in LSNRCTL, so choice B is incorrect. Choice C is incorrect because the start command itself is the one that will be password-protected. In order to configure password authentication, the change_password command is used, so choice D is incorrect as well. **(Topic 3.2)**

**7.** B. SID_DESC

**Explanation** You would need to add a new SID_DESC entry to the listener.ora file in order to have the listener serving the database you need it to serve. The SID_DESC entry is a subcomponent of the SID_LIST entry, making it a challenge not to get hung up on choice C. In this situation, be careful to choose the answer choice that most accurately answers the question. Choices A and D are both incorrect because ADDRESS and DESCRIPTION_LIST are both part of the area in listener.ora in which you define the protocols that the listener tunes into. **(Topic 3.2)**

> **8.** A and D.   Network protocols the listener serves and Service names the listener serves

**Explanation**   When you issue the LSNRCTL services command, LSNRCTL returns specific information about all the databases this listener serves. This information includes whether the listener is for shared or dedicated servers and how many connections have been made and refused by this listener for users attempting to connect to Oracle. Choice A is also correct because in order to show information about the databases served by this listener, LSNRCTL will attempt to connect to the listener via each of the network protocols identified for the listener in order to do so. Choices C and D are both incorrect—the services command does not identify whether connection pooling or concentration is configured for this listener. **(Topic 3.4)**

> **9.** D.   start *name*

**Explanation**   When you specify the name of a listener on the same line as the start command, then you can start named listeners using LSNRCTL. If you do not specify the name of the listener you wish to start, as in choice A, the default listener called LISTENER will be started. Since you have multiple listeners in this situation, you will have to give each of your listeners a distinct name in order for each of them to start correctly. Thus, choice A is incorrect. Choice B is incorrect because although you can use the set current_listener command to define the listener name for a later issuance of start within LSNRCTL, you will need to execute this as two steps because the set command does not actually start the listener. Choice C is incorrect because the show command only displays the value for whatever parameter was defined on the same line as the show command. **(Topic 3.4)**

> **10.** C and D.   The alias name defined on the machine name and global database name match and the listener must be running on TCP/IP.

**Explanation**   In order for host naming to work on an Oracle network, the machine name must be the same as the database name, and the listener must be running on TCP/IP. If both these criteria cannot be met, then you must either use local naming resolution or you must use Oracle Names, making choice A incorrect. If you have more than one database running on the host, then only the database whose name matches the machine name of the host system can be resolved using host naming, making choice B incorrect. **(Topic 4.1)**

**11.** A. tnsnames.ora

**Explanation** The tnsnames.ora is the locally housed file on the Oracle client machine that contains connect strings mapped to connect descriptors, which is required for local naming to work properly. The listener.ora file is stored on the server side, and configures the database listener, so choice B is incorrect. The sqlnet.ora file configures various aspects of Net8 operation on both client and server, so choice C is incorrect. The namesini.ora file is not a real file in the Net8 infrastructure, so choice D is incorrect as well. **(Topic 4.2)**

**12.** A. sqlnet.ora

**Explanation** General configuration information such as trace or log file directory destination is stored in the sqlnet.ora file, found either on the client or the server side, in the network/admin directory on the machine. Listener.ora is used for configuring the listener, so choice B is incorrect. The tnsnames.ora file is used for defining connect string to connect descriptor matching, thus making choice C incorrect. There is no net8asst.ora file, thus making choice D incorrect. **(Topic 4.3)**

**13.** D. Name resolution order must be changed using Net8 Assistant.

**Explanation** The order of precedence that the Oracle client will use for resolving a connect string into connect descriptor is defined in sqlnet.ora. If you want Oracle Names to be used by default, you must change the order precedence either manually in the file or via Net8 Assistant. Thus, choice D is correct. Oracle clients don't use Names first by default, so choice A is wrong. The tnsnames.ora file does not identify the location of the Names server, either, so choice B is incorrect. Finally, the order precedence is not specified in the listener.ora file, either, so choice C is incorrect. **(Topic 5.1)**

**14.** C. sdns.ora

**Explanation** The sdns.ora file is where configuration information about Oracle Names can be found. This file is located in the network/names directory on the machine hosting Oracle Names. In it, you can find information like the port on which the Names server should be listening. Choice A is incorrect because the tnsnames.ora file is used for local-naming resolution and has no bearing on Oracle Names. Choice B is incorrect because listener.ora identifies what port the database listener is tuned to. Choice D is incorrect because snmp_ro.ora identifies key information about the Intelligent Agent. **(Topic 5.2)**

**15.** A.  snmp.ora

**Explanation**   If you want Intelligent Agent to dynamically modify the Oracle Names server with information about new databases coming online within that host machine, you need to set the value for nmi.register_with_names to TRUE in the snmp.ora file. By default, the value for this parameter is FALSE. Choice B is incorrect because the snmp_ro.ora file identifies the location of the ifile used for configuring Intelligent Agent at startup. Choice C is incorrect because that file defines other parameters used by Intelligent Agent to define its operation at startup. Choice D is incorrect because listener.ora defines characteristics of the listener. **(Topic 6.1)**

**16.** D.  network/names

**Explanation**   The network/names directory is where scripts for generating your region database objects for Oracle Names can be found, so choice D is correct. The rdbms/admin directory is where most DBA administrative scripts can be found—however, not the namesini.sql script. So, choice A is incorrect. The network/admin directory is where you will find the sdns.ora configuration file for the Names server, but not where you will find the SQL script for creating the region database objects, so choice B is incorrect, too. Finally, choice C is incorrect because there is no names/admin directory in the Oracle file system. **(Topic 5.3)**

**17.** B and C.  namesctl and Net8 Assistant

**Explanation**   You can start the Oracle Names server using either namesctl or the Net8 Assistant, so choices B and C are the answers. The lsnrctl utility is used for starting the Net8 listener and the Intelligent Agent, but not Names, making choice A incorrect. The svrmgrl utility is used for starting your Oracle database, making choice D incorrect also. **(Topic 5.4)**

**18.** B.  LSNRCTL

**Explanation**   The LSNRCTL utility is used for startup of Intelligent Agent. Net8 Assistant is not capable of starting the agent, thus making choice C incorrect. The NAMESCTL utility is used for starting the Oracle Names server, making choice A incorrect. Finally, there is no AGNTCTL utility, making choice D incorrect. **(Topic 6.2)**

**19.** D.  Restoration of Names data in event of host system failure

**Explanation**   The Intelligent Agent is not equipped to handle restoration of Oracle Names server data in the event of host system failure by default. The only way this is possible is if you have stored your Names information in a database, and set up a recovery job in the OEM console to be run in the event of a disaster. However, without this additional information, there is no way for you to know whether Intelligent Agent is set up to handle recovery, so choice D is your answer. The rest of the choices identify features on Intelligent Agent. **(Topic 6.1)**

**20.** D.   NMO_NAMES

**Explanation**   The answer to this question is tricky, and requires that you have an intimate understanding of the objects you add to your database using namesini.sql. You should review the contents of that file. In it, you will see definitions for NMO_MASTER, ONRS_SERIAL, and ONRS_CONFIG, making those choices incorrect. However, you will not see any definition to a table called NMO_NAMES. **(Topic 5.3)**

**21.** B.   nmi

**Explanation**   In the snmp.ora file, you will find all your parameters that affect Intelligent Agent's integration with Oracle Names prefixed with nmi. Thus, choice B is the answer. Be careful about the strong distracter choice A. The snmp prefix, though found in snmp.ora, is for general agent setup and configuration. The dbsnmp prefix can also be found in the snmp.ora file, making choice D a strong distracter choice as well. Finally, no parameters in the snmp.ora file have the ora prefix. **(Topic 6.3)**

**22.** C.   LSNRCTL

**Explanation**   Be careful when reading this question—you are asked to supply the operating system command to shut down the Intelligent Agent, which is lsnrctl. Although the dbsnmp_stop command within LSNRCTL actually stops the agent, that command is one within the utility, not available from the command prompt except as a parameter to lsnrctl. Thus, choice B is incorrect. The stop parameter stops the Oracle Net8 listener, making choice A incorrect. Finally, the NAMESCTL utility is for starting and stopping Oracle Names, not the Intelligent Agent. **(Topic 6.2)**

**23.** A.   Failover between hardware nodes

**Explanation**   Oracle Enterprise Manager will not handle failover between two machines. You will need a high-availability product for executing this task. You can, however, use OEM to restart a database on the host machine, eliminating choice B. You can also use OEM to handle extension of a table, which eliminates choice C. Finally, Enterprise Manager can also take care of rerunning failed batch jobs, as long as the job is scheduled in the Oracle job scheduler. **(Topic 6.1)**

**24.** D. Response queue

**Explanation** After obtaining information from the database on behalf of users, the shared server process places data results into the response queue for users to obtain. The user process places a request for the shared server to process information on the request queue maintained by that user, thus making choice C incorrect. Though information for a user process is stored privately in a dedicated server's PGA, this is not the case for Oracle MTS configuration, making choice A incorrect. Also, although data requested can be found in the Oracle buffer cache, the actual response from a query is found in the response queue. Thus, choice B is incorrect **(Topic 7.1)**

**25.** A. MTS_DISPATCHERS

**Explanation** MTS_DISPATCHERS is used by Net8 to define the number of dispatchers tuned in for user connections from various networks. This feature allows the listener to assign user processes to shared servers. The MTS_SERVICE parameter is used for defining the instance a dispatcher will tune in for, making choice B incorrect. Choice C is incorrect because MTS_SERVERS identifies the number of shared servers that will be run when the database starts. Finally, choice D is incorrect because MTS_MAX_DISPATCHERS identifies the maximum number of dispatchers allowed to run on the database. **(Topic 7.2)**

**26.** B. MTS_SERVICE

**Explanation** In Oracle8, the MTS_SERVICE parameter identifies the database to its dispatchers, and will default to the value set for DB_NAME if not explicitly set in the INIT.ORA file. Choice A is incorrect because MTS_DISPATCHERS is used by Net8 to define the number of dispatchers tuned in for user connections from various networks. This feature allows the listener to assign user processes to shared servers. Choice C is incorrect because MTS_SERVERS identifies the number of shared servers that will be run when the database starts. Finally, choice D is incorrect because MTS_MAX_SERVERS identifies the maximum number of dispatchers allowed to run on the database. **(Topic 7.2)**

**27.** D. After the server has sat idle for a while.

**Explanation** When users are actively engaging the Oracle database, Oracle will spawn new shared servers until the maximum number of shared servers permitted by MTS_MAX_SERVERS has been reached. Once user activity dies down, Oracle will begin killing servers that sit idly for too long. Oracle will not kill a shared server when a particular user process terminates, because other user processes may be utilizing the services of the shared server. Thus, choice C is incorrect. While the number of shared servers will downsize when you bounce the database, choice B does not fit with the context of the question and is therefore incorrect. Choice A, by virtue of the correctness of other choices, is also incorrect. **(Topic 7.3)**

**28.  A.  MTS_LISTENER_ADDRESS**

**Explanation**   The MTS_LISTENER_ADDRESS parameter defines the port and protocol for the MTS listener. It is set in the INIT.ORA file. Choices B, C, and D all identify settings in the listener.ora file, which is needed for defining and starting the listener. But, those choices are incorrect because choice A indicates what must be set in the database in order to use MTS and shared servers. **(Topic 7.4)**

> **NOTE**
> Both the MTS_SERVICE and MTS_LISTENER_ ADDRESS parameters were made obsolete in Oracle8i. Be sure you know this difference before taking the Oracle8i version of this exam!

**29.  C.  POOL**

**Explanation**   The POOL option is set as part of the MTS_DISPATCHERS parameter in the INIT.ORA file in order to set up connection pooling, the feature of Net8 described by the question. Of the choices given, only choice D identifies an actual option available for setting within the MTS_DISPATCHERS parameter in Oracle. All choices other than C are incorrect. **(Topic 7.5)**

**30.  A.  Connection Manager**

**Explanation**   Connection Manager is the Net8 feature that replaced multiprotocol interchange from SQL*Net version 2. Connection Pooling is incorrect because although pooling connections by temporarily disconnecting physical connections while maintaining logical sessions is available in Net8, the Connection Manager is the tool or product, while connection pooling is only a feature of that product. Connection Concentration is a new feature within Net8 Connection Manager as well, making it subject to the same logic in why Connection Pooling is incorrect. Finally, Connection Exchange is not a valid answer. **(Topic 8.1)**

**31.  B.  Connection Concentration**

**Explanation**   Connection Concentration is a new feature in Net8, which is configured using the MULTIPLEX option for MTS_DISPATCHERS in your INIT.ORA file. The "on" setting is but one setting that can be used for configuring this option. Connection Manager is the Net8 feature that replaced multiprotocol interchange from SQL*Net version 2. Connection Pooling is incorrect because pooling connections by temporarily disconnecting physical connections while maintaining logical sessions is available only in Net8. Finally, Connection Exchange is not a valid answer. **(Topic 8.2)**

**32.** B.  IN

**Explanation** The IN setting for MULTIPLEX defines connection concentration from client to server, but not from server to client. The OUT setting is for that, making choice C incorrect. The two options BOTH and YES configure connection concentration in the direction of both client and server, so choices A and D are both wrong as well. **(Topic 8.2)**

**33.** B.  SOURCE_ROUTE

**Explanation** The SOURCE_ROUTE parameter is set in tnsnames.ora in order to configure the connection concentration functionality for the client side. Choice A is incorrect because MULTIPLEX is defined in order to set up connection concentration on the server side. Both DESCRIPTION and ADDRESS are incorrect because they define configuration settings in the listener.ora file, not cman.ora, where client-side connection concentration is defined. **(Topic 8.2)**

**34.** C.  CMAN_RULES, cman.ora

**Explanation** The CMAN_RULES parameter in the cman.ora file is where you identify both the parameter you need to configure and the file in which you need to configure it for the network access control feature in Net8. Choice A is incorrect because NAC_START is not a real setting in any configuration file. Choices B and D are incorrect because network access control configuration is managed with the cman.ora file, not the sqlnet.ora file or listener.ora file. **(Topic 8.3)**

**35.** D.  1610

**Explanation** Port 1610 is where Connection Manager network access control is defined to listen by default. Thus, choice D is correct. Choice A is incorrect because 1492 is not a port used by any Net8 feature by default. Choice B is incorrect because 1521 is the default listener port. Choice C is incorrect because 1575 is the default port for Oracle Names. **(Topic 8.3)**

**36.** A.  srv

**Explanation** The srv option is used for ensuring that the destination database SID is configured. Choice B is incorrect because src identifies the machine hosting the client, while choice C is incorrect because dst identifies the machine hosting the server. Finally, act is used for defining a network access control rule, making choice D incorrect as well. **(Topic 8.3)**

**37.** A. Configure connection concentration for clients.

**Explanation** After setting up rules for network access control on your Oracle network, you must configure connection concentration for clients. This sets the SOURCE_ROUTE parameter in the client's tnsnames.ora file, the critical second step for network access control to work. Choice C is incorrect because Oracle Names is an external setup factor that would not be affected if you used local name resolution. Choices B and D are both incorrect because the network listener is not affected by this setup. **(Topic 8.3)**

**38.** A. src

**Explanation** Choice A is correct because src identifies the machine hosting the client. Choice C is incorrect because the srv file is used for ensuring that the destination database SID is configured. Choice B is incorrect because dst identifies the machine hosting the server. Finally, act is used for defining a network access control rule, making choice D incorrect as well. **(Topic 8.3)**

**39.** B. cman.log

**Explanation** The cman.log file is used for logging the Connection Manager gateway execution information, making choice B the correct answer. Choice A is incorrect because cmgw.log is not a real log file used in Net8 for the Connection Manager gateway. Beware, as this choice is a strong distracter if you haven't reviewed all the configuration information before taking the OCP exam. Choice C is incorrect because cmadm.log is the log file for the Connection Manager administrator. Finally, choice D is incorrect because the sqlnet.log file is for logging general Net8 errors for client and server. **(Topic 9.1)**

**40.** D. Connection Manager

**Explanation** Connection Manager does not allow you to identify a name other than cman.log for logging information. You may only change the logging level, not the directory name or the filename used for storing the log. Choice A is incorrect because you can change the log directory and filename for the listener. Choice C is incorrect because you can change the log directory and filename for the Oracle Names as well. Finally, choice B is incorrect because you can change the log directory and filename for Connection Manager administrator from cmadm.log. **(Topic 8.1)**

**41.** A. CMAN

**Explanation** The CMAN parameter in cman.ora is used for configuring multiprotocol functionality. Choice B is incorrect because CMAN_RULES is used for setting up network access control in the cman.ora file. Choice C is incorrect because CMAN_PROFILE is used for setup of basic configuration for Connection Manager in the cman.ora file. Finally, choice D is incorrect because the choice doesn't refer to configuration of a Connection Manager feature. **(Topic 8.4)**

**42.** A. Add a new address to the cman.ora file.

**Explanation** Multiprotocol functionality in Connection Manager simply refers to setup of the Connection Manager to tune into more than one network protocol. This simply involves adding a new address to the cman.ora file that does not associate with the TCP/IP protocol, the default protocol used for Connection Manager. Choice B is incorrect because multiprotocol functionality refers to adding new addresses for Connection Manager, not the listener. Choices C and D are incorrect because they both refer to connection resolution between client and server. **(Topic 8.4)**

**43.** C. act=reject

**Explanation** There are only two valid settings for the act option—accept for accepting connections, and reject for rejecting them. The other settings given for choices A, B, and D are all settings for other parameters within Connection Manager. Thus, those other choices are all incorrect. **(Topic 8.3)**

**44.** C. Fluffy's access to the food database on RFRGRTOR is rejected.

**Explanation** The settings in this question refer to limiting access on the FOOD database running on host RFRGRTOR for the client software running on host FLUFFY. Thus, choice B is logically incorrect. The other choices refer to incorrect interpretation of the settings shown in the question. **(Topic 8.3)**

**45.** D. SUPPORT

**Explanation** The SUPPORT setting for listener tracing is the highest level of tracing available for Oracle Net8 listeners. OFF is the lowest, making choice A incorrect. USER is a low-level setting that shows enough information for most users, making choice B incorrect. ADMIN is a mid-level setting to give information for DBAs, making choice C incorrect. **(Topic 9.1)**

**46.** B.   LOG_LEVEL

**Explanation**   When configuring tracing for Connection Manager, you will use the LOG_LEVEL parameter to define a level of tracing using the values 1, 2, 3, or 4—4 being the highest tracing level available. Choice A refers to tracing in the listener, and therefore is incorrect. Choice C indicates tracing within Oracle Names, and is also wrong. Finally, Choice D indicates general Net8 tracing set in sqlnet.ora, and is wrong as well. **(Topic 9.1)**

**47.** C.   As soon as you restart the listener

**Explanation**   Changes to the tracing settings on a listener take effect when you stop and restart that listener. Choice A is therefore incorrect. Simply restarting the database won't cut it, because the listener stays up while your database gets bounced. Choice B is wrong. Finally, choice D is also wrong. **(Topic 9.1)**

**48.** C.   TRCASST

**Explanation**   Trace Assistant is used for formatting the output stored in a tracing log file to view the contents in a more readable manner. Choice A is wrong because DBVERIFY verifies database files for block corruption. Choice B is wrong because Net8 Assistant is used for configuring Net8 via a GUI interface. Finally, choice D is wrong because the TKPROF utility is used for configuring the output file produced by session tracing into a readable format. **(Topic 9.3)**

**49.** D.   sqlnet.ora

**Explanation**   The sqlnet.ora file is used for configuring encryption and checksums in Net8. Choices A, B, and C are all incorrect because they refer to configuration files not used for setup of encryption and checksums. **(Topic 10.4)**

**50.** A.   CRYPTO_SEED

**Explanation**   The CRYPTO_SEED parameter in sqlnet.ora is used for setup and configuration of the cryptography seed of between 10 and 70 characters for security in Net8. All other choices are incorrect. **(Topic 10.4)**

# Answers to Practice Exam 2

**1.** B and E.  Low distribution cost *and* centralized code management

**Explanation**  Choices A, C, and D all describe features of client/server applications. Their visual design makes them easy to use, their substantial application size puts client machine resources to work, and their use of networking makes them as scalable as the server side can handle. They are not inexpensive to distribute to your user populations, however, and the code is distributed over every single client machine, making code management difficult, if not impossible, to centralize. **(Topic 1.1)**

**2.** C.  Internet computing

**Explanation**  *n*-tier applications with multiple application servers all handling specialized tasks reserved for clients in client/server or two-tier architecture are part of the Oracle network computer architecture (for Internet computing). Mainframes make sure all processing happens on one centralized machine, while, as noted, client/server is typically referred to as two-tier architecture. Uniprocessor architecture usually denotes that clients and servers all run on the same machine. **(Topic 1.1)**

**3.** B.  Transparent Network Substrate

**Explanation**  The ability Net8 has to manage connections independent of any network protocol other than its own is gained with the Transparent Network Substrate, or TNS. Oracle Call Interface is part of the client side that applications call to handle data processing operations. Oracle Processing Interface is part of the server side that handles RDBMS operations. Network Interface is the part of Net8 that establishes the session layer and accepts information from the client OCI or server OPI and passes that information to the transport layer. Oracle Protocol Adapters are at the link layer, and pass data transmission requests from the Transparent Network Substrate to the network protocol on the physical layer. **(Topic 1.2)**

**4.** A.  Two-Task Common

**Explanation**  The Two-Task Common process handles converting character-set and datatype information at the presentation layer, within the RDBMS rather than by Net8. Choices B, C, and D all identify components from Net8, which you were supposed to exclude, according to the question. Also, because the question mentions server-side, not client-side, processing, you should eliminate choice E, because the Oracle Call Interface is part of client-side application processing. **(Topic 1.2)**

**5.** C.   Provides the ability to handle connections to one Oracle server from multiple networks

**Explanation**   The Oracle Connection Manager utility in Net8 provides the ability to handle connections for one Oracle server coming in from multiple networks. Oracle Names is used to centralize management of naming services, eliminating choice A. TNS offers independence from standard networking protocols, eliminating choice B. High overall network scalability is facilitated by implementing connection pooling and concentration, but ultimately you need a more comprehensive network solution than a solution provided by and for Oracle. This fact eliminates choice D. Native Naming Adapters are meant to allow interconnectivity between Oracle and external naming services, eliminating choice E. **(Topic 2.1)**

**6.** E.   Oracle SID resolution

**Explanation**   Since the question basically says that the error was encountered while trying to resolve the Oracle SID, the answer has to be Oracle SID resolution. The question states that the host name resolved successfully, eliminating choice A. Because connect-string lookup happens before host-name resolution, choice C must be eliminated as well. Since the Oracle SID has not been resolved, no password authentication has taken place, eliminating Choice B. And because listener availability is checked before the SID is resolved and the failure was with the SID, you can assume there was a listener available on the specified port, eliminating choice D. **(Topic 2.1)**

**7.** A.   Listener

**Explanation**   The listener process connects user processes with prespawned servers. A dispatcher is only used when the multithreaded server architecture is in place, eliminating choice B. The DBWR process is not involved in networking, eliminating choice D, while the Assistant process is fiction, eliminating choice C. **(Topic 2.1)**

**8.** D.   Transport

**Explanation**   The Network Routing component of Net8 resides at the transport layer of the OSI network model. No Net8 component resides at the physical layer, eliminating choice A. Oracle Protocol Adapters handle tasks at the link layer, eliminating choice B. TNS handles things at the network layer, eliminating choice C. The Network Interface completes tasks at the session layer, eliminating choice E. **(Topic 2.2)**

**9.** C. LSNRCTL, followed by SET PASSWORD, followed by STOP

**Explanation** By issuing only the LSNRCTL command by itself on the command prompt, you run LSNRCTL in interactive mode, which is required to stop the listener because of the password requirement. First, you issue the SET PASSWORD command, and then you issue the STOP command. Choice A starts a listener, and therefore is incorrect. Choice B simply lists the running services, and therefore is incorrect. Choice D is almost correct, but because you run both commands in batch mode, your second iteration doesn't actually have the password you set available to it, because the SET PASSWORD command sets it only session-wide. **(Topic 3.2)**

**10.** A. General Parameters

**Explanation** Trace directory and filename information are both set in the General Parameters list box of Net8 Assistant. Listening Locations is used to determine what host machine addresses the listener will tune in to for connection requests, and therefore is incorrect. Database Services is used to determine the databases this listener will connect users to, while Other Services is used to determine what nondatabase services, such as application servers, the listener will connect users to. **(Topic 3.1)**

**11.** C. listener.ora

**Explanation** Since the default listener name is LISTENER, having your only listener named SPACEMAN means you changed the name of the listener. The way to do so is to set the LISTENER parameter for your listener equal to something in your listener.ora file. Neither the tnsnames.ora nor the sqlnet.ora files will assist in setting the listener name, because these files handle client configuration while the listener resides on the server side. Finally, snmp.ora is used for setting up the Intelligent Agent. **(Topic 3.1)**

**12.** B. Batch

**Explanation** When you issue the LSNRCTL command from the command line, along with the name of the LSNRCTL executable, you are running LSNRCTL in batch. Interactive execution means you issued the executable from the command line only, and are now at a LSNRCTL prompt. Choices C and D are not valid modes of the LSNRCTL operation. **(Topic 3.2)**

**13.** D. The listener you attempted to stop isn't running.

**Explanation** "No listener" messages mean only one thing—there is no listener running by the name of the one you just tried to stop. Choice A is incorrect because there really is no such thing as protected mode when it comes to the listener. Choice B is incorrect because if you didn't supply a password, the errors would state that the addresses associated with that listener didn't recognize the password. You wouldn't receive "no listener" errors if the LSNRCTL and listener versions were incompatible. **(Topic 3.3)**

14.  B.   SERVICES

**Explanation** The SERVICES command gives you information about the connections that were successful and the ones refused for each address. The HELP command lists all LSNRCTL commands and gives basic syntax for each, eliminating choice A. The RELOAD command reloads listener.ora information without stopping the listener, eliminating choice C. The SPAWN command starts another process, such as a dedicated server, eliminating choice D. The STATUS command gives listener version, start time, run duration, trace enabled, and the name of the file used to initialize the listener, but no information about connections accepted and refused, eliminating choice E. **(Topic 3.4)**

15.  C.   Your database is using dedicated servers.

**Explanation** Host naming makes no assumptions about whether you are using MTS or dedicated servers. Choices A, B, and D, however, are all things that host naming does make assumptions about. **(Topic 4.1)**

16.  A.   tnsnames.ora

**Explanation** Whenever local naming is used, all Oracle database host names are stored in the tnsnames.ora file on the client machine. The listener.ora file is used for configuration on the server, eliminating choice C, while sqlnet.ora is used to configure client preferences, eliminating choice B. Choice D is wrong because Net8 Assistant is used to configure client preferences and listener services, but not local client host-name lookup information. Net8 Assistant is used for that purpose. **(Topic 4.2)**

17.  D.   MTS_SERVERS

**Explanation** The number of shared servers running when a database is idle returns to the initial number of servers that are automatically started when the instance starts, and this number of servers is determined by the MTS_SERVERS parameter. Choice C would have been right an hour before, when the database was experiencing a heavy transaction load, because Oracle automatically starts more servers to handle the work in this situation. The PROCESSES and OPEN_CURSORS parameters have no bearing on this discussion. **(Topic 7.3)**

**18.** B.  The database on node DB01, because Oracle attempts local-naming resolution first by default

**Explanation**  Choices A and B both get the part about the database on node DB01 right, but only choice B correctly explains why. When the default name-resolution order is used, Net8 attempts local-name resolution first, followed by Oracle Names, followed by host naming. Thus, Choice C should be eliminated along with choice A. There is no mention of external naming methods in the question, and external naming is only used if you configure it—never by default. **(Topic 4.3)**

**19.** C.  Best for Oracle networks consisting of workgroup configurations

**Explanation**  Workgroup configurations are usually small networks in one local office, and these configurations rarely need more than one Names server. Local naming can even replace Oracle Names if the Names server goes down. All other features listed are ones that regional database repositories are useful for. **(Topic 5.1)**

**20.** A.  Net8 Assistant

**Explanation**  The Net8 Assistant is used for defining the location of your Names server on the Oracle network. LSNRCTL is used for the network listener, as well as for Intelligent Agent, while Oracle Expert is used for tuning. Oracle Enterprise Manager is used as a console for database management activities. **(Topic 5.1)**

**21.** D.  names.ora

**Explanation**  The names.ora file is where information about the Names server configuration is stored. The listener.ora file is used for configuration of the network listener. The tnsnames.ora file is used for local naming resolution on client machines. The snmp.ora file is used for configuring Intelligent Agent. **(Topic 5.1)**

**22.** A.  Run the namesini.sql script.

**Explanation**  After creating the repository owner, you create the repository using the namesini.sql script. You may optionally want to create a special tablespace to hold this repository, but since this wasn't given as a choice, you should forego the option and choose A instead. Choices B and C both indicate Net8 Assistant tasks, but you do not use Net8 Assistant to configure the Names server to use the database repository until after you have created the repository in Oracle. Choice D is not something you would do, because you don't manually modify the names.ora file when you have a GUI that does it for you. **(Topic 5.3)**

**23.** B and D.   NAMESCTL *and* Net8 Assistant

**Explanation**   To start Oracle Names, you can use the Names Control utility (NAMESCTL), or the Net8 Assistant. Oracle Enterprise Manager, Server Manager, and Instance Manager are used for startup and shutdown of the database, while LSNRCTL is used for starting and stopping the Net8 listener process. **(Topic 5.4)**

**24.** A.   REGISTER

**Explanation**   The REGISTER command is used to manually register a service on the Oracle network with your Names server. The REORDER_NS command is used for changing the order of preferred Names servers in Oracle. The VERSION command is used to display the version of the Names server. The LOG_STATS command is used for capturing log statistics, and the SET command is used to define the NAMESCTL session-wide or Names server value for an option. **(Topic 5.2)**

**25.** C.   SET

**Explanation**   Changing the name of the trace file is done by using the SET TRACE_FILE_NAME command, thus making SET the right answer. The REORDER_NS command is used for changing the order of preferred Names servers in Oracle. The VERSION command is used to display the version of the Names server. The SHOW command is used to display the value you set for various options configured with the SET command, such as TRACE_FILE_NAME. The REGISTER command is used to manually register a service on the Oracle network with your Names server. **(Topic 5.1)**

**26.** B, D, and E.   Identifying events occurring on the database, allowing you to take backups of your database remotely, *and* managing SNMP on your database host

**Explanation**   Oracle Intelligent Agent is used to identify events occurring on your database from the OEM console and to manage SNMP on your database host. It does not increase system scalability. Connection pooling and connection concentration are used for that purpose. Intelligent Agent is also not used for stopping and restarting your Oracle database remotely. Server Manager and Instance Manager are used for that purpose. Finally, backups are managed with Backup Manager or Recovery Manager, which can be scheduled as a job using Oracle Enterprise Manager. Intelligent Agent can then give you event status for that job. **(Topic 6.1)**

**27.** C.  LSNRCTL

**Explanation**   LSNRCTL is used to start and stop Intelligent Agent and the network listener. To start Oracle Names, you can use the Names Control utility (NAMESCTL), or the Net8 Assistant. Oracle Enterprise Manager, Server Manager, and Instance Manager are used for startup and shutdown of the database. Net8 Assistant is used to configure and manage network services other than Intelligent Agent. **(Topic 6.2)**

**28.** A, C, and F.   Listeners, dispatchers, *and* shared servers

**Explanation**   Listeners, dispatchers, and shared servers are all part of the multithreaded server architecture in Oracle. Dedicated servers, the DBW0 process, and Names servers are not part of the MTS architecture. **(Topic 7.1)**

**29.** B.  2

**Explanation**   Since MTS_MAX_DISPATCHERS is set to 8, and you already have 6 dispatchers configured, you can add 2 more for DECnet, and that's it. The number of dispatchers configured for each protocol is indicated by the PROTOCOL option for MTS_DISPATCHERS. **(Topic 7.2)**

**30.** B.  50

**Explanation**   In general, you should have one shared server for every 10–20 concurrent users on your database. In this case, 500 divided by 20 would be 25, and 500 divided by 10 is 50. So, since choice B is 50, that must be the right answer. Choices A, C, and D are all far outside the range. Choice A is far too small, while choices C and D are too large. If you are going to run hundreds of shared servers for hundreds of concurrent users, you might as well use dedicated servers. **(Topic 7.3)**

**31.** D.  MTS_DISPATCHERS

**Explanation**   Connection pooling is configured with the POOL option on the INIT.ORA parameter MTS_DISPATCHERS. MTS_MAX_SERVERS is used to define the maximum number of multithreaded servers that may be run on Oracle, while MTS_SERVERS determines how many shared servers will be started when the database is started. MTS_LISTENER_ADDRESS is used to configure listeners on your database. **(Topic 7.5)**

**32.** C.  MTS_DISPATCHERS

**Explanation**   The MULTIPLEX option for MTS_DISPATCHERS is how connection concentration is configured. MTS_SERVERS and MTS_MAX_SERVERS are only used to configure the number of shared servers for your database. The initialization parameter MTS_LISTENER_ADDRESS is used to configure the addresses on your host machine to which listeners will tune in for connections. **(Topic 8.2)**

**33. A.** CMNS

**Explanation** This utility is entirely made-up. The components of Connection Manager include CMCTL, the Connection Manager control utility, CMADM, the Connection Manager administrative utility, and CMGW, the Connection Manager gateway. **(Topic 8.1)**

**34. D.** Returns status of Connection Manager administrative utility only

**Explanation** The command STATUS ADM is used to return status from CMADM. If STATUS by itself was used, you would obtain status for all Connection Manager components, which eliminates choice C. The STATS command is used to obtain statistics for Connection Manager components, eliminating choices A and B. **(Topic 8.1)**

**35. B.** MULTIPLEX

**Explanation** The MULTIPLEX option for MTS_DISPATCHERS is how connection concentration is configured. The PROTOCOL option defines which network protocol this dispatcher works with, while CONCENTRATE is not an actual option for this parameter. The PARTIAL option is not used for this purpose. **(Topic 8.2)**

**36. A.** 1

**Explanation** You need at least two different protocols with listeners tuned to them to have multiprotocol interchange taking place. The actual number of networks handled is entirely dependent on the hardware of the network and the machine hosting Oracle. Only one network does not constitute multiprotocol interchange, however, making choice A the correct answer. **(Topic 8.4)**

**37. D.** cman.ora

**Explanation** Since Connection Manager is used to manage network access control, the CMAN_RULES parameter in cman.ora is used to configure network-access control. The listener is not used for this purpose, so listener.ora is eliminated. Your instance is not used for this purpose, so INIT.ORA must be eliminated, too. The Names server is not involved, so eliminate names.ora. Finally, sqlnet.ora is not used for this purpose either. **(Topic 8.3)**

**38.** D. SUPPORT

**Explanation** SUPPORT-level tracing is the only level of tracing that can be used in conjunction with Trace Assistant processing. USER-level and ADMIN-level tracing cannot be used, nor can no trace level at all. After all, tracing must be enabled in order to obtain a trace file for Trace Assistant to use. **(Topic 9.1)**

**39.** B. LSNRCTL

**Explanation** The LSNRCTL utility is used to restart the listener, which is the source of the problem identified in this question. You know this because the question states you have already set up your listener, thus eliminating the need to use Net8 Assistant to set up the listener, and eliminating choice A along with it. NAMESCTL manages Oracle Names, which is not involved, and CMCTL manages Connection Manager, which also is not involved. **(Topic 9.2)**

**40.** C. Network Session

**Explanation** Recall that the first two letters of every procedure or function listed in the output of a trace file indicates the Net8 network layer component that procedure is called from. In this case, NSPRECV( ) is from the Network Session layer, because the first two letters in the procedure are NS. **(Topic 9.2)**

**41.** D. -s

**Explanation** The -s option is used to obtain statistics, and when used by itself, Trace Assistant will display statistic information from the trace file only. Though the default set of options will include statistics, that won't be the only thing included, so choice E is eliminated. For this same reason, choice C is eliminated as well. Finally, choices A and B should be eliminated because they don't even contain -s. **(Topic 9.3)**

**42.** A. Uses LDAP for authentication

**Explanation** LDAP is not available for authentication with the advanced security option. Instead, advanced security option makes it possible to use third-party authentication services listed for choices B, C, and D. **(Topic 10.2)**

**43.** E. DES_40 encryption will be used

**Explanation** Since both sides will agree to use encryption according to the parameters listed in the question, the only problem becomes which technology to use. The advanced security option determines the answer to this question by finding out which technology is shared between both client and server. In this case, DES 40-bit encryption is the only shared technology, so choice E has to be the answer. **(Topic 10.2)**

Chapter 5: OCP Exam 5: Network Administration  **329**

**44.** B. sqlnet.ora

**Explanation** The parameters for configuring authentication, encryption, and checksums for the advanced security option are all found in sqlnet.ora. The listener is not used in configuring the advanced security option, so choice A is eliminated. Your instance is also not used for this purpose, so INIT.ORA must be eliminated, too. The Names server is not involved, so eliminate names.ora. Connection Manager is not used, so cman.ora is eliminated. Finally, access.ora is not used for this purpose, either, because this configuration file is made-up. **(Topic 10.4)**

**45.** C. AUTHENTICATION_SERVICES

**Explanation** AUTHENTICATION_SERVICES is the parameter used to determine the authentication service used by the advanced security option in the sqlnet.ora file. All the other choices identify parameters used to configure encryption and checksum technology, not authentication. **(Topic 10.4)**

**46.** C. catoctk.sql

**Explanation** The Oracle-supplied packages that come with Oracle Cryptography Toolkit are found in the catoctk.sql script. This script does not get run automatically by catproc.sql, so choice A is incorrect; catalog.sql plays no part in Oracle-supplied packages other than to create the dictionary table into which the PL/SQL source code will be placed, so choice B is incorrect also. Finally, choice D is incorrect because catrexp.sql is used for generating database objects and Oracle-supplied packages for replication. **(Topic 10.3)**

**47.** D. Plain text

**Explanation** TCP/IP transmits packets of information across a network, with the data in each packet stored in unencrypted, plain text format. Thus, any packet sent across a TCP/IP network is in plain view to any user of the network. There is no available security whatsoever, at least not by default. Choices A, B, and C are all incorrect because although they define security methods that you might use to encrypt TCP/IP traffic, none is implemented by default on an Oracle network. **(Topic 10.1)**

**48.** B INIT.ORA

**Explanation** The MTS_LISTENER_ADDRESS parameter in the INIT.ORA file defines the port location to which the MTS listener will tune in for connections to the database running in MTS mode (Review earlier NOTE on obsolescence of this parameter in Oracle8*i*.) The listener.ora file is used for defining where the listener tunes in when dedicated servers are being used, making choice C incorrect. The sqlnet.ora file defines some general characteristics of Net8 on both client and server, but plays no part in defining where the listener tunes in, making choice A incorrect. Finally, tnsnames.ora resides on the client, and is used for mapping a connect string to the appropriate connection descriptor, making choice D incorrect. **(Topic 7.4)**

**49.** A.   snmp_ro.ora

**Explanation**   The ifile parameter, used by Intelligent Agent to identify the location of the configuration file where many key parameters for startup and operation, is found in the snmp_ro.ora file. This file is found in the network/admin directory under the Oracle software home directory. Before taking OCP, it is important that you review the snmp_ro.ora and snmp_rw.ora files to understand their contents. The snmp_rw.ora file is the ifile referenced in snmp_ro.ora, thus making choice B incorrect. There is an snmp.ora file in the network/admin/sample directory, where you can configure some aspects of the Intelligent Agent before starting it for the first time. But, you needn't configure snmp.ora before starting the Intelligent Agent for the first time if you do not plan to have Intelligent Agent update an Oracle Names server. **(Topic 6.3)**

**50.** B.   Returns a memory address where the dedicated server can be found

**Explanation**   The listener will send a memory address back to the user process where the dedicated server can be found. The user process will then connect with the dedicated server and perform whatever work is required. Thus, choice B is correct. Choices A and C are both incorrect because they refer to steps that occur during MTS operation. Since the question specifically discusses dedicated servers, you know that MTS is not in use at this time. Finally, choice D is incorrect. At no time does the listener queue messages for the user process at defined intervals. **(Topic 2.1)**

# CHAPTER 6

## OCP Oracle8*i* Upgrade Exam: New Features for Administrators

OCP Oracle8*i* Upgrade Exam covers issues related to Oracle8*i* new features. To pass this exam, you need to demonstrate an understanding of the new features available in Oracle8*i* for PL/SQL, database administration, backup and recovery, user password management, fine-grained access control, two-dimensional partitioning, and other areas. You will also need to demonstrate an understanding of the special features available in Oracle8*i* for mining redo logs. In more recent editions of the OCP Oracle8*i* Upgrade Exam, the focus has been on use of GUI tools for enterprise database management as well.

## OCP Upgrade Exam Topic Areas

The following topic areas are tested in the OCP Oracle8*i* Upgrade Exam. These topics are taken from the OCP Candidate Guide published by Oracle and are up-to-date as of this printing. You should download the Candidate Guide for the OCP DBA track before taking this exam to ensure these topic areas are still current by accessing the Oracle University Web site at **education.oracle.com/certification**. The topics are as follows:

1. Oracle8*i* New Features
    1.1. Identify which features are new to Oracle8*i*
    1.2. Identify which features are enhanced in Oracle8*i*
    1.3. Describe new and changed features
2. Java in the Database
    2.1. Describe Oracle Java components
    2.2. Describe *i*FS
3. Memory Management
    3.1. Create and manage a large pool
    3.2. Create and manage a segmented buffer cache
4. Optimizer and Query Improvements
    4.1. Describe the features of optimizer plan equivalence and stored plans
    4.2. Describe the contents of the DBMS_STATS stored package
    4.3. Explain top-*N* SQL queries

- **4.4.** Identify new SQL keywords for computing subtotals
- **4.5.** Describe how to use the TRIM function
- **4.6.** Identify new sort processing options

5. Summary Management
    - **5.1.** Explain how to build and manage materialized views
    - **5.2.** Explain how to build and manage summaries
    - **5.3.** Explain how to build and manage dimensions

6. Indexes and Index-Organized Tables
    - **6.1.** Describe the improvements in bitmap indexes
    - **6.2.** Describe the uses for reverse-key indexes
    - **6.3.** Describe a function-based index
    - **6.4.** Explain a descending index
    - **6.5.** Rebuild an index online
    - **6.6.** Compute index statistics
    - **6.7.** Describe an index-organized table (IOT)
    - **6.8.** Create an IOT
    - **6.9.** Explain row overflow in IOTs
    - **6.10.** List IOT and data dictionary information
    - **6.11.** List IOT restrictions
    - **6.12.** Explain logical ROWIDs
    - **6.13.** Create multiple indexes on an IOT

7. Defining Object Relational Features
    - **7.1.** Define an object relational database
    - **7.2.** Describe the object concepts in Oracle8*i*
    - **7.3.** Create a basic object type
    - **7.4.** Create a collection object
    - **7.5.** Create and use an object view

8. Manage Large Objects
    8.1. Compare and contrast LONGs and LOBs
    8.2. Choose the appropriate LOB type
    8.3. Implement Oracle directory objects
    8.4. Create storage for LOB columns
    8.5. Appropriately set PCTVERSION and CHUNK
    8.6. Explain LOB read-consistency issues
9. Basic Partitioning Concepts
    9.1. Describe the benefits of table and index partitioning
    9.2. Describe the general partitioning rules
    9.3. Implement range and hash partitioning
    9.4. Identify parallel DDL statements
    9.5. Describe partitioning locks
10. Partition Maintenance Operations
    10.1. Explain the various commands to support partition management
    10.2. Describe restrictions that apply to certain operations
    10.3. Describe the privileges required for manipulating partitioned tables and indexes
    10.4. Describe data dictionary tables that provide information on partitions
11. Composite Partitioning
    11.1. Implement composite partitioned tables and indexes
    11.2. Maintain composite partitioned tables and indexes
12. Partitioned Index-Organized Tables, LOBs, and Object Types
    12.1. Implement and maintain partitioned tables containing LOBs
    12.2. Implement and maintain partitioned object tables
    12.3. Implement and maintain partitioned tables containing object types
    12.4. Implement and maintain partitioned tables containing VARRAY columns

# Chapter 6: OCP Oracle8i Upgrade Exam: New Features for Administrators

13. Parallel DDL, Parallel DML, and Parallel Queries
    - 13.1. List the supported parallel operations
    - 13.2. Describe the advantages of parallel data manipulation language (PDML)
    - 13.3. Enable parallel DML for a session
    - 13.4. Use hints and the PARALLEL clause to set the degree of parallelism for a DML statement
    - 13.5. Execute a PARALLEL INSERT statement using the direct path mode
    - 13.6. Execute PARALLEL UPDATE and DELETE operations on partitioned tables
    - 13.7. Discuss the restrictions of using parallel DML
    - 13.8. Use the data dictionary views associated with parallel operations
    - 13.9. Describe parallel transaction recovery
    - 13.10. Describe partition-wise joins
    - 13.11. Tune parallel query
14. Installation, Configuration, and Migration
    - 14.1. List the features of the Universal Installer
    - 14.2. List the features of the Software Packager
    - 14.3. Identify the configuration improvements
    - 14.4. Perform silent mode installs
    - 14.5. List the features of the Database Configuration Assistant
    - 14.6. Describe the Installer's use of Optimal Flexible Architecture (OFA)
    - 14.7. Migrate or upgrade a database to Oracle8*i*
15. Tablespace Management
    - 15.1. Discuss extended ROWIDs and tablespace sizing
    - 15.2. Create locally-managed tablespaces
    - 15.3. Create transportable tablespaces
    - 15.4. Use read-only tablespace enhancements

16. Database Resource Manager
    16.1. List the features of the database resource manager
    16.2. Limit the use of resources using the database resource manager
17. Miscellaneous Manageability Features
    17.1. List the new database limits
    17.2. Relocate and reorganize tables
    17.3. Remove unused columns from a table
    17.4. Define temporary tables
    17.5. Identify SQL*Loader enhancements
    17.6. Monitor long-running operations
18. Recovery Manager
    18.1. Describe Recovery Manager features and operations
    18.2. Create a recovery catalog
    18.3. Create and run backup scripts
    18.4. Use Recovery Manager interactively
    18.5. Perform database recovery with RMAN
    18.6. Use RMAN with Enterprise Manager
    18.7. Create reports and lists for backup and recovery management
19. Miscellaneous Availability and Recoverability Features
    19.1. Implement duplexed and multiple archived logs
    19.2. Set up a standby database in sustained recovery mode
    19.3. Start up a database for read operations
    19.4. Describe the functionality of LogMiner
    19.5. Implement fast-start parallel rollback
    19.6. List the features of fast-start parallel rollback
    19.7. Manage corrupt block detection and repair

# Chapter 6: OCP Oracle8i Upgrade Exam: New Features for Administrators **337**

20. Features of Net8
    - **20.1.** Describe the new and enhanced Net8 features in Net8 and the listener
    - **20.2.** Describe the new and enhanced Net8 features in scalability
    - **20.3.** Describe the new and enhanced Net8 features in connectivity
    - **20.4.** Describe the new and enhanced Net8 features in manageability
    - **20.5.** Describe the new and enhanced Net8 features in security
21. SQL*Plus, PL/SQL, and National Language Support
    - **21.1.** Use SQL*Plus for database management
    - **21.2.** Describe the use of PL/SQL for event triggers
    - **21.3.** Describe the use of PL/SQL for external procedures
    - **21.4.** Describe other PL/SQL enhancements
    - **21.5.** Describe the National Language Support enhancements
22. Advanced Queuing
    - **22.1.** List the features used to manage queue tables and queues
    - **22.2.** Start a Queue Monitor process to support message expiration, retry, and delay
    - **22.3.** Start an SNP process to propagate messages
    - **22.4.** Create roles and objects to support AQ
23. Database Security
    - **23.1.** Implement password management
    - **23.2.** Describe invoker's rights security management
    - **23.3.** Implement fine-grained access control
    - **23.4.** Implement application context areas
    - **23.5.** Incorporate LDAP support for global roles
    - **23.6.** Use the Wallet Manager
    - **23.7.** Describe *n*-tier authentication

24. Oracle Enterprise Manager Version 2
    24.1. Describe the new architectural structure of Oracle Enterprise Manager version 2
    24.2. Manage administrators, permissions, and preferred credentials
    24.3. Explain advanced notification
    24.4. Manage groups
    24.5. Describe job enhancements
    24.6. Describe event enhancements
    24.7. Use the DBA Management Pack with or without an Oracle Management Server
    24.8. Describe new features in Instance Manager
    24.9. Explain the Table Data Editor
    24.10. Describe new wizards for backup and data management
25. Constraints
    25.1. Implement new types of constraint checking and enforcement
    25.2. Manage a nonunique index for unique constraints and primary keys

# Practice Exam 1

1. You are configuring your `tnsnames.ora` file for Net8 connectivity to an Oracle8*i* database. Which of the following parameters can be used to replace SID in the CONNECT_DATA area?

    A. SERVICE_NAME

    B. LOCAL_LISTENER

    C. MTS_DISPATCHERS

    D. INSTANCE_NAME

2. You would like to configure load balancing in Net8. Which of the following files will contain settings for this operation, if you have multiple listeners?

    A. sqlnet.ora

    B. init.ora

    C. tnsnames.ora

    D. listener.ora

3. You would like to configure Oracle8*i* to accept non-Net8 connections. Which of the following parameters are used for this purpose?

    A. SERVICE_NAME

    B. MTS_DISPATCHERS

    C. LOCAL_LISTENER

    D. INSTANCE_NAME

4. A server-to-server connection must be established between Oracle8*i* and a Java program. To support this connectivity, you have installed Oracle8*i* Client on the machine running the Java program. Which of the following drivers is most appropriate for this configuration?

    A. JDBC Thin Driver

    B. JDBC OCI

    C. JDBC KPRB

    D. SQLJ

5. You are explaining the Java Virtual Machine architecture to a junior DBA. Which of the following components of JVM is used to permit movement of Java classes into and out of the Oracle8i database?

   A. Library Manager

   B. SQLJ Translator

   C. Bytecode Compiler

   D. Java Class Loader

6. You are developing a Java procedure for storage in the Oracle8i database and loading it using the LOADJAVA utility. Which of the following are required steps for using this function within a SQL statement?

   A. Issuing the CREATE OR REPLACE JAVA statement

   B. Issuing the CREATE FUNCTION AS LANGUAGE JAVA statement

   C. Running the Java source through SQLJ

   D. Compiling the procedure

7. What issue will you encounter if you already have a prior version of Oracle installed on your machine and you want to use the existing Oracle home directory for Oracle8i?

   A. You will need to change ownership of the Oracle software home directory.

   B. You will need to remove the older version of Oracle.

   C. You will need to install Oracle8i to another home directory.

   D. There are no issues with installing Oracle8i to an Oracle software home directory.

8. Which of the following choices identifies the user created by the OEM Management Server for owning the Oracle repository?

   A. OEMADMIN

   B. SYS

   C. SYSTEM

   D. SYSMAN

Chapter 6: OCP Oracle8i Upgrade Exam: New Features for Administrators **341**

9. Which of the following choices best identifies a feature in OEM 2.0 that was not present in OEM 1.6?

   **A.** Pager notification of job status

   **B.** Interprocess dependencies between jobs

   **C.** Email notification of job status

   **D.** Event messaging in OEM console

10. You are managing primary keys in Oracle8i. Which of the following choices best describes the aspect or feature of the Oracle8i database that allows for use of nonunique indexes for a primary key?

    **A.** Constraint deferability

    **B.** Fine-grained access control

    **C.** Materialized views

    **D.** INSTEAD-OF triggers

11. You issue the ALTER TABLESPACE READ ONLY command against an Oracle8i database. Which of the following choices best describes what happens next?

    **A.** Oracle immediately puts the tablespace into read-only mode.

    **B.** Oracle puts the tablespace into read-only mode after the last user logs off.

    **C.** Oracle puts the tablespace into read-only mode after the last prior transaction against that tablespace commits while preventing subsequent DML until the change happens.

    **D.** Oracle returns an error.

12. You are attempting to transport a tablespace from one database to another in Oracle8i. In which two of the following situations is this process not possible?

    **A.** All database indexes and tables in one tablespace

    **B.** Partitions of a table in many tablespaces

    **C.** LOB overflow information stored in a different tablespace from inline LOB data

    **D.** The TRANSPORT_SET_VIOLATIONS view contains no data

    **E.** External BFILE references copied along with tablespace

13. You are using locally managed tablespaces in Oracle8*i*. Which of the following choices best describes the way Oracle implements this feature in the database?

   A. Using a bitmap in the space header segment

   B. Using the data dictionary on the local database

   C. Using a flat file in the local directory storing the datafile

   D. Using the data dictionary in a distributed database

14. You are configuring Oracle's large pool feature. Which of the following choices best describes information that gets stored in the large pool if one is defined for your database?

   A. Parse trees for SQL statements

   B. Session memory for MTS configuration

   C. Session memory for dedicated server configuration

   D. Block buffer overflow

15. You are developing triggers around new trigger types in Oracle. Which of the following new types are not available in Oracle8*i*?

   A. ALTER

   B. DROP

   C. SERVERERROR

   D. IOWAIT

16. You are performing DBA tasks against your Oracle8*i* database. Which of the following tools does Oracle recommend using for this task in Oracle8*i* and later releases of the database software?

   A. SQL*Plus

   B. Server Manager

   C. Storage Manager

   D. Schema Manager

17. You are implementing transaction control in a PL/SQL block. Which of the following choices best describes the use of autonomous transactions in your database?

- A. A developer wants records to be added to an EXIT_STATUS table regardless of whether the transaction completed successfully or not.
- B. Two users on the Oracle database are modifying records in different tables at the same time.
- C. Two users on the Oracle database are modifying different records in the same table at the same time.
- D. Two users on the Oracle database are modifying the same records in the same table at the same time.

18. You are tuning parallel query processing in your Oracle8*i* database. Which two of the following INIT.ORA parameters are set to TRUE if you have the PARALLEL_AUTOMATIC_TUNING parameter set?

    - A. PARALLEL_MAX_INSTANCES
    - B. DEGREE_PARALLELISM
    - C. PARALLEL_ADAPTIVE_MULTI_USER
    - D. PARALLEL_THREADS_PER_CPU

19. You are defining resource management in an Oracle database. Which of the following procedures in DBMS_RESOURCE_MANAGER cannot be performed after you have executed create_plan_directive( ) for your Oracle8*i* database resource plans?

    - A. create_consumer_group( )
    - B. set_initial_consumer_group( )
    - C. submit_pending_area( )
    - D. switch_current_consumer_group( )

20. You are managing performance in the Oracle database through the use of stored plans. Which of the following users will own the objects in which information about groups to which stored plans are members are stored in your database?

    - A. SYS
    - B. OUTLN
    - C. SYSTEM
    - D. DBA

21. You need to generate statistics for a partitioned table in parallel. Which of the following choices best identifies the method you will use in order to perform this operation?

    A. The ANALYZE command

    B. DBMS_RESOURCE_MANAGER

    C. DBMS_STATS

    D. DBMS_ROWID

22. You are optimizing SQL queries through the use of the ORDER BY clause in an inline view. Which of the following types of queries are you most likely attempting to tune?

    A. Star query

    B. Single-row subquery

    C. Multiple-row subquery

    D. Top-N query

23. You need to compute an N-dimensional cross-tabulation in your SQL statement output for reporting purposes. Which of the following Oracle8i clauses can be used for this purpose?

    A. HAVING

    B. CUBE

    C. ROLLUP

    D. TRIM

24. You need to remove a column from a table. Which of the following choices best identifies how to do so if your objective is to quickly execute the task without necessarily freeing up space in your tablespace?

    A. ALTER TABLE DROP COLUMN

    B. ALTER TABLE SET UNUSED COLUMN

    C. ALTER TABLE MODIFY COLUMN

    D. TRUNCATE TABLE

25. When generating temporary tables, which of the following places in your Oracle database is the actual data used by your temporary table stored in?

    A. PGA

    B. Buffer cache

    C. SYSTEM tablespace

    D. RBS tablespace

26. You are using SQL*Loader to insert data into your database quickly. Which of the following features allows you to define a row of data in your datafile to begin at a point other than the beginning of a line?

    A. FIELDS SEPARATED BY

    B. FIELDS TERMINATED BY

    C. TRAILING NULLCOLS

    D. RECSEPARATOR

27. You are rebuilding indexes in Oracle8*i*. Which of the following activities cannot be combined with rebuilding your index in an Oracle8*i* database, but must instead be performed as a separate operation?

    A. Estimate statistics

    B. Compute statistics

    C. Move index to another tablespace

    D. Rebuilding online

28. Your application issues the following query: SELECT * FROM EMP WHERE SALARY/5 = 2000. Which of the following choices best explains a way to enhance performance of this query?

    A. Performance of this query cannot be enhanced.

    B. Performance can be enhanced using a bitmap index.

    C. Performance can be enhanced using a descending index.

    D. Performance can be enhanced using a function-based index.

29. You have already created an index-organized table, but need to enhance performance on a column that is not part of the composite index organizing the table. Which of the following choices best describes your options in this situation?

    A. No indexes can be created on an IOT.

    B. Only B-tree indexes can be created on an IOT.

    C. Only standard B-tree and bitmap indexes can be created on an IOT.

    D. All B-tree variants and bitmap indexes can be created on an IOT.

30. Which of the following choices places Oracle database files in danger of being tampered with via users of your database?

    A. Materialized views with the same data as an underlying dictionary table

    B. Directory objects in Oracle for directories containing database files

    C. BFILE objects in separate file systems from the database

    D. PL/SQL objects packaged using the wrapper utility

31. You are implementing hash partitioning in Oracle8*i*. If you are following appropriate partitioning conventions, how many partitions would you allocate for a table in order to ensure smooth distribution of data between partitions?

    A. 8

    B. 9

    C. 10

    D. 11

32. You are managing partitioned tables and indexes. Which of the following statements will not render an associated index invalid when issued against a partitioned table in your database?

    A. ALTER TABLE RENAME PARTITION

    B. ALTER TABLE SPLIT PARTITION

    C. ALTER TABLE DROP PARTITION

    D. ALTER TABLE MOVE PARTITION

Chapter 6: OCP Oracle8*i* Upgrade Exam: New Features for Administrators **347**

33. You are managing a partitioned table that has composite partitions in Oracle8*i*. Which of the following choices identifies the keyword you must use in order to manage composite partitions in DDL operations?

    A. COMPOSITE

    B. LEAF

    C. SUBPARTITION

    D. PARTNUM

34. You are managing a data warehouse in Oracle. Which of the following choices best describes composite partitioning of objects in Oracle8*i*?

    A. Matching index partitions to their associated table partitions

    B. Partition by range and hash functions

    C. Partition by a value, such as a date or number

    D. Allowing Oracle to perform all partition management transparently

35. You wish to use parallel processing in your Oracle8*i* database. Which of the following choices identifies a feature that parallel DML offers to users of Oracle8*i* applications? (Choose three)

    A. Reduced memory requirements

    B. Enhanced performance for insert operations

    C. Reduced demand on developers to configure multisession transactions

    D. Automatic degree parallelism definition based on available instances

36. You are developing an application against an Oracle8*i* database. Which of the following hints can be used to improve performance on your UPDATE statement so that more than one I/O process is used?

    A. /*+STAR */

    B. /*+INSERT */

    C. /*+APPEND */

    D. /*+PARALLEL */

**37.** Which of the following dictionary views contains a column that will tell you whether parallel DML is enabled for the session?

  **A.** V$SESSION

  **B.** V$SESSTAT

  **C.** V$SYSTEM

  **D.** V$PX_SESSTAT

**38.** An IOT is created using the following syntax:
```
CREATE TABLE prglang_keywords
(keyword VARCHAR2(30) PRIMARY KEY,
page_number NUMBER(10))
ORGANIZATION INDEX
PCTTHRESHOLD 25
PARTITION BY RANGE(keyword)
(PARTITION PK1 VALUES LESS THAN('GET')
TABLESPACE DATA_1,
PARTITION PK2 VALUES LESS THAN('PUT')
TABLESPACE DATA_2,
PARTITION PK3 VALUES LESS THAN('STRING')
TABLESPACE DATA_3,
PARTITION PK4 VALUES LESS THAN(MAXVALUE))
TABLESPACE IOT_1;
```

If no tablespace is defined for partition PK4, where does Oracle8*i* place the partition?

  **A.** DATA_1

  **B.** DATA_2

  **C.** DATA_3

  **D.** IOT_1

**39.** You are partitioning an object table in Oracle8*i*. Which of the following choices correctly describes a restriction you must adhere to when partitioning an object table in Oracle8*i*?

  **A.** All partitions must be stored in the same tablespace.

  **B.** No partition should be stored in the same tablespace.

  **C.** Your range partition should be on a scalar-type column.

  **D.** Your composite partition should be on nested table columns only.

**Chapter 6: OCP Oracle8i Upgrade Exam: New Features for Administrators** **349**

40. You are defining IOTs in Oracle8*i*. Which of the following choices best describes how Oracle governs the storage of IOT data in an overflow tablespace?

    A. Anything over 4,000 bytes

    B. Value for CHUNK

    C. Value for PCTTHRESHOLD

    D. Value for IOT_OVERFLOW

41. You are creating IOTs in Oracle8*i*. Which of the following choices does not identify a restriction against IOTs that you must adhere to?

    A. No indexes on the IOT other than primary key

    B. No unique constraints on the IOT other than primary key

    C. No LONG columns in an IOT

    D. No replication of an IOT

42. You want to maintain multiple archive log destinations in Oracle8*i*. Which of the following parameters can be used to indicate how many ARCH processes Oracle8*i* needs to run in order to manage storage of archive logs to multiple destinations?

    A. LOG_ARCHIVE_PROCESSES

    B. LOG_ARCHIVE_MAX_PROCESSES

    C. LOG_ARCHIVE_MIN_SUCCEED_DEST

    D. LOG_ARCHIVE_START

43. You are using LogMiner within Oracle8*i*. Which of the following choices identifies the INIT.ORA parameter that defines the location where you can find output from this tool?

    A. UTL_FILE_DIR

    B. BACKGROUND_DUMP_DEST

    C. LOG_ARCHIVE_DEST

    D. USER_DUMP_DEST

44. You need to fix corrupted data blocks in an Oracle8*i* database, release 8.1.5. Which of the following choices identifies a way that you can fix corruption in a database block?

    A. DB_BLOCK_CHECKING

    B. DBVERIFY

    C. DBMS_REPAIR

    D. None of the above

45. You are implementing standby database functionality in Oracle8*i*. Which of the following choices identifies the parameter that can be specified in order to identify to the standby database where it can find redo logs to apply during sustained recovery?

    A. LOG_ARCHIVE_DEST

    B. LOG_ARCHIVE_DUPLEX_DEST

    C. STANDBY_ARCHIVE_DEST

    D. LOG_ARCHIVE_MIN_SUCCEED_DEST

46. You need to improve recovery time for your Oracle8*i* database. Which of the following choices identifies how to specify bounded instance recovery time by allowing SMON to instantiate parallel I/O slaves for better rollback performance after fast warmstart?

    A. FAST_START_PARALLEL_ROLLBACK

    B. LOG_CHECKPOINT_INTERVAL

    C. LOG_CHECKPOINT_TIMEOUT

    D. FAST_START_IO_TARGET

47. You are managing your Net8 listener in Oracle8*i*. Which of the following choices identifies a way that Oracle8*i* Database Configuration Assistant notifies the listener of new databases created on the machine hosting the Oracle databases that the listener should be listening for?

    A. Automatically

    B. Via Net8 Assistant

    C. Via Net8 Easy Config

    D. Via Server Manager

48. You are using OEM 2.0 to manage your Oracle database. Which of the following tools replaces SQL*Worksheet as the method used for issuing SQL directly against your database?

    A. OEM Console

    B. Instance Manager

    C. Table Data Editor

    D. Recovery Manager

49. You are using summaries in the Oracle8*i* database for data warehousing. Which of the following clauses is implicitly added by Oracle8*i* to queries in order to take advantage of summary management?

    A. ORDER BY

    B. GROUP BY

    C. CUBE

    D. ROLLUP

50. You are managing a data warehouse using Oracle8*i*. Which of the following choices identifies a key aspect of dimension creation that must be addressed when the dimension is created?

    A. CUBE operation

    B. ROLLUP operation

    C. Summary management

    D. Level hierarchy

51. You are attempting to create an object table in Oracle's object-relational paradigm. Which of the following choices identifies the step that must take place first in doing so?

    A. Issue CREATE TABLE command

    B. Issue CREATE TYPE command

    C. Create an INSTEAD-OF trigger

    D. Install the Java Option

52. You need to define a collection type for student exam records in an Oracle8*i* database. Each record will consist of student vital information, along with the answers each student gave on every exam they took in the class. You want the ability to reference specific questions on exams for individual students for comparison purposes. Which of the following choices identifies the best way to do it?

    A. Scalar datatypes

    B. User-defined type

    C. VARRAY

    D. Nested table

53. You are starting a standby of your Oracle8*i* database for reporting access. Which of the following choices identifies the database opening command you might use for doing so?

    A. OPEN

    B. FORCE

    C. READ ONLY

    D. RESTRICT

54. You want to rebuild an index for a heavily used table within an online transaction processing application. Which of the following choices identifies the way to do so in Oracle8*i*?

    A. Schedule downtime with users and perform when users aren't around

    B. Copy the table somewhere else and create a synonym to point users to the copy

    C. Use an index-organized journal table

    D. Start the database in restricted mode to rebuild without interference

55. You are indexing Oracle data in an application. The index will be on a column containing sequential numbers with at least seven significant digits. Most, if not all, entries will start with 1. Which of the following indexes would be best suited for the task?

    A. B-tree indexes

    B. Reverse-key indexes

C. Bitmap indexes

D. Descending indexes

**56.** You have installed Oracle8*i* and used the Database Configuration Assistant to create a database in a Windows environment. Where would you find the datafiles for your database that you just created?

A. %ORACLE_BASE%\admin

B. %ORACLE_BASE%\rdbms\admin

C. %ORACLE_BASE%\database

D. %ORACLE_BASE%\oradata

**57.** You need to store a large block of text data in Oracle. These text blocks will be around 3,500 characters in length. Which datatype would you use for storing these large objects?

A. VARCHAR2

B. CLOB

C. BLOB

D. BFILE

**58.** You need to modify partitions associated with a table. Which of the following permissions are required if you are not the owner of the partition?

A. ALTER ANY TABLE

B. ALTER ANY PARTITION

C. ALTER ANY INDEX

D. ALTER ANY OBJECT

**59.** You need to be able to administer message passing using the Advanced Queuing feature in your Oracle8*i* database. Which of the following roles must be granted to you?

A. SELECT_CATALOG_ROLE

B. DBA

C. AQ_USER_ROLE

D. AQ_TM_PROCESSES

60. You are configuring your tnsnames.ora file for accessing Oracle Parallel Server. Which two of the following choices identify items you can configure in that file in order to allow Net8 to handle access to OPS instances transparently to the application?

   A. PROTOCOL
   B. LOAD_BALANCE
   C. FAILOVER
   D. SERVICE_NAME
   E. HOST
   F. PORT

# Practice Exam 2

1. **Two users exist on an Oracle8*i* system, named FLUFFY and MUFFY. MUFFY owns a PL/SQL procedure called FOOBAR( ), defined as follows:**

   ```
   create procedure FOOBAR
   authid current_user
   is
    var1 number;
   begin
    select * into var1 from foo;
   end;
   ```

   **To use procedure FOOBAR( ), what privileges does FLUFFY need granted to her (choose as many as appropriate)?**

   **A.** CREATE PROCEDURE on schema MUFFY

   **B.** EXECUTE on procedure FOOBAR

   **C.** UPDATE on table FOO

   **D.** SELECT on table FOO

2. **You issue the following statement on an Oracle8*i* database where DB_BLOCK_SIZE is 4K:**

   ```
   CREATE TABLESPACE orgdbindex
   DATAFILE '/oracle/disk_8/index01.dbf'
   SIZE 300M
   EXTENT MANAGEMENT LOCAL
   UNIFORM SIZE 100K
   ONLINE;
   ```

   **How many blocks will each bit represent in the bitmap area of the locally managed datafiles?**

   **A.** 25

   **B.** 50

   **C.** 80

   **D.** 250

3. You are using the Universal Installer and Packager to install Oracle8*i* on a server that already hosts an Oracle7 database. Which of the following should not be performed when installing Oracle8*i* on a machine already hosting earlier editions of the Oracle database?

   A. Shut down the network listener.

   B. Shut down the database.

   C. Make a backup of existing databases.

   D. Install Oracle8*i* software to the same directory used for Oracle7 software.

4. You are reconfiguring your INIT.ORA parameter file to upgrade to Oracle8*i*. Which of the following parameters will cause problems if it is not removed?

   A. DB_NAME

   B. JOB_QUEUE_INTERVAL

   C. CONTROL_FILE_RECORD_KEEP_TIME

   D. DB_BLOCK_LRU_EXTENDED_STATISTICS

   E. CHECKPOINT_PROCESS

5. Your DBA team has one person assigned to manage a particular backup job and three people who need to know the job completed. If OMS is employed in conjunction with Enterprise Manager 2.0, what permission level is required for users who need to know about the job completion?

   A. None

   B. View

   C. Modify

   D. Full

   E. Notify

6. You wish to transport a tablespace from one database to another in Oracle8*i*. Which of the following tasks is not required for doing so?

   A. Making the tablespace status read-only

   B. Transferring datafiles to the target machine

   C. Offloading row data from objects in the tablespace using EXPORT

   D. Loading tablespace information into the target-database data dictionary using IMPORT

   E. Running the DBMS_TTS.transport_set_check( ) procedure

7. You want to specify fine-grained access control on a database object. Which two of the following tasks are not required for doing so?

   A. Issuing the CREATE CONTEXT statement

   B. Developing a security package

   C. Executing the DBMS_RLS.add_policy( ) procedure

   D. Building explicit calls to fine-grained access control in your application

8. You are assessing the impact of migrating an Oracle7 application to Oracle8*i*. Which of the following is not a difference between extended and restricted ROWID formats in Oracle8*i*?

   A. Extended ROWID format permits duplicate datafile numbers in the database, while restricted ROWID format does not.

   B. Extended ROWID format identifies the row location in each block, while restricted ROWID format does not.

   C. Extended ROWID format contains a unique identifier for the database object, while restricted ROWID format does not.

   D. Extended ROWID format is base-64, while restricted ROWID format is base-16.

9. You are implementing fine-grained access control in your Oracle database. Which of the following best describes the use of sys_context( ) in this context?

   A. Obtains information about application context for security enforcement

   B. Sets information about application context for security enforcement

   C. Indicates whether invoker's or owner's rights should be used to execute security enforcement

   D. Implements *n*-tier authentication in Oracle8*i*

10. You are designing a migration strategy for your Oracle8 version 8.0.3 database to Oracle8*i*. Which of the following scripts would be involved in this task?

    A. u0800060.sql

    B. u0800050.sql

    C. u0800040.sql

    D. u0800030.sql

11. You are using OEM 2.0 in conjunction with the OMS. Which of the following is not a feature or benefit for using this three-tier architecture?

    A. Ability to administer only one database at a time

    B. Using your Web browser to administer Oracle8*i*

    C. Centralized management of repository information

    D. Shared administrative responsibility modeled within OEM

12. You are trying to determine which tablespaces have been transported from one Oracle8*i* database into this database. Which of the following columns in the dictionary view DBA_TABLESPACES can help?

    A. PLUGGED_IN

    B. CONTENTS

    C. LOGGING

    D. STATUS

13. You have assigned three tables to the keep pool. How should you determine the appropriate size for your keep pool?

    A. Based on the size of your shared pool

    B. Based on the number of blocks in the table only

    C. Based on the number of blocks in the table plus blocks in associated indexes

    D. Based on the number of blocks in associated indexes only

    E. None of the above

14. You need to store fixed-width text data that is 20 characters long. You want to ensure that when the data to be stored in this column is less than 20 characters, Oracle8*i* pads to 20 characters with blanks. Which of the following datatypes is best for this purpose?

    A. NCHAR(20)

    B. NVARCHAR2(20)

    C. CHAR(20)

    D. VARCHAR2(20)

15. A DBA in Germany needs to ensure that both the German mark and the euro will be supported in the latest currency conversion application. Which of the following NLS parameters will work best for this purpose?

    A. NLS_TERRITORY

    B. NLS_LANG

    C. NLS_COMP

    D. NLS_DUAL_CURRENCY

16. Your developers want to use C sort routines in their server-side packages. Which of the following files must contain support for this functionality using the EXTPROC_CONNECTION_DATA parameter?

    A. listener.ora

    B. tnsnames.ora

    C. sqlnet.ora

    D. init.ora

17. User MILTON issues the following code block in his SQL*Plus session:

    ```
    CREATE OR REPLACE PROCEDURE upd_tran
    ( PVAL1 IN VARCHAR2) IS
      PRAGMA AUTONOMOUS_TRANSACTION;
      MY_VAL2 NUMBER(10);
    BEGIN
      SELECT COL_1 INTO MY_VAL2
      FROM TAB_2 WHERE COL_2 = PVAL1;
      UPDATE TAB_1 SET COL_1 = PVAL1
      WHERE COL_2 = PVAL2;
      COMMIT;
    END;
    ```

    Later, another procedure called my_tran( ) is defined by user GOETHE, which calls upd_tran( ) as part of an application. Which of the following statements is true about this application?

    A. Any transaction in progress in my_tran( ) when upd_tran( ) is called will be committed when upd_tran( ) completes.

    B. Any uncommitted changes made to table TAB_2 by my_tran( ) will not be seen by upd_tran( ).

**C.** Procedure upd_tran( ) has no problem updating TAB_1 if my_tran( ) has already done so without issuing a commit before the call to upd_tran( ).

**D.** User GOETHE needs to have update privileges on TAB_1 to execute procedure upd_tran( ).

18. You are about to begin parallel-query tuning. Which of the following INIT.ORA parameters is used to specify default values for the other two?

    **A.** PARALLEL_ADAPTIVE_MULTI_USER

    **B.** PARALLEL_THREADS_PER_CPU

    **C.** PARALLEL_AUTOMATIC_TUNING

19. Consumer group EXECUTIVES needs to have highest priority whenever it issues a query against the data warehouse application. The DBA wants to use a plan called WHSE_PLAN to manage resource allocation. Several other groups exist on the database, two of which are MANAGERS and ANALYSTS. In order for the DBA to delegate configuration of this to user JOE, which of the following procedures will be used?

    **A.** create_consumer_group( )

    **B.** create_plan_directive( )

    **C.** create_plan( )

    **D.** grant_system_privilege( )

20. After putting a database-resource-management configuration in place at lunch time, the DBA gets a call from user BUXTON, who is irate that the same query that ran in less than 1 second this morning now takes over 2 minutes. To see if the issue is BUXTON's consumer group, which of the following views is appropriate?

    **A.** DBA_RSRC_CONSUMER_GROUPS

    **B.** V$RSRC_PLAN

    **C.** DBA_RSRC_PLANS

    **D.** V$RSRC_CONSUMER_GROUP

21. You notice that there are over 200 stored outlines on your database, and you want to get rid of the ones that have never been used. Which of the following packages contains procedures you can use for this purpose?

    **A.** DBMS_STATS

    **B.** DBMS_RESOURCE_MANAGER

C. DBMS_OLAP

D. OUTLN_PKG

22. A materialized view is created that will always be refreshed fully every hour. After creation, the materialized view remains unpopulated until the first refresh. Which of the following refresh and build clauses accomplishes all these goals?

    A. BUILD IMMEDIATE REFRESH FAST ON COMMIT

    B. BUILD DEFERRED REFRESH COMPLETE NEXT SYSDATE + 1/24

    C. BUILD DEFERRED REFRESH COMPLETE ON DEMAND

    D. BUILD IMMEDIATE REFRESH FORCE NEXT SYSDATE + 1/4096

23. The user attempts to insert data into a column that would violate a nondeferrable constraint. The user has issued the ALTER SESSION SET CONSTRAINTS = DEFERRED statement. What happens on INSERT?

    A. The INSERT succeeds at the time it is issued, but the transaction will roll back later.

    B. The INSERT fails at the time it is issued and the transaction will end.

    C. The INSERT succeeds at the time it is issued and the transaction will not roll back later.

    D. The INSERT fails at the time it is issued, but the transaction will continue.

24. The value stored in an index for a column is '596849'. The DBA then issues the ALTER INDEX REVERSE statement. What does the data in the index now look like?

    A. '596849'

    B. '849596'

    C. '948695'

    D. '695948'

25. The best choice for decreasing size requirements for tables that need only be accessed via the primary key is which of the following?

    A. Create more indexes on the table.

    B. Create an index-organized table to store the data.

C. Drop the primary key.

D. Increase the PCTFREE value set for table blocks.

26. The DBA creates a directory object specifying a path name that doesn't currently exist on the file system. She or he should expect to receive an error when?

    A. The CREATE OR REPLACE DIRECTORY statement is executed.

    B. The CREATE OR REPLACE DIRECTORY statement is committed.

    C. The BFILE object is created.

    D. The BFILE object is accessed.

27. The number of blocks that comprise a chunk is defined by which of the following?

    A. The DB_CHUNK_SIZE initialization parameter

    B. The CHUNK clause used in the LOB storage definition

    C. The CREATE TABLESPACE statement

    D. The CREATE DATAFILE statement

28. The two components of a large object are which of the items listed?

    A. Value and type

    B. Value and locator

    C. Type and locator

    D. Value and control

29. The DBA should not define a directory object on a directory in the file system containing which files?

    A. Oracle datafiles

    B. Operating system utilities

    C. Word processing software

    D. Web pages

30. The DBA creates a table containing two LOB columns: a BLOB and a CLOB. What is the maximum number of tablespaces that contain data for this table?

    A. 2

    B. 3

C. 5

D. 7

31. Which of the following statements do *not* describe features of the VARRAY type? (Choose three)

    A. VARRAY allows indexes on attributes.

    B. VARRAY limits the number of elements placed in the object.

    C. VARRAY stores data in segments separate from the main object.

    D. VARRAY stores all data over 4K inline.

32. The user attempts the following INSERT statement on the EMPLOYEES relational table defined with the ADDRESS_TYPE object type: INSERT INTO EMPLOYEES VALUES('30493','405 RIVER STREET', 'BARNES','OK','12345'). Which of the following reasons is most likely why the statement fails?

    A. The ADDRESS_TYPE constructor was not used.

    B. The column values specified are out of order.

    C. The VALUES keyword is incorrectly placed.

    D. Object data cannot be inserted into a relational table.

33. When an attribute of an object is defined with the REF type, what data is actually stored in the attribute?

    A. The original data

    B. A copy of the data

    C. A pointer to the data

    D. A pointer to the copy of the data

34. The DBA chooses to allow the use of objects on relational tables in an Oracle8 database. To ease the migration effort, which of the following things might the DBA create?

    A. Object views and INSTEAD OF triggers

    B. Scalar types and index-organized tables

    C. Reverse-key indexes and table partitions

    D. None of the above

**35.** The most likely cause for a local index partition to be in the INDEX UNUSABLE state is which of the following?

    **A.** A user deleted one row from the table partition.

    **B.** The DBA issued an ALTER TABLE ADD PARTITION statement.

    **C.** The DBA issued an ALTER INDEX REBUILD PARTITION statement.

    **D.** The DBA issued an ALTER TABLE TRUNCATE PARTITION statement.

**36.** Which of the following operations should the DBA execute to load data into ten partitions of a table simultaneously?

    **A.** Execute SQL*Loader ten times in parallel.

    **B.** Execute SQL*Loader once with the parameter DEGREE=10.

    **C.** Execute SQL*Loader once with the parameter PARALLEL=TRUE.

    **D.** Execute SQL*Loader five times with the parameter INSTANCES=2.

**37.** The DBA creates a table called EXPENSES whose partition key is the EXPENSE_DATE column. The partitions are called EXP_JUNE, EXP_JULY, EXP_AUGUST, and EXP_SEPTEMBER. The DBA then drops the first partition, covering the month of June. Later, a user adds a row to the table with the EXPENSE_DATE column equal to '15-JUN-1999'. To which partition is the row added?

    **A.** EXP_JULY

    **B.** EXP_AUGUST

    **C.** EXP_SEPTEMBER

    **D.** None. The partition-key value is out of range.

**38.** Which of the following is not a benefit of partitioning?

    **A.** Partition independence

    **B.** Greater data availability

    **C.** Inability to access one partition when another is unavailable

    **D.** Scalable performance with data growth

**39.** Which of the following are not partitioned indexes available in Oracle? (Choose two)

    **A.** Global prefixed indexes

**B.** Global nonprefixed indexes

**C.** Local prefixed indexes

**D.** Global equipartitioned indexes

40. The EXPENSES table uses a partition key called EXPENSE_DATE of datatype DATE, representing the date the sale was entered. The DBA splits the EXP_JULY partition of the SALES table into two partitions, EXP_JULY1-15 and EXP_JULY16-31. All rows in the EXP_JULY partition had a value greater than July 17 for the partition key. Which of the following statements is *true* regarding the local prefixed indexes produced by the table-partition split?

    **A.** EXP_JULY1-15 will be unusable, but EXP_JULY16-31 will be valid.

    **B.** Both EXP_JULY1-15 and EXP_JULY16-31 will be valid.

    **C.** Both EXP_JULY1-15 and EXP_JULY16-31 will be unusable.

    **D.** EXP_JULY1-15 will be valid, but EXP_JULY16-31 will be unusable.

41. The DBA wants to eliminate partition X1 from table EMPLOYEES. If partition X1 contains 65 percent of the rows for the table and there are global indexes on the table, what is the fastest way for the DBA to eliminate partition X1 and make the global indexes available for use again?

    **A.** Merge the partition, rebuild the index

    **B.** Drop the partition, rebuild the index

    **C.** Delete all rows from the partition, drop the partition, rebuild the index

    **D.** Split the partition, drop the partition, rebuild the index

42. Which statement can be used to move partition X1 on table EXPENSES from tablespace DATA_01 to tablespace DATA_05?

    **A.** ALTER TABLE EXPENSES MODIFY PARTITION X1 FROM DATA_01 TO DATA_05;

    **B.** ALTER TABLE EXPENSES RENAME PARTITION X1 TO DATA_05;

    **C.** ALTER TABLE EXPENSES MOVE PARTITION X1 TABLESPACE DATA_05;

    **D.** ALTER TABLE EXPENSES DROP PARTITION X1 INTO DATA_05;

43. If the DBA wants to determine the partition key for a table, which of the following dictionary views can be used?

    A. DBA_PART_TABLES

    B. DBA_TAB_HISTOGRAMS

    C. DBA_TAB_COLUMNS

    D. DBA_TAB_COL_STATISTICS

44. To execute parallel DML on the Oracle database, the DBA must do which of the following?

    A. Specify PARALLEL clauses in the CREATE TABLE statement

    B. Execute the ALTER TABLE *NAME* NOLOGGING statement

    C. Execute the ALTER SESSION ENABLE PARALLELL DML statement

    D. COMMIT the transaction

45. An UPDATE statement on a partitioned table will parallelize by which of the following?

    A. PARTITIONS

    B. ROWID RANGES

    C. SLAVE I/O PROCESSES

    D. THE /*+APPEND */ HINT

46. Which of the following can parallel DML not operate on? (Choose three)

    A. Range partitioned tables

    B. Index-organized tables

    C. Clustered tables

    D. Tables containing object types

47. Finish the following statement: "The ALLOCATE CHANNEL command used in conjunction with COPY must ___."

    A. Name the resource explicitly

    B. Use the DISK clause

    C. Use the FOR DELETE clause

    D. Be run after the COPY is complete

**48.** Which of the following maintenance operations should the DBA run after adding a datafile?

   **A.** REGISTER DATABASE

   **B.** RESET DATABASE

   **C.** CATALOG

   **D.** RESYNC CATALOG

**49.** A full backup consists of which of the following elements?

   **A.** All blocks in a datafile except unused blocks

   **B.** Changed blocks in a datafile

   **C.** All datafiles in the database

   **D.** Changed datafiles in the database

**50.** In the absence of the recovery catalog, where can RMAN find most of the information it needs?

   **A.** Backup sets

   **B.** Datafiles

   **C.** Password file

   **D.** Control file

**51.** The DBA issues the ALTER DATABASE BACKUP CONTROLFILE TO '/DISK1/ORACLE/HOME/DBCONTROL.CTL' statement. What can the DBA do to use this control-file backup in conjunction with RMAN?

   **A.** Issue the CATALOG command.

   **B.** Copy the file to tape.

   **C.** Issue the COPY command.

   **D.** Nothing. The control-file backup can be used as is.

**52.** What effect does setting CONTROL_FILE_RECORD_KEEP_TIME to 0 have?

   **A.** Forces Oracle8 to keep no information for RMAN

   **B.** Decreases backup and recovery performance

   **C.** Limits growth of the control-file size

   **D.** Has no effect on control-file size

**53.** The DBA identifies that the backups necessary for media recovery are on tape. What command should be executed first to perform the recovery?

   **A.** COPY

   **B.** SWITCH

   **C.** ALLOCATE CHANNEL

   **D.** RESTORE

**54.** Once the DBA defines attributes in a RUN command, how long will they be defined?

   **A.** Permanently

   **B.** For the duration of the instance

   **C.** For the duration of the session

   **D.** For the duration of the RUN command

**55.** By default, how many errors will occur in a RUN command before RMAN terminates?

   **A.** 1

   **B.** 5

   **C.** 25

   **D.** Operating-system specific

**56.** The DBA completes incomplete recovery to a system change number and then opens the database. What recovery-catalog maintenance command must be executed?

   **A.** REGISTER DATABASE

   **B.** RESET DATABASE

   **C.** RESYNC CATALOG

   **D.** CHANGE DATABASE

**57.** Which command can the DBA issue to determine which datafiles in the database are in the most serious need of backup?

   **A.** REPORT UNRECOVERABLE

   **B.** REPORT NEED BACKUP

- **C.** LIST INCARNATION
- **D.** LIST COPY OF DATAFILE

58. **Which of the following best describes multiplexing in backup sets?**
    - **A.** One archive log in one backup set with file blocks stored contiguously
    - **B.** Multiple control files in one backup set with file blocks for each stored noncontiguously
    - **C.** Multiple datafiles in one backup set with file blocks for each stored noncontiguously
    - **D.** One datafile in multiple backup sets with file blocks stored contiguously

59. **The DBA has run the `start_time_manager( )` process, but several of the expiration features in queuing still don't work. Which of the following may solve the problem?**
    - **A.** The DBMS_LOB package hasn't been created.
    - **B.** The AQ_TM_PROCESSES initialization parameter hasn't been set.
    - **C.** The DBA ran the grant_type_access( ) procedure.
    - **D.** Queuing is not available in Oracle8.

60. **What parameter is used to carry a message into the queue with the `enqueue( )` procedure?**
    - **A.** message
    - **B.** msgid
    - **C.** queue_data
    - **D.** payload

# Answers to Practice Exam 1

**1. A.** SERVICE_NAME

**Explanation** The SERVICE_NAME parameter is used to replace SID in your `tnsnames.ora` file for Oracle8i. Choices B, C, and D all identify `init.ora` parameters used in Oracle8i for enhanced networking and connectivity. **(Topic 20.1)**

**2. C.** tnsnames.ora

**Explanation** To configure load balancing, the LOAD_BALANCE parameter must be set in the `tnsnames.ora` file. The `sqlnet.ora` file is not used, nor is `init.ora`, nor is `listener.ora`. Review the explanation of load balancing in the chapter for more information about the use of `tnsnames.ora` for this purpose. **(Topic 20.2)**

**3. B.** MTS_DISPATCHERS

**Explanation** To set up connectivity to Oracle8i without Net8, a dispatcher must be configured that handles GIOP or IIOP protocol connectivity. This is accomplished using the MTS_DISPATCHERS parameter in your `init.ora` file. Although choices C and D identify INIT.ORA parameters in Oracle8i, these are not the parameters used to configure dispatchers. Choice A, SERVICE_NAME, is incorrect because this is a `tnsnames.ora` parameter. **(Topic 20.3)**

**4. B.** JDBC OCI

**Explanation** When you install the Oracle8i Client OCI software on the machine running the client or server software, server-to-server or robust client connectivity is handled using JDBC OCI. JDBC Thin is for Web browsers calling Oracle8i, eliminating choice A. JDBC KPRB is used for Java stored procedures in the Oracle8i database, eliminating choice C. SQLJ is a Java precompiler, not a JDBC driver, eliminating choice D. **(Topic 2.1)**

**5. D.** Java Class Loader

**Explanation** The Java Class Loader is the utility used for loading Java classes into Oracle8i. Library Manager is used to manage Java libraries, eliminating choice A. The SQLJ Translator is used for embedding SQL into Java, eliminating choice B. The Bytecode Compiler is used for converting Java source code into executable classes, eliminating choice C. **(Topic 2.1)**

**6.** B. Issuing the CREATE FUNCTION AS LANGUAGE JAVA statement

**Explanation** The CREATE FUNCTION AS LANGUAGE JAVA statement is used to publish a Java stored procedure so that it can be used in SQL and PL/SQL. The statement in choice A is used to actually create the Java stored procedure, not publish it. The rest of the statements require you to understand that LOADJAVA only loads compiled Java code. If the Java is not compiled, you should use the statement in choice A to compile it. The use of SQLJ is not required for stored procedures that are already compiled, eliminating choice C. Finally, since the procedure is already compiled before you load it into Oracle8*i* using LOADJAVA—you do not need to compile it again—eliminating choice D. **(Topic 2.1)**

**7.** C. You will need to install Oracle8*i* to another home directory.

**Explanation** Oracle8*i* comes with the new Universal Installer and Packager, which requires that you install Oracle to a new home directory. There is no way to install Oracle using Universal Installer and Packager to an Oracle home directory to which the old Oracle Installer installed Oracle prior. Changing software owners won't cut it, so choice A is incorrect. However, the host machine can have multiple versions of Oracle on it, so choice B is incorrect. And, obviously, choice D is incorrect as well. **(Topic 14.2)**

**8.** D. SYSMAN

**Explanation** The SYSMAN user is created as part of the Oracle Management Server (OMS) for management of the OEM repository. OEMADMIN, while a great name for owning a repository, is not the default name, eliminating choice A. SYS and SYSTEM are both users created when Oracle8*i* is installed, but not by the OMS, eliminating choices B and C. **(Topic 24.7)**

**9.** B. Interprocess dependencies between jobs

**Explanation** OEM 2.0 introduced interprocess dependencies as a new feature for the OEM software. No prior version of Enterprise Manager allowed you to define jobs that would run based on whether or not another job completed successfully. OEM 1.6 allowed for both email and pager notification of job failure, eliminating choices A and C. Choice D is incorrect because OEM 1.6 provided users with event notification in the OEM console as well. **(Topic 24.5)**

**10.** A. Constraint deferability

**Explanation** Using constraint deferability, Oracle8*i* allows you to have a nonunique index managing a primary-key constraint. Fine-grained access control allows for complex security management, eliminating choice B. Materialized views are similar to snapshots in earlier versions of Oracle, eliminating choice C. Finally, INSTEAD-OF triggers support migration of relational databases to the object-relational paradigm, eliminating choice D. **(Topic 25.2)**

11. C. Oracle puts the tablespace into read-only mode after the last prior transaction against that tablespace commits while preventing subsequent DML until the change happens.

**Explanation** Only after the last transaction commits does Oracle put the tablespace into read-only mode. The tablespace cannot be put into read-only mode before a transaction against data in that tablespace commits due to the locks on mutating database objects held by the incomplete transaction. This point eliminates choice A. Oracle does not need to wait until the users all log off, however—Oracle can change tablespace status after the transaction commits, eliminating choice B. Finally, choice D is incorrect because Oracle returning an error is the behavior Oracle demonstrated in versions prior to Oracle8*i*. **(Topic 15.4)**

12. B and C. Partitions of a table in many tablespaces and LOB overflow information stored in a different tablespace from inline LOB data

**Explanation** In choices B and C, situations where the tablespace being transported is not self-contained are being described by the given answer. Thus, these choices identify times where the tablespace is not transportable, because only self-contained tablespaces can be transported from one tablespace to another. Choice A is incorrect because the choice describes a situation where the tablespace is self-contained. Choices D and E are incorrect for the same reason. **(Topic 15.3)**

13. A. Using a bitmap in the space header segment

**Explanation** The principle behind locally managed tablespaces is that the space management is handled using a bitmap stored in the datafile header rather than by storing available space information in the data dictionary. Thus, choice B is incorrect. The locality of the database into which the information is stored is not relevant, either, so choice D is also incorrect. Finally, choice C is incorrect because Oracle does not store information integral to the operation of your database in a flat file, due to complex recovery issues inherent in doing so. **(Topic 15.2)**

14. B. Session memory for MTS configuration

**Explanation** The large pool, when configured, will be used by Oracle to store session memory for MTS configuration. This relieves the burden on the shared pool to store this information when MTS is in use, leaving more room for SQL parse trees. Only the shared pool may be used for storing SQL parse trees, so choice A is incorrect. Choice C is also incorrect because session memory in the dedicated server configuration is always stored in a private area seen only by that process. Finally, choice D is incorrect because the buffer cache is used for storing all block buffers, and there is no real concept of "overflow" with respect to this memory area. **(Topic 3.1)**

**15.** D. IOWAIT

**Explanation** There is no trigger that fires when an I/O wait occurs, and thus choice D is the correct answer. However, the other database-level triggers identified as choices do exist in Oracle8*i*. The ALTER trigger fires whenever you alter the DDL for a database object, thus making choice A incorrect. The DROP trigger fires whenever you drop a database object, thus making choice B incorrect. Finally, the SERVERERROR trigger fires whenever a server error occurs, making choice C incorrect. **(Topic 21.2)**

**16.** A. SQL*Plus

**Explanation** As of Oracle8*i*, Oracle incorporated all the functionality formerly available in Server Manager into SQL*Plus, so that DBAs might use SQL*Plus to manage activities like startup and shutdown. Server Manager, while still functioning in all of its current ability, is now an obsolete product, and will go the way of SQL*DBA in a future database release, so choice B is incorrect. Choices C and D are both incorrect as well, for although they are useful products for database activities like object and tablespace management, they do not allow you to start up or shut down your database the way Server Manager and SQL*Plus do. **(Topic 21.1)**

**17.** A. A developer wants records to be added to an EXIT_STATUS table regardless of whether the transaction completed successfully or not.

**Explanation** Autonomous transactions allow for procedures to execute their own transaction within the scope of their procedure, without interfering with the transaction that may have been going on within the calling procedure. This feature would allow the developer to create a procedure to add records to an EXIT_STATUS table and commit those records without disrupting the rollback of the transaction that would need to occur in the calling procedure if that transaction failed. Normal transaction processing in Oracle allows two users to make changes to different rows in different or same tables at the same time. Thus, choices B and C are eliminated. No user can make a change to the same row at the same time as another user. Table locks in Oracle prevent it. Thus, choice D is also eliminated. **(Topic 21.4)**

**18.** C and D.   PARALLEL_ADAPTIVE_MULTI_USER and
PARALLEL_THREADS_PER_CPU

**Explanation**   One of the parameters set automatically by PARALLEL_ AUTOMATIC_TUNING is a parameter designed to enable automatic management of the degree of parallelism by Oracle8*i*. This INIT.ORA parameter is the PARALLEL_ADAPTIVE_MULTI_USER parameter. If PARALLEL_AUTOMATIC_ TUNING is set to TRUE, then PARALLEL_ADAPTIVE_MULTI_USER will also be set to TRUE automatically. Another new INIT.ORA parameter set automatically by PARALLEL_AUTOMATIC_TUNING is the PARALLEL_THREADS_PER_CPU parameter. The value indicates how many parallel processes a CPU on your machine can handle. PARALLEL_MAX_INSTANCES must be set manually in the INIT.ORA file to define the maximum number of instances that may attach to this database, thus making choice A incorrect. DEGREE_ PARALLELISM is not an INIT.ORA parameter. **(Topic 13.11)**

**19.** A. create_consumer_group( )

**Explanation**   Once you have created a plan directive in your Oracle8*i* database, you are basically done with resource plan definition, and are ready to submit the plan to the database. Thus, consumer groups should already have been created, making choice A the correct answer, insofar as you cannot issue create_consumer_ group( ) after defining your plan directive. You may submit the plan to Oracle using submit_pending_area( ), making choice C incorrect. Once your plan is in place, you may begin managing user's consumer groups using set_initial_consumer_group( ) and switch_current_consumer_group( ), thus making choices B and D incorrect, too. **(Topic 16.2)**

**20.** B.   OUTLN

**Explanation**   The OUTLN user owns two tables, OL$ (plus two indexes associated with this table) and OL$HINTS (plus one index associated with this table). These objects are used for holding stored plan or stored outline information. Thus, if you remember that stored plans and stored outlines are synonymous, then you will have no problem identifying the correct answer. SYS and SYSTEM own dictionary and system-wide database objects other than stored outlines in the Oracle8*i* database, making choices A and D incorrect. Finally, DBA is usually a role, not a user, in the Oracle8*i* database. **(Topic 4.1)**

**21.** C.   DBMS_STATS

**Explanation**   The DBMS_STATS table offers a significant advantage over the ANALYZE command—it can gather statistics on objects other than indexes in parallel. Thus, it is the right choice for partitioned tables where statistics generation may take a long time—and choice A is incorrect. Choices B and D are incorrect because DBMS_RESOURCE_MANAGER is used for managing resource plans in Oracle8*i*, and DBMS_ROWID is used for restricted- to extended-ROWID conversion activities. **(Topic 4.2)**

22. D. Top-*N* query

**Explanation** ORDER BY clauses are now supported in inline views in SQL queries. An inline view is a subquery found in the FROM clause of a SELECT statement, where a subset of data is predefined for search criteria. The ORDER BY clause enhances selection of the top *n* number of rows (thus, the meaning of a "top-*N* query"). Though the inline view represents one form of subquery, this does not mean that the inline view enhances performance of either type of subquery identified in choices B and C. Thus, those choices are incorrect. Oracle also offers a separate new feature for star query optimization, so choice A is incorrect as well. **(Topic 4.3)**

23. B. CUBE

**Explanation** The CUBE keyword included in a GROUP BY clause of SQL statements in Oracle8*i* allows you to perform *N*-dimensional cross-tabulations within the Oracle database, returning the result set directly to the client with ease. This keyword is useful in queries within data warehouses and makes choice B correct. Choice C is incorrect because even though the ROLLUP keyword was also added to SQL queries in Oracle8*i*, this keyword supports subtotal and grand total calculations of grouped data. Although the HAVING expression is also available in group operations, choice A is incorrect because you needn't define a HAVING clause in order to use either CUBE or ROLLUP. Finally, choice D is incorrect because the trim( ) function combines the abilities of ltrim( ) and rtrim( ). **(Topic 4.4)**

24. B. ALTER TABLE SET UNUSED COLUMN

**Explanation** The ALTER TABLE SET UNUSED COLUMN command marks a column as being unused in the table without actually removing any data from the column or table. The operation executes quickly, because the only change actually made is to the data dictionary in the Oracle database. The ALTER TABLE DROP COLUMN command is more extensive and long-running, but also removes the actual data from the table, thus freeing up space, so choice A is incorrect. Choice C is used for changing the datatype definition of a column, and is thus incorrect. Choice D deallocates all storage for a table, leaving only the definition intact, which is also incorrect. **(Topic 17.3)**

**25.** A. PGA

**Explanation** Data in temporary tables in Oracle8*i* is stored in the sort area, and the sort area is a part of your PGA. Since the table is temporary, there is no way for Oracle to store the data either in your buffer cache or in any tablespace other than TEMP. Thus, choices B, C, and D are all incorrect. The reason temporary table data might be stored in your TEMP tablespace is because the temporary table data might fill your sort area. In this situation, Oracle8*i* behaves as every version of Oracle behaved, and puts overflow in the temporary tablespace used for disk sorts. **(Topic 17.4)**

**26.** D. RECSEPARATOR

**Explanation** The RECSEPARATOR keyword in your SQL*Loader control file allows you to define a character other than "NEWLINE" that separates records. Thus, multiple rows of data can be stored on one line, or a single line of data can be found spanning multiple lines. Choice A is incorrect because the FIELDS SEPARATED BY clause defines the column separation delimiter, not the line delimiter. The FIELDS TERMINATED BY clause defines a character to be found when SQL*Loader reaches the end of a column, making choice B incorrect as well. Finally, TRAILING NULLCOLS identifies to SQL*Loader that, if additional columns are found in the table for which there are no records in the load file, then SQL*Loader will place a NULL value for that column. Thus, choice C is incorrect. **(Topic 17.5)**

**27.** A. Estimate statistics

**Explanation** You can compute statistics, but not estimate statistics, on Oracle8*i* indexes when you rebuild them. Thus, choice A is correct, and choice B is incorrect. The REBUILD clause does allow you to rebuild in another tablespace as well by simply specifying the TABLESPACE clause in the ALTER INDEX REBUILD command. This feature was actually implemented in Oracle8. Thus, choice C is incorrect as well. Finally, choice D indicates that the index can be rebuilt online, while users are still modifying data in the table. This is a new feature in Oracle8*i*, and thus choice D is incorrect. **(Topic 6.6)**

**28.** D. Performance can be enhanced using a function-based index.

**Explanation** A function-based index is designed to enhance performance on a SELECT statement in which the WHERE clause contains a column modified by a function. The function must produce a repeatable result in order to be indexable. Thus, choice D is correct. The query performance can be enhanced in Oracle8*i*, though not in prior versions of Oracle, making choice A incorrect. However, neither bitmap index nor descending index will do the trick the way a function-based index would, so choices B and C are wrong as well. **(Topic 6.3)**

**29.  D.**  All B-tree variants and bitmap indexes can be created on an IOT.

**Explanation**   In Oracle8*i*, all types of B-tree indexes including descending, function-based, and reverse-key indexes, as well as bitmap indexes, can be created on an IOT. This contrasts with Oracle8, where no index other than the one organizing the table could be created on an IOT, thus making choice A incorrect. Choices B and C are logically incorrect as well, given the validity of choice D. **(Topic 6.13)**

**30.  B.**  Directory objects in Oracle for directories containing database files

**Explanation**   You should never create directory objects in your database that correspond to directories containing Oracle datafiles. This could lead to users being able to tamper with and corrupt your Oracle datafiles. Thus, choice B is the correct answer. Though it is not advisable to create materialized views of dictionary table data, there is no harm in doing so other than the potential impact on database performance, so choice A is incorrect. Choices C and D are both incorrect because it is highly recommended from a security perspective to both store BFILE objects on file systems separate from your database and to wrap PL/SQL code using the Oracle wrapper utility. **(Topic 8.3)**

**31.  A.**  8

**Explanation**   Oracle recommends that when you use hash partitioning, you should use 2 to the power of *n* partitions in order to ensure proper distribution of data across multiple partitions. Thus, appropriate numbers of partitions include 2, 4, 8, 16, 32, and so on. Thus, of the choices given, only choice A conforms to this guideline. Thus, choices B, C, and D are not correct. Beware of choice C in this situation, because 10 looks like a nice, round number, and could easily fool you into making the wrong choice if you do not understand Oracle's recommendations. **(Topic 9.3)**

**32.  A.**  ALTER TABLE RENAME PARTITION

**Explanation**   Renaming a partition from something obscure to something more meaningful will not invalidate either the entire partitioned index or any partition of that index, thus making choice A your correct answer. Choices B, C, and D are all incorrect because dropping a partition, splitting a partition, and moving a partition from one tablespace to another will all invalidate either the associated index partition or the entire index associated with the table. **(Topic 10.2)**

**33.** C. SUBPARTITION

**Explanation** The SUBPARTITION keyword is used in Oracle8*i* to identify the composite subpartition that you will perform DDL operations upon. Choice A is incorrect because even though composite partitioning refers to the type of partitioning being used, there is no COMPOSITE keyword found in the DDL for creating or managing the partition. Choice B is also incorrect, because LEAF is not a valid keyword in partition object DDL, either. Finally, choice D is incorrect because PARTNUM is not a valid keyword in partition object DDL, either. **(Topic 11.2)**

**34.** B. Partition by range and hash functions

**Explanation** Composite partitioning means that you have partitioned by range, then subpartitioned by hash function, rendering choice B the correct answer. Choice A is wrong because the answer given describes equipartitioning between tables and indexes, not composite partitioning. Choice C is wrong because the choice given describes range partitioning only. Choice D is wrong because the choice given describes hash partitioning only. Remember, composite partitioning is a combination of range and hash partitioning. **(Topic 11.1)**

**35.** B, C, and D. Enhanced performance for insert operations, reduced demand on developers to configure multisession transactions, and automatic degree parallelism definition based on available instances

**Explanation** Oracle8*i* supports enhanced performance for insert operations, reduced demand on developers to configure multisession transactions, and automatic degree parallelism definition based on available instances as part of its support for parallel DML operations in the database. The only drawback for parallel DML is increased memory requirements, both for the additional instances running on the same or multiple servers and for the I/O processes needed to execute the DML operations in parallel. **(Topic 13.2)**

**36.** D. /*+PARALLEL */

**Explanation** The parallel hint allows for multiple I/O processes to get involved in the processing of a DML operation in Oracle8*i*. Thus, choice D is the correct answer. Choice A is incorrect because the star hint is used for optimizing star queries in data warehouses, not for parallel DML operations. Though the insert and/or append hints can encourage Oracle to use the direct path for inserting data into the database, the DML operation being performed according to the question is an update. Thus, choices B and C are incorrect. **(Topic 13.4)**

## Chapter 6: OCP Oracle8i Upgrade Exam: New Features for Administrators

**37.** A. V$SESSION

**Explanation** The V$SESSION view gives comprehensive information for the current session, including whether parallel DML has been enabled for the session. Thus, choice A is correct. Choice B is incorrect because V$SESSTAT is designed for capturing statistics about the session, not for capturing current session-level statuses like whether parallel DML is enabled. Choice C is incorrect because V$SYSTEM captures general system-wide statistics. Finally, choice D is incorrect because V$PX_SESSTAT is designed to capture system-wide statistics for parallel DML operations. **(Topic 13.8)**

**38.** D. IOT_1

**Explanation** Since Oracle8*i* tablespace storage precedence for partitions is from partition level to table level, the PK4 partition gets placed in IOT_1, where the storage allocation for the table level is defined. DATA_1, DATA_2, and DATA_3 are the tablespaces defined for storing the partitions; however, those definitions are at the partition level for each of the respective partitions. Each definition is out of scope with respect to the other definitions. Thus, Oracle8*i* will not use DATA_1, DATA_2, and DATA_3 for storing PK4, making choices A, B, and C incorrect. **(Topic 12.2)**

**39.** C. Your range partition should be on a scalar-type column.

**Explanation** Range partitioning should be done on scalar-type columns in Oracle8*i* when partitioning an object table; however, the column may be part of an object type so long as the element being used for range partitioning is scalar (i.e., a VARCHAR2, NUMBER, DATE, etc.). You cannot partition on a nested table column, so choice D is wrong. Also, no restriction exists in Oracle8*i* either way regarding placement of partitions of an object table either in one tablespace or in many different tablespaces, so choices A and B are also both wrong. **(Topic 12.3)**

**40.** C. Value for PCTTHRESHOLD

**Explanation** The PCTTHRESHOLD storage option defines a percentage threshold for row data in a data block. If one row of data in an IOT data block takes up more than the percentage of space in that data block defined by PCTTHRESHOLD, then all the nonkey data for that row is stored in an overflow tablespace. Choices A and B are both incorrect because they refer to Oracle8*i* features related to large object data. The CHUNK storage option is used for LOB data so that Oracle can treat several database blocks as one contiguous unit for substantial amounts of data. Also, the LOB limit for inline data is 4,000 bytes. Finally, IOT_OVERFLOW is not a reserved word in Oracle, but may be used as the name for an IOT overflow tablespace. **(Topic 6.9)**

**41.** A. No indexes on the IOT other than primary key

**Explanation** Not having indexes on an IOT other than the primary key is not a restriction that exists on IOTs anymore. When IOTs were first introduced in Oracle8, this restriction was present, but after Oracle8, the restriction went away. You cannot have a unique constraint on any IOT column other than the primary key, so choice B is incorrect. You also may not define a column of LONG datatype in an IOT, so choice C is incorrect. Finally, you cannot replicate an IOT column due to the lack of ROWID information in an IOT, so choice D is incorrect as well. **(Topic 6.11)**

**42.** B. LOG_ARCHIVE_MAX_PROCESSES

**Explanation** This question is tricky because one of the choices looks deceptively similar to the correct answer. Choice B is the correct name for the parameter used to define how many ARCH processes Oracle8*i* should run. Choice A does not identify an actual INIT.ORA parameter, but looks like it "should" be right. It is important that you can distinguish the real from the imaginary on your OCP exam. Choice C is incorrect because although you can define how many archive destinations Oracle8*i* should maintain with LOG_ARCHIVE_MIN_SUCCEED_DEST, Oracle8*i* does not automatically start a specific number of ARCH processes based on the value for this parameter. Finally, choice D is incorrect because the LOG_ARCHIVE_START parameter merely tells Oracle8*i* that an ARCH process should be started at the time the instance is started, but by itself LOG_ ARCHIVE_START tells Oracle8*i* to start only one ARCH process. **(Topic 19.1)**

**43.** A. UTL_FILE_DIR

**Explanation** The LogMiner tool will write output into flat files on the machine hosting your Oracle database. But, in order to do so, you must define a directory using UTL_FILE_DIR, the parameter used by Oracle8*i* to define a directory where PL/SQL can write output to a flat file. Information will not be dumped to either BACKGROUND_DUMP_DEST or USER_DUMP_DEST automatically, thus eliminating choices B and D. Finally, choice C is also incorrect because the LOG_ARCHIVE_DEST is where archive logs are written to, not where output from LogMiner is written to. **(Topic 19.4)**

**44.** D. None of the above

**Explanation** Though DBMS_REPAIR contains many procedures and functions that can be used for detecting block corruption, no function or procedure in that package will actually fix the block corruption. This is a feature that has yet to be implemented in Oracle8*i*, release 8.1.5, though it is scheduled for implementation in later releases. For now, you will simply have the ability to tell Oracle8i to skip a corrupted block. So, choice D is right, and choice C is wrong. Other choices given simply allow for block corruption detection, so they are wrong as well. **(Topic 19.7)**

**45.** C. STANDBY_ARCHIVE_DEST

**Explanation** The STANDBY_ARCHIVE_DEST parameter defines to the standby database where to find redo logs to apply during sustained recovery operation. Choices A and B identify locations where archive logs will be stored in the production database and in the standby, but neither alone will be enough information for the standby database to know where to find its redo to apply, so both choices are incorrect. Finally, choice D is incorrect because LOG_ARCHIVE_MIN_ SUCCEED_DEST tells an Oracle8i database how many destinations must be maintained with archive logs in order for proper operation of the database. **(Topic 19.2)**

**46.** A. FAST_START_PARALLEL_ROLLBACK

**Explanation** In prior versions of Oracle, although database recovery time was reduced because Oracle could open the database after the instance roll-forward process completed, the transaction rollback could still take a long time—particularly for parallel DML operations—because rollback had to happen serially. In Oracle8i, you can specify the FAST_START_PARALLEL_ ROLLBACK parameter to low or high to allow SMON to use parallel-query slaves for parallel rollback, thus speeding up the rollback process. Choices B, C, and D all combine to reduce the time needed for faster warmstart, but none affect transaction rollback after instance recovery the way choice A will. **(Topic 19.5)**

**47.** A. Automatically

**Explanation** You can choose to allow Oracle8i to automatically propagate changes to the listener.ora file as well when new databases are created using the Database Configuration Assistant. Although choices B and C both identify ways for you to manually change the listener to tune into connections for a new Oracle8i database, they are both incorrect. Choice D is also incorrect because Server Manager is an obsolete product for managing Oracle8i, and furthermore, was never used for managing the listeners anyway. **(Topic 20.4)**

**48.** C. Table Data Editor

**Explanation** The Table Data Editor tool in OEM 2.0 was used to replace SQL*Worksheet, the SQL manipulation tool (sometimes called SQL*Plus GUI mode) available in prior versions of Enterprise Manager for changing data or doing other things directly in SQL against your database. Instance Manager remains in OEM, making choice B incorrect. The OEM Console never gave you command-line access to a database, so choice A is wrong. Finally, Recovery Manager is used for recovering a database either in command-line or GUI mode, not for issuing SQL directly against the database, making choice D incorrect, too. **(Topic 24.9)**

**49.** B.   GROUP BY

**Explanation**   The GROUP BY clause is added by Oracle8*i* within the scope of summary management implicitly. This allows for query rewrite, and thus enhanced performance in the data warehouse. The ORDER BY clause is not implicitly added, thus making choice A incorrect. And, though CUBE and ROLLUP may be used to add additional information to the output of the grouped query, this information is not added implicitly by summary management. **(Topic 5.2)**

**50.** D.   Level hierarchy

**Explanation**   When creating a dimension, two aspects must be defined. First, the various levels must be defined for the dimension. Second, the hierarchy between those levels must be defined. CUBE and ROLLUP operations do not need to be defined, so choices A and B are incorrect. Also, summary management is not defined as part of the dimension definition, so choice C is incorrect. **(Topic 5.3)**

**51.** B.   Issue CREATE TYPE command

**Explanation**   Before creating an object table, you must define the table type to be used for the object table. Note that no error will occur if you define a table where you didn't define a table type first—this is more of a best practice than a hard and fast rule. After a table type has been created, you will issue the CREATE TABLE command, so choice A is incorrect. You shouldn't need to define INSTEAD-OF triggers unless you are migrating a relational design to an object-relational design, so choice C is incorrect as well. Finally, choice D is wrong because object tables are part of the objects option, not the Java Option. **(Topic 7.3)**

**52.** D.   Nested table

**Explanation**   Oracle recommends that, if individual items in the collection object must be accessed, you use TABLE; otherwise, use VARRAY. Since you want to access individual items in the collection object, choice D is correct and choice C is wrong. Choice A is wrong because although you'll want to use scalar types in the definition of the nested table type, the overall type will be a nested table, not scalar. Finally, choice B is wrong because even though the table type will be user-defined, there are more specific choices available that more accurately reflect the answer. **(Topic 7.4)**

**53.** C. READ ONLY

**Explanation** Oracle8*i* offers DBAs the ability to open a database in read-only mode for report or query access. This feature is useful for opening database clones or standby databases for reporting purposes. Choice A is incorrect because simply opening the database allows both read and write traffic into the database. Choice B is incorrect because forcing the database to OPEN is used in situations where a normal OPEN doesn't work because shutdown didn't complete normally beforehand. Finally, choice D is incorrect because opening the database in restricted mode is used for giving database access to users with the restricted session privilege only, but still permits writes to the database by those users. **(Topic 19.3)**

**54.** C. Use an index-organized journal table

**Explanation** The rebuild online feature in Oracle8*i* allows indexes to be rebuilt online in the following way. Oracle8*i* will create an index-organized copy of your table called a journal table, which is used for obtaining data while the index rebuild occurs. After the index is rebuilt, Oracle8*i* copies the changes made to data during the rebuild into the new index. This feature reduces the need for downtime in support of rebuilding indexes in Oracle8*i*, which makes choices A and D wrong. Choice B is wrong as well because you will not need to manually move, replicate, or do any of the repointing yourself—Oracle8*i* handles it for you. **(Topic 6.5)**

**55.** B. Reverse-key indexes

**Explanation** A reverse-key index is one where the contents of the indexed column are reversed. This gives a higher amount of lead-in selectivity than a straight B-tree index would, because the cardinality of the root node in the B-tree would be low. This is based on the fact that most records would begin with 1 (recall the question content if you don't understand why), whereas the reverse of that key would have greater cardinality. Be careful of choice A, because although cardinality is high, choice B gives a better option for performance. Choice C is incorrect because bitmap indexes are designed for low-cardinality records like status or gender. Finally, choice D indicates an index type that wouldn't suit this situation. **(Topic 6.2)**

**56.** D. %ORACLE_BASE%\oradata

**Explanation** Oracle8*i* significantly enhanced its support of the Optimal Flexible Architecture (OFA). Database Configuration Assistant now installs all Oracle datafiles under an oradata\<SID> directory within the software home tree in NT environments. In contrast, prior versions of Oracle would place all datafiles under the database directory, so choice C is incorrect for Oracle8*i*. Choice A is incorrect because only the admin components will be placed under the admin directory in the ORACLE_HOME tree. However, this is also an OFA-compliant way to set up the Oracle environment, so it is also important to understand. Finally, choice B is incorrect because Oracle-supplied DBA scripts are found in the rdbms\admin area. **(Topic 14.6)**

**57.  A.  VARCHAR2**

**Explanation**  Since the text blocks are within the size limits imposed in Oracle8*i* for the VARCHAR2 datatype, it is best to use the scalar type rather than a LOB for simplicity sake. If the block was larger than 4,000 bytes, you would most likely use CLOB, but since the size requirement is less than 4,000 bytes, choice B is incorrect. You would use BLOB to store binary large objects, making choice C incorrect. Finally, since the text block is not stored as an external file (you would not use the BFILE type), making choice D incorrect. **(Topic 8.2)**

**58.  A.  ALTER ANY TABLE**

**Explanation**  No new privileges are introduced to Oracle8*i* with respect to partitions because partitions are merely another type of table. Thus, the permission you will need in order to modify table DDL for a table owned by another user is the alter any table privilege. Choice A is then the right answer, and choice B is eliminated. Choice C refers to permissions on modifying indexes, making it incorrect, and choice D is incorrect because no alter any object privilege exists in the database. **(Topic 10.3)**

**59.  C.  AQ_USER_ROLE**

**Explanation**  The AQ_USER_ROLE must be granted to Advanced Queuing users for message processing using the procedures and packages supplied by Oracle for this purpose. Choice A is incorrect because the SELECT_CATALOG_ROLE is used for administering the ability to select data from the data dictionary. Choice B is incorrect because DBA is a role used for administering the ability for a user to perform every action available in the database. Finally, choice D is incorrect because AQ_TM_PROCESSES is actually an INIT.ORA parameter used for setup of advanced queuing. **(Topic 22.4)**

**60.  B and C.  LOAD_BALANCE and FAILOVER**

**Explanation**  The LOAD_BALANCE and FAILOVER items in your tnsnames.ora file are used for transparently configuring Net8 load balancing and failover between two or more instances connected to the same database in an OPS setup. Choice A is incorrect because PROTOCOL is used for identification of network protocol this

Oracle database service can be found on. SERVICE_NAME is designed to replace SID, thus making choice D incorrect as well. Finally, HOST and PORT are used within TCP/IP to identify the actual machine and port number where the Oracle listener can be found. Thus, choices E and F are wrong also. **(Topic 20.3)**

# Answers to Practice Exam 2

**1.** B and D.   EXECUTE on procedure FOOBAR *and* SELECT on table FOO

**Explanation**   Since the procedure contains the line AUTHID CURRENT_USER, this procedure will use invoker's rights execution. Thus, FLUFFY not only needs permission to run the procedure, but the user needs permission to perform all actions specified within the procedure, as well. Since no procedure is being created, choice A is incorrect. Since no table is being updated, choice C is incorrect. **(Topic 23.2)**

**2.** A.   25

**Explanation**   The bits in the local-management bitmap in each datafile will either represent one block or many blocks. The bit will represent many blocks only if UNIFORM SIZE is used, in which case the number of blocks represented by one bit equals the number of blocks in each extent. In this case, the block size is 4K, while the uniform extent size is 100K, meaning that each extent contains, and each bit represents, 25 blocks. **(Topic 15.2)**

**3.** D.   Install Oracle8*i* software to the same directory used for Oracle7 software.

**Explanation**   Using Universal Installer and Packager, you cannot install Oracle8*i* to the same directory that contains a prior release of Oracle installed with an earlier release of Oracle Installer. You should shut down any existing databases and listeners and make a backup of the existing database before installing a new version of Oracle on a machine already hosting an Oracle database. **(Topic 14.1)**

**4.** E.   CHECKPOINT_PROCESS

**Explanation**   The CHECKPOINT_PROCESS parameter was rendered obsolete in Oracle8 because CKPT now runs all the time in support of LGWR. DB_NAME is still used, eliminating choice A, while JOB_QUEUE_INTERVAL is the parameter that replaced SNAPSHOT_REFRESH_INTERVAL, eliminating choice B. Choice C indicates a parameter introduced in Oracle8 that still is used in Oracle8*i*, while choice D indicates a parameter that has not changed since Oracle7. **(Topic 1.2)**

**5.** E.   Notify

**Explanation**   The Notify permission in OEM indicates that an administrator should be informed via email or page about the status of a particular job. None indicates the administrator has no privileges on a job, eliminating choice A. View indicates the administrator can see but not change information about a job, eliminating choice B. Modify indicates that the administrator can change the status or aspects of job execution, eliminating choice C. Full means the administrator can alter all aspects of job execution, eliminating choice D. **(Topic 24.2)**

## Chapter 6: OCP Oracle8i Upgrade Exam: New Features for Administrators 387

**6.** C.  Offloading row data from objects in the tablespace using EXPORT

**Explanation**  Transporting a tablespace in Oracle8i eliminates the need to transfer data between databases using SQL*Loader and EXPORT. You will still need EXPORT and IMPORT to transfer dictionary information about the tablespace and its object contents, however, eliminating choice D. You will also need to make the tablespace read-only before moving it, eliminating choice A. Transporting a tablespace involves moving the actual datafiles to another machine, eliminating choice B. Finally, you will use DBMS_TTS.transport_set_check( ) to determine whether your tablespace is self-contained, eliminating choice E. **(Topic 15.3)**

**7.** A and D.  Issuing the CREATE CONTEXT statement *and* building explicit calls to fine-grained access control in your application

**Explanation**  When specifying fine-grained access control on a database object, you do not need to create a context or to code support into your application. Oracle8i automatically enforces the fine-grained access control based on rules for access to a database object that you define within a security package. You bind that package to the database object using the DBMS_RLS.add_policy( ) package. **(Topic 23.3)**

**8.** B.  Extended ROWID format identifies the row location in each block, while restricted ROWID format does not.

**Explanation**  Both restricted and extended ROWID formats contain information about the location of a row in a particular block, although extended ROWID format refers to this information as a "slot." All other statements made about extended and restricted ROWIDs made for this question are true. **(Topic 15.1)**

**9.** A.  Obtains information about application context for security enforcement

**Explanation**  The sys_context( ) function can be used to obtain information about application context in a security policy package. Choice B is incorrect because application context information is set using the set_context( ) procedure in the DBMS_SESSION package. Choice C is incorrect because invoker's rights are handled with the authid *option* clause in PL/SQL procedure specifications. Choice D is incorrect because *n*-tier authentication in Oracle8i is handled with the Advanced Security Option. **(Topic 23.4)**

**10.** D.  u0800030.sql

**Explanation**  The scripts for upgrading Oracle8 to Oracle8i can be found in the rdbms/admin subdirectory under the Oracle software home directory, and the file you use depends on the version of Oracle you run. For example, for Oracle8 version 8.0.3, you use u0800030.sql. **(Topic 14.7)**

**11.** A. Ability to administer only one database at a time

**Explanation** With OEM 2.0 running in conjunction with the Oracle Management Server (OMS), you have the ability to administer multiple databases at the same time, not just one. You can also administer Oracle from within your Web browser. OMS manages repository information centrally, and also allows for the sharing of administrative responsibility, eliminating choices C and D. **(Topic 24.1)**

**12.** A. PLUGGED_IN

**Explanation** The PLUGGED_IN column indicates whether the tablespace was transported into this database or not. Choice B is incorrect because CONTENTS indicates whether the tablespace contains permanent or temporary objects or not. Choice C is incorrect because LOGGING is used to identify whether the objects created in this tablespace that don't specify LOGGING for themselves will log transaction information. Choice D is incorrect because STATUS indicates whether the tablespace is online or offline. **(Topic 15.3)**

**13.** C. Based on the number of blocks in the table plus blocks in associated indexes

**Explanation** When sizing the keep pool, ensure that there is enough room for the entire table plus all associated indexes. If one or the other is omitted, then you may size the keep pool too small and lose blocks, resulting in I/O operations later to read either table or index data back into memory. You wouldn't base the size of the keep pool on anything from your shared pool. **(Topic 3.2)**

**14.** C. CHAR(20)

**Explanation** Since the requirement is for fixed-width text data storage, all NLS datatype equivalents can be eliminated, since they are designed to store variable-width character sets. Additionally, the requirement is for fixed-length strings padded to the full size of the datatype if the data is not as long as the width. Thus, VARCHAR2 can be eliminated, leaving you with the CHAR datatype. **(Topic 21.5)**

**15.** D. NLS_DUAL_CURRENCY

**Explanation** NLS_DUAL_CURRENCY is used for EU countries supporting two currencies so that dual currencies can be identified in the database. NLS_TERRITORY may identify their national currency, but not necessarily the euro, eliminating choice A. The NLS_LANG parameter is used to identify the national language, but not the currency, making choice B incorrect. NLS_COMP is used for enhanced comparison operations, not to support dual currencies, eliminating choice C. **(Topic 21.5)**

## Chapter 6: OCP Oracle8i Upgrade Exam: New Features for Administrators 389

**16.** B.  tnsnames.ora

**Explanation**  You have to set up EXTPROC_CONNECTION_DATA so that EXTPROC can be found by Oracle8i. This is done in the tnsnames.ora file. All other choices identify parameter files, but EXTPROC_CONNECTION_DATA is not configured in those files, so choices A, C, and D are all incorrect. **(Topic 21.3)**

**17.** B.  Any uncommitted changes made to table TAB_2 by my_tran( ) will not be seen by upd_tran( ).

**Explanation**  Any uncommitted transaction in a procedure that calls a second procedure defined to use autonomous transactions will not be seen by that second procedure. Since the transaction in upd_tran( ) is autonomous, however, it will not COMMIT changes made in my_tran( ), eliminating choice A. The upd_tran( ) procedure will also encounter a deadlock if my_tran( ) already has a lock on TAB_1, eliminating choice C. Finally, this procedure does not define invoker's rights execution, eliminating choice D. **(Topic 1.1)**

**18.** C.  PARALLEL_AUTOMATIC_TUNING

**Explanation**  The PARALLEL_AUTOMATIC_TUNING parameter is used to set values automatically for the other parameters, PARALLEL_ADAPTIVE_MULTI_USER and PARALLEL_THREADS_PER_CPU. Of course, you can set values for those parameters that will override the defaults set by PARALLEL_AUTOMATIC_TUNING. **(Topic 13.1)**

**19.** D.  grant_system_privilege( )

**Explanation**  To delegate appropriate privileges for execution of procedures identified in choices A, B, and C to user JOE, you need to execute the grant_system_privilege( ) procedure. **(Topic 1.3)**

**20.** D.  V$RSRC_CONSUMER_GROUP

**Explanation**  The V$RSRC_CONSUMER_GROUP view contains information about which sessions are using which consumer groups. The DBA_RSRC_CONSUMER_GROUPS view shows information about the consumer groups themselves, along with their current status, eliminating choice A. The V$RSRC_PLAN shows the resource plan in use in the instance, eliminating choice B. The DBA_RSRC_PLANS view shows information about available resource plans and the status for those plans, eliminating choice C. **(Topic 16.1)**

**21.** D.  OUTLN_PKG

**Explanation**  The OUTLN_PKG package contains procedures used to manage outlines. DBMS_STATS manages statistics generation and collection, eliminating choice A. The DBMS_RESOURCE_MANAGER package is for managing resource usage, eliminating choice B. The DBMS_OLAP package contains advisory functions for summaries, eliminating choice C. **(Topic 1.1)**

**22.** B. BUILD DEFERRED REFRESH COMPLETE NEXT SYSDATE + 1/24

**Explanation** Since the materialized view will not be populated until the first refresh, you must use the BUILD DEFERRED syntax in the CREATE MATERIALIZED VIEW statement. This eliminates choices A and D. Since you want a full refresh every time this action is performed, the COMPLETE keyword is required in the REFRESH clause, preserving both choices. However, to perform mathematical operations using SYSDATE, you must use fractional values if you want to increment by less than one day at a time. In this case, 1/24 indicates you want the refresh to happen every hour, while 1/4096 would have the refresh occurring approximately once every 17.6 seconds, thus eliminating choice C. **(Topic 5.1)**

**23.** D. The INSERT fails at the time it is issued, but the transaction will continue.

**Explanation** A nondeferrable constraint cannot be deferred by the ALTER SESSION SET CONSTRAINTS=DEFERRED statement. Therefore, the INSERT statement will fail. However, statement failure does not cause a transaction to fail. Therefore, choice D is correct. **(Topic 25.1)**

**24.** C. '948695'

**Explanation** The data in a reverse-key index is actually reversed within the index, but not in the table. **(Topic 6.2)**

**25.** B. Create an index-organized table to store the data.

**Explanation** Index-organized tables take less space to store than a comparable table-plus-primary-key setup. Since the table will only be accessed via the primary key, there is no need for additional indexes. Furthermore, for storage reasons, the DBA won't want to create more indexes, eliminating choice A. Choice C is incorrect because dropping the primary key will reduce storage but has the unwanted effect of making data difficult to access. Choice D is incorrect because increasing PCTFREE makes a table require more storage to store the same number of rows. Review the discussion of index-organized tables. **(Topic 6.7)**

**26.** D. The BFILE object is accessed.

**Explanation** Oracle does not check the path specified at directory creation time to see if it exists. Therefore, choice A is incorrect. The CREATE OR REPLACE DIRECTORY statement is DDL, and therefore does not need to be committed, eliminating choice B. The BFILE object is created externally from Oracle, so there is no check performed at that time either, eliminating choice C. **(Topic 8.3)**

Chapter 6: OCP Oracle8i Upgrade Exam: New Features for Administrators **391**

**27.** B.   The CHUNK clause used in the LOB storage definition

**Explanation**   All information, options, and clauses pertaining to the definition for storage of internal LOBs, such as BLOBs, CLOBs, and NCLOBS, can be found in the storage clause of the object storage definition. Review the creation of large objects. **(Topic 8.5)**

**28.** B.   Value and locator

**Explanation**   Every LOB has a locator, which is stored inline with the table. The locator is a pointer to the value, which is stored in a segment away from the main table information or external to the database, as in the case of BFILE. **(Topic 8.4)**

**29.** A.   Oracle datafiles

**Explanation**   The users of the database should not have access to the files of the Oracle database or their directories through any other method than the Oracle RDBMS. To allow access in any other way jeopardizes the integrity of the system. **(Topic 1.3)**

**30.** C.   5

**Explanation**   A table containing two LOB columns can have as many as five tablespaces containing its data. Consider the following. The first tablespace stores the inline table data, including locator data for the LOBs. The second and third are used to store the LOB value data. The fourth and fifth are used to store index data for the LOBs. Indexes are used to manage the contents of the LOB. Since table partitioning is not allowed on tables containing LOB columns, there can be no more tablespaces used than these five. **(Topic 8.1)**

**31.** A, C, and D.   VARRAY allows indexes on attributes, VARRAY stores data in segments separate from the main object, *and* VARRAY stores all data over 4K inline.

**Explanation**   VARRAY types do not allow the indexing of elements in the object. In addition, the data is stored in the same extents as the parent table ("inline"), as long as it isn't over 4K. If over 4K, the data is stored in a different segment. A VARRAY type does require a limit on the number of elements that can be placed in the array. Therefore, choice B is the only one that accurately describes the VARRAY type. **(Topic 7.3)**

**32.** A.   The ADDRESS_TYPE constructor was not used.

**Explanation**   When inserting data into an object type, the name of the object type must be referenced. This reference is called a constructor. There is no way to know the order of the attributes in an object without seeing the object type, so choice B is incorrect. The VALUES keyword is properly placed, so choice C is incorrect. And, object data can definitely be put into relational tables, as long as the relational table has a column defined with an object type, making choice D incorrect as well. **(Topic 7.2)**

**33.** C. A pointer to the data

**Explanation** The data in a REF type is a pointer to the referenced object, not to the actual data or even a copy of the data, eliminating choices A and B. Choice D is incorrect because no copy of the data is made; thus, no pointer to the copy can be made. **(Topic 7.2)**

**34.** A. Object views and INSTEAD OF triggers

**Explanation** The use of object views and INSTEAD OF triggers is designed to support easier migration to object applications. The use of scalar types, index-organized tables, reverse-key indexes, and partitions are all relational in nature, and therefore not part of the transition to object-relational databases, eliminating choices B and C. Obviously, choice D is also incorrect. **(Topic 7.5)**

**35.** D. The DBA issued an ALTER TABLE TRUNCATE PARTITION statement.

**Explanation** Several operations on table partitions will cause the index partition to become unusable. One of these operations is to truncate the table partition. Adding a new table partition creates a new index partition, and since the added partition is empty, the corresponding index partition is automatically valid. Choice A will simply remove a row from the index and the table, while choices B and C create or fix indexes, leaving them valid. **(Topic 10.1)**

**36.** A. Execute SQL*Loader ten times in parallel.

**Explanation** An individual SQL*Loader run can operate against a single partition of the Oracle database. Another execution of SQL*Loader can operate against a different partition at the same time. This is the best way to run a data load against multiple partitions of a table. Choices B and D are incorrect because the parameters named are not actual SQL*Loader parameters. Choice C is incorrect because the PARALLEL parameter simply runs a parallel load on the single partition, not a load on multiple partitions in parallel. **(Topic 9.2)**

**37.** A. EXP_JULY

**Explanation** After a partition is dropped, all rows inserted into the table that would have been stored in that partition go into the next highest partition. If the partition dropped had been the highest partition, Oracle would not allow the row to be inserted. **(Topic 10.2)**

**38.** C.   Inability to access one partition when another is unavailable

**Explanation**   Creating partitions creates partition independence, and this choice contradicts the definition of partition independence—namely, that the availability of each partition is independent of the availability of another partition. All of the other choices are features of partitioning. **(Topic 9.1)**

**39.** B and D.   Global nonprefixed indexes *and* global equipartitioned indexes

**Explanation**   Answering this question requires some memorization. The global nonprefixed index is not an index in the Oracle database. Since the partition key for the global index doesn't have to be tied to the partition key of the table, the DBA can create all prefixed global indexes. Choice D is a little more obvious—remember that an index cannot simultaneously be global and equipartitioned. **(Topic 12.1)**

**40.** D.   EXP_JULY1-15 will be valid, but EXP_JULY16-31 will be unusable.

**Explanation**   When Oracle splits the table partition, a similar split occurs in the associated local (equipartitioned) index. Since one of the resultant table partitions will be empty, the associated index for that partition will be valid while the other one remains unusable. If the table partition had been empty, both resulting index partitions would have been valid. **(Topic 9.1)**

**41.** B.   Drop the partition, rebuild the index

**Explanation**   The most efficient means for making the global index available quickly in this situation is to drop the partition and rebuild the index. Had the partition not contained so much of the row data for the table, the DBA might consider choice C. Choices A and D are both incorrect. Choice A is wrong because there is no option for merging two partitions together except by the SQL-processing mechanism in a SELECT statement. **(Topic 10.1)**

**42.** C.   ALTER TABLE EXPENSES MOVE PARTITION X1 TABLESPACE DATA_05;

**Explanation**   The ALTER TABLE MOVE PARTITION statement is used to move partitions from one tablespace to another. Choice A is incorrect because the MODIFY operation allows the DBA to modify other storage parameters but not to move the partition to a different tablespace. Choice B renames the partition but does not move it. Choice D is not a valid statement. **(Topic 10.1)**

**43.** A.   DBA_PART_TABLES

**Explanation**   The dictionary view containing the information about partition keys is the DBA_PART_TABLES view. Choice B, DBA_TAB_HISTOGRAMS, gives data distribution information for columns in the tables of the database. Choice C,

DBA_TAB_COLUMNS, lists all columns in all tables in the database. Choice D, DBA_TAB_COL_STATISTICS, gives column statistics for tables in the database for purposes of cost-based optimization. **(Topic 10.4)**

**44. C.** Execute the ALTER SESSION ENABLE PARALLEL DML statement

**Explanation** Parallel hints can be used in DML statements, but in order for a statement to be executed in parallel, the session must have parallel-DML processing enabled. **(Topic 13.3)**

**45. A.** PARTITIONS

**Explanation** An UPDATE or DELETE statement on a partitioned table will parallelize by partition. Parallelism by ROWID ranges is used for SELECT statements, eliminating choice B. Slave I/O parallelism and the direct path INSERT managed by the APPEND hint are both used in database INSERT statements, eliminating choices C and D. **(Topic 13.6)**

**46. B, C, and D.** Index-organized tables, clustered tables, *and* tables containing object types

**Explanation** Parallel DML cannot operate on index-organized tables, tables with object types, or clustered tables. It can operate on partitioned tables. Review the limitations on parallel DML. **(Topic 13.7)**

**47. B.** Use the DISK clause

**Explanation** The COPY command can only work in conjunction with the DISK specification because an image copy can be made only to disk. Review the discussion of the COPY command. Naming the resource explicitly will not work in situations where the DBA names a tape resource, eliminating choice A. The FOR DELETE clause is mainly used to allocate a channel to delete a backup, eliminating choice C. The channel must be allocated before issuing the COPY command, eliminating choice D. **(Topic 18.3)**

**48. D.** RESYNC CATALOG

**Explanation** The catalog must be synchronized with the database every time the control file changes. This includes changes made by the log switch and changes made by adding or removing datafiles or redo logs. Choice A is incorrect because the database need only be registered when RMAN is first run. Choice B is incorrect because the database needs to be RESET only when the redo-log sequence is reset, as after incomplete recovery. Choice C is incorrect because CATALOG is used to include copies of database components with the recovery catalog if the copy was made using a method other than RMAN. **(Topic 18.1)**

## Chapter 6: OCP Oracle8i Upgrade Exam: New Features for Administrators

**49.** A.   All blocks in a datafile except unused blocks

**Explanation**   Full backup means the full datafile will be backed up except for unused data blocks, while incremental refers to the backup of only those blocks in a datafile that have changed. Thus, other choices are incorrect. Review the discussion of full and incremental backup. **(Topic 18.3)**

**50.** D.   Control file

**Explanation**   The control file contains a great deal of information to support RMAN. If the maintenance of the recovery catalog is not possible, the next best thing is to let RMAN use the control file. Review the introduction to RMAN and the recovery catalog. **(Topic 18.4)**

**51.** A.   Issue the CATALOG command.

**Explanation**   To include a backup file in the recovery catalog that has been created using tools other than RMAN, the DBA can issue the CATALOG command. Simply copying the file to tape will not record its existence in the recovery catalog, eliminating choice B. Executing the COPY command on the current version of the file the DBA has already made a copy of externally is fine, but does nothing to include the first copy made by the DBA in the recovery catalog. Choice D is simply incorrect. **(Topic 18.2)**

**52.** C.   Limits growth of the control-file size

**Explanation**   The CONTROL_FILE_RECORD_KEEP_TIME initialization parameter determines how long certain time-sensitive information will be kept to support RMAN in the control file. If set to zero, Oracle will eliminate this information from the control file as often as necessary to make room for new information, thereby limiting the growth of the control-file size. Review information about the enhanced Oracle8 control-file support for backup and recovery. **(Topic 18.1)**

**53.** C.   ALLOCATE CHANNEL

**Explanation**   The first step on almost all RUN commands is to allocate a channel to communicate with the operating system. **(Topic 18.3)**

**54.** D.   For the duration of the RUN command

**Explanation**   The SET statements issued during a RUN command are valid for the entire RUN command, but no longer than that. **(Topic 18.3)**

**55.** A.   1

**Explanation**   RMAN has low error tolerance. As soon as it encounters an error of any sort, it will terminate. This is default behavior and can't be changed. **(Topic 18.1)**

**56.** B.   RESET DATABASE

**Explanation**   Incomplete recovery requires the DBA to recover the database to a point in time in the past. After completing that recovery, the DBA must discard all archived redo logs that contained changes made after that point in time by opening the database with the RESETLOGS option. After opening the database in this way, the recovery catalog must be reset with the RESET DATABASE command in RMAN. **(Topic 18.5)**

**57.** A.   REPORT UNRECOVERABLE

**Explanation**   This report will list all datafiles that are not recoverable with the current backups and archived redo information—the files that are in most dire need of backup. **(Topic 18.7)**

**58.** C.   Multiple datafiles in one backup set with file blocks for each stored noncontiguously

**Explanation**   Multiplexing is when multiple datafiles are stored noncontiguously in a backup set to prevent the backup of any datafile from reducing online performance on that datafile. Choices A and B are incorrect because archived redo logs and control files are not multiplexed in backup sets. Choice D doesn't describe multiplexing. **(Topic 18.1)**

**59.** B.   The AQ_TM_PROCESSES initialization parameter hasn't been set.

**Explanation**   Several features of the Oracle advanced queuing system use time-based features. For the time-based features to work, the Time Manager process must be running on the Oracle instance. Although the start_time_manager( ) process is used to activate the Time Manager for use, this process doesn't actually start the execution of the Time Manager process. Only setting the AQ_TM_PROCESSES initialization parameter to 1 can do that. **(Topic 22.1)**

**60.** D.   payload

**Explanation**   Answering this question requires experience with the enqueue( ) and dequeue( ) operations. Although the information carried by the queue is called a message, the variable that carries it into the queue or out of the queue is called the PAYLOAD. Review the discussion of enqueue( ) and dequeue( ). **(Topic 22.4)**

# PART II

## OCP Key Terms and Concepts

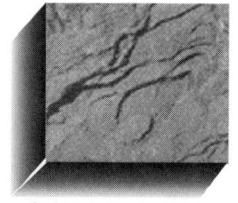

# CHAPTER 7

## OCP Exam I Terms and Concepts

The following key terms and concepts summarize facts and ideas tested in OCP Exam 1. They are meant to act as crib notes for your accelerated preparation and review, not as thorough coverage of all test matter. You may find them useful in the final days before taking the OCP Exam, preparing to take the practice exams appearing later in the chapter, or simply to jog your thoughts within your overall preparation strategy.

# Overview of Relational Databases, SQL and PL/SQL

- Advantages of the Oracle RDBMS over flat file systems include the following:
    - Easier to change system in the event of changing business requirements
    - Flexibility to model data relationships other than parent/child
    - Permits easier data manipulation and retrieval using SQL
- The RDBMS in an Oracle database handles the following tasks:
    - Implicit datatype conversion
    - Disk reads or disk writes
    - Filtering table data according to search criteria
    - Index lookups for faster response time
    - Sorting and formatting data returned
- SQL is the language used by Oracle users to communicate what data they would like to see, create, change, or remove from the Oracle database. These are DML commands and queries.
- SQL also contains commands that allow you to create, change, or remove database objects like tables, and commands for managing the database. These are DCL and DDL commands.
- There are more than these three types of categories:
    - Data definition language (DDL) statements

- Data manipulation language (DML) statements
- Transaction control statements (COMMIT, ROLLBACK)
- Session control statements (ALTER SESSION)
- System control statements (ALTER SYSTEM)

- PL/SQL is Oracle's programmatic extension to SQL, allowing you to code control structures, loops, and variable declarations around SQL operations.
- Two types of PL/SQL blocks are available in Oracle—named blocks and anonymous blocks.
- The four types of named PL/SQL blocks are procedures, functions, packages, and triggers.

# Writing Basic SQL Statements

- Data is retrieved from Oracle using SQL SELECT statements.
- Syntax for a SELECT statement consists of `select .. from ..;`.
- When entering a SELECT statement from the prompt using SQL*Plus, a semicolon (;) at the end of the statement, or slash (/) in the first position of the line must be used to end the statement.
- Arithmetic operations can be used to perform math operations on data selected from a table, or on numbers using the DUAL table.
- The DUAL table is a table with one column and one row used to fulfill the syntactic requirements of SQL SELECT statements.
- Values in columns for particular rows may be NULL.
- If a column contains the NULL value, you can use the `nvl( )` function to return meaningful information instead of an empty field.
- Aliases can be used in place of the actual column name or to replace the appearance of the function name in the header.
- Output from two columns can be concatenated together using a double-pipe (||).

## Restricting and Sorting Data

- The ORDER BY clause in a SELECT statement is a useful clause to incorporate sort order into the output of the file.
- Sort orders that can be used are ascending or descending, abbreviated as ASC and DESC. The order is determined by the column identified in the order by clause.
- The WHERE clause is used in SQL queries to limit the data returned by the query.
- The WHERE clauses contain comparison operations that determine whether a row will be returned by a query.
- There are several logical comparison operations, including =, >, >=, <, <, <=, <>, !=, ^=.
- In addition to the logical operations, there is a comparison operation for pattern matching called LIKE. The % and _ characters are used to designate wildcards.
- There is also a range operation called BETWEEN.
- There is also a fuzzy logic operation called soundex.
- The WHERE clause can contain one or more comparison operations linked together by using AND, OR, and preceded by NOT.

## Single-Row Functions

- Several SQL functions exist in Oracle.
- SQL functions are broken down into character functions, number functions, and date functions.
- A few functions can be used on many different types of data.
- There are also several conversion functions available for transforming data from text to numeric datatypes and back, numbers to dates and back, text to ROWID and back, and so on.

# Displaying Data from Multiple Tables

- SELECT statements that obtain data from more than one table and merge the data together are called joins.

- In order to join data from two tables, there must be a common column.

- A common column between two tables can create a foreign key, or link, from one table to another. This condition is especially true if the data in one of the tables is part of the primary key—the column that defines uniqueness for rows on a table.

- A foreign key can create a parent/child relationship between two tables.

- One type of join is the inner join, or equijoin. An equijoin operation is based on an equality operation linking the data in common columns of two tables.

- Another type of join is the outer join. An outer join returns data in one table even when there is no data in the other table. The "other" table in the outer join operation is called the outer table.

- The common column that appears in the outer table of the join must have a special marker next to it in the comparison operation of the SELECT statement that creates the table.

- The outer join marker is as follows: (+).

- If the column name is the same in both tables, common columns in tables used in join operations must be preceded either with a table alias that denotes the table in which the column appears or the entire table name.

- The data from a table can be joined to itself. This technique is useful in determining whether there are rows in the table that have slightly different values but are otherwise duplicate rows.

- Table aliases must be used in self join SELECT statements.

# Aggregating Data Using Group Functions

- Data output from table SELECT statements can be grouped together according to criteria set by the query.

- A special clause exists to assist the user in grouping data together. That clause is called GROUP BY.

- There are several grouping functions that allow you to perform operations on data in a column as though the data were logically one variable.

- The grouping functions are max( ), min( ), sum( ), avg( ), stddev( ), variance( ), and count( ).

- These grouping functions can be applied to the column values for a table as a whole or for subsets of column data for rows returned in GROUP BY statements.

- Data in a GROUP BY statement can be excluded or included based on a special set of WHERE criteria defined specifically for the group in a HAVING clause.

- The data used to determine the HAVING clause can either be specified at runtime by the query or by a special embedded query, called a subquery, which obtains unknown search criteria based on known search methods.

# Subqueries

- Subqueries can be used in other parts of the SELECT statement to determine unknown search criteria, as well. Subqueries are generally included in this fashion in the WHERE clause.

- Subqueries can use columns in comparison operations that are either local to the table specified in the subquery or use columns that are specified in tables named in any parent query to the subquery.

- Subqueries that use equality comparison operations are referred to as single-value subqueries. The subquery must return only one row.

- Subqueries that use other comparison operations like <, >, or IN are referred to as multiple-value subqueries. The subquery can return one or many rows.

- Subqueries can be correlated—that is to say, a subquery may refer to a column in the parent query.

## Multiple-Column Subqueries

- The columns selected in the multiple-column subquery must reference back to the same number and types of columns in the parent query.
- Multiple-column subqueries are often used in conjunction with UNION, INTERSECT, and MINUS operations.

## Producing Readable Output from SQL*Plus

- SQL commands can be entered directly into SQL*Plus on the command line.
- You can edit mistakes in SQL*Plus with the change command. If a mistake is made, the change (c/*old*/*new*) command is used.
- Alternatively, the edit (ed) command can be used to make changes in your favorite text editor.
- You can specify a favorite text editor by issuing the define_editor command at the prompt.
- Variables can be set in a SELECT statement at runtime with use of runtime variables. A runtime variable is designated with the ampersand character (**&**) preceding the variable name.
- The special character that designates a runtime variable can be changed using the set define command.
- A command called define can identify a runtime variable value to be picked up by the SELECT statement automatically.
- Once defined, the variable remains defined for the rest of the session or until undefined by the user or process with the undefine command.
- A user can modify the message that prompts the user to input a variable value. This activity is performed with the accept command.

## Manipulating Data

- New rows are put into a table with the INSERT statement. The user issuing the INSERT statement can insert one row at a time with one statement, or do a mass insert with `insert into` *table_name* `(select ...)`.

- Existing rows in a database table can be modified using the UPDATE statement. The UPDATE statement may contain a WHERE clause similar in function to the WHERE clause of SELECT statements.

- Existing rows in a table can be deleted using the DELETE statement. The DELETE statement also may contain a WHERE clause similar in function to the WHERE clause in UPDATE or SELECT statements.

- Transaction processing controls the change of data in an Oracle database.

- Transaction controls include commands that identify the beginning, breakpoint, and end of a transaction, and locking mechanisms that prevent more than one user at a time from making changes in the database.

## Creating and Managing Tables

- Tables are created without any data in them, except for tables created with the CREATE TABLE AS SELECT statement. These tables are created and prepopulated with data from another table.

- The built-in datatypes available for creating columns in tables are CHAR, VARCHAR2, NUMBER, DATE, RAW, LONG, LONG RAW, ROWID, BLOB, CLOB, NCLOB, and BFILE, NCHAR, NVARCHAR2, and UROWID.

- A table column can be added or modified with the ALTER TABLE statement.

- Columns can be added with little difficulty if they are nullable, using the `alter table add (column_name datatype)` statement. If a NOT NULL constraint is desired, add the column, populate the column with data, and then add the NOT NULL constraint separately.

- Column datatype size can be increased with no difficulty by using the `alter table modify (column_name datatype)` statement. Column size can be decreased, or the datatype can be changed, only if the column contains NULL for all rows.

- If the table is dropped, all constraints, triggers, and indexes created for the table are also dropped.

- Removing all data from a table is best accomplished with the TRUNCATE command rather than the `delete from table_name` statement because TRUNCATE will reset the table's high-water mark and deallocate all the table's storage quickly, improving performance on `select count( )` statements issued after the truncation.

- An object name can be changed with the RENAME statement or with the use of synonyms.

## Including Constraints

- A table can be created with five different types of integrity constraints: PRIMARY KEY, FOREIGN KEY, UNIQUE, NOT NULL, and CHECK.

- Referential integrity often creates a parent/child relationship between two tables, the parent being the referenced table and the child being the referring table. Often, a naming convention that requires child objects to adopt and extend the name of the parent table is useful in identifying these relationships.

- Constraints can be added to a column only if the column already contains values that will not violate the added constraint.

- Primary-key constraints can be added with a table constraint definition by using the `alter table add (constraint constraint_name primary key (column_name))` statement, or with a column constraint definition by using the `alter table modify (column_name constraint constraint_name primary key)` statement. An index will be created.

- Unique constraints can be added with a table constraint definition by using the `alter table add (constraint constraint_name unique (column_name))` statement, or with a column constraint definition by using the `alter table modify (column_name constraint constraint_name unique)` statement.

- Foreign-key constraints can be added with a table constraint definition by using the `alter table add (constraint constraint_name foreign key (column_name) references OWNER.TABLE` (`column_name`) [`on delete cascade`]) statement, or with a column constraint definition by using the `alter table modify (column_name constraint constraint_name references OWNER.TABLE (column_name) [on delete cascade])` statement. No index will be automatically created.

- Check constraints can be added with a table constraint definition by using the `alter table add (constraint constraint_name check (check_condition))` statement, or with a column constraint definition by using the `alter table modify (column_name constraint constraint_name check (check_condition))` statement.

- The check condition cannot contain subqueries, references to certain keywords (such as USER, SYSDATE, ROWID), or any pseudocolumns.

- NOT NULL constraints can be added with a column constraint definition by using the `alter table modify (column_name NOT NULL)` statement.

- A named primary-key, unique, check, or foreign-key constraint can be dropped with the `alter table drop constraint constraint_name` statement. A NOT NULL constraint is dropped using the `alter table modify (column_name NULL)` statement.

- In addition there is an ALTER TABLE DROP PRIMARY KEY (CASCADE) and ALTER TABLE DROP UNIQUE constraint_name.

- If a constraint that created an index automatically (primary keys and unique constraints) is dropped, then the corresponding index is also dropped.

## Creating Views

- A view is a virtual table defined by a SELECT statement.

- Views can distill data from tables that may be inappropriate for some users, and can hide the complexity of data from several tables or on which many operations have been performed.

- There are two types of views: simple and complex.

- Simple views are those that have only one underlying table.

- Complex views are those with two or more underlying tables that have been joined together.
- Data may be inserted into simple views except in the following cases:
    - If the WITH CHECK OPTION is used, the user may not INSERT, DELETE, or UPDATE data on the table underlying the simple view if the view itself is not able to SELECT that data for the user.
    - The user may not INSERT, DELETE, or UPDATE data on the table underlying the simple view if the SELECT statement creating the view contains GROUP BY, ORDER BY, or a single-row operation.
    - No data may be inserted in simple views that contain references to any virtual column, such as ROWID, CURRVAL, NEXTVAL, and ROWNUM.
    - No data may be inserted into simple views that are created with the READ ONLY option.
- Data may be inserted into complex views when all of the following conditions are true:
    - The statement affects only one of the tables in the join.
    - For UPDATE statements, all columns changed are extracted from a key-preserved table. In addition, if the view is created with the WITH CHECK OPTION clause, join columns and columns taken from tables that are referenced more than once in the view are not part of the UPDATE.
    - For DELETE statements, there is only one key-preserved table in the join. This table may be present more than once in the join, unless the view has been created with the WITH CHECK OPTION clause.
    - For INSERT statements, all columns where values are inserted must come from a key-preserved table, and the view must not have been created with the WITH CHECK OPTION clause.
- The WITH CHECK OPTION clause on creating a view allows the simple view to limit the data that can be inserted or otherwise changed on the underlying table by requiring that the data change be selectable by the view.
- Modifying the data selected by a view requires re-creating the view with the CREATE OR REPLACE VIEW statement, or dropping the view first and issuing the CREATE VIEW statement.

- An existing view can be recompiled by executing the ALTER VIEW statement if for some reason it becomes invalid due to object dependency.
- A view is dropped with the DROP VIEW statement.

## Oracle Data Dictionary

- There is information available in the Oracle database to help users, developers, and DBAs know what objects exist in the Oracle database. The information is in the Oracle data dictionary.
- To find the positional order of columns in a table, or what columns there are in a table at all, the user can issue a DESCRIBE command on that table. The Oracle data dictionary will then list all columns in the table being described.
- Data dictionary views on database objects are divided into three categories based on scope of user visibility: USER_, for what is owned by the user; ALL_, for all that can be seen by the user; and DBA_, for all that exists in the database, whether the user can see it or not.
- A comment can be added to the data dictionary for a database object with the COMMENT ON command. The comment can subsequently be viewed in DBA_TAB_COMMENTS or DBA_COL_COMMENTS.

## Other Database Objects

- Indexes are created automatically in conjunction with primary-key and unique constraints. These indexes are named after the constraint name given to the constraint in the definition of the table.
- Other indexes are created manually to support database performance improvements.
- Indexes created manually are often on nonunique columns.
- B-tree indexes work best on columns that have high cardinality—a large number of distinct values and few duplicates in the column.
- B-tree indexes improve performance by storing data in a binary search tree, and then searching for values in the tree using a "divide and conquer" methodology outlined in the chapter.

Chapter 7: OCP Exam 1 Terms and Concepts **411**

- Bitmap indexes improve performance on columns with low cardinality—few distinct values and many duplicates on the column.
- Columns stored in the index can be changed only by dropping and re-creating the index.
- Indexes can be deleted by issuing the DROP INDEX statement.
- A sequence generates integers based on rules that are defined by sequence creation.
- Options that can be defined for sequences are the first number generated, how the sequence increments, the maximum value, the minimum value, whether the sequence can recycle numbers, and whether numbers will be cached for improved performance.
- Sequences are used by selecting from the CURRVAL and NEXTVAL virtual columns.
- The CURRVAL column contains the current value of the sequence.
- Selecting from NEXTVAL increments the sequence and changes the value of CURRVAL to whatever is produced by NEXTVAL.
- The rules that a sequence uses to generate values can be modified using the ALTER SEQUENCE statement. You can only change the increment, minimum and maximum values, cached numbers, and behavior of an existing sequence, not the start value.
- A sequence can be deleted with the DROP SEQUENCE statement.

## Controlling User Access

- The Oracle database security model consists of two parts: limiting user access with password authentication and controlling object use with privileges.
- Available privileges in Oracle include system privileges for maintaining database objects and object privileges for accessing and manipulating data in database objects.
- Changing a password can be performed by a user with the ALTER USER IDENTIFIED BY statement.
- Granting system and object privileges is accomplished with the GRANT command.

- Taking away system and object privileges is accomplished with the REVOKE command.
- Creating a synonym is accomplished with the CREATE SYNONYM command.

## Declaring Variables

- PL/SQL is a programming environment that is native to the Oracle database. It features seamless integration with other database objects in Oracle and with SQL.
- There are three parts to a PL/SQL program: the declaration area, the execution area, and the exception handler.
- There are two categories of PL/SQL blocks: named and anonymous blocks. Named blocks include procedures, functions, packages, and triggers.
- Procedures allow the developer to specify more than one output parameter, while functions only allow one return value. Other than that, the two PL/SQL blocks are similar in function and use.
- Variables are defined in the declaration section.
- Variables can have a scalar datatype, such as NUMBER or VARCHAR2, or a referential datatype defined by a table and/or column reference followed by %TYPE or %ROWTYPE.
- Constants are declared the same way as variables, except for the fact that the CONSTANT keyword is used to denote a constant and the constant must have a value assigned in the declaration section.
- Variables can have values assigned anywhere in the PL/SQL block using the assignment operator, which is a colon followed by an equal sign (:=).

## Write Executable Statements

- The SHOW ERRORS command can be used in conjunction with application development to determine compilation problems. That shows only the errors from the last compiled program. If you need to check all errors, use USER_ERRORS.

## Interacting with the Oracle Server

- Any SQL statement is valid for use in PL/SQL. This includes all SQL statements, such as SELECT and DELETE, and transaction control statements, such as COMMIT and ROLLBACK.
- There is a SELECT INTO command as well.

## Writing Control Structures

- Conditional processing is handled in PL/SQL with IF-THEN-ELSE statements.
- IF-THEN-ELSE statements rely on Boolean logic to determine which set of statements will execute. If the condition is TRUE, the statements in the THEN clause will execute. If the condition is FALSE, the statements in the ELSE clause will execute.
- The IF statements can be nested into ELSE clauses.
- Several loops control the repetition of blocks of PL/SQL statements.
- The LOOP-EXIT statement is a simple definition for a loop that marks the beginning and end of the loop code. An IF-THEN statement tests to see whether conditions are such that the loop should exit. An EXIT statement must be specified explicitly.
- The IF-THEN statement can be replaced with an EXIT WHEN statement, which defines the EXIT condition for the loop.
- The WHILE statement eliminates the need for an EXIT statement by defining the EXIT condition in the WHILE LOOP statement.
- If the programmer wants the code to execute a specified number of times, the FOR LOOP can be used.

## Working with Composite Datatypes

- To develop a composite datatype in PL/SQL, you use the TYPE declaration to define the datatype, then declare a variable of that type.

## Writing Explicit Cursors

- Every SQL statement executes in an implicit cursor. An explicit cursor is a named cursor corresponding to a defined SQL statement.

- An explicit cursor can be defined with the `cursor cursor_name is` statement. Cursors can be defined to accept input parameters that will be used in the WHERE clause to limit the data manipulated by the cursor.

- Once declared, a cursor must be opened, parsed, and executed in order to have its data used. This task is accomplished with the OPEN statement.

- In order to obtain data from a cursor, the programmer must FETCH the data into a variable. This task is accomplished with the FETCH statement.

- The variable used in the FETCH can either consist of several loose variables for storing single-column values or a record datatype that stores all column values in a record.

## Advanced Explicit Cursor Concepts

- A special loop exists to simplify use of cursors: the CURSOR FOR loop.

- The CURSOR FOR loop handles the steps normally done in the OPEN statement, and implicitly fetches data from the cursor until the %NOTFOUND condition occurs. This statement also handles the declaration of the variable and associated record type, if any is required.

## Handling Exceptions

- The exception handler in PL/SQL handles all error handling.

- There are user-defined exceptions, predefined exceptions, and pragma exceptions in PL/SQL.

- Only user-defined exceptions require explicit checks in the execution portion of PL/SQL code to test to see if the error condition has occurred.

- A named exception can have a WHEN clause defined in the exception handler that executes whenever that exception occurs.

- The OTHERS exception is a catchall exception designed to operate if an exception occurs that is not associated with any other defined exception handler.

# CHAPTER 8

## OCP Exam 2 Terms and Concepts

The following key terms and concepts summarize facts and ideas tested in OCP Exam 2. They are meant to act as crib notes for your accelerated preparation and review, not as thorough coverage of all test matter. You may find them useful in the final days before taking the OCP Exam, preparing to take the practice exams, or simply to jog your thoughts within your overall preparation strategy.

# Oracle Architectural Components

- Several structures are used to connect users to an Oracle server. They include memory structures like the System Global Area (SGA) and Program Global Area (PGA), network processes like listeners and dispatchers, shared or dedicated server processes, and background processes like DBW0 and LGWR.

- The SGA consists of the buffer cache for storing recently accessed data blocks, the redo log buffer for storing redo entries until they can be written to disk, and the shared pool for storing parsed information about recently executed SQL for code sharing.

- The fundamental unit of storage in Oracle is the data block.

- SQL SELECT statements are processed in the following way: a cursor or address in memory is opened, the statement is parsed, bind variables are created, the statement is executed, values are fetched, and the cursor is closed.

- SQL DML statements such as UPDATE, DELETE, and INSERT are processed in the following way: a cursor or address in memory is opened, the statement is parsed, the statement is executed, and the cursor is closed. You will want to use bind variables as well.

- Several background processes manage Oracle's ability to write data from the buffer cache and redo log buffer to appropriate areas on disk. They are DBW0 for writing data between disk and buffer cache, and LGWR for writing redo log entries between the redo log buffer and the online redo log on disk.

- DBW0 writes data to disk when LGWR tells it to (during a checkpoint), and when the buffer cache is full and a server process needs to make room for buffers required by user processes.

- Server processes are like genies from the story of Aladdin because they retrieve data from disk into the buffer cache according to the user's command.

- There are two configurations for server processes: shared servers and dedicated servers. In dedicated servers, a listener process listens for users connecting to Oracle. When a listener hears a user, the listener tells Oracle to spawn a dedicated server. Each user process has its own server process available for retrieving data from disk.

- In shared server configurations (also called multithreaded server or MTS), a user process attempts to connect to Oracle. The listener hears the connection and passes the user process to a dispatcher process. A limited number of server processes, each handling multiple user requests, are monitored by a dispatcher, which assigns user processes to a shared server based on which has the lightest load at the time of user connection. The dispatcher outs the request in the request queue and the shared server with the lightest load will process the request and put the result in the response queue.

- The COMMIT statement may trigger Oracle to write changed data in the buffer cache to disk, but not necessarily. It only makes a redo log buffer entry that says all data changes associated with a particular transaction are now committed.

- Two user authentication methods exist in Oracle: operating system authentication and Oracle authentication.

- There are two privileges DBAs require to perform their functions on the database. In Oracle authentication environments, they are called SYSDBA and SYSOPER.

- To use Oracle authentication, the DBA must create a password file using the ORAPWD utility.

- To start and stop a database, the DBA must connect as INTERNAL or SYSDBA.

# Using Administrative Tools

- The tool used to start and stop the database is called Server Manager. This tool is usually run in line mode.

- Another tool for managing database administration activity is Oracle Enterprise Manager (OEM). OEM has many administrative tools available, including Backup Manager, Data Manager, Daemon Manager, Instance Manager, Replication Manager, Schema Manager, Security Manager, SQL Worksheet, Storage Manager, Net8 Assistant, and Software Manager.

## Managing an Oracle Instance

- There are several options for starting a database:
    - **STARTUP NOMOUNT** Starts the instance and does not mount a database
    - **STARTUP MOUNT** Starts the instance and mounts but does not open the database
    - **STARTUP OPEN** Starts the instance and mounts and opens the database
    - **STARTUP RESTRICT** Starts the instance, mounts and opens the database, but restricts access to those users with RESTRICTED SESSION privilege granted to them
    - **STARTUP RECOVER** Starts the instance, leaves the database closed, and begins recovery for disk failure scenario
    - **STARTUP FORCE** Makes an instance start that is having problems either starting or stopping
- When a database is open, any user with a username and password and the CREATE SESSION privilege can log into the Oracle database.
- Closing or shutting down a database must be done by the DBA while running Server Manager and while the DBA is connected to the database as INTERNAL or SYSDBA.
- There are four options for closing a database:
    - **SHUTDOWN NORMAL** No new existing connections are allowed, but existing sessions may take as long as they want to wrap up.
    - **SHUTDOWN IMMEDIATE** No new connections are allowed, existing sessions are terminated, and their transactions are rolled back.
    - **SHUTDOWN ABORT** No new connections are allowed, existing sessions are terminated, and transactions are not rolled back.
    - **SHUTDOWN TRANSACTIONAL** Existing transactions are allowed to complete, and then terminated. Idle connections are terminated.
- Instance recovery is required after SHUTDOWN ABORT is used.
- You can obtain values for initialization parameters from several sources:
    - V$PARAMETER dynamic performance view

- SHOW PARAMETER command in Server Manager
- OEM Instance Manager administrative tool

■ Several important runtime-logging files exist on the machine hosting Oracle. Each background process, such as LGWR and DBW0, will have a trace file if some error occurs in their execution, and the instance has a special trace file called the *alert log*. Trace files are written whenever the background process has a problem executing. The alert log is written whenever the instance is started or stopped, whenever the database structure is altered, or whenever an error occurs in the database.

■ Trace files and alert logs are found in the directory identified by the BACKGROUND_DUMP_DEST parameter in the init*sid*.ora file.

# Creating a Database

■ Before creating the database, assess according to the following things on the OS level:
  - Are there enough individual disk resources to run Oracle without I/O bottlenecks?
  - Is there enough CPU, memory, and disk space for Oracle processing?
  - Are disk resources for different Oracle databases on the same host in separate directories?
  - Are environment settings correct for the database creation?

■ The first step in creating a database is to back up any existing databases already on the host machine.

■ The second step in creating a database is for the DBA to create a parameter file with unique values for several parameters, including the following:
  - **DB_NAME**   The local name for the database.
  - **DB_DOMAIN**   The network-wide location for the database.
  - **DB_BLOCK_SIZE**   The size of each block in the database.
  - **DB_BLOCK_BUFFERS**   The number of blocks stored in the buffer cache.
  - **PROCESSES**   The maximum number of processes available on the database.

- **ROLLBACK_SEGMENTS** Named rollback segments the database acquires at startup.

- **LICENSE_MAX_SESSIONS** The maximum number of sessions that can connect to the database.

- **LICENSE_MAX_WARNING** The sessions trying to connect above the number specified by this parameter will receive a warning message.

- **LICENSE_MAX_USERS** The maximum number of users that can be created in the Oracle instance.

- LICENSE_MAX_SESSIONS and LICENSE_MAX_WARNING are used for license tracking or LICENSE_MAX_USERS is used, but not both, usually.

- After creating the parameter file, the DBA executes the CREATE DATABASE command, which creates the datafiles for the SYSTEM tablespace, an initial rollback segment, SYS and SYSTEM users, and redo log files. On conclusion of the CREATE DATABASE statement, the database is created and open.

- The default password for SYS is CHANGE_ON_INSTALL.

- The default password for SYSTEM is MANAGER.

- The number of datafiles and redo log files created for the life of the database can be limited with the MAXDATAFILES and MAXLOGFILES options of the CREATE DATABASE statement.

- The size of a datafile is fixed at its creation, unless the AUTOEXTEND option is used.

- The size of a control file is directly related to the number of datafiles and redo logs for the database, and the usage of RMAN and the usage of Control file space for RMAN purposes.

- Understand all Oracle physical disk resources, and they are control files, redo logs, and datafiles.

# Data Dictionary Views and Standard Packages

- The catalog.sql script creates the data dictionary. Run it after creating a database, while connected to Oracle administratively through Server Manager.

# Chapter 8: OCP Exam 2 Terms and Concepts

- The catproc.sql script creates the Oracle-supplied packages used often in PL/SQL development. Run it after creating a database, while connected to Oracle administratively through Server Manager.

## Maintaining the Control File

- Control files are used to tell the Oracle instance where to find the other files it needs for normal operation.

- The contents of a control file can be found in the script to create it, which Oracle generates with an ALTER DATABASE BACKUP CONTROLFILE TO TRACE. This file is then found in the directory specified by the USER_DUMP_DEST initialization parameter.

- You will find information about control files, such as where they are located on your host machine, in V$CONTROLFILE, V$CONTROLFILE_RECORD_SECTION, and V$DATABASE.

- It is important to multiplex control files in order to reduce dependency on any single disk resource in the host machine. This is done using the CONTROL_FILES parameter in init*sid*.ora.

## Maintaining Redo Log Files

- The Oracle redo log architecture consists of the following components: redo log buffer to store redo entries from user processes, LGWR to move redo entries from memory onto disk, and online redo logs on disk to store redo entries taken out of memory.

- Online redo logs are referred to as groups. The group has one or more files, called members, where LGWR writes the redo log entries from memory. There must be at least two online redo log groups for the Oracle instance to start.

- Checkpoints are events in which LGWR tells DBWR to write all changed blocks to disk. They occur during log switches, which are when LGWR stops writing a full log and starts writing a new one. At this point, LGWR will also write the redo log file sequence change to datafile headers and to the control file. That's not the only event. See also LOG_CHECPOINT_INTREVAL and LOG_CHECKPOINT_TIMEOUT.

- Understand the process LGWR uses to write redo data from one log to another and then back again, what happens when archiving is used, what the role of the ARCH process is, and how LGWR can contend with ARCH.

- Understand how to multiplex redo logs using both the CREATE DATABASE and ALTER DATABASE statements, and why it is important to do so.

## Managing Tablespaces and Datafiles

- Understand how tablespaces and datafiles relate to one another. A tablespace can have many datafiles, but each datafile can associate with only one tablespace.

- At database creation, there is one tablespace—SYSTEM. The DBA should *not* place all database objects into that tablespace, because often their storage needs conflict with each other. Instead, the DBA should create multiple tablespaces for the different segments available on the database and place those objects into those tablespaces.

- Some logical disk resources map to Oracle physical disk resources, and they are tablespaces, segments, extents, and blocks.

- The different types of segments (and tablespaces you need) are: *table*, *index*, *rollback*, and *temporary*. Two other segment types, *cluster* and *IOT*, will not be used frequently, and thus can probably be placed into your data tablespace without interfering with the other objects. You can have more than one table or index tablespace. See also partitioning.

- A final tablespace you should create to separate your application data from objects created in support of your Oracle database administrative tools, such as Oracle Enterprise Manager, is the TOOLS tablespace.

## Storage Structures and Relationships

- When a segment containing a database object cannot store any more data for that table, Oracle will obtain an extent to store the data. This adversely affects performance. Understand the discussion of how to weigh segment preallocation against allowing Oracle to acquire new extents.

- Understand how Oracle allows the DBA to control space usage at the block level with PCTFREE and PCTUSED.

- Know what dictionary views are used to find information about storage structures, including DBA_SEGMENTS, DBA_TABLESPACES, DBA_TS_QUOTAS, DBA_EXTENTS, DBA_FREE_SPACE, and DBA_FREE_SPACE_COALESCED.

- Understand the inverse proportional relationship between the lifespan of extents and fragmentation in the tablespace—the shorter the lifespan, the higher potential for fragmentation in the tablespace.

# Managing Rollback Segments

- Rollback segments allow transaction processing to occur by storing the old version of data that has been changed but not committed by the users. Once transactions are committed, the information in a rollback segment remains there until Oracle overwrites it with new uncommitted transaction information. In other words, Oracle does not remove committed information immediately.

- Rollback segments should consist of equally sized extents.

- The PCTINCREASE option is not permitted on rollback segments.

- Rollback segments must be brought online in order to use them.

- A rollback segment cannot be taken offline until all active transactions writing rollback entries have completed. This same restriction applies to tablespaces containing active rollback segments.

- Entries are associated with transactions in the rollback segment via the use of a system change number (SCN).

- When Oracle Parallel Server is used, the number of public rollback segments allocated by Oracle when the database is started is equal to the quotient of TRANSACTIONS / TRANSACTIONS_PER_ROLLBACK_SEGMENT. This can also be used for single instance.

- Specific private rollback segments can be allocated at startup if they are specified in the ROLLBACK_SEGMENTS parameter in INIT.ORA.

- The number of rollback segments required for an instance is determined by the Rule of Four—divide concurrent user processes by 4; if the result is less than 4 + 4, round up to the nearest multiple of 4.

- Monitor performance in rollback segments with V$ROLLSTAT and V$WAITSTAT.

# Managing Temporary Segments

- There are two types of temporary segments: temporary segments for permanent tablespaces and temporary segments for temporary tablespaces.

- Oracle's use of temporary segments was reworked to make disk sorts more efficient. Sort segments in temporary tablespaces are allocated for the first disk sort and then persist for everyone's use for the duration of the instance. The result is less fragmentation than is the case in temporary segments in permanent tablespaces.

- A new memory area called the *sort extent pool* manages how user processes allocate extents for disk sorts in temporary tablespaces.

- SMON handles deallocation of temporary segments in permanent tablespaces when the transaction no longer needs them.

- You cannot create permanent database objects, such as tables, in temporary tablespaces. You also cannot convert permanent tablespaces into temporary ones unless there are no permanent objects in the permanent tablespace.

- You can get information about temporary segments and sort segments from the DBA_SEGMENTS, V$SORT_SEGMENT, and V$SORT_USAGE dictionary views.

- A sort segment exists in the temporary tablespace for as long as the instance is available. All users share the sort segment.

- The size of extents in the temporary tablespace should be set to a multiple of SORT_AREA_SIZE, plus one additional block for the segment header, in order to maximize disk sort performance.

# Managing Tables

- There are four types of tables: regular tables, partitioned tables, cluster tables, and index-organized tables.

- There are two categories of datatypes: user-defined and built-in.

- There are three classes of built-in types: scalar, collection, and relationship types.

- The "regular size" scalar types include CHAR, NCHAR, VARCHAR2, NVARCHAR2, DATE, RAW, ROWID, and NUMBER.

- The "large size" scalar types include LONG and LONG RAW from Oracle7, and CLOB, NCLOB, BLOB, and BFILE.
- The collection types include VARRAY or variable-length array, and TABLE, which is a nested table type.
- The relationship type is REF, and it is a pointer to other data in another table.
- Collection and relationship types require the Objects Option installed on your Oracle database.
- Remember how to use each of the options for defining storage and table creation. They are as follows:
    - **INITIAL** First segment in the table
    - **NEXT** Next segment allocated (not simply the second one in the table)
    - **PCTINCREASE** Percentage increase of next extent allocated over NEXT value
    - **MINEXTENTS** Minimum number of extents allocated at table creation
    - **MAXEXTENTS** Maximum number of extents the object can allocate
    - **PCTFREE** How much of each block stays free after INSERT for row UPDATE
    - **PCTUSED** Threshold that usage must fall below before a row is added
    - **INITRANS** Number of concurrent changes that can happen per block
    - **MAXTRANS** Maximum number of transactions that are likely to touch the same data blocks at any given time
    - **LOGGING/NOLOGGING** Whether Oracle will store redo for the CREATE TABLE statement
    - **CACHE/NOCACHE** Whether Oracle allows blocks to stay in the buffer cache after full table scans
- Row migration is when an UPDATE makes a row too large to store in its original block.
- Chaining is when a row is broken up and stored in many blocks. Both require multiple disk reads/writes to retrieve/store, and, therefore, are bad for performance.

## Managing Indexes

- Indexes are used to improve performance on database objects in Oracle. The types of indexes in Oracle are bitmap, B-tree, and reverse-key.

- Bitmap indexes are best used for improving performance on columns containing static values with low cardinality, or few unique values in the column.

- B-tree indexes are best used for improving performance on columns containing values with high cardinality.

- The decision to create an index should weigh the performance gain of using the index against the performance overhead produced when DML statements change index data.

- Reverse-key indexes store the index values in reverse sort order.

- The PCTUSED parameter is not available for indexes, because every index block is always available for data changes as the result of Oracle needing to keep data in order in an index.

- DBA_INDEXES and DBA_IND_COLUMNS are dictionary views that store information about indexes.

## Maintaining Data Integrity

- Data integrity constraints are declared in the Oracle database as part of the table definition.

- There are five types of integrity constraints:
    - **PRIMARY KEY** Identifies each row in the table as unique
    - **FOREIGN KEY** Develops referential integrity between two tables
    - **UNIQUE** Forces each non-NULL value in the column to be unique
    - **NOT NULL** Forces each value in the column to be not NULL
    - **CHECK** Validates each entry into the column against a set of valid value constants

- There are different constraint states in Oracle, including deferrable constraints or nondeferrable constraints.

- In addition, a constraint can be enabled on a table without validating existing data in the constrained column using the ENABLE NOVALIDATE clause.

- Oracle uses unique indexes to enforce UNIQUE and PRIMARY KEY constraints when those constraints are not deferrable. If the constraints are deferrable, then Oracle uses nonunique indexes for those constraints.

- When a constraint is created, every row in the table is validated against the constraint restriction.

- The EXCEPTIONS table stores rows that violate the integrity constraint created for a table.

- The EXCEPTIONS table can be created by running the utlexcpt.sql script.

- The DBA_CONSTRAINTS and DBA_CONS_COLUMNS data dictionary views display information about the constraints of a database.

- Triggers are PL/SQL programs that allow you to define a DML statement event that causes the code to execute.

- There are two types of triggers: row triggers and statement triggers.

- Triggers and constraints can be enabled or disabled. If enabled, constraints will be enforced and triggers will fire. If disabled, constraints will not be enforced and triggers will not fire.

# Using Clusters and Index-Organized Tables

- Index-organized tables (IOTs) are tables that are stored in B-tree index structures.

- ROWID information is not stored in IOTs because the row data is stored along with the index.

- IOTs store all row data in a B-tree structure, while regular tables store table data in table segments and index data in indexes.

- IOT rows have no ROWID; regular table rows do.

- Uniqueness for IOT data is determined by the primary key, rather than by ROWID.

- A full table scan on a regular table guarantees no return order on row data, while index scans on IOTs return data in primary-key order.

- IOTs cannot be partitioned or replicated, or participate in a distributed transaction, because ROWIDs are not used. This restriction is removed in Oracle8*i*.

- There can be no index on an IOT, other than the implicit IOT index structure. This restriction includes indexes created as part of unique keys, so unique keys other than the primary key are not supported in IOTs, either.

- Index clusters improve performance on queries that join two or more tables with static data by storing related data from the tables in the same physical data blocks. This reduces the number of I/O reads required to retrieve the data.

- Determining space requirements for clusters is accomplished by doing the following:
    - Determine the number of rows that will associate with each individual cluster entry.
    - Determine the number of cluster entries that will fit into one block.
    - Determine the number of blocks required for the cluster.

- Clusters should not be used to store tables whose data is dynamic or volatile.

- The steps to create a cluster, once proper sizing has taken place, are as follows:
    1. Create the cluster with the CREATE CLUSTER statement.
    2. Place tables in the cluster with the CLUSTER option of the CREATE TABLE command.
    3. Create the cluster index with the CREATE INDEX ON CLUSTER command.
    4. Populate tables with data. This step cannot be done until step 3 is complete.

- Hash clustering is similar to regular clusters because data from multiple tables are stored together in data blocks. However, there is an additional key to search for data, called a *hash key*.

- Data is retrieved from a hash cluster by Oracle applying a hash function to the value specified in equality operations in the WHERE clause of the table join. Ideally, this allows for data retrieval in one disk read.

- Hash clusters only improve performance on queries when the data is static, and the SELECT statements contain equality operations *only*. Range queries are not allowed.

# Loading and Reorganizing Data

- A hint is a directive you pass to the Oracle RDBMS telling it to process your statement in a certain way.
- Direct-path INSERT is accomplished using hints. They are specified as follows:
    - **/*+append */** Add records to the end of the table, above the high-water mark.
    - **/*+parallel(*tablename, integer*) */** Add records in parallel, using multiple I/O processes.
- SQL*Loader loads data from a flat file to a table.
- There are several file components:
    - **Datafile** Contains all records to be loaded into the database
    - **Control file** Identifies how SQL*Loader should interpret the datafile
    - **Parameter file** Gives runtime options to be used by SQL*Loader
    - **Discard file** Holds records that SQL*Loader might reject, based on WHEN conditions defined in the control file
    - **Bad file** Holds records that SQL*Loader might reject, based on constraint violations defined in your database
    - **Log file** Stores information about the execution of a SQL*Loader run, such as record counts and why records were rejected
- Data in the datafiles can be structured into fixed- or variable-length fields.
- The positional specifications for fixed-length fields are contained in the control file, along with other specifications for the data load.
- For variable-length data fields, appropriate delimiters must be specified.
- The two types of delimiters used are terminating delimiters and enclosing delimiters.

- There are two data load paths: *conventional* and *direct*.
- Conventional loads use the same SQL interface and other Oracle RDBMS processes and structures that other processes use.
- Conventional-path loading updates indexes as rows are inserted into the database, and also validates integrity constraints and fires triggers at that time.
- Direct-path loads bypass most of the Oracle RDBMS, writing full database blocks. A direct-path load parses the input records according to the field specifications, converts the input field data to the column datatype, and builds a column array.
- The column array is passed to a block formatter, which creates data blocks in Oracle database block format. The newly formatted database blocks are written directly to the database, bypassing most RDBMS processing.
- Direct-path loading disables indexes, INSERT triggers, and constraints until all data is loaded. Constraints and indexes are rechecked and built after data load.
- The direct-path load may occasionally leave an index in direct-path state. This often is due to load failure or the loading of a data record that violates the table's integrity constraints.
- EXPORT pulls data out of your Oracle database and puts it into a file in binary format. The IMPORT tool is used to read files produced by EXPORT into the database.

# Managing Users

- New database users are created with the CREATE USER statement.
- A new user can have the following items configured by the CREATE USER statement:
    - Password
    - Default tablespace for database objects
    - Temporary tablespace
    - Quotas on tablespaces
    - User profile

- Account lock status
- Whether the user must specify a new password on first logging on
- User definitions can be altered with the ALTER USER statement and dropped with the DROP USER statement. Users can issue the ALTER USER statement only to change their password and default roles.
- Information about a database user can be found in the following data dictionary views:
  - DBA_USERS
  - DBA_PROFILES
  - DBA_TS_QUOTAS
- Users in operating system authenticated database environments generally have their usernames preceded by OPS$ at user-creation time.

# Managing Profiles

- User profiles help to limit resource usage on the Oracle database.
- The DBA must set the RESOURCE_LIMIT parameter to TRUE in order to use user profiles.
- The resources that can be limited via profiles include the following:
  - Sessions connected per user at one time
  - CPU time per call
  - CPU time per session
  - Disk I/O per call
  - Disk I/O per session
  - Connection time
  - Idle time
  - Private memory (only for MTS)
  - Composite limit

- Profiles should be created for every type or class of user. Each parameter has a resource limit set for it in a user profile, which can then be assigned to users based on their processing needs.

- Oracle installs a special profile granted to a user if no other profile is defined. This special profile is called DEFAULT, and all values in the profile are set to UNLIMITED.

- Any parameter not explicitly set in another user profile defaults in value to the value specified for that parameter in DEFAULT.

## Managing Privileges

- New Oracle8 and Oracle8i features in password administration are also available:
    - **FAILED_LOGIN_ATTEMPTS** Number of unsuccessful attempts at login a user can make before the account locks; the default is 3.
    - **PASSWORD_LIFE_TIME** Number of days a password will remain active; the default is 60.
    - **PASSWORD_REUSE_TIME** Number of days before the password can be reused; the default is 1,800 (approximately five years).
    - **PASSWORD_REUSE_MAX** Number of times the password must be changed before one can be reused; the default is UNLIMITED.
    - **PASSWORD_LOCK_TIME** Number of days after which Oracle will unlock a user account locked automatically when the user exceeds FAILED_LOGIN_ATTEMPTS; the default is 1/1,440 (one minute).
    - **PASSWORD_GRACE_TIME** Number of days during which an expired password must be changed by the user or else Oracle permanently locks the account; the default is 10.
    - **PASSWORD_VERIFY_FUNCTION** Function used for password complexity verification; the default function is called verify_function( ).

    These defaults are only valid if you did run utlpwdmg.sql.

- Database privileges govern access for performing every permitted activity in the Oracle database.

- There are two categories of database privileges: *system privileges* and *object privileges*.

- System privileges allow for the creation of every object on the database, along with the ability to execute many commands and connect to the database.

- Object privileges allow for access to data within database objects.

- There are three basic classes of system privileges for some database objects: CREATE, ALTER, and DROP ANY. These privileges give the grantee the power to create database objects in their own user schema.

- Some exceptions exist to the preceding rule. The ALTER TABLE privilege is an object privilege, while the ALTER ROLLBACK SEGMENT privilege is a system privilege. The INDEX privilege is an object privilege as well.

- Three oddball privileges are GRANT, AUDIT, and ANALYZE. These privileges apply to the creation of all database objects and to running powerful commands in Oracle.

- The ANY modifier gives the user extra power to create objects or run commands on any object in the user schema.

- The final system privilege of interest is the RESTRICTED SESSION privilege, which allows the user to connect to a database in RESTRICTED SESSION mode.

- Object privileges give the user access to place, remove, change, or view data in a table or one column in a table, as well as to alter the definition of a table, create an index on a table, and develop FOREIGN KEY constraints.

- When system privileges are revoked, the objects a user has created will still exist.

- A system privilege can be granted WITH ADMIN OPTION to allow the grantee to administer others' ability to use the privilege.

- When object privileges are revoked, the data placed or modified in a table will still exist, but you will not be able to perform the action allowed by the privilege anymore.

- An object privilege can be granted WITH GRANT OPTION to another user in order to make them an administrator of the privilege.

- The GRANT OPTION cannot be used when granting a privilege to a role, or the other way: the WITH ADMIN OPTION can be used when granting a privilege to a role.

## Managing Roles

- Roles are used to bundle privileges together and to enable or disable them automatically.
- A user can create objects and then grant the object privileges to the role, which then can be granted to as many users as require it.
- There are roles created by Oracle when the software is installed:
    - **CONNECT**  Can connect to the database and create clusters, links, sequences, tables, views, and synonyms. This role is good for table schema owners and development DBAs.
    - **RESOURCE**  Can connect to the database and create clusters, sequences, tables, triggers, and stored procedures. This role is good for application developers.
    - **DBA**  Can use any system privilege WITH ADMIN OPTION.
    - **EXP_FULL_DATABASE**  Can export all database objects to an export dump file.
    - **IMP_FULL_DATABASE**  Can import all database objects from an export dump file to the database.
    - **DELETE_CATALOG_ROLE**  Extends DELETE privileges on SYS-owned dictionary tables, in response to the new restriction on DELETE ANY TABLE privileges that prevents grantees from removing rows from SYS-owned dictionary tables.
    - **EXECUTE_CATALOG_ROLE**  Allows grantee EXECUTE privileges on any SYS-owned package supplied with the Oracle software.
    - **SELECT_CATALOG_ROLE**  Allows grantee to SELECT data from any SYS-owned dictionary table or view. These are examples of predefined roles. There are more than these (e.g., RECOVERY_ CATALOG_ OWNER).
- Roles can have passwords assigned to them to provide security for the use of certain privileges.
- Users can alter their own roles in a database session.

- When a privilege is granted to the user PUBLIC, then every user in the database can use the privilege. However, when a privilege is revoked from PUBLIC, then every stored procedure, function, or package in the database must be recompiled.

## Auditing

- Auditing the database can be done either to detect inappropriate activity or to store an archive of database activity.
- Auditing can collect large amounts of information. In order to minimize the amount of searching, the person conducting the audit should limit the auditing of database activities to where he or she thinks a problem may lie.
- Any activity on the database can be audited, either by naming the privilege or by naming an object in the database.
- The activities of one or more users can be singled out for audit; or, every access to an object or privilege, or every session on the database, can have their activities audited.
- Audits can monitor successful activities surrounding a privilege, unsuccessful activities, or both.
- In every database audit, starting and stopping the instance, and every connection established by a user with DBA privileges as granted by SYSDBA and SYSOPER, are monitored regardless of any other activities being audited.
- Audit data is stored in the data dictionary in the AUD$ table, which is owned by SYS.
- Several dictionary views exist for seeing data in the AUD$ table. The main ones are as follows:
    - DBA_AUDIT_EXISTS
    - DBA_AUDIT_OBJECT
    - DBA_AUDIT_SESSION
    - DBA_AUDIT_STATEMENT
    - DBA_AUDIT_TRAIL

- If auditing is in place and monitoring session connections, and if the AUD$ table fills, then no more users can connect to the database until the AUD$ table is (archived and) emptied.

- The AUD$ table should be audited, whenever in use, to detect tampering with the data in it.

## Using National Language Support

- Oracle uses the database character set for data stored in CHAR, VARCHAR2, CLOB, and LONG column identifiers such as table names, column names, and PL/SQL variables entering and storing SQL and PL/SQL.

- In some cases, you may wish to have the ability to choose an alternate character set for the database because the properties of a different character encoding scheme may be more desirable for extensive character processing operations, or to facilitate ease of programming. In particular, the following datatypes can be used with an alternate character set: NCHAR, NVARCHAR2, NCLOB.

- Specifying an NCHAR character set allows you to specify an alternate character set from the database character set for use in NCHAR, NVARCHAR2, and NCLOB columns. This can be particularly useful for customers using a variable-width multibyte database character set because NCHAR has the capability to support fixed-width multibyte encoding schemes, whereas the database character set cannot. The benefits in using a fixed-width multibyte encoding over a variable-width one are optimized string processing performance on NCHAR, NVARCHAR2, and NCLOB columns, and ease of programming with a fixed-width multibyte character set as opposed to a variable-width multibyte character set.

# CHAPTER 9

## OCP Exam 3 Terms and Concepts

The following key terms and concepts summarize facts and ideas tested in OCP Exam 3. They are meant to act as crib notes for your accelerated preparation and review, not as thorough coverage of all test matter. You may find them useful in the final days before taking the OCP Exam, preparing to take the practice exams, or simply to jog your thoughts within your overall preparation strategy.

# Backup and Recovery Considerations

- The three axioms of database backup and recovery for a DBA are these: maximize database availability, maximize recovery performance, and maximize data recoverability.

- Without backups, database recovery is not possible in the event of a database failure that destroys data.

- Three factors that should be considered when developing a backup strategy are the business requirements that affect database availability, whether the database should be recoverable to the point in time of the database failure, and the overall volatility of data in the database.

- Disaster recovery for any computer system can have the following impact: loss of time spent recovering the system, loss of user productivity correcting data errors or waiting for the system to come online again, the threat of permanent loss of data, and the cost of replacing hardware.

- The final determination of the risks an organization is willing to take with regard to their backup strategy should be handled by management. The DBA should advise management of any and all risks and the impact of any plan that management wants to enact regarding recovery.

- Complete recovery of data is possible in the Oracle database, but it depends on a good backup strategy.

- Testing backup and recovery strategy has three benefits: weaknesses in the strategy can be corrected, data corruption in the database that is being copied into the backups can be detected, and the DBA can improve his or her own skills and tune the overall process to save time.

# Oracle Recovery Structures and Processes

- The background processes involved in Oracle database backup and recovery are as follows:
    - **SMON** Handles instance recovery at database startup and periodically coalesces free space in tablespaces, and cleans up temporary segments that are no longer in use
    - **PMON** Performs process recovery on dedicated servers when associated user processes crash
    - **CKPT** Handles aspects of checkpoint processing
    - **ARCH** Handles automatic archiving of redo logs
    - **LGWR** Writes redo entries from memory to disk
    - **DBW0** Writes dirty buffers from memory to disk
- File structures for Oracle database recovery include online and archived redo logs, and backup copies of datafiles, control files, init*sid*.ora files, and password files.
- Memory structures for Oracle database backup and recovery include the redo log buffer, buffer cache, and large pool.
- Checkpoints are opportunities for Oracle to synchronize the data stored in redo logs with data stored in datafiles.
- Multiplexing online redo logs and control files reduces the dependency you have on any one disk, which could crash and make your database unrecoverable.

# Oracle Backup and Recovery Configuration

- The difference between logical and physical backups is the same as the difference between the logical and physical view of Oracle's use of disk resources on the machine hosting the database.

- Logical backups are used to copy the data from the logical Oracle database objects, such as tables, indexes, and sequences.
- The EXPORT and IMPORT tools are used for logical database object export and import.
- Physical backups are used to copy Oracle database files that are present from the perspective of the operating system. This includes datafiles, redo log files, control files, the password file, and the parameter file.

## Oracle Recovery Manager Overview

- The new architecture for backup and recovery in Oracle8 consists of Recovery Manager (RMAN) and a recovery catalog.
- Recovery Manager is a utility that allows DBAs to manage all aspects of backup and recovery using an Oracle-supported tool.
- There are some enhancements to the control file, and it is much larger in Oracle8 to support RMAN. RMAN information is stored for a period of time corresponding to the CONTROL_FILE_RECORD_KEEP_TIME initialization parameter.
- RMAN has four sets of commands: recovery catalog maintenance commands, reporting commands, scripting commands, and RUN commands.

  To run RMAN, type **rman** at the OS command prompt. One mandatory option and four optional ones are used:

  - **TARGET (Mandatory)**   Used to identify the production or target database
  - **RCVCAT**   Used to identify the recovery catalog database
  - **CMDFILE**   Used to execute RMAN in batch mode with a command script
  - **MSGLOG**   Used to keep a log of all activity
  - **APPEND**   Permits RMAN to append information to an old log file for the current RMAN session
- Communication with the operating system is possible in RMAN with the ALLOCATE CHANNEL command.

# Oracle Recovery Catalog Maintenance

- A recovery catalog runs on a database, other than the production database containing all your user data, and it tracks all backup and archived redo logs produced for the database.

- Recovery catalog management commands include the following:

    - **REGISTER DATABASE**   Used to register a target database

    - **RESET DATABASE**   Used when the target database is opened and the redo log sequence needs to be reset

    - **RESYNC CATALOG**   Used after log switches in target database

    - **CHANGE**   Used to alter the control file or other database filenames used

    - **LIST INCARNATION**   Used to show the current database data version

    - **CATALOG**   Used to identify copies of files made outside of RMAN

- RMAN reporting and listing commands give information about the current database and its recovery status.

- Reports show information about database files and recoverability. One of the reports that can be used is REPORT NEED BACKUP to show the files of the database that need to be backed up. Options for this report include INCREMENTAL = *num* to show the files that need *num* incremental backups to be recovered, and DAYS *num* to show the files that haven't been backed up in *num* days. Another report includes REPORT UNRECOVERABLE to show files that are not recoverable.

- Lists show information about the backups that are available in the database. Some lists that can be used are LIST COPY OF TABLESPACE, LIST COPY OF DATAFILE, LIST BACKUPSET, and LIST INCARNATION OF DATABASE.

- There are several commands available in RMAN for script creation. They are CREATE SCRIPT, REPLACE SCRIPT, DELETE SCRIPT, and PRINT SCRIPT.

- The final set of commands in RMAN are RUN commands. These commands handle most of the processing in RMAN, such as execution of scripts, SQL, and backup and recovery operations.

# Physical Backups Without Oracle Recovery Manager

- To determine what datafiles are present in the database, use the V$DATAFILE dictionary view.

- To determine what control files are present in the database, use the SHOW PARAMETERS CONTROL_FILES command from Server Manager, or look in the V$CONTROLFILE view.

- To determine what redo log files are available in the database, use the V$LOGFILE dictionary view.

- There are two types of physical backups: offline backups and online backups.

- Offline backups are complete backups of the database taken when the database is closed. In order to close the database, use the SHUTDOWN NORMAL, SHUTDOWN TRANSACTIONAL, or SHUTDOWN IMMEDIATE command.

- Online backups are backups of tablespaces taken while the database is running. This option requires that Oracle be archiving its redo logs. To start an online backup, the DBA must issue the ALTER TABLESPACE *name* BEGIN BACKUP statement from Server Manager. When complete, the DBA must issue the ALTER TABLESPACE *name* END BACKUP statement.

- Archiving redo logs is crucial for providing complete data recovery to the point in time that the database failure occurs. Redo logs can only be used in conjunction with physical backups.

- When the DBA is not archiving redo logs, recovery is only possible to the point in time when the last backup was taken.

- Databases that must be available 24 hours a day generally require online backups because they cannot afford the database downtime required for logical backups or offline backups.

- Database recovery time consists of two factors: the amount of time it takes to restore a backup, and the amount of time it takes to apply database changes made after the most recent backup.

- If archiving is used, then the time spent applying the changes made to the database since the last backup consists of applying archived redo logs. If not, then the time spent applying the changes made to the database since

Chapter 9: OCP Exam 3 Terms and Concepts  **443**

the last backup consists of users identifying and manually reentering the changes they made to the database since the last backup.

- The more changes made after the last database backup, the longer it generally takes to provide full recovery to the database.

- Shorter recovery time can be achieved with more frequent backups.

- Each type of backup has varied time implications. In general, offline physical database backups require database downtime.

- Only online database backups allow users to access the data in the database while the backup takes place.

- The more transactions that take place on a database, the more redo information that is generated by the database.

- An infrequently backed-up database with many archived redo logs is just as recoverable as a frequently backed-up database with few online redo logs. However, the time spent handling the recovery is longer for the first option than the second.

- Read-only tablespaces need to be backed up only once, after the database data changes and the tablespace is set to read only.

- init*sid*.ora parameters involved in archiving include the following:

    - **LOG_ARCHIVE_DEST**   Identifies primary archive destination

    - **LOG_ARCHIVE_START**   Makes ARCH start running

    - **LOG_ARCHIVE_FORMAT**   Determines format conventions for archived redo logs

    - **LOG_ARCHIVE_DUPLEX_DEST**   Identifies the multiplexed archive destination

    - **LOG_ARCHIVE_MIN_SUCCEED_DEST**   Identifies in how many locations an archived redo log will need to be stored

- The five steps for setting up archiving of redo logs include

    - Shutting down the database using IMMEDIATE, NORMAL, or TRANSACTIONAL options

    - Configuring LOG_ARCHIVE_DEST, LOG_ARCHIVE_START, and LOG_ARCHIVE_FORMAT init*sid*.ora parameters

    - Mounting the database

- Changing archiving status with ALTER DATABASE ARCHIVELOG
- Opening the database
- Take control-file backups whenever you issue the ALTER DATABASE command or CREATE, ALTER, or DROP TABLESPACE commands. This is done with the ALTER DATABASE BACKUP CONTROLFILE TO [TRACE|*filename*] command.
- Make sure you know how to take online and offline database backups.
- Never take an online backup of multiple tablespaces at the same time. Instead, take tablespace backups serially.
- Dictionary views to use for database backup include V$DATABASE, V$TABLESPACE, V$DATAFILE, V$LOGFILE, V$CONTROLFILE, V$BACKUP, and V$DATAFILE_HEADER.

# Physical Backups Using Oracle Recovery Manager

- The BACKUP command runs backups. RMAN creates incremental or full copies of files for the entire database, the files of a tablespace, or individual datafiles.
- The backups of files and archived redo logs are placed into collections called backup sets. A backup can contain only archived redo logs or only datafiles and control files.
- Datafiles can be multiplexed into a backup set, meaning that the blocks of datafiles are stored noncontiguously on the sequential offline storage media, such as tape.
- Backup sets are composed of backup pieces. The number of pieces in a backup set depends on the parallelism of the backup, the number of tapes required for the backup, and other factors.
- Oracle8 and RMAN support the incremental backup of datafiles, which store only the blocks of a datafile that have been changed since the last full backup. A full backup reads the entire file and copies all blocks into the backup set, skipping only datafile blocks that have never been used. That means that it is not containing all blocks of datafiles.

- There are four levels of incremental backup available in RMAN GUI mode, as well as a level-0 backup, which is a full backup. RMAN line mode offers eight levels of incremental backup.

- To recover a database component from backup, the component must first be restored.

- The COPY command will create an image copy of a database file component. This component is immediately usable for recovery.

- The COPY command only produces image copies to disk, while BACKUP can send database file components directly to tape.

# Types of Failures and Troubleshooting

- The types of database failure are user error, statement failure, process failure, instance failure, and media failure.

- User error is when the user permanently changes or removes data from a database in error. Rollback segments give supplemental ability to correct uncommitted user errors, but usually the DBA will need to intervene for recovery.

- Statement failure occurs when there is something syntactically wrong with SQL statements issued by users in the database. Oracle rolls back these statements automatically and issues an error to the user indicating what the statement problem was.

- Process failure occurs when the user session running against the database is terminated abnormally. Statement rollback, release of locks, and other process cleanup actions are performed automatically by PMON.

- Instance failure occurs when the instance is forced to shut down due to some problem with the host machine or an aborted background process. Recovery from this problem occurs when the instance is restarted. Instance recovery is handled automatically by the SMON process.

- Media failure occurs when there is some problem with the disks that store Oracle data, and the data is rendered unavailable. The DBA must manually intervene in these situations to restore lost data from backups.

- Temporary media failure usually results from the failure of hardware other than the actual disk drive. After the problem is corrected, the database can access its data again.

- Permanent media failure is usually the result of damage to data itself. Usually, the drive will need to be replaced and the DBA will need to recover the data on the disk from backup.
- The DBVERIFY utility is helpful for identifying block corruption in datafiles on your database. The LOG_BLOCK_CHECKSUM parameter in your INIT.ORA file is useful for identifying block corruption in your redo logs before they are archived.
- Background processes like PMON and DBW0 produce trace files whenever an error occurs in their operation.
- A special trace file called the alert log contains information about several database-wide operations, including
  - Database startup and shutdown
  - INIT.ORA parameter values
  - Tablespaces being created, altered, and dropped
  - Databases being altered
  - Rollback segments being created, altered, and dropped
  - Internal errors
  - Log switch activities

# Oracle Recovery Without Archiving

- Recovery when the database runs in NOARCHIVELOG mode is only possible to the point in time at which the most recent backup was taken.
- The advantage of running your database in NOARCHIVELOG mode, from a recovery perspective, is simplicity of backup and recovery.
- The disadvantage of NOARCHIVELOG mode is that you lose any data changes made after the most recent backup. This database operation mode is effective for development and testing environments.
- Database recovery for NOARCHIVELOG mode databases must be accomplished from full offline backups. *All* files must be restored from backup, not just damaged ones, to ensure that the database is consistent at a single point in time.

# Complete Oracle Recovery with Archiving

- Recovery when the database runs in ARCHIVELOG mode is possible to the point in time of media failure.

- The advantage of running your database in ARCHIVELOG mode is that you have that additional level of recoverability, and can run your database 24 hours a day, 7 days a week, while still being able to take backups.

- The disadvantage of ARCHIVELOG mode is that recovery is somewhat more complex, and you need to make sure you have all the archived redo logs—from the time your backup was taken to the time of media failure. This database operation mode is effective for production database operation.

- Two components of database recovery when archiving is enabled are the database file backups and archived redo logs that can be applied in order to restore data changes made after the most recent backup.

- Database recovery is performed in Server Manager with the RECOVER command. You can perform database, tablespace, and datafile recovery.

- Automatic recovery can be used to reduce the amount of interaction required for database recovery and is specified with the AUTOMATIC keyword. When enabled, Oracle will automatically apply its suggestions for archive logs.

- Automatic archiving needs the LOG_ARCHIVE_DEST and LOG_ARCHIVE_FORMAT parameters to be set in init*sid*.ora to help formulate and apply redo log suggestions:

    - **LOG_ARCHIVE_DEST**   Determines where redo log archives will be placed

    - **LOG_ARCHIVE_FORMAT**   Determines the nomenclature for the archived redo information

- When archiving is enabled and recovery is necessary, you only need to restore the damaged datafiles, except when the datafile damaged was part of the SYSTEM or a ROLLBACK tablespace with active rollback segments, in which case database recovery will be accomplished from full offline backups.

- Recovery of an Oracle database running in ARCHIVELOG mode can consist of the following six situations:

- Recovery from damage to datafiles in SYSTEM or ROLLBACK tablespaces.
- Recovery from deleted datafiles in non-SYSTEM or non-ROLLBACK tablespaces.
- Recovery from damaged datafiles in non-SYSTEM or non-ROLLBACK tablespaces.
- Recovery from deleted datafiles in non-SYSTEM or non-ROLLBACK tablespaces when there is no backup datafile.
- Recovery from media failure occurring while the datafiles were being backed up; for this situation, you can circumvent a long recovery using the ALTER DATABASE DATAFILE *name* END BACKUP statement.
- Recovery when an unused online redo log is removed accidentally.

■ Information about the status of a database recovery and the files you need can be found in the following views:

- **V$RECOVER_FILE**   Used for locating datafiles needing recovery.
- **V$LOG_HISTORY**   Used for identifying the list of all archived redo logs for the database
- **V$RECOVERY_LOG**   Used for identifying the list of archived redo logs required for recovery
- **V$RECOVERY_FILE_STATUS**   Used for identifying the files that need recovery and the status of that recovery
- **V$RECOVERY_STATUS**   Used for identifying overall recovery information, such as start time, log sequence number needed for recovery, status of previous log applied, and reason recovery needs user input

■ The AUTOMATIC keyword reduces the amount of interaction between Oracle and the DBA by having Oracle automatically apply redo logs to the database. You cannot use this option with the RECOVER UNTIL CANCEL command. The logs Oracle uses are based on the contents of V$LOG_HISTORY and on the settings for two init*sid*.ora parameters, LOG_ARCHIVE_DEST and LOG_ARCHIVE_FORMAT.

■ Information about the SCN range contained in archived redo logs is in V$LOG_HISTORY.

■ For complete or incomplete recovery, the database cannot be available for users. For complete recovery of a tablespace only, the undamaged or unaffected parts of the database can be available for use.

- In some cases, it may be necessary to move datafiles as part of recovery. If this is required, the control file must be modified with the ALTER DATABASE RENAME FILE statement.

## Incomplete Oracle Recovery with Archiving

- Incomplete recovery may be required when the DBA loses an archived redo log file. For example, suppose there are three archived redo logs for a database, numbered 1, 2, and 3. Each archive contains information for 10 transactions (SCN 0–9, 10–19, and 20–29), for a total of 30 transactions. If archive sequence 3 is lost, the DBA can only recover the database through SCN 19, or archive sequence 2. If 2 is lost, then the DBA can only recover the database through SCN 9; and if archive sequence 1 is lost, then *no* archived redo log information can be applied.

- There are three types of incomplete recovery: time based, change based, and cancel based. They are differentiated in the RECOVER DATABASE option by what follows the UNTIL clause. Cancel-based incomplete recovery uses UNTIL CANCEL, change-based incomplete recovery uses UNTIL CHANGE *scn*, and time-based incomplete recovery uses UNTIL '*yyyy-mm-dd:hh24:mi:ss*'.

- You need to use incomplete recovery when tables get dropped or when incorrect data is committed to a table by someone. You could also use an export if available.

- Incomplete recovery might be your only choice if you do not have all your archived redo logs, when you have to use a backup control file, or when you lose all unarchived redo logs and one or more datafiles.

- Incomplete recovery from offline backups is accomplished with the following steps. Don't omit any steps or you will have to go through an even more lengthy process to recover to the point at which you reset the logs and after that point as well.

    1. Do a SHUTDOWN ABORT operation.
    2. Restore all backup copies of datafiles.
    3. Start up and mount, but do not open, the database.

4. Execute a RECOVER DATABASE operation, applying appropriate archived redo logs. Use the appropriate incomplete recovery option: cancel-based incomplete recovery uses UNTIL CANCEL, change-based incomplete recovery uses UNTIL CHANGE *scn*, time-based incomplete recovery uses UNTIL '*yyyy-mm-dd:hh24:mi:ss*'.

5. Open the database using the RESETLOGS option to discard archives and reset sequence numbers. Investigate to see if your recovery was successful—don't just assume it was.

6. Shut down with TRANSACTIONAL, IMMEDIATE, or NORMAL options.

7. Back up your database.

8. Open the database and make it available to users.

# Oracle Export and Import Utilities

- EXPORT and IMPORT can be used for a logical data-backup strategy. However, you will not be able to plan a full-fledged recovery strategy using EXPORT and IMPORT alone, because these tools do not save or restore SYS-owned objects.

- If you lost the SYSTEM tablespace on a database that you only backed up with exports, you would first have to drop and re-create the database, and then create the tablespaces and users needed. After that, you could start loading the database objects from the EXPORT dump file using IMPORT.

- You already learned the basics of EXPORT and IMPORT in Chapter 8. You can use EXPORT for logical backup, running it in FULL mode.

- Review EXPORT command-line parameters from Chapter 8 before taking OCP Exam 3!

- The benefit of cumulative and incremental exports is that they take less space and less time to generate because they only contain the objects that changed since the last complete or any EXPORT, respectively.

- EXPORT can run in the direct path when the DIRECT parameter on the command line or in the parameter file is set to TRUE. In this way, blocks read from the database skip most stages of SQL statement processing and get written to the dump file quickly.

- EXPORT direct path has several restrictions:

- It cannot be invoked interactively.
- Character sets for the client and server must be the same.
- The BUFFER parameter has no impact on performance (it does for conventional path).
- No datatypes introduced in Oracle8 can be exported in EXPORT direct path.
- You can use earlier versions of EXPORT on later versions of Oracle, or later versions of IMPORT on files produced by earlier versions of EXPORT. You should avoid using later versions of EXPORT and IMPORT against earlier versions of the Oracle database.
- Review the use of IMPORT command-line parameters, IMPORT object sequence, and NLS considerations from Chapter 8 before taking OCP Exam 3!

## Additional Oracle Recovery Issues

- There are several methods for minimizing downtime on your database, including the following:
    - **Fast warmstart**  The database will start quickly after recovery because recovery ends at the end of the roll-forward process, and user processes implicitly roll back any uncommitted changes before manipulating recovered blocks.
    - **Parallel recovery**  Oracle allows multiple processes to handle recovery at once, though this requires support from the host for multiple processes writing to the same or different disks at the same time. Review the chapter to see the init*sid*.ora parameters and RECOVER PARALLEL command options used for parallel recovery.
    - **Start with missing datafiles**  You can do this when the database supports multiple applications using datafiles of different tablespaces. Starting your database in this way increases availability for unaffected applications while allowing you to recover the damaged parts.
- You need to back up read-only tablespaces after their read/write status changes to read-only, or after the data in a read-only tablespace is changed. If you lose datafiles in read-only tablespaces and your only backup is from a time when the tablespace was not read-only, you will have to restore the

file, apply archive logs, and change the tablespace status accordingly, after it is restored.

- You need to re-create your database control files in three situations. They are when all control files are lost due to media failure, when the name of the database must be changed, and when you want to change option settings for your database in the control file (using the CREATE DATABASE statement). Option settings that can be set with the CREATE DATABASE statement include MAXDATAFILES, MAXLOGFILES, MAXLOGMEMBERS, and others.

- There are two ways to recover a control file. One is to use a backup control file created with the ALTER DATABASE BACKUP CONTROLFILE TO *filename* statement. Another is to re-create the control file using a CREATE CONTROLFILE statement. This statement can be found in a script generated by the ALTER DATABASE BACKUP CONTROLFILE TO TRACE command.

- ORA-1578, or the use of the DBVERIFY command, indicates when there is corruption in data blocks of a datafile. The most effective way to correct the problem is to recover the corrupted datafiles as though they were lost in media failure. You could also re-create the segment.

- The loss of your recovery catalog can be remedied by using the CATALOG command to reregister all the datafiles, backup control files, and archive redo logs. Alternatively, you can use the RESYNC CATALOG command to draw this information from the control file; but the problem is that all the files listed there may not exist anymore, so you may need to use the UNCATALOG command.

- The SWITCH command will substitute a datafile copy for a current file. The switched datafile will then need media recovery.

- The RESTORE command will retrieve files from the backup copy and put them where the DBA specifies.

- The RECOVER command will conduct media recovery using backups restored in combination with archived redo logs.

- Several old and new dictionary views exist in Oracle8 to support RMAN:

    - **V$ARCHIVED_LOG**   Displays names and information from the control file about archived redo logs

    - **V$BACKUP_CORRUPTION**   Displays information from the control file about corrupt datafile backups

- **V$BACKUP_DATAFILE** Offers information from the control file about backup datafiles and control files
- **V$BACKUP_DEVICE** Offers operating-system-specific information about supported third-party vendors for RMAN in Oracle8
- **V$BACKUP_REDOLOG** Displays information about archived redo logs in backup sets
- **V$BACKUP_SET** Displays information from the control file about all backup sets
- **V$BACKUP_PIECE** Displays information from the control file about all pieces in all backup sets
- **V$DATAFILE** Lists information about datafiles in the Oracle8 database
- **V$DATAFILE_HEADER** Lists information about datafile headers in the Oracle8 database

- Create a new control file, if required, by using the CREATE CONTROLFILE statement before initiating recovery. Be sure to specify RESETLOGS and ARCHIVELOG. If available, use the control file script created when the TRACE option is used in backing up the control file.

- Back up your control file regularly using the ALTER DATABASE BACKUP CONTROLFILE TO [TRACE|*filename*] statement.

- You can recover your database with both the ALTER DATABASE RECOVER command or simply with the RECOVER command.

- Always make sure to clear your alert log out periodically, because it will continue to grow in size at all times the database is operational. However, ensure that you save what you clear out, because you might need it later for database recovery.

- If you don't take a backup after you finish your recovery, and your database fails again, you will have to do a lot of work to recover. First, you'll have to recover to the point at which you reset your log sequence number, and then you will have to recover using the sequence number for the current control file.

- Incomplete recovery with RMAN takes much the same form as when using operating system commands, except all commands are put into a RUN script, not executed interactively. Also, archive logs and datafiles must be registered in the recovery catalog. However, in graphical mode, RMAN could find the most recent backup for you and then the recovery is much easier.

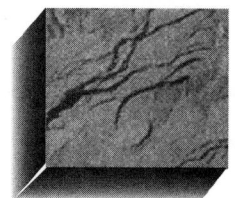

# CHAPTER 10

## OCP Exam 4 Terms and Concepts

The following key terms and concepts summarize facts and ideas tested in OCP Exam 4. They are meant to act as crib notes for your accelerated preparation and review, not as thorough coverage of all test matter. You may find them useful in the final days before taking the OCP Exam, preparing to take the practice exams, or simply to jog your thoughts within your overall preparation strategy.

# Business Requirements and Tuning

- Three goals of performance tuning are improving the performance of particular SQL queries, improving the performance of applications, and improving the performance of the entire database.

- The steps for performance tuning are as follows:

    1. Tune application configuration.
    2. Tune operating system structures.
    3. Tune memory structures.
    4. Tune I/O.
    5. Detect and resolve contention.

- The preceding performance-tuning steps should be executed in the order given to avoid making sweeping database changes that cause things to break in unanticipated ways.

# Oracle Alert, Trace Files, and Events

- Oracle maintains several log files for user and background processes, and for system-wide events. The log files for user and background processes are called trace files, and they can be found in the directories specified by USER_DUMP_DEST and BACKGROUND_DUMP_DEST INIT.ORA parameters.

- Background trace files are created when background processes fail. They offer little value in the goal of tuning an Oracle database.

- The system-wide event log file is called the alert log. This file can be found in the directory identified by the BACKGROUND_DUMP_DEST parameter.

- The alert log doesn't offer much information for database tuning, but it will help identify system-wide events.
- Events are occurrences in Oracle that substantially alter the behavior or performance of the database.
- If you are running Oracle Intelligent Agent, you can track events using the Oracle Enterprise Manager console.

# Utilities and Dynamic Performance Views

- V$ performance views are used in Oracle to collect and review statistics for database performance and operation. These views are owned by SYS and are accessible to users who have the SELECT_CATALOG_ROLE role granted to them, or the SELECT ANY TABLE privilege.
- System events and their statistics in Oracle can be identified using the V$SYSTEM_EVENT view. Session events and their statistics in Oracle can be identified using the V$SESSION_EVENT view.
- The UTLBSTAT and UTLESTAT utilities are frequently used by DBAs to identify performance issues on the Oracle database.
- The UTLBSTAT and UTLESTAT utilities require the user executing these scripts to be connected to Oracle as the INTERNAL user.
- UTLBSTAT is the utility that begins statistics collection. Executing this file creates special tables for database-performance statistics collection and begins the collection process.
- UTLESTAT is the utility that ends statistics collection. It concludes the statistics-collection activity started by UTLBSTAT and produces a report of database activity called report.txt.
- The report.txt file consists of the following components:
  - Statistics for file I/O by tablespace and datafiles. This information is useful in distributing files across many disks to reduce I/O contention.
  - SGA, shared pool, table/procedure, trigger, pipe, and other cache statistics. Used to determine whether there is contention for any of the listed resources.

- Latch wait statistics for the database instance. Used to determine whether there is contention for resources using latches.
- Statistics for how often user processes wait for rollback segments, which is used to determine whether more rollback segments should be added.
- Average length of dirty buffer write queue, which is used to determine whether DBW0 is having difficulty writing blocks to the database.
- Initialization parameters for the database, including defaults.
- Start time and stop time for statistics collection.
- OEM Tuning Pack is a tool that can be used for advanced tuning and event detection in Oracle using Enterprise Manager.

# Tuning Considerations for Different Applications

- Online transaction processing (OLTP) applications are systems generally used by large user populations, and these databases have frequently updated data and constantly changing data volume.
- OLTP application performance is adversely affected by increases in processing overhead for data changes. This includes excessive use of indexes and clusters.
- Decision-support systems (DSS) are systems that store large volumes of data for generating reports for users.
- DSS system performance is adversely affected by processing overhead associated with complex SELECT statements. This may include a lack of proper indexing, clustering, data migration, or chaining.
- Systems can be reconfigured on a temporary basis for application requirements.
- Multiple copies of initialization parameter files (INIT.ORA) can be used to manage this need for on-the-fly reconfiguration.
- You can also store multiple parameter configurations in Instance Manager for reconfiguring the database temporarily.

# SQL Tuning

- SQL tuning is the most important step in all database performance tuning, and it should always happen as the first step in that tuning process.

- The DBA's role in tuning depends on how large the IT organization is and how many applications the DBA administers. The larger the organization or DBA instance workload, the more likely that application tuning falls into the hands of developers.

- There are several tools available for diagnosing tuning problems in SQL*Plus, the command line, and Enterprise Manager, including the following:

    - **EXPLAIN PLAN** Used to determine the execution plan for SQL statements.

    - **SQL Trace and TKPROF** Used to determine execution statistics for SQL statements.

    - **AUTOTRACE** Offers execution plan and execution statistics for statements in SQL*Plus sessions as they are executed.

    - **Performance Manager** This tool collects and displays information about the performance of your database, allowing you to tune memory, minimize disk I/O, and avoid resource contention. It is a graphical tool with drill-down capability that allows both real-time monitoring and recording of statistics over time for replay later.

    - **TopSessions** This tool allows you to gather information about the top Oracle user sessions quickly, such as file I/O, CPU, and other metrics, allowing you to determine which users are utilizing the most Oracle resources.

    - **Oracle Trace** This tool allows a detailed level of performance-data collection at the level of every server, network, and host machine activity associated with an application. (This is not the same as SQL Trace, which offers the ability to trace SQL processing in a SQL*Plus session.)

    - **Tablespace Manager** This tool allows you to analyze block usage in tablespaces, and to perform tablespace defragmentation dynamically.

- **Oracle Expert** This tool provides performance tuning handled automatically by Oracle. Oracle Expert analyzes and solves problems detected via Performance Manager, TopSessions, and Oracle Trace in areas of access methods, INIT.ORA parameters, and object sizing and placement.

- There are two optimizer modes in Oracle: rule-based and cost-based optimization. Optimizer mode is set with the OPTIMIZER_MODE parameter. Within cost-based optimization, there are two different optimizer goals: ALL_ROWS for maximizing throughput, and FIRST_ROWS for minimizing response time. The default setting for OPTIMIZER_MODE is CHOOSE, allowing Oracle to determine dynamically what the goal will be. Rule-based optimization is provided for backward compatibility.

- Use of the following new features in Oracle require cost-based optimization:
    - Partitioned and index-organized tables
    - Reverse-key indexes
    - Parallel queries, star queries, and star transformations

- Star queries, star transformations, and star schemas relate to data warehouse applications. Oracle can optimize star queries to run efficiently when cost-based optimization is in place.

- Hash joins are special operations the RDBMS can perform in which two tables are joined together using dynamic partitions in memory, where Oracle will use the smaller partition to probe data in the larger one.

- To permit hash joins, the HASH_JOIN_ENABLED INIT.ORA parameter must be set to TRUE, or the /*+USE_HASH(emp dept) */ hint must be included in the SQL statement.

- SQL Trace can be enabled at the instance level by setting the SQL_TRACE parameter to TRUE and starting the instance.

- SQL Trace can be enabled at the session level with the ALTER SESSION SET SQL_TRACE=TRUE statement.

- SQL Trace tracks the following statistics for SQL statements: CPU time and real elapsed time; parse, execute, and fetch counts; library cache misses; data block reads; and number of rows processed.

- To use SQL Trace properly, several initialization parameters should be set in the INIT.ORA file:
    - TIMED_STATISTICS = TRUE

- MAX_DUMP_FILE_SIZE=(*appropriate size to capture all contents, default 500, expressed in operating system–size blocks*) (optional)
- USER_DUMP_DEST=*absolute_pathname_on_your_system* (optional)

■ TKPROF takes as input the trace file produced by SQL Trace and produces a readable report summarizing trace information for the query.

■ DBMS_APPLICATION_INFO is used to register various blocks of code with the database for performance-tuning purposes. When the code is registered, you can find performance information for procedures, functions, packages, and triggers in the V$SESSION and V$SQLAREA views.

■ SQL is a flexible language in which the same data result can be generated from different statements. There is usually an efficient and an inefficient way to construct your SQL statements. The following rules offer a methodology for optimizing SQL statements:

- Use (NOT) EXISTS instead of (NOT) IN
- Avoid functions on indexed columns in WHERE clauses if you want Oracle to use the index on that column.
- Include leading columns from composite indexes in WHERE clauses if you want Oracle to utilize the index.
- Avoid the misuse of views, such as using views where they weren't intended to be used and constructing joins using views.
- Construct separate SQL statements for different purposes.
- Use hints when appropriate.
- Avoid the DISTINCT keyword.

■ When tuning join statements, observe the following rules:

- Construct joins with equality comparisons and AND operations.
- Avoid full table scans.
- Construct WHERE clauses that use small tables as driving tables. If you need to, review the chapter to understand what a driving table is.
- Put the most selective comparison operations first in WHERE clauses because of the composite index usage.
- Filter operations on single tables belong before join operations.

■ Oracle performance often depends on the capabilities of the host machine.

# Generic Operating System Tuning Issues and Oracle

- Memory tuning consists of ensuring the Oracle SGA always resides in real memory.
- I/O configuration consists of enabling I/O cache write-through on the operating system or hardware level, using I/O devices with rapid read/write capability (such as fast disk spindles or solid-state disk media), and using hardware mirroring instead of striping for Oracle resources—particularly redo logs.
- Process-schedule tuning means that all Oracle processes should have the same priority at the OS level so that no Oracle process gets less or more attention from the CPU scheduler than another.
- A process is a program currently executing on a machine that handles a defined task. CKPT, LGWR, and other background operations are handled as processes in UNIX.
- In Windows, all these operations are handled in one process called oracle.exe. Each individual operation is handled as a thread within that process.
- Many machines that run Oracle support real and virtual memory. Real memory is directly accessible by a process or thread at any given time, while virtual memory is an area or file on disk storing information that hasn't been used by an executing process in a while.
- Oracle SGA consists of five parts: the shared pool, the redo log buffer, the buffer cache, large pool, and the java pool.
- You tune your host machine in three areas: memory configuration, I/O, and process scheduling.

# Tuning the Shared Pool

- The shared pool contains the dictionary (row) cache and the library cache.
- The dictionary cache stores row data from the Oracle data dictionary in memory to improve performance when users select dictionary information.

- Performance on the dictionary cache is measured by the hit ratio calculated from data in the V$ROWCACHE view, using the formula (SUM ( GETS – GETMISSES) / SUM(GETS)) * 100. Be sure you understand what each of the referenced columns means in the V$ROWCACHE view.

- Row-cache hit ratio should be 99 percent or more, or else there could be a performance problem on the database. This ratio is improved by increasing the SHARED_POOL_SIZE init*sid*.ora parameter.

- The library cache stores parse information for SQL statements executing in the Oracle database for sharing purposes.

- Library cache performance is measured by the library-cache hit ratio, calculated from data in the V$LIBRARYCACHE view using the formula (SUM(PINS – RELOADS) / SUM(PINS)) * 100. Be sure you understand what each of the referenced columns means in the V$LIBRARYCACHE view.

- The library-cache hit ratio should be 99 percent or more, or else a performance problem may exist on the database. This ratio is improved by increasing the SHARED_POOL_SIZE parameter, using more identical SQL queries in the database, or pinning objects in the shared pool.

## Tuning the Buffer Cache

- The size of your buffer cache is configured in Oracle using the DB_BLOCK_BUFFERS parameter.

- Access to the buffer cache is managed by LRU latches. Set the number of latches managing the buffer cache with the DB_BLOCK_LRU_LATCHES parameter so that the ratio of buffers to latches is 50 to 1.

- Performance on the buffer cache is measured by the buffer cache hit ratio, calculated from the statistics in the VALUE column of the V$SYSSTAT view where NAME is db block gets, consistent gets, and physical reads.

- Buffer cache hit ratio is calculated as (db block gets + consistent gets – physical reads) / (db block gets + consistent gets) * 100. The result should be at least 90 percent for effective database performance.

- You can assess the impact of adding buffers to the buffer cache using the V$RECENT_BUCKET view. Statistics will be collected in this view from the V$SYSSTAT view if the DB_BLOCK_LRU_EXTENDED_STATISTICS parameter is greater than 0.

- You can assess the impact of removing buffers from the buffer cache by using the V$CURRENT_BUCKET view. Statistics will be collected in this view from the V$SYSSTAT view if the DB_BLOCK_LRU_EXTENDED_STATISTICS parameter is set to TRUE. These parameters are obsolete in Oracle8*i*.

- Oracle8 and Oracle8*i* allows you to configure your buffer cache to have multiple buffer pools. A keep pool contains object blocks you want to persist in memory, and a recycle pool contains object blocks you want eliminated from memory as quickly as possible.

- Multiple buffer pools are configured using INIT.ORA parameters, allocating their space and dedicated latches from the overall totals set for the buffer cache:

    - **BUFFER_POOL_KEEPs**  Configures the keep pool. You set it as follows: BUFFER_POOL_KEEP = (buffers:*n*, lru_latches:*n*).

    - **BUFFER_POOL_RECYCLEs**  Configures the recycle pool. You set it as follows: BUFFER_POOL_RECYCLE = (buffers:*n*, lru_latches:*n*).

- The total allocation for buffers and latches in both pools cannot exceed the overall allocation for space and latches for the buffer cache. All space left over in the buffer cache configuration goes to the default pool.

- Blocks are stored in either pool depending on which one you assign the block to be stored in by using the ALTER *object name* STORAGE (BUFFER_POOL *pool*) command, where *object* is the type of object that permits a storage clause, such as table, index, cluster, or partition. The *name* variable indicates the name of the object you are assigning to one of the buffer pools, and *pool* is the name of the pool you want to assign the object to (KEEP, RECYCLE, or DEFAULT).

- Table caching is done using the ALTER TABLE *name* CACHE statement.

# Tuning the Redo Log Buffer

- The redo log buffer cache stores redo entries in memory until LGWR can write them to disk.

- If the redo log buffer fills with redo information faster than LGWR can write it to online redo logs, user processes will have to wait for space to write redo to the redo log buffer.

- You can identify whether user processes are waiting for redo log buffer space by using the V$SYSSTAT view. Select the VALUE column where the NAME column is redo buffer allocation retries; and if this statistic is not zero and it increases regularly, increase the size of the redo log buffer using the LOG_BUFFER parameter.

- If the value for redo log space requests is not near zero, the DBA should increase the redo log buffer cache until redo log space requests and redo buffer allocation retries are near zero. The redo log buffer-cache size is determined by the parameter LOG_BUFFERS.

- There is only one redo allocation latch in your database, and it must be acquired by a user process so that process can write to the redo log buffer. You can reduce contention for the redo allocation latch by decreasing the setting for LOG_SMALL_ENTRY_MAX_SIZE to a smaller value.

# Database Configuration and I/O issues

- Five types of tablespaces commonly found on the Oracle database are SYSTEM, DATA, INDEX, ROLLBACK, and TEMP. You can use the DBA_SEGMENTS view to determine when objects are inappropriately placed in various tablespaces.

- The SYSTEM tablespace should contain data dictionary tables and initial rollback segments only. It is inappropriate to place any other objects in them as they may fill the SYSTEM tablespace, causing maintenance problems.

- The DATA tablespaces should contain table data only. Other types of segments, such as rollback segments or temporary segments, could cause tablespace fragmentation, making it hard for the tables to acquire extents.

- The INDEX tablespaces should contain indexes to table data only.

- The ROLLBACK tablespaces should contain rollback segments only.

- The TEMP tablespaces should be available for the creation of temporary segments for user queries. No other objects should be placed in this tablespace.

- Detecting I/O problems with datafiles is handled with the V$FILESTAT view. Look for high values in the PHYRDS, PHYWRTS, and AVGIOTIM columns of this view to identify hotspots and I/O issues. V$SESSION_WAIT can be used to identify I/O problems with online redo logs and control files, as well.

- Files should be distributed to reduce I/O contention:
  - Acceptable combinations of resources on the same disk include the following: multiple control files can be on the same disks as online redo logs or datafiles, and temporary tablespace datafiles can be combined with other disk resources only when enough memory is available to ensure that all sorts occur in memory.
  - Unacceptable combinations of resources on the same disk include the following: DATA and INDEX tablespace datafiles, ROLLBACK tablespace datafiles and any other tablespace datafiles, DATA or INDEX tablespace datafiles and the SYSTEM tablespace, and online redo logs and any other tablespace datafiles.
- You can stripe in two ways:
  - Object striping is taking a large table, dividing it into partitions, and putting the partitions on separate disks.
  - Hardware striping is configured at the OS level, and it involves copying identical segments or stripes of information across several different disks to avoid dependence on any single disk.
- Checkpoints occur at least as frequently as log switches, but can occur more frequently in two cases:
  - LOG_CHECKPOINT_INTERVAL is set to a number representing the number of blocks that can be written to an online redo log before the checkpoint occurs.
  - LOG_CHECKPOINT_TIMEOUT is set to a number representing the number of seconds between checkpoints.
- More frequent checkpoints improve database recoverability by copying dirty buffers to disk more frequently, but can reduce online performance because LGWR stops clearing out the log buffer more frequently to handle checkpoint processing.
- You can improve process I/O on the DBW0 background processes by using the same number of database writers as CPUs on the machine by changing DB_WRITER_PROCESSES to a value from 2 to 9. Be sure the number of LRU latches set with the INIT.ORA parameter DB_BLOCK_LRU_LATCHES in the buffer cache is set to a multiple of the number of DB_WRITER_PROCESSES on the system.

# Using Oracle Blocks Efficiently

- Block size is determined by the DB_BLOCK_SIZE initialization parameter.
- Block size cannot be changed once the database is created.
- Oracle block size should be a multiple of operating system block size.
- The use of space within a block to store row data is determined by PCTFREE and PCTUSED. The PCTFREE option is the amount of space Oracle leaves free in each block for row growth. The PCTUSED option is the amount of space that must be freed after the block initially fills in order for Oracle to add that block to the freelist.
- A high PCTFREE means the block leaves a lot of room for rows to grow. This is good for high-volume transaction systems with row growth, but has the potential to waste disk space.
- A low PCTFREE maximizes disk space by leaving little room for rows to grow. Space is well utilized but potential is there for chaining and row migration.
- Row migration is where a row has grown too large for the block it is currently in, so Oracle moves it to another block.
- Chaining is where Oracle tries to migrate a row, but no block in the freelist can fit the entire row because the row is larger than the entire block size (for example, one of the columns in the table is type LONG), so Oracle breaks it up and stores the pieces where it can find room in several blocks).
- The ANALYZE command places ROWIDs for chained rows in the CHAINED_ROWS table created by utlchain.sql. This table must be present for ANALYZE to work, though you can also use your own precreated table instead of CHAINED_ROWS.

# Optimizing Sort Operations

- SQL operations that use sorts include GROUP BY, ORDER BY, SELECT DISTINCT, MINUS, INTERSECT, UNION, min( ), max( ), count( ), CREATE INDEX, and *sort merge join* RDBMS operations and the creation of indexes.

- Sorting should be done in memory. The V$SYSSTAT view can be queried to find the number of sorts done in memory vs. the number of sorts done using disk space.

- To increase the number of sorts taking place in memory, increase the value set for the SORT_AREA_SIZE initialization parameter.

- If a disk sort is performed, the DBA should ensure that all temporary segments allocated for that sort are placed in a temporary tablespace. This is ensured by creating users with a temporary tablespace named in CREATE USER.

- If no temporary tablespace is named, the default tablespace used for storing temporary segments will be SYSTEM—this can lead to problems, because temporary segments fragment tablespaces and SYSTEM is critical to the proper functioning of the database.

- If memory and disk resources permit, set the database to use SORT_DIRECT_WRITES. This parameter is set to TRUE if the database is to use direct writes to the database for sorting.

- The SORT_WRITE_BUFFERS parameter determines the number of buffers that will be used for direct writes, and the SORT_WRITE_BUFFER_SIZE parameter will be used to determine the size of the buffers.

## Rollback Segment Tuning

- When an instance starts, it acquires by default TRANSACTIONS/TRANSACTIONS_PER_ROLLBACK_SEGMENT rollback segments. If you want to ensure that the instance acquires particular rollback segments that have particular sizes or particular tablespaces, specify the rollback segments by name in the ROLLBACK_SEGMENTS parameter in the instance's parameter file.

- The instance acquires all the rollback segments listed in this parameter, even if more than TRANSACTIONS/TRANSACTIONS_PER_ROLLBACK_SEGMENT segments are specified. The rollback segments can be either private or public.

- All extents of a rollback segment are the same size. This is enforced by Oracle with the removal of the PCTINCREASE storage clause in the CREATE ROLLBACK SEGMENT syntax.

- Rollback segments should have an OPTIMAL size specified by the OPTIMAL storage clause.

- If a data transaction forces the rollback segment to grow more than one extent past its OPTIMAL setting, Oracle will shrink the rollback segment automatically after the transaction commits, when the rollback segment header detects that an entire segment is inactive.

- Shrinks and extends cause additional processing overhead on the Oracle instance.

- The DBA can query the V$ROLLSTAT dynamic performance view to determine whether a high number of extends and shrinks are happening to the rollback segment.

- If a high number of shrinks are occurring, as reflected by the SHRINKS column of V$ROLLSTAT, the DBA should increase the OPTIMAL storage clause for that rollback segment.

- Index use in retrieving table data can be monitored using the V$SYSSTAT view or by executing EXPLAIN PLAN on every SQL statement in an application.

- Database objects should be sized so that all data in the object fits into one extent or a few extents. When using partitioned objects and parallel execution, the number of extents should match the number of anticipated parallel processes.

# Monitoring and Detecting Lock Contention

- Levels of locking include row share, row exclusive, share, exclusive, share row exclusive.

- Causes of lock contention are when a process doesn't relinquish a lock it holds, when a process holds a higher level of lock than it really needs, and when a user process drops while holding a lock in the client/server architecture.

- The UTLLOCKT procedure is used to detect lock contention.

- The method to eliminate contention is to kill sessions that are deadlocked. The Session ID and serial number from V$SESSION are required for this activity. To kill a session, execute ALTER SYSTEM KILL SESSION.

- Preventing deadlocks is done at the application level by changing the application to relinquish locks it obtains or using locks with the least amount of scope required to complete the transaction.

- Oracle errors arising from deadlocks can be found in the alert log, a special file the Oracle database uses to track all errors on that instance. The error "deadlock detected while waiting for a resource" corresponds to a deadlock.

- Application developers can also prevent deadlocks by designing the application to acquire locks in the same order in all processes, and to use the minimum locking capability required to complete the transaction.

- V$LOCK lists the processes that are holding object locks on the system. This is useful for finding processes that may be causing waits on the system.

## Latch and Contention Issues

- Latches are similar to locks in that they are used to control access to a database resource. Latch contention is when two (or more) processes are attempting to acquire a latch at the same time.

- There are dozens of different latches available in the Oracle database.

- Latches are used in conjunction with restricting write access to online redo logs, among other things. The two types of latches for this purpose are redo-allocation latches and redo-copy latches.

- Some processes that make requests for latches are willing to wait for the latch to be free. Other processes move on if they cannot obtain immediate access to a latch.

- V$LATCH is used for latch-performance monitoring. It contains GETS, MISSES, SLEEPS, IMMEDIATE_GETS, and IMMEDIATE_MISSES statistics required for calculating wait ratios.

- V$LATCHNAME holds a readable identification name corresponding to each latch number listed in V$LATCH.

- V$LATCHHOLDER lists the processes that are currently holding latches on the system. This is useful for finding the processes that may be causing waits on the system.

- Latch performance is measured by the wait ratio. For processes willing to wait, the wait ratio is calculated as (MISSES / GETS) * 100.

- For processes wanting immediate latch access, the wait ratio is calculated as (IMMEDIATE_MISSES / IMMEDIATE_GETS) * 100.

## Tuning with Oracle Expert

- Oracle Expert is a tool that helps diagnose and resolve tuning problems on your Oracle database. You should understand basic usage of this tool before taking OCP Exam 4.

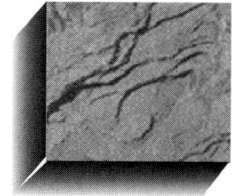

# CHAPTER 11

## OCP Exam 5
## Terms and Concepts

The following key terms and concepts summarize facts and ideas tested in OCP Exam 5. They are meant to act as crib notes for your accelerated preparation and review, not as thorough coverage of all test matter. You may find them useful in the final days before taking the OCP Exam, preparing to take the practice exams appearing later in the chapter, or simply to jog your thoughts within your overall preparation strategy.

## Overview

- Network computing combines centralized code location with scalability, ease of use, low distribution costs, and widespread dissemination of content.

## Basic Net8 Architecture

- Net8 base and add-on components offer many features for network and client/server computing, including the following:
    - Enhanced security with advanced security option
    - Centralized management of database naming with Oracle Names server
    - Scalability with connection pooling and connection concentration
    - Independence from standard networking protocols with the use of Oracle Protocol Adapters
    - Ability to handle connections from multiple network protocols for the same Oracle server using Oracle Connection Manager
    - Simplified network administration via Net8 Assistant, running stand-alone or from the OEM console
    - Reduced reliance on locally maintained tnsnames.ora files through the use of host naming
    - Diagnosis of network performance using Oracle Trace Assistant
    - Interconnectivity with third-party vendor standard name services with Native Naming Adapters

- The basic procedure Net8 uses to connect client and server is as follows:

    1. You provide username, password, and connect string via a database tool.

    2. Net8 looks in tnsnames.ora, Oracle Names, or uses the host-naming method to resolve the connect string into a connect descriptor.

    3. Net8 looks for the machine specified. When it is found, Net8 attempts to connect to the listener and Oracle SID using the information specified or using established assumption patterns if the host-naming method is used.

    4. The listener either accepts the connection or refuses it, depending on database availability and the correctness of the connect descriptor information.

    5. If the connection is accepted, the listener passes the user process either to a dispatcher process or a preexisting dedicated server, or the listener generates a dedicated server for that process and passes the process to that server.

- User connections are ended voluntarily with the appropriate command or by attempting to establish a new connection.

- User connections may end involuntarily when a listener, shared server, dispatcher, or dedicated server fails to operate properly.

- The components of the Net8 architecture for supporting network connections are congruent with the OSI network model, described in the book, and include the following components:

    - Oracle Protocol Adapter for your network protocol (link layer)
    - Transparent Network Substrate (network layer)
    - Network Routing, Network Authentication, and Network Names (transport layer)
    - Network Interface (session layer)

- The components of the Oracle RDBMS that are also mapped to the OSI network model include the following:

    - Two-Task Common and OCI/OPI (presentation layer)
    - Forms, Reports, SQL*Plus, OEM, Tuning Pack, and others (application layer)

- The remaining layer of the OSI model is the physical layer. Your network protocol, such as TCP/IP, resides at that level.

- Connections between client and server travel from the application layer down through other layers, across the physical layer of your network, and then back up through the layers of the OSI model in reverse, in order to be processed on your Oracle database.

# Basic Net8 Server-Side Configuration

- Net8 Assistant can be used to configure your network listeners in the following areas:

    - **General parameters** General, logging and tracing, and authentication.

    - **Listening locations** Addresses this listener will receive connection requests from on your host machine.

    - **Database services** Oracle databases this listener will manage user connections for.

    - **Other services** Other Oracle services, such as Oracle Application Server or EXTPROC, that this listener will manage user connections for.

- The name of your listener is LISTENER by default, but can be changed by changing the parameter *listener_name = description ...*, where listener_name is the new name, to your listener.ora file, where *name* is a short alphanumeric text string.

- The LSNRCTL utility is also used to configure and manage your Net8 listener processes. This tool is run either interactively or in batch from the host system command line of your application.

- Starting and stopping the listener process using LSNRCTL is handled with the START and STOP commands.

- Review LSNRCTL commands like SET and SHOW commands. The latter set of commands can be used for configuring the listener or session options and displaying those listener/session configuration settings.

- Net8 listener configuration information is stored in the listener.ora configuration file, found in the network/admin subdirectory under your Oracle software home directory on the machine hosting the Oracle database.

- Recall the need to provide password information to shut down the listener by default, if you set up the password. You can change this requirement in Net8 Assistant.

# Basic Net8 Client-Side Configuration

- Host naming allows a connection to be made between client and server without a tnsnames.ora file or Oracle Names server being present. Net8 assumes the following about the server it attempts to connect to when host naming is specified:
    - The listener is tuned to a well-known network protocol-specific service of TCP and port location of 1521 for Net8 client connections.
    
    If these conditions are not met, then host naming shouldn't be used.

- The local naming method is handled with the tnsnames.ora file stored and managed locally on your client machine. This file is configured with the Net8 Assistant tool.

- The other client-side configuration file, sqlnet.ora, contains settings for default network-database naming conventions and for whether client-side tracing is enabled. This file can be managed with Net8 Assistant.

- Both tnsnames.ora and sqlnet.ora can be found in the network/admin directory under the Oracle software home directory on your client machine (by default, however, you could also choose another directory).

- When you use local naming on your client, Net8 engages in the following process for connecting to Oracle when you provide a username, password, and connect string:
    - Looks in tnsnames.ora for the connect string that is provided.
    - Finds the host machine defined in the associated connect descriptor.
    - Finds the listener defined in the associated connect descriptor on that host.
    - Finds the SID defined in the associated connect descriptor associated with that listener on that host.
    - Oracle authenticates user and password information.

- You can define client-side preferences in areas of general preferences, naming methods used, and referential order.

# Usage and Configuration of Oracle Names

- Oracle Names is used as an *n*-tier server solution for centralized administration of services available on the Oracle network.

- Net8 Assistant is used to configure centralized naming. Client preferences for using Oracle Names are set in the Profiles node of that tool.

- Oracle Names can be run on the same machine hosting the Oracle database, or on a different machine.

- Names server locations can be defined with Net8 Assistant using the wizard available when you create the Names server. Review the chapter to recall the process for doing so.

- When you configure your first Names server on the Oracle network, Oracle calls that network the root region. This is used later for administrative purposes when new subregions are created.

- Review how to define a preferred Names server in the chapter.

- Review the storage of Names information on the local file system, and the use of Net8 Assistant for this purpose, both covered in the chapter.

- You can configure listeners to register their services with Oracle Names using Net8 Assistant. Review the chapter to understand how.

- The sdns.ora configuration file supports Oracle Names by identifying the name of the Names server and its location on the network.

- You can store naming information in a repository on your Oracle database. To configure the database, you must create a user for the Names server to use to log in and maintain the repository information, and then run namesini.sql to store that information, which is found in the net80/names directory on Windows machines, network/admin on UNIX.

- To set up your Names server to use that regional database, you perform a series of steps using Net8 Assistant. Review the chapter to understand the process.

- NAMESCTL is a utility you can run interactively or from the command line to perform many activities also done using Net8 Assistant.

- To start the Names server, use the NAMESCTL START command. For Windows, use NAMESCTL80 START.

- To stop the Names server, use the NAMESCTL STOP command. For Windows, use NAMESCTL80 STOP.

# Usage and Configuration of Oracle Intelligent Agent for OEM

- Intelligent Agent is used in conjunction with Oracle Enterprise Manager to enhance the DBA's ability to centrally administer multiple Oracle databases and resources on the Oracle network.

- Intelligent Agent runs on the same machine that is hosting your Oracle database and helps you administer that database by detecting when certain occurrences or events arise that may change your database performance.

- LSNRCTL can be used to start Intelligent Agent with the DBSNMP_START command.

- LSNRCTL can be used to stop Intelligent Agent with the DBSNMP_STOP command.

- LSNRCTL can be used to determine the current status of Intelligent Agent with the DBSNMP_STATUS command.

- The main configuration file for Intelligent Agent is snmp.ora, but even this file is only used when you plan on registering Intelligent Agent with Oracle Names on your network.

# Usage and Configuration of the Multithreaded Server

- The components of Oracle's multithreaded server architecture include dispatchers and shared servers.

- Dispatchers maintain two work queues to handle user processing. The dispatcher processes place user process data-processing requests on the dispatcher request queue for processing by the next available shared server. The shared server places the results of the user-processing request on the response queue.

- Dispatchers are configured with several parameters in init*sid*.ora:
  - MTS_DISPATCHERS is used to define the protocol the dispatcher listens to, and the number of dispatchers for that protocol.
  - MTS_MAX_DISPATCHERS is used for limiting the number of dispatcher processes on the machine.
- Shared servers are also configured with init*sid*.ora parameters:
  - MTS_SERVERS determines the number of shared servers on the system that will be started when the database starts. Oracle may start more shared servers automatically if the workload for the database gets too large.
  - MTS_MAX_SERVERS determines the maximum number of servers Oracle will start automatically.
- You can assign dispatchers to certain listeners using the LISTENER option in the MTS_DISPATCHERS parameter.

# Usage and Configuration of Connection Manager

- Connection pooling is when Net8 releases transport connections that have been idle to establish a physical connection to a new client connection, while still preserving the logical session with the previous client.
- Connection pooling is configured with the POOL option in the MTS_DISPATCHERS parameter.
- Connection Manager allows Net8 to integrate two or more networks connected to one machine into one logical Oracle network.
- Connection Manager can also filter connections between different clients and servers using network-access control.
- Connection Manager offers connection concentration to connect many logical client sessions through a single transport, thereby increasing scalability for an application.

- There are three components to Connection Manager:
    - **CMGW** The Connection Manager gateway process, which acts as a liaison between clients and the Net8 listener.
    - **CMADM** The Connection Manager administrator process, which maintains address information in the Oracle Names server for Net8 clients.
    - **CMCTL** The Connection Manager control utility, similar to NAMESCTL or LSNRCTL in that you can set many options for Connection Manager interactively or from the command line using this tool.

- Configuring connection concentration on the server side is handled using the MTS_DISPATCHERS parameter in init*sid*.ora using the MULTIPLEX or MULTIPLEXING option. This option is set to 1, TRUE, YES, ON, IN, OUT, or BOTH.

- To configure connection concentration on the client side, you use Net8 Assistant's Routing tab in the General work area in the Profile node. Click the Use Source Route Addresses checkbox to set this up.

- To configure multiprotocol functionality, you must add multiple protocol addresses to the CMAN parameter in cman.ora.

- Configuring network access control is a two-part process:
    1. Set up the SRC, DST, SRV, and ACT options for the CMAN_RULES parameter in cman.ora.
    2. Use Net8 Assistant's Routing tab in the General work area in the Profile node. Click the Use Source Route Addresses checkbox to set this up.

- If CMAN_RULES is configured in cman.ora, then you must define explicitly all client and server connections you want to connect and reject. If a client/server combination is not defined in CMAN_RULES, Connection Manager will assume it should reject the combination.

# Troubleshoot the Network Environment

- Log and trace files assist in determining network problems occurring in your Oracle network environment. You configure their use in the configuration file appropriate to the network component you want to monitor:
    - **Net8 listener**   listener.ora
    - **Oracle Names**   names.ora
    - **Connection Manager**   cman.ora
    - **Client/server profile**   sqlnet.ora

- The parameters for configuring log and trace filename and location for each of the various configuration files are listed here:
    - **listener.ora**   LOG_DIRECTORY_listener_name, LOG_FILE_listener_name where listener_name is the name of the listener, TRACE_DIRECTORY_listener_name, and TRACE_FILE_listener_name
    - **names.ora**   NAMES.LOG_FILE, NAMES.LOG_DIRECTORY, NAMES.TRACE_FILE, NAMES.TRACE_DIRECTORY
    - **cman.ora**   CMAN_PROFILE permits defining LOG_LEVEL and TRACING options
    - **sqlnet.ora**   LOG_FILE_SERVER, LOG_DIRECTORY_SERVER, TRACE_FILE_SERVER, TRACE_DIRECTORY_SERVER, LOG_FILE_CLIENT, LOG_DIRECTORY_CLIENT, TRACE_FILE_CLIENT, TRACE_DIRECTORY_CLIENT

- TNSPING is a service that operates in the same way as the PING command in the UNIX or Windows operating systems works. It allows you to determine whether an Oracle service is running or not, and how long it takes that service to send a response to a request.

- TRACE_LEVEL is another important parameter for configuring tracing that determines how much trace information is written to the trace file as part of the trace. Valid values for TRACE_LEVEL include OFF, USER, ADMIN, and SUPPORT.

- You may need to restart your network component in order to have trace settings take hold.
- The four steps for diagnosing network problems include the following:
    1. Review the log file first.
    2. Look at the error stack at the end of the file.
    3. Diagnose and resolve the problem using the error stack in the log file.
    4. If the log-file error stack doesn't provide enough information, enable tracing and use the trace file for further information.
- Some common network errors and possible causes and resolutions include the following:
    - **ORA-3113**  End of file on communication channel. This means you were disconnected unexpectedly. Attempting to reconnect usually indicates more accurately what the problem is.
    - **ORA-12154**  TNS couldn't resolve service name. Ensure that you entered the connect string properly, and that there is an associated connect descriptor in Oracle Names or tnsnames.ora.
    - **ORA-12203**  TNS was unable to connect to the destination. The host machine information was probably incorrect in the connect descriptor, or else there is no DNS service on your network.
    - **ORA-12224**  TNS detected no listener on your host specified. Make sure the listener is running and the port information in the connect descriptor is correct.
    - **ORA-12500**  The listener couldn't start a dedicated server on the host. There is probably something wrong with the SID_LIST parameter in listener.ora, or possibly an error in the connect descriptor.
    - **ORA-12533**  There were incorrect parameters in the ADDRESS portion of the connect descriptor specified locally or on the Names server.
    - **ORA-12545**  TNS experienced a general lookup failure. Check to see that the connect descriptor is valid, the listener is running, and that the DNS server maps the host name given to the appropriate network address for the machine hosting Oracle.
    - **ORA-12560**  There is a problem with the Oracle Protocol Adapter. Turn on tracing for more info.

- Your trace file tells you a great deal of information about the types of packets that traverse the Oracle network, such as identifying the procedures used by various OSI network components:
  - **NSPTCN** Connect packet
  - **NSPTAC** Accept connection packet
  - **NSPTRF** Refuse connection packet
  - **NSPTRS** Resend data packet
  - **NSPTMK** Marker packet
  - **NSPDA** Data packet
  - **NSPCNL** Control packet
- Your trace file tells you a great deal of information about the functions and procedures doing work in the layers of Net8 corresponding to the OSI network model. These functions and procedures are prefixed with two characters to indicate the OSI layer they correspond to. The layers are as follows:
  - **NA** Network authentication
  - **NI** Network interface
  - **NN** Network name resolution
  - **NR** Network routing
  - **NS** Network session
  - **NT** Network transport
- You can identify the trace-error information corresponding to the network error you received in your application (such as SQL*Plus) by looking at the end of your trace file.
- In UNIX, the OERR utility gives you more information about how to identify problems. You may use this utility on the UNIX command line by entering **oerr *abc nnnnn***, where *abc* is the three-character sequence at the beginning of the error code you see (such as ORA) and *nnnnn* is the error number (such as 12203). This utility is not available in Windows.

- Trace Assistant can be used to format the contents of a trace file into something more readable. The command-line syntax for Trace Assistant is trcasst *options filename*, where `filename` is replaced with the name of your trace file and `options` is replaced with zero or more of the following command-line options: -o, -e, -s. Each of these options, in turn, has a set of options you can specify. Review the chapter for more information.

- If you specify no options for Trace Assistant, then the default options of -odt -e -s are used.

# Security in the Network Environment

- Some security issues associated with network data transfer include the following:
    - Sensitive data being transported in plain text, and thus being viewable by third parties
    - Data being intercepted en route by third parties without being discovered by sender or recipient
    - Rogue servers configured either through DNS or by IP address piracy

- Effects of security issues include credit fraud, loss of competitive advantage, or ruined reputation.

- Two Oracle networking products are designed to provide layers of security over network protocols: Cryptographic Toolkit and advanced security option.

- Oracle Cryptographic Toolkit allows you to build support for security features used in Oracle Security Server into your application via the Cryptographic Toolkit OCI.

- Oracle advanced security option provides enhanced security and functionality by enabling you to use third-party authentication and encryption technologies to keep data private.

- Advanced security option provides support for the use of the following third-party technologies:
  - RSA 40-bit, 56-bit (U.S. only), and 128-bit (U.S. only) encryption technologies
  - DES 40-bit and 56-bit (U.S. only) encryption technologies
  - RSA MD5 data-integrity checksum algorithm technology
  - Kerberos 5, Identix, CyberSAFE, ACE/Server, and SecurID for centralized authentication
- The sqlnet.ora parameters used for configuring encryption/checksum use, and their valid values, include the following:
  - `ENCRYPTION_CLIENT` Accepted, requested, rejected, required
  - `ENCRYPTION_SERVER` Accepted, requested, rejected, required
  - `ENCRYPTION_TYPES_CLIENT` RC4_40, RC4_56, RC4_128, DES, DES40
  - `ENCRYPTION_TYPES_SERVER` RC4_40, RC4_56, RC4_128, DES, DES40
  - `CRYPTO_CHECKSUM_CLIENT` Accepted, requested, rejected, required
  - `CRYPTO_CHECKSUM_SERVER` Accepted, requested, rejected, required
  - `CRYPTO_CHECKSUM_TYPES_CLIENT` MD5
  - `CRYPTO_CHECKSUM_TYPES_SERVER` MD5
- CRYPTO_SEED is a special parameter that defines the 10 to 70-character cryptographic key used to verify data integrity. Use only random sequences of characters for setting this parameter, and try to make the character sequence as long as possible to ensure Oracle uses the strongest key possible.
- Be sure you understand how to configure authentication parameters used by advanced security option in your sqlnet.ora file, and how to use Net8 Assistant to configure advanced security option.

# CHAPTER 12

## OCP Oracle8*i* Upgrade Exam Terms and Concepts

The following key terms and concepts summarize facts and ideas tested in OCP Oracle8*i* Upgrade Exam. They are meant to act as crib notes for your accelerated preparation and review, not as thorough coverage of all test matter. You may find them useful in the final days before taking the OCP Exam, preparing to take the practice exams, or simply to jog your thoughts within your overall preparation strategy. You will also cover Oracle8 new features, which will help you if you are taking the Oracle8 OCP DBA upgrade exam as well.

## Oracle8*i* New Features

- Recall that the ROWID format in Oracle8 was different from Oracle7. Oracle8*i* uses the new extended ROWID format, as well.
- You can convert between extended ROWID and restricted ROWID formats using the DBMS_ROWID package created by the dbmsutil.sql script run automatically by catproc.sql. DBMS_ROWID also contains a host of procedures and functions for obtaining the components of an extended ROWID.
- The library and file system location of your external parameters must be defined using the CREATE LIBRARY and CREATE DIRECTORY statements.
- New OLAP operators available in GROUP BY clauses of SELECT statements include CUBE and ROLLUP.
- The new trim( ) single-row function combines features of rtrim( ) and ltrim( ) into one function.
- The following sort-related parameters in Oracle8*i* are now obsolete, due to implicit use of direct writes when sorting:
  - SORT_DIRECT_WRITES
  - SORT_WRITE_BUFFERS
  - SORT_WRITE_BUFFER_SIZE

## Java in the Database

- Three methods exist for using Java in Oracle8*i*:
  - JDBC, a driver similar to ODBC for calling the database from within Java programs

- SQLJ, a precompiler for embedding SQL statements in Java programs
- JDeveloper, an integrated development environment combining JDBC and SQLJ

■ Three types of Oracle8*i* Java drivers exist in Oracle8*i*: JDBC Thin for Web-enabled Java applications using Oracle, JDBC OCI for robust clients and server-to-server connectivity, and JDBC KPRG for Java stored procedures in Oracle8*i*.

■ You can load Java stored procedures into Oracle using CREATE PROCEDURE AS JAVA statements or using the LOADJAVA utility.

■ *i*FS is a Java-based tool that allows you to use your Oracle8*i* database as a file system.

■ The Java virtual machine in Oracle8*i* is JDK 1.1 compatible and consists of the following components:

- **Bytecode Compiler** Converts a Java-language program into a Java class. Java classes are binary programs, which can be executed on the host machine.
- **Native Compilation** Used for optimizing Java bytecode programs so that they will run faster.
- **Java Runtime Interpreter** Used for executing a Java class.
- **Java Class Loader** Permits the movement of Java classes into and out of the Oracle8*i* database.
- **Library Manager and Standard Libraries** Support functionality required for basic use of Java and for use of Java within Oracle8*i*.
- **SQLJ Translator** Enables embedded SQL in Java programs by precompiling SQL into Java language constructs.
- **Object Memory Management** Allocates and frees memory in blocks called *object memories*.
- **Memory Manager and Garbage Collector** Handles Object Memory Management and other JVM memory-related functions.

■ You should run the initjvm.sql script in Oracle8*i* as user SYS to load required Java classes into the Oracle8*i* database, unless you installed JAVA Server. This script is found in javavm/install and creates the JAVASYSPRIV and JAVAUSERPRIV roles (which are not required in 8.1.6 anymore), as well as the DBMS_JAVA package.

- The following INIT.ORA parameters are used in support of Java on your Oracle8*i* database:
    - **SHARED_POOL_SIZE**  Defines the size of your shared pool in bytes. This should be set to at least 50MB to run initjvm.sql.
    - **JAVA_POOL_SIZE**  Defines the size of the Java pool, a new area of the SGA in Oracle8*i* used to store shared Java objects. Should be set to 50MB when running initjvm.sql, but can be as low as 20MB for normal use of Java stored procedures.
    - **JAVA_SOFT_SESSIONSPACE_LIMIT**  Identifies a soft limit on memory used by Java in a session. Default is 1MB. If this limit is exceeded, a warning is written to the alert log.
    - **JAVA_MAX_SESSIONSPACE_SIZE**  Identifies the maximum amount of memory that can be used by a Java procedure; the default is 4GB. When the limit set by this parameter is exceeded, the executing Java procedure is killed by Oracle8*i* automatically.
- The three steps for loading and publishing Java classes as stored procedures in Oracle8*i* are as follows:
    1. Write the Java program using a Java development environment, such as JDeveloper.
    2. Load the Java program into Oracle8*i* using either the CREATE OR REPLACE JAVA SOURCE command or the LOADJAVA utility.
    3. Publish your Java procedure to SQL. This step identifies your Java procedure to SQL and PL/SQL by exposing the procedure entry point, mapping datatypes in Java to PL/SQL or SQL, and indicating parameter passing between Java and PL/SQL or SQL.

# Memory Management

- The large pool in Oracle8*i* is used to store session information for MTS configuration and information supporting I/O processes for backup and recovery.
- The LARGE_POOL_SIZE INIT.ORA parameter is used to define the total size of the large pool.
- The LARGE_POOL_MIN_ALLOC (which is obsolete in 8.1.6) INIT.ORA parameter is used to define the minimum amount of space that processes can allocate in the large pool.

- Oracle8*i* allows you to configure your buffer cache to have multiple buffer pools. A keep pool contains object blocks you want to persist in memory, and a recycle pool contains object blocks you want eliminated from memory as quickly as possible.
- Multiple buffer pools are configured using INIT.ORA parameters, allocating their space and dedicated latches from the overall totals set for the buffer cache:
  - BUFFER_POOL_KEEP configures the keep pool. You set it as follows: BUFFER_POOL_KEEP = (buffers:*n*, lru_latches:*n*).
  - BUFFER_POOL_RECYCLE configures the recycle pool. You set it as follows: BUFFER_POOL_RECYCLE = (buffers:*n*, lru_latches:*n*).
  - The total allocation for buffers and latches in both pools cannot exceed the overall allocation for space and latches for the buffer cache. All space left over in the buffer cache configuration goes to the default pool.
- Which pool blocks are stored in depends on which one you assign the block to, using the ALTER *object name* STORAGE (BUFFER_POOL *pool* ), where *object* is the type of object that permits a storage clause, such as table, index, cluster, or partition. The *name* variable indicates the name of the object you are assigning to one of the buffer pools, and *pool* is the name of the pool you want to assign the object to (keep, recycle, or default).

# Optimizer and Query Improvements

- Stored outlines are database objects containing execution plans for statements. These outlines can be used to control plan stability across database versions or conditions.
- To create and use stored outlines, the CREATE_STORED_OUTLINES and USE_STORED_OUTLINES INIT.ORA parameters must be set either to the name of the category you want the outline to belong to, or to DEFAULT to place the outline in the default category.
- The text of a SQL query must match the text in the stored outline for the query (including hints, but not bind variables) in order for Oracle8*i* to use the outline to process the query.
- Information about outlines is stored in tables owned by user OUTLN called OL$HINTS and OL$, which contain hints used by the outlines and information about the outline itself, respectively.

- The contents of OL$HINTS and OL$ can also be found in your data dictionary, in the DBA_OUTLINES and DBA_OUTLINE_HINTS views, respectively.
- The OUTLN_PKG is used to manage outlines with the following procedures:
  - **drop_unused( )**   Removes outlines that have never been used
  - **drop_by_cat( )**   Removes all outlines in a specified category
  - **update_by_cat( )**   Moves all outlines in one category to another
- Change the password for user OUTLN (which is OUTLN by default) to avoid security problems.
- The DBMS_STATS package has procedures that perform the same task as the ANALYZE command, and it provides additional functionality.
- Review the procedures available for gathering, setting, showing, and moving statistics with DBMS_STATS in the chapter.
- Oracle8*i* is able to optimize top-*n* queries (a top-*n* query is one that obtains the top *n* values from the result set using ROWNUM and returns them to the user) to produce results faster than its predecessors could.

# Summary Management

- Materialized views replace snapshots in Oracle8*i*. They store as one database object both the definition of a regular view and the data obtained by that view at a particular point in time. They are created using the CREATE MATERIALIZED VIEW statement.
- Materialized views must be refreshed in order to get the data changes made in underlying base tables populated into the materialized view. The REFRESH clause defines the type of refresh used. The types include COMPLETE, FAST, FORCE, and NEVER.
- Materialized views can be refreshed automatically when the underlying data is changed, or at regular intervals. You can refresh materialized views using DBMS_MVIEW package procedures, as well. Review the chapter to understand which procedures are available.
- Query rewrite is when Oracle automatically changes the query to use a materialized view instead of using the base tables. This feature is enabled using the init*sid*.ora parameter QUERY_REWRITE_ENABLED.

- Review the chapter to understand all privileges associated with creating, maintaining, removing, and using materialized views and query rewrite.

- The following dictionary views are used to find information for materialized views:

  - **ALL_REFRESH_DEPENDENCIES**   This view shows tables that materialized views and summaries depend on for data refresh.

  - **DBA_MVIEW_AGGREGATES**   If a materialized view contains grouping functions, this dictionary view gives information about it.

  - **DBA_MVIEW_ANALYSIS**   This view gives information about materialized views supporting query rewrites.

  - **DBA_MVIEW_DETAIL_RELATIONS**   This view identifies all objects referenced in a materialized view.

  - **DBA_MVIEW_JOINS**   This view identifies columns joined from base tables in the materialized view.

  - **DBA_MVIEW_KEYS**   This view offers more information about the relationships between objects identified in DBA_MVIEW_DETAIL_RELATIONS.

- A summary is a materialized view containing a GROUP BY statement that can be used in data warehouses to represent data multidimensionally as a summary of fact and dimension-table information.

- A dimension can be created on dimension-table information in Oracle8i to allow different options for query rewrite. They identify the different levels of hierarchy between columns in a dimension table or between dimension tables, and they are created using the CREATE DIMENSION statement.

- Information about your dimension objects in Oracle8i can be found in the following dictionary views:

  - **DBA_DIMENSIONS**   Offers information about dimension objects

  - **DBA_DIM_LEVELS**   Indicates the levels within a dimension

  - **DBA_DIM_LEVEL_KEY**   Includes information about the column defined as part of a dimension level

  - **DBA_DIM_HIERARCHIES**   Shows data about the hierarchies defined for a dimension

  - **DBA_DIM_CHILD_OF**   Indicates the hierarchy between levels in the dimension object

- **DBA_DIM_JOIN_KEY** Describes join information between two dimension tables, if more than one table is used in the dimension

- **DBA_DIM_ATTRIBUTES** Represents the relationship between dimension level and functionally dependent column, if one is present

■ The following stored procedures are available in DBMS_OLAP as advisory functions for summaries:

- **evaluate_utilization( )** Evaluates the utilization of a summary using workload estimates

- **evaluate_utilization_w( )** Evaluates the utilization of a summary using actual workload statistics

- **estimate_summary_size( )** Estimates the space requirement for a summary

- **recommend_mv_w( )** Assesses the usage of the summary and recommends whether you should keep it, or recommends where you could create new summaries to improve performance

## Indexes and Index-Organized Tables

■ Index creation can be combined with statistics generation in the CREATE INDEX COMPUTE STATISTICS statement. Index rebuilds can be combined with statistics generation in the ALTER INDEX REBUILD COMPUTE STATISTICS statement.

■ Only computing of statistics (not estimating) may be performed in conjunction with the CREATE INDEX or ALTER INDEX statement.

■ Function-based indexes can be used to circumvent situations in which Oracle8*i* will not use an index on a column to process a query or data change because the column referenced in the WHERE clause has some function performed on it.

■ The creation of function-based indexes uses the same CREATE INDEX statement as B-tree indexes. Instead of defining only a column to be indexed, you define the function operating on the column, as well as the column itself.

■ To use a function for a function-based index, the results of the function must be repeatable if given the same inputs. For example, given column SALARY, SALARY + 8 is repeatable.

- To use function-based indexes within your session, you must first issue ALTER SESSION SET QUERY_REWRITE_ENABLED = TRUE within your session:
    - Descending indexes can be used to improve sort operations when columns are sorted in descending order. Again, the CREATE INDEX statement is used to create the descending index, but when the indexed column is defined, you specify the ASC or DESC keywords to indicate sort order.
    - Function-based indexes can be combined with descending indexes.
- The following is the improvement from bitmap indexes:
    - Before 8.1.5, Oracle looks at the table definition to compute the maximum possible number of records that can be stored in a block of that table.
    - Therefore, bitmap indexes using this value have lots of unnecessary artificial 0 bits on the end of every block.
    - A new alternative, the ALTER TABLE option MINIMIZE RECORDS_PER_BLOCK, causes Oracle to scan a table and determine the largest number of records in any block. The resulting value is then used as the maximum number of records allowed in *any* block of that table. This reduces the size of bitmap indexes. The maximum number of rows per block no longer depends on the table's definition, and thus users can modify the table structure without invalidating bitmap indexes.
- Reverse-key indexes can be used to improve performance in Oracle Parallel Server environments by storing the actual key data reversed within the index. The CREATE INDEX REVERSE or ALTER INDEX REVERSE keywords are used in this situation.
- Oracle8*i* supports online building or rebuilding of indexes using less restrictive locking mechanisms and journal tables to allow users to continue to make data changes to the table while the index is being created. Review the chapter content to ensure you understand how this works.
- The syntax used for online rebuilding of an index is ALTER INDEX *name* REBUILD ONLINE, and the syntax used for online building of the index the first time is to use the ONLINE keyword with the CREATE INDEX statement.
- Bitmap and cluster indexes cannot be built or rebuilt online.
- To minimize storage on tables that will only be accessed via the primary key, an index-organized table (IOT) can be used.

- An IOT is created with the CREATE TABLE ORGANIZATION INDEX statement. Since the index is the table, there is no need for a ROWID on the row data stored in an IOT.

- A threshold limit for storage of any particular row in the blocks of the IOT can be set using the PCTTHRESHOLD num OVERFLOW TABLESPACE tblspc clause.

- A new column on DBA_, ALL_, and USER_TABLES, called IOT, indicates whether the table is index organized. This column can contain *IOT* for the IOT segment, *IOT_OVERFLOW* for the IOT overflow segment, and NULL for any other table.

- Secondary indexes can be created on index-organized tables using the CREATE INDEX statement. Oracle8*i* release 2's concept of logical ROWIDs is used to support secondary indexes on IOTs.

# Defining Object Relational Features

- Oracle8 and Oracle8*i* supports object-relational databases with the incorporation of object types for creating user-defined datatypes, more built-in datatypes, larger capacity, faster performance, and use of data cartridges for add-on functionality.

- Users may define their own datatypes with object types.

- The two components of an object type are attributes and views. Object types are created with the CREATE OR REPLACE TYPE *name* AS OBJECT statement.

- Attributes are data-storage components of the object defined to have either predefined scalar, collection, and reference datatypes, or other user-defined types.

- A scalar datatype is any datatype available in Oracle7 (object types cannot include LONG, LONG RAW, NCHAR, and NVARCHAR2 attributes or attributes defined with referential datatypes using the %TYPE keyword) and the new LOB datatypes available in Oracle8.

- A collection datatype can be either a variable-length array (VARRAY) or a nested table (TABLE).

- Though similar in that both variable arrays and nested tables can store multiple object "rows" in connection to a single "row" of data in another object, there are key differences between the two.

- If the amount of data to be stored in the collection object is under 4K, well defined, and limited in number, use VARRAY; otherwise, use TABLE.

- If individual items in the collection object must be accessed, use TABLE; otherwise, use VARRAY.

- If the data in the collection object must be indexed for performance, use TABLE; otherwise, use VARRAY.

- A reference type allows the developer to create pointers in one row of one object table to objects in another object table. The reference type doesn't contain the actual data; rather, it contains a pointer to the data in another object table.

- To obtain the actual data in another table using the pointer, the deref( ) operation can be used for a relational table, and the value( ) operation can be used in object tables.

- Along with types, methods are another component of an object. They are used to define activities that can be performed in association with the object.

- Defining methods is similar to using packages, with a specification included in the type definition and a body containing the application logic. The type body is defined with a separate CREATE TYPE BODY statement.

- To INSERT data into a relational table or object table defined with an object type, that object type must be referenced by name in the INSERT statement. This reference is called a constructor.

- Object views are designed to ease the transition from relational databases to object databases by creating an object structure over underlying relational tables.

- To INSERT data into the underlying relational data using object views, special triggers can be created, called INSTEAD OF triggers. The syntax used is CREATE TRIGGER *name* INSTEAD OF.

# Manage Large Objects

- The new LOB datatypes available in Oracle8*i* databases are BLOB, CLOB, NCLOB, and BFILE. There is no implicit conversion between LOB datatypes.

- LOBs have two components: value and locator.

- Differences between LONG and LONG RAW datatypes and LOB datatypes are size (2GB vs. 4GB), multiple LOB columns per table vs. one LONG or

LONG RAW, LONG data is stored inline in the table vs. only LOB locators being stored inline, and object types support LOBs (except NCLOB) and not LONG or LONG RAW. Finally, access to LOB data is nonsequential, while LONG and LONG RAW data only permits sequential access to data in the column.

- LOBs have several storage considerations over and above normal objects. LOBs may have a tablespace defined to store the LOB value and another tablespace for the associated index. This is not true in Oracle8*i* release 2.

- Oracle supports data storage for LOB datatypes with a new structure—a chunk. A chunk is a collection of blocks used to store LOB data. The blocks in the chunk must be contiguous, but the chunks used to store LOB data needn't be.

- The number of blocks in a chunk is defined with the object containing the LOB.

- Oracle will attempt to reclaim unused blocks in a chunk if the amount of data changed in the space of the chunk exceeds a certain threshold.

- The LOB column can have a NULL value assigned to it with either the empty_blob( ) or empty_clob( ) procedure.

- Access to internal LOB data is managed by the DBMS_LOB PL/SQL package or the Oracle Call Interface (OCI).

- The BFILE type is not stored in the Oracle database. Only the locator is stored in the database. BFILE objects are READ ONLY.

- To access an external object, a directory object must be created to identify its file-system location. Creation of a directory object is done with the CREATE OR REPLACE DIRECTORY *name* AS '*path*' STATEMENT.

- Creating a directory object in Oracle doesn't create the underlying directory path in the operating system. There is also no check at the time the directory object is created to verify whether the path exists. An error only occurs at the time the BFILE is referenced.

- The to_LOB( ) procedure is used to convert LONG columns to LOBs.

## Basic Partitioning Concepts

- Tables and indexes in Oracle8*i* can be partitioned.

- Table and index partitions are defined with three new parts to the CREATE TABLE and CREATE INDEX statements: PARTITION BY RANGE(*column*), which defines the partition key; VALUES LESS THAN (*value*), which defines the upper bound for each partition subrange; and tablespace location and storage parameters. Only the storage parameters need be preceded by the STORAGE clause.

- Tables and indexes can have up to 64,000 partitions.
- Oracle8*i* can store up to 512 petabytes of data.
- The following restrictions apply to changing column and constraint definitions on a partitioned table:
  - The partition key's datatype or size cannot be changed.
  - All values for the partition-key column must be accommodated by a partition.
  - If no partition defined for the partitioned object contains VALUES LESS THAN (MAXVALUE), the partition-key column cannot contain NULL values.
  - An INSERT on the table will fail if the value specified for the partition is outside any range specified for any partition on the table.
  - The partitioned table may not contain a column declared with the LONG or LONG RAW datatypes.
  - The value in a partition-key column cannot be changed if the change will cause the row to move partitions.
  - The individual partitions of the table cannot be referenced through a database link or a synonym.
  - A PL/SQL block may not contain SQL that refers directly to a partition in a table. However, the user can create dynamic SQL, using the DBMS_SQL package, that references individual partitions in PL/SQL blocks, or can use views that reference an individual partition in a table. Only table partitions can be directly referenced, not index partitions.
- The EXPLAIN PLAN utility has several new features to support partitioned tables:
  - Three new columns for the PLAN_TABLE are PARTITION_START, PARTITION_STOP, and PARTITION_ID.
  - EXPORT and IMPORT can handle partitioned tables. EXPORT can create export files containing only the named partition if used in TABLE mode.
  - The ANALYZE statement can be executed either on individual partitions or on entire partitioned database objects.

- SQL*Loader can run multiple conventional or direct-path loads on different partitions in the object. For direct-path loads, the load on each partition can be executed using the PARALLEL=TRUE parameter, which sets the direct load to run in parallel when loading one partition.

- To load all partitions of the table with one load, SQL*Loader allows a sequential load. Only one sequential load can operate on a partitioned table at one time.

## Partition Maintenance Operations

- A table's partitions can be altered in several ways:
    - The ALTER TABLE DROP PARTITION statement drops a named partition and its contents.
    - The ALTER TABLE ADD PARTITION statement adds a partition over and above the highest range currently existing on a partition in the table.
    - The ALTER TABLE RENAME PARTITION statement renames a partition.
    - The ALTER TABLE MODIFY PARTITION statement first allows the DBA to change physical storage parameters, and sets the equipartitioned index data to UNUSABLE.
    - The ALTER TABLE TRUNCATE PARTITION statement deletes all data from the table partition.
    - The ALTER TABLE SPLIT PARTITION statement splits one partition into two.
    - The ALTER TABLE MOVE PARTITION statement moves the partition to another extent in the same tablespace or into another tablespace.
    - The ALTER TABLE EXCHANGE PARTITION statement is an easy method of inserting information from a nonpartitioned table into a partition.
- The ALTER INDEX DROP PARTITION statement drops the named partition and its contents.
- The ALTER INDEX RENAME PARTITION statement renames the partition.
- The ALTER INDEX REBUILD PARTITION statement fixes an INDEX UNUSABLE index partition.

- The ALTER INDEX MODIFY PARTITION statement changes physical storage parameters for a partition.
- The ALTER INDEX SPLIT PARTITION statement splits one partition into two.
- The ALTER INDEX UNUSABLE statement makes an index partition unusable.
- The ALTER INDEX PARALLEL statement defines parallelism for the index.

## Composite Partitioning

- Hash partitioning is defined using the PARTITION BY HASH(*column*) syntax. You should remember to define the number of partitions and the tablespaces Oracle8*i* should use to store them, or explicitly name your partitions and where you want them to be stored.
- Composite partitioning is range and hash partitioning combined, which gives you a two-dimensional partitioning/subpartitioning option, as well as more partition-key columns to choose from for partition-wise joins. It's also for PDML.

## Parallel DDL, Parallel DML, and Parallel Queries

- Oracle8*i* allows DML operations to run in parallel.
- Parallel DML offers performance benefits, automatic parallelism, and affinity between partitions and disks.
- There are three types of parallelism: parallelism by ROWID range, parallelism by partition, and parallelism by I/O process:
    - Parallelism by ROWID range is used in SELECT statements.
    - Parallelism by partition is used in parallel UPDATE and DELETE statements.
    - Parallelism by I/O process is used in parallel INSERT statements.
- The ALTER SESSION ENABLE PARALLEL DML statement is used to enable parallel DML in a session.

- There is no way to institute parallel DML for an entire instance.
- When using parallelism by partition, only one parallel-query process can operate on a partition.
- When using parallelism by parallel-query process or by ROWID range, multiple parallel-query processes can access a single partition, or a nonpartitioned table, at once.
- Only one parallel-DML operation is allowed per transaction on the same table.
- No DML or SELECT statements can be issued on the changed table after a successful parallel-DML operation in a transaction. A SELECT statement can be issued on another table, however.
- Even though all DML statements issued after parallel DML is enabled are considered for parallelism, not all statements will be executed in parallel. To guarantee parallelism in a DML statement, use the PARALLEL hint, specified with the /*+PARALLEL (*tablename, degree_parallel*) */ syntax.
- The degree of parallelism defined in the CREATE TABLE statement specifies the degree of parallelism in DML and SELECT statements issued on that table later.
- Parallel hints can be specified for both the INSERT and the SELECT statement in an INSERT AS SELECT statement.
- The APPEND and NOAPPEND hints are also available for INSERT statements, telling Oracle to use the INSERT direct path or not, respectively.
- The INSERT direct path is similar to the direct path available in SQL*Loader.
- New features have been added in support of parallel DML to the V$SESSION, V$PX_SESSTAT, and V$PX_SYSSTAT views in the form of new statistics collected in the latter two views and a new PDML_ENABLED column in the former view.
- Redo logging can be turned on and off on a per-table basis for INSERT statements only with the ALTER TABLE *name* LOGGING and ALTER TABLE *name* NOLOGGING statements, respectively.
- Transaction and process recovery takes longer for parallel DML because usually the ROLLBACK process executes serially.
- No parallel DML is allowed on index-organized tables, tables with LOBs or object types, or clustered tables; parallel DML must be committed or rolled back before executing another DML statement.
- No parallel INSERT on any global index is allowed in Oracle8*i*.

- Parallel-query optimization can be performed in Oracle8*i* using the new init*sid*.ora parameter PARALLEL_AUTOMATIC_TUNING. This parameter will automatically configure other parameters and settings to eliminate the need to define parallel query at the table or transaction level.

- Another parameter, PARALLEL_ADAPTIVE_MULTI_USER, allows for automatic management of the degree of parallelism in Oracle8*i*.

- Another parameter, PARALLEL_THREADS_PER_CPU, indicates how many parallel processes can be handled on each CPU at once.

- Monitoring query parallelism is done using the following views:

    - **V$PX_PROCESS**   Lists identification information about parallel-query processes running in various sessions

    - **V$PX_PROCESS_SYSSTAT**   Details statistics for parallel-query processing

    - **V$PX_SESSION**   Identifies more information about sessions running parallel-query processing

    - **V$PX_SESSTAT**   Shows a combination of data from the V$PX_SESSION view and the V$SESSTAT view

# Installation, Configuration, and Migration

- Universal Installer and Packager is the new software installer for Oracle products. It is written in Java and runs on multiple platforms.

- Universal Installer and Packager permits automated, noninteractive software installation through the use of a response file.

- When installing Oracle8*i* on certain platforms, you will need to ensure that you install the software to a separate home directory. This is a requirement of the new version of Universal Installer and Packager.

- If you are attempting to perform a Typical Installation of Oracle8*i* Enterprise Edition, ensure that you have more than the 128MB minimum RAM requirement. If your installation fails, try a Minimal Installation instead.

- The Net8 listener is compatible with SQL*Net version 2.3 and higher. If any database on the machine hosting Oracle8*i* does not meet this requirement, you should upgrade to that version of SQL*Net.

- You can have Universal Installer and Packager install a preconfigured database for you with minimal user interaction. In this case, all scripts, such as catalog.sql and catproc.sql, are run automatically, and a few basic tablespaces, such as DATA, INDEX, and ROLLBACK, are created with the following information:
  - SID is ORC0 or ORCL
  - INTERNAL password is oracle
  - SYS password is change_on_install
  - SYSTEM password is manager
- You can also use the Database Configuration Assistant to set up a database. This is a wizard-driven interface in which you define the tablespaces you want, along with the desired SGA size and other INIT.ORA characteristics. The wizard generates your tablespace datafiles and INIT.ORA file.
- Several parameters have been renamed or rendered obsolete between Oracle7, Oracle8, and the latest version of Oracle8*i*. Some common ones are
  - DB_WRITERS in Oracle7 was renamed DBWR_IO_SLAVES in Oracle8 and higher.
  - SNAPSHOT_REFRESH_INTERVAL in Oracle7 was renamed JOB_QUEUE_INTERVAL in Oracle8 and higher.
  - CHECKPOINT_PROCESS was rendered obsolete in Oracle8 and higher. The CKPT process now always runs.
- The migration and upgrade path for earlier versions of Oracle to Oracle8*i* is to migrate from Oracle7 to Oracle8 and then upgrade from Oracle8 to Oracle8*i*.
- The six steps of database migration are
  1. Prepare for migration by understanding the new features of Oracle8 and Oracle8*i*.
  2. Make sure you have plenty of disk space—the Oracle8 and Oracle8*i* software distribution takes between 550 and 750MB of space on disk.
  3. Develop a test plan for ensuring your migration is successful.
  4. Preserve your data source by taking a backup beforehand.

5. Perform the migration.
  6. Back up your converted database, test to see if the database works, modify your applications as necessary, and make the whole thing available to the users.

- The upgrade path for Oracle8 to Oracle8*i* is as follows:
  1. Modify your INIT.ORA file according to parameters changed or eliminated between Oracle8 and Oracle8*i*.
  2. Change environment variables, such as ORACLE_HOME, to point to your Oracle8*i* installation home directory.
  3. Start the instance and open the database in restricted session mode.
  4. Run the Oracle8*i* upgrade script found in rdbms/admin under your Oracle8*i* software home directory appropriate to your version of Oracle8.
  5. Back up the database and open it for general use.

# Tablespace Management

- Oracle8*i* offers several features for extended tablespace management. One of these features is the ability to make a tablespace read-only. You do not have to wait for transactions to complete before issuing the ALTER TABLESPACE...READ ONLY statement. When the statement is issued, the target tablespace goes into a transitional read-only mode in which no further DML statements are allowed, though existing transactions that modified the tablespace will be allowed to commit or roll back. Once this occurs, the tablespace is quiesced, with respect to active transactions.

- Moving data between databases is simplified by the new transportable tablespaces in Oracle8*i*. To use this feature, the target database must be a replica of the source, or else you must copy the tablespace dictionary information as well as dictionary information for the contents of a tablespace using the EXPORT and IMPORT tools.

- To transport a tablespace, the contents must be self-contained. This means all partitions for an object must be in the same tablespace, LOB overflow information must be in the same tablespace as the table with the LOB column defined, and several other restrictions.

- The DBMS_TTS package contains a procedure called transport_set_check( ) that can be used to determine whether a tablespace is self-contained or not. The package is created with the dbmsplts.sql script, automatically run by catproc.sql.

- Management of free space in tablespaces can be handled centrally with the data dictionary or locally within the datafiles with Oracle8*i*.

- Locally managed tablespaces are better because they reduce the need to reorganize tables to fit into fewer extents, reduce the need for coalesced free space, and reduce contention for dictionary information regarding tablespace storage allocation.

- Locally managed tablespaces consist of each datafile having a small area where each block in the datafile is represented by a bit. The bit is set to 0 or 1 to specify whether the block is free or used, respectively.

- To specify local management of tablespaces, you must use the EXTENT MANAGEMENT LOCAL keywords in the CREATE TABLESPACE command.

- You can also define two new methods for segment and extent allocation in the tablespace. Each will override the default storage clause for the tablespace and any storage definition in the CREATE *object* statement:

  - The database can manage its own tablespace extent allocation based on your setting for INITIAL when you specify for it to do so with the AUTOALLOCATE keyword.

  - You can specify that all extents will be the same size using the UNIFORM SIZE keywords. In addition, if you use UNIFORM SIZE space allocation, the bits in the bitmap storage-management area of locally managed tablespaces will represent the number of blocks that is equivalent to the size of each extent set by UNIFORM SIZE.

## Database Resource Manager

- Database Resource Manager is a new feature in Oracle8*i* that complements profiles to limit overall usage of a machine hosting the Oracle database.

- Database Resource Manager is a PL/SQL package.

# Miscellaneous Manageability Features

- Columns can be dropped in two ways in Oracle8i—logically and physically:
    - Logical column removal consists of marking the column as unused with the ALTER TABLE SET UNUSED COLUMN statement.
    - Physical column removal consists of dropping the column with the ALTER TABLE DROP COLUMN statement. Review the coverage in the chapter to be sure you understand the options that can be specified for physical column removal.

- Temporary tables in Oracle8i can be created to support complex transactions or reporting. The data in them persists either until the end of the transaction or the session; for as long as data appears in that table, the data is available to every user connected to the database, and users that have privileges to access this table.

- Temporary tables are created with the CREATE GLOBAL TEMPORARY TABLE statement. Any column and constraint definition permitted in a permanent table is also permitted in a temporary table. Indexes created to support those constraints (if any) will also be temporary.

- The ON COMMIT [DELETE|PRESERVE] ROWS clause will indicate whether the data in a temporary table will be deleted or preserved, respectively, after the transaction is committed.

- Temporary-table creation and DML activity generates no redo to recover the data changes, but they do generate rollback so that Oracle can roll back any changes in the event of session or instance failure.

- Information about temporary tables can be found in the TEMPORARY and DURATION columns of DBA_TABLES.

- Moving tables is handled with the ALTER TABLE MOVE statement. This statement causes Oracle8i to place the table into a new segment in the same tablespace. If the TABLESPACE name clause is added to the ALTER TABLE MOVE statement, then the table gets moved to the tablespace indicated.

- The ALTER TABLE MOVE statement also moves related objects, such as constraints, indexes, and triggers.

- SQL*Loader now permits use of column-data delimiters longer than one character and the use of a recseparator character that indicates the end of a logical record in the SQL*Loader data file.

# Recovery Manager

- The new architecture for backup and recovery in Oracle8 and Oracle8i consists of Recovery Manager and a recovery catalog.
- Recovery Manager (RMAN) is a utility that allows DBAs to manage all aspects of backup and recovery using an Oracle-supported tool.
- A recovery catalog is a dictionary run on another Oracle database that tracks all backup and archived redo logs produced for the database.
- There are some enhancements to the control file and a much larger control file in Oracle8 to support RMAN. RMAN information is stored for a period of time corresponding to the CONTROL_FILE_RECORD_KEEP_TIME initialization parameter.
- RMAN is created with the catrman.sql script, found in rdbms/admin under the Oracle software home directory.
- RMAN has four sets of commands: recovery catalog maintenance commands, reporting commands, scripting commands, and RUN commands.
- To run RMAN, type **rman** at the OS command prompt. One mandatory option and three optional ones are used: TARGET to identify the production or target database; RCVCAT to identify the recovery catalog database; CMDFILE to execute RMAN in batch mode with a command script; and MSYGLOG to keep a log of all activity with APPEND, allowing RMAN to append information to an old log file for the current RMAN session.
- Communication with the operating system is possible in RMAN with the ALLOCATE CHANNEL command.
- Recovery-catalog management commands include the following:
    - **REGISTER DATABASE** Registers a target database
    - **RESET DATABASE** Resets the redo log sequence when the target database is opened
    - **RESYNC CATALOG** Resynchronizes the recovery catalog after log switches in the target database

# Chapter 12: OCP Oracle8i Upgrade Exam Terms and Concepts

- **CHANGE** Alters the control file or other database filenames used
- **LIST INCARNATION** Shows the current database data version
- **CATALOG** Identifies copies of files made outside of RMAN

- RMAN reporting and listing commands give information about the current database and its recovery status.

- Reports show information about files of the database and recoverability. One of the reports that can be used is REPORT NEED BACKUP, which shows the files of the database that need backup. Options for this report include INCREMENTAL = *num*, which shows the files that need *num* incremental backups to be recovered, and DAYS *num*, which shows the files that haven't been backed up in *num* days. Another report includes REPORT UNRECOVERABLE, which shows files that are not recoverable.

- Lists show information about the backups that are available in the database. Some lists that can be used are LIST COPY OF TABLESPACE, LIST COPY OF DATAFILE, LIST BACKUP, and LIST INCARNATION OF DATABASE.

- There are several commands available in RMAN for script creation. They are CREATE SCRIPT, REPLACE SCRIPT, DELETE SCRIPT, and PRINT SCRIPT.

- The final set of commands in RMAN are RUN commands. These commands handle most of the processing in RMAN, such as execution of scripts, SQL, and backup and recovery operations.

- The BACKUP command runs backups. RMAN creates incremental or full copies of files for the entire database, the files of a tablespace, or individual datafiles.

- The backups of files and archived redo logs are placed into collections called *backup sets*. A backup can contain only archived redo logs or only datafiles and control files.

- Datafiles can be multiplexed into a backup set, meaning that the blocks of datafiles are stored noncontiguously on the sequential offline storage media, such as tape.

- Backup sets are composed of backup pieces. The number of pieces in a backup set depends on the parallelism of backup, number of tapes required for the backup, and other factors.

- Oracle8*i* and RMAN support the incremental backup of datafiles, which store only the blocks of a datafile that have been changed since the last full backup. A full backup reads the entire file and copies all blocks into the backup set, skipping only datafile blocks that have never been used.

- There are eight levels of incremental backups and a level-0 backup, which is a full backup.
- To recover a database component from backup, the component must first be restored.
- The COPY command will create an image copy of a database file component. This component is immediately usable for recovery.
- The COPY command only produces image copies to disk, while BACKUP can send database file components directly to tape.
- The SWITCH command will substitute a datafile copy for a current file. The datafile switched will then need media recovery.
- The RESTORE command will retrieve the files from the backup copy and put them where the DBA specifies.
- The RECOVER command will conduct media recovery using backups restored in combination with archived redo logs.
- Several old and new dictionary views exist in Oracle8*i* to support RMAN.
    - V$ARCHIVED_LOG displays name and information in the control file about archived redo logs.
    - V$BACKUP_CORRUPTION displays information in the control file about corrupt datafile backups.
    - V$BACKUP_DATAFILE offers information from the control file about backup datafiles and control files.
    - V$BACKUP_DEVICE offers operating-system–specific information about supported third-party vendors for RMAN in Oracle8 and Oracle8*i*.
    - V$BACKUP_REDOLOG displays information about archived redo logs in backup sets.
    - V$BACKUP_SET displays information from the control file about all backup sets.
    - V$BACKUP_PIECE displays information from the control file about all pieces in all backup sets.
    - V$DATAFILE lists information about datafiles in the Oracle8 and Oracle8*i* database.
    - V$DATAFILE_HEADER lists information about datafile headers in the Oracle8 database.

# Miscellaneous Availability and Recoverability Features

- There are two ways in Oracle8*i* to specify maintenance of multiple archive-log destinations, which are mutually exclusive:
    - LOG_ARCHIVE_DUPLEX_DEST and LOG_ARCHIVE_DEST
    - LOG_ARCHIVE_DEST_*n*, where *n* is an integer between 1 and 5, indicating up to 5 archive destinations.

- LOG_ARCHIVE_DEST_*n* can be set with several options: LOCATION, SERVICE, MANDATORY, REOPEN, and OPTIONAL. Some locations can be made mandatory or optional. Review the chapter contents to make sure you understand what each means and which are mutually exclusive.

- LOG_ARCHIVE_MIN_SUCCEED_DEST can be used to make some optional locations mandatory, but not to make a mandatory location optional.

- The availability of archive-log destinations can be changed using the LOG_ARCHIVE_DEST_STATE_*n* parameter, where *n* is set to the number of the archive log destination identified with LOG_ARCHIVE_DEST_*n*. The destination state can be DEFER or ENABLE to defer or enable its maintenance, respectively.

- Multiple ARCH processes are enabled by specifying a number for LOG_ARCHIVE_MAX_PROCESSES and setting LOG_ARCHIVE_START to TRUE.

- You can find information about your archive destinations and processes using the V$ARCHIVE_DEST and V$ARCHIVE_PROCESSES views, respectively.

- LogMiner allows you to examine the contents of your online and archived redo logs.

- Two packages are used by you to run LogMiner: DBMS_LOGMNR_D to manage the LogMiner dictionary file, and DBMS_LOGMNR to manage LogMiner itself.

- The build( ) procedure in DBMS_LOGMNR_D builds the LogMiner dictionary file as a text file external to Oracle. Before running this

- procedure, you will need to set the directory you want your dictionary file written in for the UTL_FILE_DIR parameter.

- To analyze specific log files, you must identify them to LogMiner by means of a list. The add_logfile( ) procedure in DBMS_LOGMNR is used for that. Make sure you understand the parameters passed for this procedure.

- To start and stop LogMiner usage, you must issue the start_logmnr( ) and stop_logmnr( ) procedures. Be sure you understand parameter passing for start_logmnr( ).

- Information about the contents of your redo logs can be found in V$LOGMNR_CONTENTS.

- You can only find information in LogMiner for DML statements that acted on nonchained rows, where the datatypes manipulated were scalar (VARCHAR2, for example—not LOB or VARRAY). Only the session running LogMiner can see the contents of V$LOGMNR_CONTENTS.

- Bounded recovery time is specified using the FAST_START_IO_TARGET parameter.

- The principle behind bounded recovery is to keep the DBW0 process more active, so that there are few dirty blocks in memory to minimize processing in the event of an instance failure.

- The LOG_CHECKPOINT_INTERVAL and LOG_CHECKPOINT_TIMEOUT parameters have new meanings in Oracle8*i*, allowing you more control over the number of dirty blocks in memory at any given time.

- The FAST_START_PARALLEL_ROLLBACK INIT.ORA parameter allows for SMON to execute parallel rollback using parallel-query slave processes. This activity will occur when starting the Oracle8*i* database after instance failure when a parallel transaction was taking place.

- You can detect block corruption in Oracle8*i* using the DB_BLOCK_ CHECKING INIT.ORA parameter, the ANALYZE TABLE VALIDATE STRUCTURE statement, the DBVERIFY utility, or the DBMS_REPAIR package.

- There are several procedures you should understand how to use in DBMS_REPAIR:

    - **admin_tables( )**  Constructs repair table.
    - **check_object( )**  Validates object structure and finds corrupt blocks.

- **fix_corrupt_blocks( )** Marks block as corrupt. In later versions of Oracle8*i*, this procedure will fix the corruption.
- **skip_corrupt_blocks( )** Indicates that corrupt blocks identified should be skipped.
- **dump_orphan_keys( )** Used on indexes to eliminate references to corrupt data blocks in tables.
- **rebuild_freelists( )** Used to rebuild a table freelist if the corrupt block is a freelist header.

- Although you can use DBMS_REPAIR on tables with LOB columns, VARRAYs, and nested tables, any data for those columns not inline with the rest of the table gets ignored.

- You can't use DBMS_REPAIR on IOTs or LOB indexes. The dump_orphan_keys( ) procedure doesn't work on bitmap or function-based indexes.

- To automate sustained recovery to stop executing when no redo logs appear for a long time, you can specify the ALTER DATABASE RECOVER MANAGED STANDBY DATABASE TIMEOUT *n* command. The value *n* is the number of minutes the standby database should wait after applying the last log to see if another appears. If no log appears during that time, recovery will automatically end.

- You can open a database in read-only mode in Oracle8*i* by using the ALTER DATABASE OPEN READ ONLY statement. Only query operations will be permitted by users.

# Features of Net8

- Oracle8*i* databases automatically register with the Net8 listener. All you need to do is specify values for new INIT.ORA parameters called INSTANCE_NAME, SERVICE_NAMES, and LOCAL_LISTENER.

- Load balancing is achieved in Oracle8*i* by setting the LOAD_BALANCE tnsnames.ora parameter to ON.

- The ADDRESS specification remains the same—only the SID information is replaced with SERVICE_NAME and INSTANCE_NAME.

- The LOCAL_LISTENER parameter in your INIT.ORA file indicates a connect string from the local tnsnames.ora file that Oracle8*i* should use to identify the local listener to register with.

- Oracle8*i* allows you to connect to the database without using Net8. Instead, you can use GIOP, an implementation of the Internet Inter-ORB Protocol, or IIOP, which is a presentation layer that enhances Two-Task Common for connectivity without Net8. The TNS layer is also eliminated on the client side, but not the server side.

# SQL*Plus, PL/SQL, and National Language Support

- SQL*Plus has replaced Server Manager as the tool for Oracle database management.

- NLS datatype equivalents exist for CHAR, CLOB, and VARCHAR2 datatypes. They are NCHAR, NCLOB, and NVARCHAR2.

- The NLS_DUAL_CURRENCY parameter supports EU member countries that use and support dual currencies: their home currency and the euro.

- The NLS_COMP parameter is used to enhance comparison and sort operations in Oracle8*i*.

- Oracle8*i* NLS support extends to South African and additional Asian character sets.

- Procedures written in C or Java can now be called from PL/SQL using external procedures. Optional return values, called callbacks, are also supported.

- The EXTPROC_CONNECTION_DATA parameter in tnsnames.ora must be configured in order to use external procedures.

- Autonomous transactions are possible in Oracle8*i* using the PRAGMA AUTONOMOUS_TRANSACTION keywords in your PL/SQL block. An autonomous transaction is one that can be completed without impacting any other transaction currently underway within a session.

- Prior to Oracle8*i*, transactions were only considered autonomous if they were performed in separate sessions. Oracle8*i* offers the ability to perform autonomous transactions within a single session.

- Dynamic SQL is now possible using language constructs in PL/SQL, rather than using DBMS_SQL.

- Oracle8*i* offers the following enhanced triggering events:

- ALTER Trigger fires when database object is altered.
- CREATE Trigger fires when database object is created.
- DROP Trigger fires when database object is dropped.
- LOGOFF Trigger fires when user logs off of Oracle8*i*.
- LOGON Trigger fires when user logs on to Oracle8*i*.
- SERVERERROR Trigger fires when user receives an error from Oracle8*i*.
- SHUTDOWN Trigger fires just before the server starts the shutdown of an instance.
- STARTUP Trigger fires when the Oracle8*i* instance starts.

# Advanced Queuing

- Oracle8 and Oracle8*i* supports advanced queuing of messages between multiple processes and the deferral of executing database operations.
- The fundamental unit of queuing is a message.
- Messages have two components: user data and control information.
- Messages are stored in a queue.
- Queues are stored in a queue table.
- Messages are put into a queue with procedures from the DBMS_AQ package.
- The two procedures available in DBMS_AQ are enqueue( ) and dequeue( ).
- The management of queues and queue tables is done with the DBMS_AQADM package. The procedures of this package are create_queue_table( ), drop_queue_table( ), create_queue( ), drop_queue( ), alter_queue( ), start_queue( ), stop_queue( ), start_time_manager( ), stop_time_manager( ), add_subscriber( ), remove_subscriber( ), and queue_subscribers( ).
- The roles used for managing access to the DBMS_AQ and the DBMS_AQADM packages are AQ_USER_ROLE and AQ_ADMINISTRATOR_ROLE.
- Certain features of messaging, such as dequeue delay and message expiration, depend on the use of the Time Manager process. The Time

Manager must be turned on as part of the start of the Oracle instance, by setting the AQ_TM_PROCESSES initialization parameter to 1.

- Available dictionary views for queuing are DBA_QUEUE_TABLES for queue tables, DBA_QUEUES for queues, and AQ$QUEUE_TABLE_NAME for each queue table in the database.

# Database Security

- Review password management and administrative features introduced in Oracle8.

- Oracle8*i* allows you to specify invoker's rights execution of PL/SQL stored procedures, meaning that the user calling the procedure must have both EXECUTE privileges for that procedure and system/object privileges to perform whatever operations are involved in the procedure.

- Prior versions of Oracle used owner's rights execution for PL/SQL stored procedures, where only the owner of the procedure needed to have privileges to perform whatever operations were involved in the procedure.

- Invoker's rights execution is defined in the PL/SQL procedure or function specification by using the AUTHID *option* clause, where *option* is replaced by CURRENT_USER or DEFINER for invoker's or owner's rights execution, respectively.

- Fine-grained access control is another new security feature in Oracle8*i*. It allows you to define a security policy that is always enforced in the form of a PL/SQL package associated with a table or view.

- Fine-grained access control operates by adding a predicate or additional set of clauses to the WHERE clause of a user's SQL statement; it is designed to transparently verify or restrict the information a user is allowed to see.

- To manage aspects of security-policy PL/SQL packages being bound to tables or views, you use the add_policy( ), drop_policy( ), enable_policy( ), and refresh_policy( ) procedures found in the DBMS_RLS package.

- Fine-grained access control may use information about users called *attributes* to determine whether the user may perform a specific operation. This information may or may not come from another feature called *application context*.

- Application context is also implemented using a package of your own design. The procedures in this package are used to verify or set attributes about users that can be used by fine-grained access control to restrict access to certain data.

- The package used for application context is bound to a context object in Oracle8*i*. The context object is created using the CREATE CONTEXT *name* USING *owner.pkg* statement.

- Oracle8*i* supports all of Oracle8's integration of third-party *n*-tier authentication security tools, and moves ahead of Oracle8 by adding support for SSL, downloadable wallets via LDAP, management of wallets using Oracle Wallet Manager, and support for remote dial-up authentication using RADIUS.

# Oracle Enterprise Manager Version 2

- Oracle Enterprise Manager 2.0 underwent significant changes. It is now a Java-based, *n*-tier application that can be accessed via Web browsers.

- The middle tier in OEM 2.0 is called an Oracle Management Server (OMS). It manages the data repository stored on one of the databases in your network.

- You now have the option to log into the Oracle Management Server in order to perform administrative activities on many different Oracle databases at the same time.

- Earlier versions of OEM required you to log into each database separately and store a repository on each of them.

- OEM 2.0 also provides scalability because you can add multiple Oracle Management Servers to your network to distribute the load better and also to provide fault tolerance.

- OEM 2.0 running with OMS allows for repository sharing between DBAs, with one superuser who can create other administrators and superusers. The default username and password for the OMS superuser is SYSMAN and oem_temp, respectively.

- Multiple DBAs in OEM 2.0 are given access to manage jobs and events via a multilevel permission architecture. The five levels are *none*, *view*, *modify*, *full*, and *notify*.

- Preferred authentication credentials are also maintained for every DBA in the OMS.

- You can also run OEM 2.0 in client/server mode, as was available in OEM 1.6, but you will not be able to use the advanced features provided by the *n*-tier architecture.

# Constraints

- Integrity constraints in Oracle8*i* can be deferred. If the constraint is deferred, Oracle8*i* does not verify whether the data added to the constrained column conforms to the constraint until the transaction is committed by the user.
- The possibility to defer a constraint is defined in the table. Whether constraints are actually deferred or not is specified either in the session or in the transaction.
- The SET CONSTRAINT *name* [IMMEDIATE|DEFERRED] statement is used to make constraints deferrable or immediate within the transaction. The ALTER SESSION SET CONSTRAINT *name* [IMMEDIATE|DEFERRED] does the same within an entire session.
- The [NOT] DEFERRABLE keywords in the CREATE TABLE or ALTER TABLE statement are used to indicate whether the constraint can (or cannot) be deferred in the table.
- The INITIALLY [DEFERRED|IMMEDIATE] keywords in the CREATE TABLE or ALTER TABLE statement indicate whether the constraint is deferrable or not deferrable by default within the user session.
- Nonunique compound indexes can be used to enforce UNIQUE or PRIMARY KEY constraints.
- The DBA_CONSTRAINTS view will give information about integrity-constraint deferability, validation, and reliance.
- The enabling and disabling of constraints is handled in Oracle8*i* with the ALTER TABLE statement.
- The two options for enabling constraints in Oracle include ENABLE VALIDATE, which forces a check of all data in the column to see whether it conforms to the constraint, and ENABLE NOVALIDATE, which does not check to see whether data in the column conforms to the constraint being enabled.

- The two options for disabling constraints in Oracle include DISABLE VALIDATE to prevent any data from entering the table that might not conform to the disabled constraint. DISABLE VALIDATE disables the constraint and drops the index on the constraint, but keeps the constraint valid. This feature is most useful in data warehousing situations, when the need arises to load into a range-partitioned table a quantity of data with a distinct range of values in the unique key. In such situations, the DISABLE VALIDATE state enables you to save space by not having an index. You can then load data from a nonpartitioned table into a partitioned table using the EXCHANGE_PARTITION_CLAUSE of the ALTER TABLE statement or using SQL*Loader. All other modifications to the table (inserts, updates, and deletes) by other SQL statements are disallowed, and DISABLE NOVALIDATE, which indicates to Oracle that the column should be ignored completely, are disallowed.

- DISABLE NOVALIDATE indicates to Oracle that the column should be ignored completely.The RELY or NORELY keywords can be added to the DISABLE NOVALIDATE option for disabling constraints to indicate that the column does not contain any data that would violate the constraint, thus allowing the query optimizer to perform query rewrite.

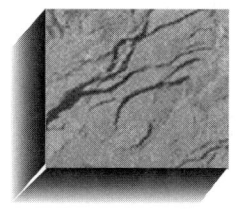

# Index

## A

ABORT option, 205
ACCEPT command, 68
access
    auditing and, 140
    managing methods for, 87
access control
    configuration of, 290, 316–317, 481
    defining rules for, 292, 318
    enabling, 303–304, 327
    host machine resources and, 86
    overview of, 7
    password authentication and, 411–412
    specifying fine-grained control, 357, 387, 516
administrative tools, 80, 417
advanced security options
    authentication and, 328
    cryptography and, 293, 319
    overview of, 485–486
ALERT file, 117, 147
alert logs
    deadlocks and, 263, 470
    errors and, 167
    function of, 446
    log switches and, 264, 272
    overview of, 214
    performance tuning and, 456–457
    periodic clearing of, 453
alias names, 310

ALTER ANY TABLE, privilege, 384
ALTER SYSTEM statement, 143
ALTER TABLE statement
    adding columns with, 56
    failure of, 137
    table management and, 406
ALTER USER statement
    changing passwords with, 60
    changing user definitions with, 430
    compared with CREATE USER statements, 112–113
    configuring new and existing users with, 92
    options of, 113
ALTER VIEW statement, 410
ALTERTABLESPACE READ ONLY, 341, 372
ANALYZE command
    chained rows and, 467
    partitioning and, 499
    performance tuning and, 272–273
AQ_TM_PROCESS, 396
AQ_USER_ROLE, 384
ARCH process
    conflicts and, 118
    redo logs and, 142, 439
architectural components, 80
archive logs
    destination of, 511
    formats of, 193
    managing, 349, 380
    multiplexing, 155, 162–163, 180, 187

ARCHIVELOG mode
    backups and, 166, 172, 183
    initialization parameters and, 182, 209
    overview of, 447–449
    recovery and, 170
    redo logs and, 90, 193
    uses of, 195–196
archiving
    automatic archiving, 447
    Oracle8i and, 208
    recovery and, 152, 447–450
    redo logs and, 154–155
attributes
    overview of, 496
    REF type and, 363, 392
auditing
    access and, 140
    data deletion and, 137
    database options for, 128–129
    enabling, 97
    explaining, 99
    locating audit information, 87
    managing, 84
    order status and, 104
    overview of, 435–436
    use of, 120
    value-based auditing and, 135
authentication
    advanced security options and, 328, 485
    configuration of, 306, 329
    listener startup and, 283
    Oracle architecture and, 417
    passwords and, 58, 96, 128
AUTHENTICATION_SERVICES, 329
AUTOTRACE
    performance tuning with, 221, 252–253
    SQL tuning tools and, 459

# B

B-tree indexes, 426
background processes
    comparing with threads, 241, 270
    free space and, 93
    maintaining, 421–422
    Oracle architecture and, 416
    performance tuning and, 227–228, 258–259
    redo logs and, 85
    synchronization and, 177–178
    trace files and, 446

BACKUP command, 444, 509
Backup Manager
    RMAN and, 193–194
    use of, 187
backup sets, 444, 509
backups
    ARCHIVELOG mode and, 172
    calculating progress of, 207
    configuration of, 150–151, 439–440
    control files and, 157, 166
    incremental levels of, 168, 179
    overview of, 438
    permissions and, 356, 386
    physical backups and, 151, 442–445
    practice exam answers for, 186–198, 199–212
    practice exams for, 154–169, 170–185
    scripts and, 178, 179
    simple alternative for, 163
    strategies for, 155, 160, 170–171, 191
    structures and processes for, 439
    synchronization and, 158
    techniques for, 367–369, 395–396
    testing, 206
    third-party interoperability and, 163
    timing of, 157, 188
    topic areas of, 150–153
    troubleshooting, 445–446
    UNIX and, 156
bad files, SQL*Loader, 139
BETWEEN statement, 402
BFILE object, 390, 497–498
bitmap indexes
    databases and, 32
    errors and, 134
    performance queries and, 219, 251
    performance tuning and, 66, 495
    uses of, 70, 426
BLOB, 497. *see also* large object datatypes (LOBs)
block size
    determining, 467
    efficient use of, 216
    OLTP and, 228, 259
    performance tuning and, 467
    space allocation and, 238, 268
buffer cache
    adding buffers to, 248, 276
    hit ratio for, 240, 269
    latch contention and, 266
    monitoring, 239, 268
    Oracle8i and, 491

performance tuning and, 215,
  224–225, 255–256, 463–464
queries and, 246, 275
saving information and, 94
size of, 63, 245, 274
buffer pools, 240, 269

# C

C sort routines, 359, 388
Cartesian products
  SQL statements and, 15
  WHERE clause and, 54
case statements, DECODE function and, 70
CATALOG command, 194–195, 395
catalog.sql script, 420
catproc.sql script, 421
CEIL function, SQL*Plus, 34–35
chaining. *see* row chaining
change-based recovery, 211
CHAR datatype
  fixed-width text and, 388
  use of, 130
character sets
  parameters for, 116
  using, 84
  variable length of, 146
CHECK constraints, 31
checkpoints
  altering, 110
  backups and, 178
  frequency of, 88, 154, 186, 206, 466
  function of, 439
  instance recovery and, 191–192
  number of datafiles and, 120–121
checksums
  corruption and, 189
  sqlnet.ora file and, 293, 319, 486
chunks, 362, 391
CKPT
  checkpoint processing with, 439
  redo logs and, 111, 141
  sequences and, 205
  synchronizing datafile headers and, 192
client/server computing
  Net8 and, 474–475
  network administration and, 294, 320
  overview of, 308
CLOB, 497. *see also* large object datatypes (LOBs)
cluster key indexes
  building, 495
  creating, 120

clusters
  querying tables and, 135
  range operations and, 121
  using, 83, 87, 428–429
CMADM (Connection Manager administrative utility, 481
CMADM (Connection Manager administrative) utility, 327
CMAN, 318
cman.log, 317
cman.ora
  access control and, 327
  parameters of, 318, 481, 482
CMAN_RULES
  access control and, 316
  configuring, 481
  defining, 291, 317
CMCTL (Connection Manager control) utility, 303, 327, 481
CMGW (Connection Manager gateway), 327, 481
collection datatypes, 425, 496
columns
  datatypes and, 99
  dropping, 144, 507
  managing, 406
  primary-key indexes and, 130
  removing from databases, 344, 375
  SQL*Loader and, 508
command-line options
  database corruption and, 159–160
  recovery and, 187
  RMAN and, 156
COMMIT statements
  data changes and, 60
  lock contention and,
    231, 262
  Oracle architecture and, 417
  resource allocation and, 267
  using, 50, 105
complex views, 409
composite datatypes, 8, 413
composite partitioning, 347, 378
configuration
  Oracle8*i* and, 335
  overview of, 503–505
CONNECT role, 129
connection concentration
  configuration of, 289–290, 316–317
  Net8 features and, 289, 315–316
  parameters for, 303, 327
  using, 302, 326
Connection Manager
  components of, 302, 327

configuration of, 281, 480–481
function of, 295, 321
multiprotocol functionality and, 290, 316
Net8 features and, 289, 315
tracing levels in, 292–293, 318–319
troubleshooting gateway problems and, 291, 317
using, 281, 480–481
Connection Manager administrative (CMADM) utility, 327, 481
Connection Manager control (CMCTL) utility, 303, 327, 481
Connection Manager gateway (CMGW), 327, 481
connection pooling
    Net8 and, 315
    overview of, 480
    using, 302, 326
connectivity
    limiting database connections, 108
    Net8 and, 294, 320
constraints
    CHECK constraints and, 31
    creating and maintaining, 6
    deferring, 371–372
    indexes associated with, 11
    integrity constraints and, 407, 426
    Oracle8*i* and, 338, 518–519
    overview of, 407–408
    removing, 31
    types of, 50–51
    using, 426–427
    violations of, 361, 390
contention, 248, 276. *see also* latch contention; lock contention
control files
    adding information to, 118
    backups and, 157, 166, 198
    creating, 192
    enhancing, 508
    limiting growth of, 367, 395
    locating, 106, 137
    maintaining, 81, 192, 421
    multiplexing, 178
    recovery and, 452–453
    recreating, 181, 199, 204
    risk of eliminating, 161
    RMAN and, 367, 395, 440
    SQL*Loader and, 112
control structures
    PL/SQL and, 43
    writing, 7–8, 413

conversion functions, PL/SQL, 16
COPY command, 445
corruption. *see* data corruption
CPUs
    connection time of, 125
    resource cost of, 93
    tuning, 222, 253
crashes. *see* failures
CREATE CONTEXT statement, 387
CREATE INDEX statements, 267
CREATE SCRIPT command, 195
CREATE SESSION privilege, 129
CREATE TABLE AS SELECT statement, 406
CREATE TYPE command, 382
CREATE USER statements
    ALTER USER statement and, 112–113
    configuring users with, 92
    creating users with, 430
    preventing conflicts and, 89
    QUOTA clause and, 144
    restricting number of tables with, 114
cryptography, 293, 319
Cryptography Toolkit, 306, 329, 485
CUBE keyword, SQL statements, 344, 375
CURRVAL, 53–54
CURSOR FOR loops
    explicit cursors and, 60–61
    functions of, 63
    keyword for opening, 48
    named cursors and, 78
    PL/SQL and, 27–28, 49
cursors. *see also* explicit cursors
    named cursors and, 78
    referencing values from, 69
    using, 47–48

# D

data
    aggregating with group functions, 5, 404
    COMMIT command and, 60
    data fields and, 429
    displaying from multiple tables, 5, 403
    loading and reorganizing, 83, 429–430
    managing access to, 23
    manipulating, 6, 406
    preventing changes in, 37
    restricting and sorting, 4, 402
    ROLLBACK command and, 35
    selecting from tables, 22, 24
    storing regional data, 286, 313

data blocks
    bitmap and, 355, 386
    chunks and, 362, 391
    fixing corruption of, 350, 380–381, 512
    Oracle architecture and, 416
    PCTFREE and, 137
    storing, 353, 383
data corruption
    correcting, 203, 350, 380–381, 512
    recovery and, 177, 205
    reducing occurrences of, 211
data definition language (DDL) statements, 400
data dictionaries
    constructing and using, 81
    creating code in, 28
    database access and, 104
    location of, 85
    overview of, 6, 408–410
    query performance and, 98
    record location in, 108
    recovery and, 176
    viewing code and, 17
    views and characteristics in, 32
data dictionary views, 420–421
    adding clauses to, 16
    adding columns to, 15
    auditing data and, 435
    buffer cache, hit ratio and, 240, 269
    buffer cache, increasing with, 246, 248, 275, 276
    buffer cache, monitoring with, 225, 239, 256, 268
    buffer cache, tuning with, 463–464
    changing or recreating, 54
    creating, 6, 16, 26, 408–410
    DBA_PROFILES and, 127
    dynamic views and, 214, 457–458
    functions of, 10, 50
    I/O issues and, 239, 268, 465
    latch-performance and, 470
    materialized views and, 361, 390
    parallel DML and, 348, 379
    partitioning and, 366, 393–394
    performance and, 218, 250, 457
    pinning objects in shared pool with, 247, 275
    queries and, 105
    recovery and, 448
    redo logs and, 465
    removing from tables, 20
    RMAN support and, 452–453, 510
    rollback segments and, 267
    scripts and, 96
    session information and, 389
    storage information and, 423
    synchronization and, 189
    transporting tablespaces and, 358, 388
    tuning session memory with, 240, 269
    tuning shared pool with, 241, 270
    wait events and, 234, 264
    wait information and, 271
data integrity
    lookups and, 98–99
    maintaining, 83, 426–427
data load, conventional path vs. direct path, 108
data manipulation language (DML) statements
    data dictionary views and, 348, 379
    executing, 366, 394
    Oracle architecture and, 416
    running in parallel, 501–502
    SQL and, 401
DATA tablespace, 465
data warehousing, 351, 382
database administration, 80–147
    practice exam answers for, 118–132, 133–147
    practice exams for, 85–101, 102–117
    topic areas of, 80–84
Database Configuration Assistant, 504
database objects
    constraints and, 11
    overview of, 6–7, 410–411
    tablespaces and, 70–71
Database Resource Manager, 336, 506
Database Services, Net8, 309
databases
    activity reports for, 457–458
    backup statements for, 210
    bitmap indexes and, 32
    configuring tablespaces for, 226, 257–258
    creating, 81, 419–420
    host naming and, 310
    initialization parameters for, 418–419
    instance recovery and, 418
    limiting connections and, 108
    logging process on, 419
    login to, 418
    modifying schemas of, 114
    objects and, 6–7, 11, 70–71, 410–411
    online backups and, 210–211
    Oracle security model for, 21, 337, 516–517

performance tuning and, 241, 270,
   465–466
preventing corruption of, 161
shutting down, 418
starting up, 418
trace files and, 419
UPDATE statement and, 17
datafiles
   backing up, 157, 201, 368–369,
      396, 444
   checkpoints and, 120–121
   directory objects and, 362, 391
   location of, 353, 383
   maintaining, 367, 394
   managing, 81, 422
   mapping physical to logical, 38
   SQL*Loader and, 123
   synchronization of, 186
   tablespaces and, 125
datatypes. *see also by type*
   categories of, 424
   columns size and, 99
   composite datatypes and, 8
   DATE functions and, 11
   determining, 115
   fixed-width text and, 358, 388
   storing, 16
   table management and, 406
DATE
   converting, 55
   datatypes and, 11
   types of, 51
date conventions, 116
DBA_PROFILES, 127
DBA_SEGMENTS, 139
DBMS_REPAIR, 512–513
DBMS_STATS, 343, 374–375
DBVERIFY
   command-line options and, 159, 191
   data block corruption and, 452
   function of, 198, 446
   RMAN and, 195
DBWO, 416, 439
DDL (data definition language) statements, 400
deadlocks
   information on, 232, 263
   preventing, 470
decision-support systems (DSS)
   performance tuning and, 458
   recovery and, 172, 200, 210
DECODE function, 51, 70
DEFAULT profile, 127

DEFAULT ROLE clause, 143
DEFINE command, 57
DELETE statement, 406
dictionary cache
   hit ratio for, 223, 245, 254, 274
   performance tuning and, 462–463
dictionary views. *see* data dictionary views
dimension objects, 493–494
directory objects
   datafiles and, 362, 391
   incorrect path and, 362, 390
   security and, 346, 377
disaster recovery plan, 160–161, 191, 438
DISK clause, 394
disk crashes
   preventing, 97
   recovery and, 177
disk sorts. *see also* sort operations
   optimizing, 230, 260
   tuning, 229
dispatchers. *see also* multithreaded server
   (MTS)
   configuration of, 301, 326, 480
   function of, 479
   Oracle architecture and, 417
   using, 145
DML statements. *see* data manipulation
   language (DML) statements
DROP TABLE
   sizing tables and, 122
   using, 65
DROP TABLESPACE command
   failure of, 133
   issuing, 102
DROP USER statement, 430
DROP VIEW statement, 410
DSS. *see* decision-support systems (DSS)
DUAL table
   overview of, 51
   statements and, 12
dynamic views, 214, 457–458

# E

encryption
   advanced security options and, 485
   clients and servers and, 305–306, 328
   sqlnet.ora file and, 293, 319, 486
equijoin operations, 403
errors. *see also* failures; troubleshooting
   common errors and resolutions, 483
   corruption and, 203

# Index 527

GROUP BY clause and, 63
insufficient privileges and, 98
LSNRCTL command and, 322–323
Net8 listeners and, 296, 322–323
ORA-00600 errors, 197
sequences and, 34
Server Manager and, 133
SQL statements and, 28, 29
events
    monitoring, 218, 250
    performance tuning and, 457
exceptions
    automatic, 66
    defining, 37
    exception handlers and, 8, 48, 59, 69, 414
    OTHERS and, 49
    procedures and, 21, 77
    using, 69, 427
EXCEPTIONS, 129
executable statements. *see also* statements
    labels and, 75
    objects and, 23
    PL/SQL and, 72
    writing, 7, 412
execution section, PL/SQL, 74
EXISTS statement, subqueries and, 67–68
EXIT statement, 78
EXPLAIN PLAN
    partitioning and, 499
    SQL tuning tools and, 459
explicit cursors. *see also* cursors
    advanced concepts for, 414
    CURSOR FOR loop and, 60–61
    overview of, 8
    reducing number of, 24
    writing, 414
EXPORT dump files, 100
EXPORT utility
    backups and, 153, 180–181
    parameters for, 181, 202–203, 209
    recovery and, 174–175
    transporting tablespaces and, 505
    using, 159–160, 190–191, 430, 450–451
extents, 229, 260

## F

failover
    hardware nodes and, 313
    tnsnames.ora and, 384

failures. *see also* errors; troubleshooting
    information on, 170
    recovery from, 204
    statement failure and, 177
    types of, 445–446
fast transaction rollback, 208
fast warmstart, 208, 451
file components, 429
file structures, 439
FOR UPDATE clause, 77
foreign-key constraints, 407
foreign-key relationships, 56
free space
    allocation of, 136–137
    SMON and, 125
freelist contention
    correcting, 276
    determining, 233, 263
FROM clause, SQL statements, 49, 69
function-based indexes, 494–495

## G

gateways, 291, 317
General Parameters, Net8 Assistant, 322
GIOP, 514
GOTO command, 74–75
GRANT clause
    privileges and, 412
    roles and, 144
GROUP BY clause
    data aggregation and, 404
    errors using, 63
    materialized views and, 493
    summary management and, 382
group operations
    creating multiple members for, 129
    data aggregation and, 404
    functions of, 404
    overview of, 13–14

## H

hardware bottlenecks, 222, 253–254
hash clusters
    HASHKEYS and, 142
    using, 428–429
hash joins, 460
hash partitioning
    implementing, 346, 377
    Oracle8*i* new features and, 501
HASHKEYS, 142

HAVING clause
    groups and, 404
    using, 23, 59
hints, 429
home directories, 340, 371
host machines
    limiting resource use on, 86
    performance tuning and, 462
host naming
    client/server connections and, 477
    conditions for, 284
    name resolution with, 282, 308
    Net8 and, 297, 323

# I

I/O
    configuring, 462
    detecting statistics of, 239, 268
    distributing, 227, 258
    performance tuning and, 216, 253, 465–466
    reducing bottlenecks, 161, 192
    using parallel processes with, 378
IDENTIFIED BY clause, 143
IF-THEN-ELSE statements, 413
image copies, 197
IMPORT utility
    moving indexes with, 175
    recovery and, 153
    transporting tablespaces and, 505
    using, 159–160, 185, 212, 430, 450–451
incomplete recovery
    RMAN and, 453
    types of, 449
incremental backup, 197–198, 207, 444–445, 510
index-organized tables (IOTs)
    overview of, 495–496
    using, 83, 348–349, 379–380, 427–428
INDEX privilege, 135
INDEX tablespace, 465
indexes
    bitmap indexes and, 32
    cluster key indexes and, 120
    enhancing performance of, 346, 359
    finding location of, 139
    function-based indexes and, 376–377
    IMPORT utility and, 175
    INDEXFILE parameter and, 203
    location and size of, 108
    managing, 82, 426
    measuring usage and performance of, 239, 268
    NOLOGGING option and, 165
    NULL values and, 37
    OLTP and, 352, 383
    Oracle8i and, 333, 494–496
    partitioning and, 346, 377
    performance tuning and, 219, 251
    query performance and, 234
    rebuilding, 345, 376
    removing from tables, 31
    reverse-key indexes and, 129, 383
    sequences and, 352
    storage parameters for, 91
    types of, 410–411
    USER_INDEXES and, 66
initialization parameters
    ARCHIVELOG mode and, 182
    databases and, 418–419
    Instance Manager and, 134
    MTS and, 287–288, 314
    performance tuning and, 458
    selecting, 116–117
    setting values for, 103
    tablespaces and, 105
    V$NLS_PARAMETERS, 146
INIT.ORA
    checkpoint frequency and, 154
    control files and, 206
    MTS_LISTENER_ADDRESS and, 329
    MULTIPLEX option, 289, 316
    multiplexing control files and, 178
    Oracle8i upgrades and, 356, 386
    parameters, 464, 490
    performance tuning and, 220, 252
    use of, 141
INSERT privilege, 138
INSERT statements
    constraints and, 390
    correct use of, 363, 391–392
    data insertion with, 497
    data manipulation with, 406
    identifying, 96
INSERT triggers, 130
installation
    memory requirements and, 503
    Oracle8i and, 335
    overview of, 503–505
Instance Manager
    database reconfiguration with, 458
    initialization parameters and, 134
    using, 187

# Index 529

instance recovery
    checkpoints and, 191–192
    databases and, 418
    shutdown options and, 178
    SMON and, 125, 184, 189
    tuning, 227, 258
instances
    failures of, 445
    managing, 80, 418–419
INSTEAD OF triggers, 392, 497
insufficient privileges errors, 98
INTEGER datatype, 55
integrity constraints
    deferring, 518
    types of, 407, 426
Intelligent Agent
    configuration of, 281, 285–287, 312, 313, 479
    operation parameters of, 307, 330
    shutdown of, 287, 301, 313, 326
    simplifying management with, 300–301, 325
    startup of, 286, 307, 312, 330
    tracking events and, 457
    using, 281, 286, 287, 312–313, 479
INVENTORY tables
    inserting records into, 18
    SQL*Plus and, 20
IOTs. *see* index-organized tables (IOTs)

## J

Java, 332, 339–340, 370–371, 488–490
Java Class Loader, 370, 489
Java Virtual Machines (JVMs), 340, 370, 489
JDBC, 488
JDeveloper, 489
join operators
    definition of, 403
    performance tuning and, 220, 252, 461
    using, 52, 57

## K

keep pool, 245, 273, 358, 388

## L

large object datatypes (LOBs)
    components of, 362, 391
    managing, 497–498

large pool feature, Oracle8*i*, 342, 373, 490
LASTNAME value, PL/SQL, 33
latch contention. *see also* lock contention
    detecting, 236–237, 266
    monitoring, 217
    overview of, 470–471
    performance tuning and, 470–471
LEVEL keyword, RMAN and, 188–189
LGWR process
    conflicts and, 118
    function of, 439
    maintaining, 421–422
    Oracle architecture and, 416
    performance tuning and, 227–228, 258–259
    redo logs and, 142, 464
library cache
    hit ratio for, 223, 245, 246, 254, 274
    performance tuning and, 462–463
    users of, 126
LIKE operators, 56
listener.ora
    defining names and, 322
    Net8 listeners and, 476
    parameters for, 482
load balancing
    Net8 and, 339, 370
    setting parameters for, 513
    views used for, 227, 258
load paths, data, 430
LOAD_BALANCE, 384
LOBs. *see* large object datatypes (LOBs)
local naming, 298, 323, 477
lock contention
    monitoring and detecting, 217
    performance tuning and, 231–232, 262, 469–470
    preventing, 263
log buffers, 225, 257, 274
log files
    performance tuning and, 456–457
    troubleshooting and, 482
log switches
    frequency of, 243, 272
    performance tuning and, 234, 264
logging. *see also* redo log files
    cman.log and, 317
    Connection Manager and, 291, 317
    databases and, 418, 419
    transactions and, 123
LOGGING option
    NOLOGGING option and, 165
    speed and recoverability and, 195
logical backups, 439–440, 450

logical data models, 38
LOGIN.SQL file, 54
LogMiner tool
    overview of, 511–512
    using, 349, 380
lookup tables
    data integrity and, 98–99
    performance tuning and, 246, 274
loop control, 413
loop exit conditions, 66
LSNRCTL command
    error messages and, 322–323
    Intelligent Agent and, 326, 479
    Net8 listeners and, 297, 476
    restarting listeners with, 328
    shutdown of Intelligent Agent with, 313
    startup of Intelligent Agent with, 312

## M

machine names, 310
maintenance operations, 367, 394
management
    data access management, 23
    memory management, 332, 490–491
    miscellaneous features for, 507–508
    password management, 94, 126
    resource management, 343, 374
    summary management, 333, 351, 382, 492–494
    table management, 406
    tablespace management, 505–506
materialized views
    dictionary views and, 493
    refresh options for, 361, 390
    replacing snapshots with, 492
media failure
    prevention of, 86
    recovery after, 200
    troubleshooting, 445–446
media management layer (MML), 193
memory
    analyzing use of, 235, 264–265
    database recovery and, 439
    installation requirements and, 503
    managing, 332, 490–491
    performance tuning and, 222, 254, 462
    sessions and, 224, 255
methods, defining, 497
migration
    migration to object applications, 363, 392
    Oracle7 to Oracle8*i*, 357, 387, 504
    Oracle8 to Oracle8*i*, 357, 387, 504–505
    overview of, 335, 503–505
    steps in process of, 504–505
MML (media management layer), 193
MTS. *see* multithreaded server (MTS)
MTS_DISPATCHERS
    configuration of, 301, 326
    connection concentration and, 326
    non-Net8 connections and, 339
    using, 314
MTS_LISTENER_ADDRESS
    port location and, 329–330
    use of, 315
MTS_SERVERS, 323
MTS_SERVICE, 314
multiple-column sub-queries, 5, 405
multiple-row queries, 39–40
MULTIPLEX option, INIT.ORA, 289, 316
multiplexing
    archive logs and, 155, 162–163, 180, 187
    backup sets and, 369, 396
    control files and, 178
    function of, 439
    redo logs and, 119
multiprotocol functionality
    CMAN parameter and, 318
    configuring, 481
    Connection Manager and, 290, 316, 318
    setting up, 291–292
    using, 303, 327
multithreaded server (MTS). *see also* dispatchers
    configuration of, 281, 479–480
    listener address and, 307, 329
    Oracle architecture and, 417
    processes in, 301, 326
    session information and, 115
    shared servers and, 298, 302, 323, 326
    using, 287–289, 314–315

## N

N-tier applications, 294, 320
name resolution. *see also* Oracle Names
    host naming and, 282, 308
    steps in process of, 285, 311
Names Control utility (NAMESCTL)
    naming functions of, 478–479

Index **531**

Oracle Names and, 300
shutting down name servers with, 312
starting names servers with, 325
namesini.sql script, 324
names.ora, 324, 482
National Language Support (NLS)
defining national languages and, 116
NLS_SORT and, 146
Oracle8*i* new features and, 337, 514
overview of, 436
parameters of, 359, 388
using, 84
NCA (network computer architecture), 320
NCLOB, 497. *see also* large object datatypes (LOBs)
nested blocks, PL/SQL and, 74
NESTED LOOPS, 271
nested tables, 382
Net8
architecture of, 474–476
client-side configuration of, 477
connection pooling and, 315
connectivity and, 294, 320
cryptography and, 293, 319
features of, 289, 315–316
host naming and, 297, 323
load balancing and, 339, 370
Oracle8*i* new features and, 337, 513–514
overview of, 280
routing and, 296, 321
server-side configuration of, 476–477
shutdown of, 296, 322
tracing with, 284, 311
Net8 Assistant
centralizing naming with, 478
defining nondefault trace directory with, 296, 322
listener configuration with, 283, 309
name resolution with, 311
network listeners and, 476
shutting down name servers with, 312
starting name servers with, 325
Net8 listeners
authentication and, 283
compatibility of, 503
configuring with Database Services, 309
connecting users to database with, 307, 330
defining names for, 296, 322
error messages and, 296, 304, 322–323, 328

LSNRCTL command and, 476
managing, 350, 381
tracing and, 292, 318
using, 283–284, 309–310
network administration, 280–330
client/server systems and, 294, 320
configuration of, 282
practice exam answers for, 308–319, 320–330
practice exams for, 282–293, 294–307
security and, 281, 485–486
topic areas of, 280–281
troubleshooting, 281, 482–485
network computer architecture (NCA), 320
network/names directory, scripts in, 312
NEXTVAL, 53–54
NLS. *see* National Language Support (NLS)
NLS_CURRENCY, 146
NLS_DUAL_CURRENCY, 388
NLS_SORT parameter, 146
NOARCHIVELOG mode
applications of, 162
compared with ARCHIVELOG mode, 188
overview of, 446
recovery and, 158–159, 171, 189–190, 192–193, 199–200, 210
reducing recovery time and, 203
RMAN and, 171
using, 182, 195–196
Node UpDown event, 250
NOLOGGING option
indexes and, 165
speed and recoverability and, 195
NOT NULL constraints, 408
Notify permissions, 386
NULL values
constraints on, 65
using, 37, 75
NVL function, 14

## O

object relational features
object tables and, 351, 382
Oracle8*i* new features and, 333, 496–497
objects
access management and, 23
database privileges and, 432–433
executable statements and, 23
large objects and, 334
Oracle databases and, 41
SYS schema and, 118

OEM. *see* Oracle Enterprise Manager (OEM)
OERR utility, 484
OFA (Optimal Flexible Architecture), 383
offline backups, 442
OLTP. *see* online transaction processing (OLTP)
OMS. *see* Oracle Management Server (OMS)
online backups, 442
online redo log files. *see* redo log files
online transaction processing (OLTP)
    block size and, 228, 259
    index for, 352, 383
    performance tuning and, 458
operating systems (OS)
    database creation and, 419
    performance tuning and, 215, 241–242, 270–271
OPS (Oracle Parallel Server), 354, 384
Optimal Flexible Architecture (OFA), 383
OPTIMAL parameter
    rollback segments and, 124
    uses of, 87
optimizer
    modes of, 460
    Oracle8*i* new features and, 332–333, 491–492
ORA-00600 errors, 197
Oracle architecture, 416–417
Oracle Cryptography Toolkit. *see* Cryptography Toolkit
Oracle Enterprise Manager (OEM)
    administrative tools of, 417
    features in OEM 2, 338, 341, 371, 517–518
    handling failover with, 313
    Intelligent Agent and, 479
    OMS and, 358, 388
    performance tools of, 218–219, 250–251
    repository and, 340, 371
    Table Data Editor tool and, 351, 381
Oracle Expert
    performance tuning and, 217, 235–236, 265–266, 471
    SQL tuning tools and, 460
Oracle Intelligent Agent. *see* Intelligent Agent
Oracle Management Server (OMS)
    OEM 2 and, 358, 388
    overview of, 517
    SYSMAN and, 371
Oracle Names
    configuration of, 281, 285, 311, 478–479
    name resolution with, 282, 308

    server location and, 299, 324
    shutting down, 286, 312
    starting up, 300, 325
    storing naming information with, 299, 324
    using, 281, 478–479
Oracle Parallel Server (OPS), 354, 384
Oracle Server, 7, 413
Oracle Trace, 459
Oracle8*i*
    archiving and, 208
    connections in, 339, 370
    installation, configuration, migration and, 503–505
    interoperability with earlier Oracle versions, 356, 386
    resource management and, 343, 374
Oracle8*i*, new features, 488
    availability and, 511–513
    composite partitioning and, 501
    constraints and, 518–519
    Database Resource Manager and, 506
    database security and, 516–517
    indexes and, 494–496
    IOTs and, 494–496
    Java and, 488–490
    LOBs and, 497–498
    memory management and, 490–491
    miscellaneous management features and, 507–508
    Net8 and, 513–514
    NLS and, 514
    object relational features and, 496–497
    OEM v. 2 and, 517–518
    optimizer and, 491–492
    parallel operations and, 501–503
    partitioning and, 498–501
    PL/SQL and, 514
    queries and, 491–492
    queuing and, 515–516
    recovery and, 511–513
    RMAN and, 508–510
    SQL*Plus and, 514
    summary management and, 492–494
    tablespace management and, 505–506
    triggers and, 514–515
Oracle8*i*, upgrades, 332–396. *see also* migration
    practice exam answers for, 370–385, 386–396
    practice exams for, 339–354, 355–369
    topic areas of, 332–338
ORAPWD utility, 417

ORDER BY clause
    optimizing queries with, 375
    overview of, 402
    using keywords with, 51
OS. *see* operating systems (OS)
OSDBA privilege, 276
OSI model
    Net8 and, 475–476
    presentation layer of, 282, 309
    trace files and, 484
    transport layer and, 296, 321
OTHERS, exceptions and, 49, 69
outlines
    eliminating stored outlines, 360–361, 389–390
    use of, 491–492
OUTLN_PKG, 389–390, 492

# P

packages
    creating, 96
    local procedures and, 74
    scripts and, 420–421
    using, 497
packet information, 484
parallel DML. *see* data manipulation language (DML) statements
parallel operations
    composite partitioning and, 501–503
    Oracle8*i* and, 335
    parallel DML and, 347, 378, 501–502
    parallel-query tuning and, 360, 389
    parallel recovery and, 451
    query processing and, 343, 374
PARALLEL_AUTOMATIC_TUNING, 389
partitioning
    composite partitioning and, 501
    DBMS_STATS and, 343, 374–375
    maintaining, 500–501
    managing, 346–348, 377–379
    Oracle8*i* and, 334
    overview of, 498–500
    techniques for, 364–366, 392–393
passwords
    administration features for, 432
    ALTER USER statement and, 60
    authentication and, 58, 96
    changing, 23
    listener startup and, 283
    managing, 94, 126
    ORAPWD utility and, 417
    problems with, 92–93
    roles and, 128
    unauthorized access and, 109
payload message, 396
PCTFREE
    block size and, 114–115, 137, 467
    controlling space usage with, 422
    high settings for, 145
    row chaining and data migration and, 244, 273
    storage requirements and, 106
    tables and, 91
    using, 119, 124
PCTINCREASE
    PCTUSED values and, 131
    rollback segments and, 119, 141, 423
PCTTHRESHOLD storage option, 379
PCTUSED
    block size and, 114–115, 467
    controlling space usage with, 422
    increasing, 131
    settings for, 121
    tables and, 91
    using, 119, 124
Performance Manager, 459
Performance Monitor (PMON), 242, 271
    process crashes and, 234, 264
    recovery and, 439
    Tuning Pack and, 242, 271
    using, 262
performance tools, OEM, 218–219, 250–251
performance tuning, 456–471
    application requirements and, 458
    basic issues of, 462
    block size and, 467
    buffer cache and, 463–464
    database configuration and, 465–466
    DSS and, 458
    dynamic views and, 457–458
    I/O issues and, 465–466
    latch and contention and, 470–471
    lock contention and, 469–470
    log files for, 456–457
    OLTP applications and, 458
    Oracle Expert and, 471
    OS and, 215
    overview of, 456
    practice exam answers for, 250–263, 264–277
    practice exams for, 218–233, 234–249
    redo log buffers and, 464–465
    rollback segments and, 468–469
    shared pool and, 462–463

        SQL and, 215, 459–461
        stored operations and, 467–468
        stored plans and, 343, 374
        topic areas of, 214–217
        utilities for, 457
performance views, 457
permissions
        altering partitions and, 353, 384
        backups and, 356, 386
        roles and, 104–105
PGA (Program Global Area), 376, 416
physical backups
        overview of, 439–440
        with RMAN, 444–445
        without RMAN, 442–444
PL/SQL, 4–78
        bulk data operations in, 46–47
        coding declarations for, 45–46
        conversion functions and, 16
        CURSOR FOR loop and, 27–28, 49
        data changes and, 24
        Data Resource Manager and, 506
        declaring table of records in, 76
        declaring variables in, 42, 412
        defining information in, 41
        executable statements and, 73
        executing code in, 29–30
        execution section of, 74
        finding errors in, 30–33, 36–37, 41–42
        LASTNAME value and, 33
        location of parse information and, 94
        nested blocks and, 74
        Oracle8i new features and, 337,
            342–343, 373, 514
        overview of, 4, 401
        performance tuning and, 221, 253
        practice exam answers for, 49–62,
            63–78
        practice exams for, 9–26, 27–48
        procedures and, 16, 42
        questions covering use of, 9–10
        reusability and, 28–29
        storing numeric datatypes in, 16
        topic areas of, 4–8
        using control structures with, 43
        using to answer questions, 43–45
        variable declaration in, 19, 20–21
PMON. *see* Performance Monitor (PMON)
power loss, backups and, 168–169
practice exam answers
        backup and recovery, 186–198,
            199–212

        database administration, 118–132,
            133–147
        network administration, 308–319,
            320–330
        Oracle8i upgrades, 370–385, 386–396
        performance tuning, 250–263,
            264–277
        SQL and PL/SQL, 49–62, 63–78
practice exams
        backup and recovery, 154–169,
            170–185
        database administration, 85–101,
            102–117
        network administration, 282–293,
            294–307
        Oracle8i upgrades, 339–354, 355–369
        performance tuning, 218–233,
            234–249
        SQL and PL/SQL, 9–1: 26, 27–48
presentation layer, OSI model, 282, 309
prespawned servers, 295, 321
primary key constraints
        constraint types and, 50
        constraint violations and, 109
        failure due to, 56
        integrity constraints types and, 407
        performance tuning and, 219, 251
        reenabling, 98
        SELECT statements and, 99–100
primary-key indexes
        column order in, 130
        IOTs and, 380
        nonunique indexes and, 341, 371
        table size and, 361–362, 390
privileges
        access methods and, 87, 411–412
        ALTER ANY TABLE privilege, 384
        CREATE SESSION privilege, 129
        database access and, 104
        granting, 58, 355, 386
        grant_system_privilege(), 389
        INDEX privilege, 135
        INSERT privilege, 107, 138
        insufficient privileges errors and, 98
        managing, 83, 110, 432–433
        OSDBA privilege, 276
        REVOKE command and, 140–141
        roles and, 120, 434
        SYSDBA privilege, 276, 417
        SYSOPER privilege, 417
        system privileges and, 104–105
        tablespaces and, 89

        users and, 91, 411–412
        WITH GRANT OPTION and, 123
procedures
        exceptions and, 21, 77
        executing in PL/SQL, 42
        package constraints and, 74
process failures, 445
process-schedule, tuning, 462
profiles
        defining profile areas, 110
        generating, 125
        host machine resources and, 119
        inability to drop, 131
        location of, 96
        managing, 83, 431–432
        resource use and, 142
        SPANKY and, 121
        specifying resource limits and, 112
Program Global Area (PGA), 376, 416
programming languages, integrating, 71

## Q

queries
        advanced database queries and, 39
        backup queries and, 168
        clusters and, 135
        data warehouse applications and, 242, 271
        datafile backup and, 157, 188
        dictionary views and, 105
        enhancements to, 98, 345, 376–377
        increasing buffer cache and, 246, 275
        inline views and, 29
        multiple-column sub-queries and, 5
        multiple-row queries and, 39–40
        optimizing, 220, 221, 252, 253, 344, 375
        Oracle8i new features and, 332–333, 491–492
        parallel query processing and, 343, 374, 503
        performance slowdown and, 250
        performance tuning and, 72, 228–230, 259
        rollback segments and, 97
        SQL*Plus and, 39–40
        sub queries and, 5
        tablespaces and, 166–167
        using indexes with, 264
queuing
        advanced features for, 353, 384

        Oracle8i new features and, 337, 515–516
        techniques for, 369, 396
QUOTA clause, 144

## R

RAID 5
        I/O distribution and, 258
        performance tuning and, 239, 268
        types of, 466
RDBMS. see relational databases (RDBMS)
records, 108
recovery
        ARCHIVELOG mode and, 170
        archiving and, 152, 447–449
        automatic recovery and, 447
        configuration of, 150–151, 439–440
        corruption and, 161, 177
        dictionaries views and, 176
        disk crashes and, 177
        incomplete recoveries and, 179, 449–450
        issues of, 451–453
        methods for, 172–174
        names restoration and, 312–313
        NOARCHIVELOG and, 158, 162, 171, 199–200
        Oracle8i new features and, 336, 511–513
        overview of, 438
        practice exam answers for, 186–198, 199–212
        practice exams for, 154–169, 170–185
        recovery time and, 175, 181, 196, 203, 350, 381
        simple alternatives for, 163
        standby functionality and, 350, 381
        steps in process of, 201
        strategies for, 155, 156, 172
        structures and processes for, 150, 439
        synchronization and, 158
        time-based, 201
        topic areas of, 150–153
        troubleshooting, 445–446
        types of, 184–185
        without archiving, 446
recovery catalog
        creation of, 156
        maintaining, 151, 194, 441
        maintenance commands in, 368, 396
        management commands in, 508–509

overview of, 508
recovering lost information and, 176
RMAN and, 194, 367, 395
roles and, 187
tape backups and, 204
UNCATALOG command and, 191
updating, 180
using, 160, 163
Recovery Manager (RMAN)
backing up to tape with, 183–184
backup queries and, 168
backup staging area and, 180
backup strategies and, 167
command-line options for, 156
commands used with, 164–165, 183, 207–208, 210
complete recovery with, 173–174
database backup and, 157
evaluating use of, 155
incremental backup levels and, 197–198, 207
LEVEL keyword and, 188–189
NOARCHIVELOG and, 158–159, 171
OEM and, 508–510
Oracle8i and, 336
overview of, 151, 440
recovery with, 176, 200
streaming and, 167–168, 197
using recovery catalogs with, 163, 194
viewing backup progress with, 179
when to use, 182, 187
RECSEPARATOR keyword, SQL*Loader and, 376
recycle pool, 273
REDO ALLOCATION, 266
redo log buffer
performance tuning and, 216, 464–465
sizing, 226, 257
redo log files
ACTIVE status and, 176–177
ARCHIVELOG mode and, 90, 193
archiving, 154–155, 186, 442
CKPT and, 111, 141
clearing unarchived logs, 112
disk crashes and, 97
hardware striping and, 239, 268
integrity of, 170, 199
maintaining, 81, 421–422
multiplexing and, 109, 111, 119
performance tuning and, 226, 257
RESETLOGS option and, 202

sustained recovery and, 350
using, 85
REF type, 363, 392
REFERENCES privilege
foreign-key relationships and, 56
tables and, 18
referential integrity, 13
REGISTER command
recovery catalog and, 194
registering services with, 325
relational databases (RDBMS)
advantages of, 400
hierarchical databases and, 71
Net8 and, 294, 320
OSI model and, 475
overview of, 4
sort operations and, 229
storage strategy for, 38–39
tasks performed by, 400
reload statistics, 274
remote administration, 90
RENAME statement, 407
replication, SNP, 170, 199
REPORT RECOVERABLE, 396
reports, tuning, 234
report.txt, 457
repository, Oracle Expert
creating, 265
storing naming information and, 299
RESET DATABASE command, 396
RESETLOGS option, 202
resources
allocating, 237, 267
costs of, 143
managing, 343, 374
profiles and, 431–432
response queue, MTS, 314
RESTRICTED SESSION, 122
reverse-key indexes
data in, 361, 389
indexes and, 129
overview of, 383
using, 426, 495
REVOKE command, 140–141
RMAN. see Recovery Manager (RMAN)
roles
allocating, 113
CONNECT role and, 129
database access and, 104
DEFAULT ROLE and, 124
defining default roles, 110–111

Index **537**

    displaying, 134
    GRANT clause and, 144
    granting permissions to, 104–105
    granting privileges to, 120
    managing, 84, 434–435
    password authentication and, 128
    performance tuning and, 235, 265
    recovery catalogs and, 187
    uses of, 60
ROLLBACK command
    data changes and, 35
    UPDATE statement and, 50
rollback segments
    assigning processes to, 109
    heavy usage and, 89
    information storage and, 113
    limiting size of, 120, 128
    managing, 82, 423
    monitoring, 238, 267
    OPTIMAL parameter and, 124
    optimizing, 230–231, 261–262
    PCTINCREASE and, 119
    performance tuning and, 217, 468–469
    SET TRANSACTION command and, 139
    sizing extents of, 97, 111, 141
    statistics and, 133
    storage parameters and, 86
    transaction distribution and, 273
    transaction wrapping and, 102
ROLLBACK tablespace, 465
routing, 296, 321
row cache, 138–139
row chaining
    avoiding, 228, 259
    block size and, 467
    correcting, 86
    definition of, 425
row migration
    block size and, 467
    definition of, 425
    performance tuning and, 244, 272–273
    prevention of, 228, 259
ROWID, 129, 488
rows
    finding number of rows in tables, 46
    inserting into tables, 33
    location of, 112
RUN command, 368, 395

## S

SAVEPOINT operations, 50, 68
scalar datatypes, 425, 496
schemas, data dictionary and, 85
SCNs (system change numbers), 423, 448
scope, sessions and, 265
scripts
    backups and, 179, 183, 206
    buffer cache and, 225, 256
    commands for, 165
    CREATE SCRIPT command and, 195
    Cryptography Toolkit and, 306, 329
    database backup and, 157
    dictionary views and, 96, 420
    generating region database with, 285, 312
    migration and, 357, 387
    packages and, 421
    performance tuning and, 247, 275
    recovery and, 183, 206
    RMAN and, 184
    row migration and, 228, 259
    SQL statements and, 35
    SQL*Plus and, 18, 21
    UTLLOCKT utility and, 267
Scripts tab, Oracle Expert, 265
sdns.ora, 311, 478
security
    advanced options for, 305
    advanced security options and, 328
    cryptography and, 293, 319
    database security model and, 20–21
    directory objects and, 346, 377
    network environment and, 281, 485–486
    password-authentication and, 96
segments. *see also* rollback segments; temporary segments
    altering size of, 89
    defining storage for, 106
    limiting extents of, 100
    system segments and, 131
    types of, 101, 422
SELECT COUNT (*) statement, 54
SELECT statements
    executable statements and, 11
    GROUP BY clause and, 404
    join operators and, 403
    Oracle architecture and, 416
    overview of, 402
    rollback segments and, 144
    subqueries and, 77
    using, 26
    WHERE clause and, 20
sequences
    CKPT and, 205
    creating, 14

errors and, 34
indexes and, 352, 383
storage of, 136
using, 124
Server Manager
administration with, 417
errors and, 133
SERVICE_NAME parameter, 370
session tracing
location of information produced by, 243, 272
performance tuning and, 220, 252
sessions
control statements for, 401
dedicated servers and, 114
dictionary views and, 389
information storage and, 115
RESTRICTED SESSION and, 122
shared pool and, 145, 274
tuning memory for, 224, 240, 255, 269
SET command
changing trace file names with, 325
password authentication with, 309
SET LONG statement
increasing buffer size with, 63
using, 55
SET TRANSACTION command
defining transactions with, 69–70
rollback segments and, 139
using, 50
SGA. *see* System Global Area (SGA)
SHARE locks, 231, 262
shared pool
flushing, 126
location of information in, 145
performance tuning and, 215, 241, 247, 270, 275, 462–463
pinning PL/SQL packages in memory and, 223, 255
session information and, 274
sort area and, 260
SORT_AREA_SIZE and, 260
tuning reserved space in, 223–224, 255
SHUTDOWN commands
immediate shutdown, 102–103
normal shutdown, 131
options for, 101
shutdown options
databases and, 418
instance recovery and, 178
SID resolution, 295, 321
simple views, 408
single-row functions, 4, 402

SMON
datafile synchronization and, 198
free space management with, 125
instance recovery and, 184, 189, 211, 439
rollback performance and, 350
temporary segments and, 424
snmp.ora, 312, 479
snmp_ro.ora, 330
SNP processes, 170, 199
sort operations. *see also* disk sorts
limiting database sorts, 238, 267
optimizing, 216, 229–230, 260
performance tuning and, 467–468
sort segments and, 424
SORT_AREA_SIZE
allocating, 229
default settings for, 238, 267
shared pool and, 260
soundex, 402
SOURCE_ROUTE parameter, 316
space utilization
block management and, 114
managing, 88
SPANKY
host machine processing and, 88
profile limiters and, 121
SPOOL command, 59
SQL, 4–78
overview of, 4, 400–401
parse information and, 94
performance tuning and, 215, 459–461
practice exam answers for, 49–62, 63–78
practice exams for, 9–26, 27–48
shared area of, 126
topic areas of, 4–8
using scripts with, 35
using subqueries with, 34
wild-card comparisons in, 18
SQL INSERT, 139
SQL queries. *see* queries
SQL statements
Cartesian products and, 15
FROM clause and, 49, 69
CUBE keyword and, 344, 375
finding errors in, 28, 29
increasing reuse of, 223, 254–255
indexes and, 249, 277
invalid statements and, 9, 36
optimizing, 461
performance tuning and, 233, 263
sort operations and, 229

## Index 539

SQL (cont.)
  use of, 22
  valid statements and, 25
  writing, 4, 401
SQL trace, 459, 460–461
SQLJ, 489
SQL*Loader
  bad files and, 139
  columns and, 508
  control files and, 112
  datafiles and, 123
  execution parameters and, 90
  loading data with, 429
  partitioning and, 500
  primary-key constraint violations and, 109
  using, 345, 376
sqlnet.ora
  authentication and, 329
  encryption and checksums and, 319, 486
  naming conventions and, 477
  Net8 tracing and, 311
  parameters for, 482
SQL*Plus
  CEIL function and, 34–35
  commands and, 25
  ending transactions and, 10
  INVENTORY tables and, 20
  NLS_DATE_FORMAT information and, 15–16
  Oracle8i new features and, 337, 342, 373, 514
  performance tuning and, 459
  producing readable output from, 5, 405
  queries and, 39–40
  uncommitted transactions and, 359–360, 389
  using scripts with, 18–19, 21
srv option, 316–317
STANDBY_ARCHIVE_DEST parameter, 381
star queries, 460
START command, 73
STARTUP command, 255
STARTUP MOUNT statement, 111
startup options, databases, 418
statements
  action required by failures in, 177, 205
  DUAL table and, 12
  executable statements and, 11–12
  failures and, 445
  reusability and, 52
  SELECT statements and, 11
  syntax of, 134–135
  timing of data changes and, 136
  writing executable statements, 7
storage
  default settings for, 133, 238, 267
  identifying parameters for, 107
  implementation strategy for, 38–39
  indexes and, 91
  PCTFREE and, 106
  regional data and, 286, 313
  rollback segments and, 86
  structures and relationships for, 82, 422–423
  tablespace settings and, 102
STORAGE clause
  improper definition of, 123
  objects not permitting storage and, 92
  rollback segments and, 86
stored outlines. *see* outlines
stored plans, 343, 374
stored procedures
  summary management and, 494
  variables and, 14
streaming
  backup sets and, 197
  datafiles and, 211
  RMAN and, 167–168
striping
  I/O distribution and, 258
  performance tuning and, 239, 268
  types of, 466
SUBPARTITION keyword, 378
subqueries
  EXISTS statement and, 67–68
  multiple-column sub-queries and, 405
  overview of, 5, 404–405
  SELECT statements and, 77
  SQL statements and, 34
  uses of, 72
  when to use, 59
  WHERE clause and, 71
summary management
  data warehousing and, 351
  GROUP BY clause and, 382
  Oracle8i new features and, 333, 492–494
SUPPORT, Net8 listeners, 318–319
synchronization
  background processes for, 177–178
  backup and recovery and, 158
  datafiles and, 186
  dictionaries views and, 189
  SMON and, 198
syntactic attributes, 25

SYS schema, 118
SYSDBA privileges, 276, 417
SYSMAN, 371, 517
SYSOPER privileges, 417
system change numbers (SCNs), 423, 448
system control statements, 401
System Global Area (SGA)
    components of, 462
    Oracle architecture and, 416
    performance tuning and, 248, 276
    sizing out of memory, 257
    tuning size of, 222, 254
system privileges, 432–433
system segments, 131
SYSTEM tablespace
    backups and, 164
    overview of, 422
    tablespace types and, 465
    using, 118

# T

table caching, 225, 256
Table Data Editor tool, 351, 381–382
TABLE datatypes, 497
table of records, PL/SQL, 76
tables
    adding columns to, 17
    CREATE USER statement and, 114
    creating, 6, 406–407
    displaying data from multiple
        tables, 403
    dropping, 58
    eliminating views in, 20
    finding number of rows in, 46
    inserting rows in, 33
    managing, 6, 82, 406–407, 424–425
    moving, 507
    obtaining data from, 22
    PCTFREE and PCTUSED values and, 91
    placing in buffer pools, 240, 269
    preventing data changes in, 37
    REFERENCES privilege and, 18
    removing indexes from, 31
    selecting data in, 24
    syntactic attributes and, 25
    temporary storage for, 345, 376
    temporary tables and, 507
    types of, 424
    using statements with, 10
    WHERE clause and, 19, 33
Tablespace Manager
    SQL tuning tools and, 459

    tablespace availability and, 95
    using, 127
tablespaces
    availability of, 95
    configuration of, 226, 257–258
    CREATE USER statement and, 114
    datafiles and, 125
    decreasing size of, 140
    free space in, 106
    initialization parameters and, 105
    LOBs and, 362–363, 391
    managing, 81, 422, 505–506
    moving between databases, 356, 387
    Oracle8i and, 335, 341–342, 372
    performance tuning and, 230, 260
    point-in-time recovery and,
        159, 190, 202
    privileges and, 89
    query access and, 166–167
    recovery and, 211
    relationships in, 93
    storage and, 85, 135
    storing database objects in, 70–71
    temporary, 122
    transporting between databases,
        358, 388
    troubleshooting, 94
    types of, 465
tape backup
    operational procedures for, 209
    recovery catalog and, 204
TEMP tablespace, 465
temporary segments, managing, 82, 424
threads
    comparing with processes, 241, 270
    UNIX and, 222
    using, 254
TKPROF
    performance tuning and, 220, 252
    SQL tuning tools and, 459, 460
    using, 244, 273
tnsnames.ora
    C sort routines and, 389
    local naming and, 323, 477
    OPS instances and, 354, 384
    overview of, 311
    parameters of, 339, 370
    using, 298, 324
TNSPING utility, 482
TOOLS tablespace, 422
topic areas, exams
    backup and recovery, 150–153
    database administration, 80–84
    network administration, 280–281

Oracle8i upgrades, 332–338
performance tuning, 214–217
SQL and PL/SQL, 4–8
TopSessions, 459
Trace Assistant, 485
trace files
background processes and, 446
databases and, 419
location of, 214, 264
OSI layers and, 484
output of, 304–305, 328
packet information and, 484
performance tuning and, 456
SET command and, 325
troubleshooting and, 482
TRACE_LEVEL, 482
tracing
Net 8 listeners and, 292–293, 318–319
Net8 tracing and, 284, 311
network settings for, 304, 328
transaction control statements, 401
transactions
allocating rollback segments to, 231, 261–262
code and, 35
rollback segments and, 244, 273
SET TRANSACTION command and, 69–70
wrapping and, 102
transport layer, OSI model, 296, 321
TRCASST (Trace Assistant), 319
triggers
INSERT trigger and, 130
INSTEAD OF triggers and, 497
Oracle8i new features and, 342, 373, 514–515
using, 427
troubleshooting. *see also* errors; failures
gateways, 291, 317
log files, 482
media failures, 445–446
network environment, 281, 482–485
tablespaces, 94
using TNSPING utility for, 482
using trace files for, 482
using TRACE_LEVEL for, 482
TRUNCATE operations, 68
tuning. *see* performance tuning
Tuning Pack, Oracle Expert, 242, 265–266, 271
Two-Task Common processes, 320
%TYPE variables, 58

## U

UNCATALOG command, 191
UNION query, 260
unique key constraints, 50, 407
Universal Installer and Packager
software installation with, 503
using, 356, 386
UNIX
backups and, 156
OERR utility and, 484
threads and, 222
UPDATE statement
data manipulation with, 406
improving performance of, 347, 378
issuing, 50
Oracle databases and, 17
parallelizing, 366, 394
processing, 105
upgrades, Oracle8i. *see* Oracle8i, upgrades
user access. *see* access control
user-defined records, 45
user profiles. *see* profiles
userid, 92–93
USER_INDEXES, 66
users
access costs and, 93
allocating roles to, 113
creating in databases, 89
data selection by, 101
DEFAULT profile and, 127
generating profile information for, 125
killing user sessions and, 103
managing, 83, 430–431
privileges and, 91
resource usage limits for, 113
V$SESSION view and, 134
utilities. *see* performance tuning
UTLBSTAT, 457
UTLESTAT, 457
UTLLOCKT
detecting lock contention with, 262, 469
using scripts with, 237, 267

## V

value-based auditing, 135
VARCHAR2 datatype
datatypes and, 145
storing large blocks with, 383

variables
    controlling declaration of, 7
    declaring, 412
    DEFINE command and, 57
    incorrect declaration of, 73
    PL/SQL and, 19, 20–21, 42
    stored procedures and, 14
    %TYPE variables and, 58
VARRAY datatypes
    features of, 363, 391
    overview of, 496–497
views. *see* data dictionary views
virtual memory, 254, 462
V$NLS_PARAMETERS, 146
V$SESSION view, 134

## W

wait events
    dictionary views and, 234, 264
    storage of, 242, 271
wait ratio, 471
WHERE clause
    Cartesian products and, 54
    Oracle databases and, 39
    overview of, 13, 402
    performance tuning and, 272
    required components and, 67
    SELECT statements and, 20
    subqueries and, 71, 404
    tables and, 19, 33
WHERE CURRENT OF clause, 77
WHILE loops
    EXIT statement and, 78
    statements and, 48
wild-cards
    LIKE operators and, 56
    SQL and, 18
WITH GRANT OPTION, 123
workgroups, 324
wrapping, rollback segments and, 133

# For Best Results on Oracle Certification, Get the Ultimate OCP Solution:

http://www.ExamPilot.Com

# ExamPilot.Com

*Everything You Need to Get Certified, From the Oracle Certification Authority.*

**Now on the Web, at
http://www.ExamPilot.Com**

ExamPilot.Com and the ExamPilot logo are trademarks of ExamPilot.Com.

# Get Your FREE Subscription to *Oracle Magazine*

*Oracle Magazine* is essential gear for today's information technology professionals. Stay informed and increase your productivity with every issue of *Oracle Magazine*. Inside each **FREE,** bimonthly issue you'll get:

- Up-to-date information on Oracle Database Server, Oracle Applications, Internet Computing, and tools
- Third-party news and announcements
- Technical articles on Oracle products and operating environments
- Development and administration tips
- Real-world customer stories

## Three easy ways to subscribe:

**1. Web** — Visit our Web site at www.oracle.com/oramag/. You'll find a subscription form there, plus much more!

**2. Fax** — Complete the questionnaire on the back of this card and fax the questionnaire side only to **+1.847.647.9735.**

**3. Mail** — Complete the questionnaire on the back of this card and mail it to P.O. Box 1263, Skokie, IL 60076-8263.

If there are other Oracle users at your location who would like to receive their own subscription to *Oracle Magazine*, please photocopy this form and pass it along.

☐ **YES! Please send me a FREE subscription to *Oracle Magazine*.**   ☐ **NO**

To receive a free bimonthly subscription to *Oracle Magazine*, you must fill out the entire card, sign it, and date it (incomplete cards cannot be processed or acknowledged). You can also fax your application to **+1.847.647.9735. Or subscribe at our Web site at www.oracle.com/oramag/**

| SIGNATURE (REQUIRED) | X | | DATE | |
|---|---|---|---|---|

| NAME | | TITLE |
|---|---|---|
| COMPANY | | TELEPHONE |
| ADDRESS | | FAX NUMBER |
| CITY | | STATE | POSTAL CODE/ZIP CODE |
| COUNTRY | | E-MAIL ADDRESS |

☐ From time to time, Oracle Publishing allows our partners exclusive access to our e-mail addresses for special promotions and announcements. To be included in this program, please check this box.

## You must answer all eight questions below.

**1 What is the primary business activity of your firm at this location?** *(check only one)*
- ☐ 03 Communications
- ☐ 04 Consulting, Training
- ☐ 06 Data Processing
- ☐ 07 Education
- ☐ 08 Engineering
- ☐ 09 Financial Services
- ☐ 10 Government—Federal, Local, State, Other
- ☐ 11 Government—Military
- ☐ 12 Health Care
- ☐ 13 Manufacturing—Aerospace, Defense
- ☐ 14 Manufacturing—Computer Hardware
- ☐ 15 Manufacturing—Noncomputer Products
- ☐ 17 Research & Development
- ☐ 19 Retailing, Wholesaling, Distribution
- ☐ 20 Software Development
- ☐ 21 Systems Integration, VAR, VAD, OEM
- ☐ 22 Transportation
- ☐ 23 Utilities (Electric, Gas, Sanitation)
- ☐ 98 Other Business and Services

**2 Which of the following best describes your job function?** *(check only one)*
**CORPORATE MANAGEMENT/STAFF**
- ☐ 01 Executive Management (President, Chair, CEO, CFO, Owner, Partner, Principal)
- ☐ 02 Finance/Administrative Management (VP/Director/ Manager/Controller, Purchasing, Administration)
- ☐ 03 Sales/Marketing Management (VP/Director/Manager)
- ☐ 04 Computer Systems/Operations Management (CIO/VP/Director/ Manager MIS, Operations)

**IS/IT STAFF**
- ☐ 07 Systems Development/ Programming Management
- ☐ 08 Systems Development/ Programming Staff
- ☐ 09 Consulting
- ☐ 10 DBA/Systems Administrator
- ☐ 11 Education/Training
- ☐ 14 Technical Support Director/ Manager
- ☐ 16 Other Technical Management/Staff
- ☐ 98 Other

**3 What is your current primary operating platform?** *(check all that apply)*
- ☐ 01 DEC UNIX
- ☐ 02 DEC VAX VMS
- ☐ 03 Java
- ☐ 04 HP UNIX
- ☐ 05 IBM AIX
- ☐ 06 IBM UNIX
- ☐ 07 Macintosh
- ☐ 09 MS-DOS
- ☐ 10 MVS
- ☐ 11 NetWare
- ☐ 12 Network Computing
- ☐ 13 OpenVMS
- ☐ 14 SCO UNIX
- ☐ 24 Sequent DYNIX/ptx
- ☐ 15 Sun Solaris/SunOS
- ☐ 16 SVR4
- ☐ 18 UnixWare
- ☐ 20 Windows
- ☐ 21 Windows NT
- ☐ 23 Other UNIX
- ☐ 98 Other
- 99 ☐ **None of the above**

**4 Do you evaluate, specify, recommend, or authorize the purchase of any of the following?** *(check all that apply)*
- ☐ 01 Hardware
- ☐ 02 Software
- ☐ 03 Application Development Tools
- ☐ 04 Database Products
- ☐ 05 Internet or Intranet Products
- 99 ☐ **None of the above**

**5 In your job, do you use or plan to purchase any of the following products or services?** *(check all that apply)*
**SOFTWARE**
- ☐ 01 Business Graphics
- ☐ 02 CAD/CAE/CAM
- ☐ 03 CASE
- ☐ 05 Communications
- ☐ 06 Database Management
- ☐ 07 File Management
- ☐ 08 Finance
- ☐ 09 Java
- ☐ 10 Materials Resource Planning
- ☐ 11 Multimedia Authoring
- ☐ 12 Networking
- ☐ 13 Office Automation
- ☐ 14 Order Entry/Inventory Control
- ☐ 15 Programming
- ☐ 16 Project Management
- ☐ 17 Scientific and Engineering
- ☐ 18 Spreadsheets
- ☐ 19 Systems Management
- ☐ 20 Workflow

**HARDWARE**
- ☐ 21 Macintosh
- ☐ 22 Mainframe
- ☐ 23 Massively Parallel Processing
- ☐ 24 Minicomputer
- ☐ 25 PC
- ☐ 26 Network Computer
- ☐ 28 Symmetric Multiprocessing
- ☐ 29 Workstation

**PERIPHERALS**
- ☐ 30 Bridges/Routers/Hubs/Gateways
- ☐ 31 CD-ROM Drives
- ☐ 32 Disk Drives/Subsystems
- ☐ 33 Modems
- ☐ 34 Tape Drives/Subsystems
- ☐ 35 Video Boards/Multimedia

**SERVICES**
- ☐ 37 Consulting
- ☐ 38 Education/Training
- ☐ 39 Maintenance
- ☐ 40 Online Database Services
- ☐ 41 Support
- ☐ 36 Technology-Based Training
- ☐ 98 Other
- 99 ☐ **None of the above**

**6 What Oracle products are in use at your site?** *(check all that apply)*
**SERVER/SOFTWARE**
- ☐ 01 Oracle8
- ☐ 30 Oracle8*i*
- ☐ 31 Oracle8*i* Lite
- ☐ 02 Oracle7
- ☐ 03 Oracle Application Server
- ☐ 04 Oracle Data Mart Suites
- ☐ 05 Oracle Internet Commerce Server
- ☐ 32 Oracle *inter*Media
- ☐ 33 Oracle JServer
- ☐ 07 Oracle Lite
- ☐ 08 Oracle Payment Server
- ☐ 11 Oracle Video Server

**TOOLS**
- ☐ 13 Oracle Designer
- ☐ 14 Oracle Developer
- ☐ 54 Oracle Discoverer
- ☐ 53 Oracle Express
- ☐ 51 Oracle JDeveloper
- ☐ 52 Oracle Reports
- ☐ 50 Oracle WebDB
- ☐ 55 Oracle Workflow

**ORACLE APPLICATIONS**
- ☐ 17 Oracle Automotive
- ☐ 35 Oracle Business Intelligence System
- ☐ 19 Oracle Consumer Packaged Goods
- ☐ 39 Oracle E-Commerce
- ☐ 18 Oracle Energy
- ☐ 20 Oracle Financials
- ☐ 28 Oracle Front Office
- ☐ 21 Oracle Human Resources
- ☐ 37 Oracle Internet Procurement
- ☐ 22 Oracle Manufacturing
- ☐ 40 Oracle Process Manufacturing
- ☐ 23 Oracle Projects
- ☐ 34 Oracle Retail
- ☐ 29 Oracle Self-Service Web Applications
- ☐ 38 Oracle Strategic Enterprise Management
- ☐ 25 Oracle Supply Chain Management
- ☐ 36 Oracle Tutor
- ☐ 41 Oracle Travel Management

**ORACLE SERVICES**
- ☐ 61 Oracle Consulting
- ☐ 62 Oracle Education
- ☐ 60 Oracle Support
- ☐ 98 Other
- 99 ☐ **None of the above**

**7 What other database products are in use at your site?** *(check all that apply)*
- ☐ 01 Access   ☐ 10 PeopleSoft
- ☐ 02 Baan   ☐ 11 Progress
- ☐ 03 dbase   ☐ 12 SAP
- ☐ 04 Gupta   ☐ 13 Sybase
- ☐ 05 IBM DB2   ☐ 14 VSAM
- ☐ 06 Informix
- ☐ 07 Ingres
- ☐ 08 Microsoft Access
- ☐ 09 Microsoft SQL Server
- ☐ 98 Other
- 99 ☐ **None of the above**

**8 During the next 12 months, how much do you anticipate your organization will spend on computer hardware, software, peripherals, and services for your location?** *(check only one)*
- ☐ 01 Less than $10,000
- ☐ 02 $10,000 to $49,999
- ☐ 03 $50,000 to $99,999
- ☐ 04 $100,000 to $499,999
- ☐ 05 $500,000 to $999,999
- ☐ 06 $1,000,000 and over

If there are other Oracle users at your location who would like to receive a free subscription to *Oracle Magazine*, please photocopy this form and pass it along, or contact Customer Service at **+1.847.647.9630**

Form 5

OPRESS

*Knowledge is power. To which we say,*

# crank up the power.

## Are you ready for a power surge?

Accelerate your career—become an **Oracle Certified Professional (OCP)**. With Oracle's cutting-edge *Instructor-Led Training*, *Technology-Based Training*, and this *guide*, you can prepare for certification faster than ever. Set your own trajectory by logging your personal training plan with us. Go to **http://education.oracle.com/tpb**, where we'll help you pick a training path, select your courses, and track your progress. We'll even send you an email when your courses are offered in your area. If you don't have access to the Web, call us at 1-800-441-3541 (Outside the U.S. call +1-310-335-2403).
**Power learning has never been easier.**

ORACLE®
University

©2000 Oracle Corporation. All rights reserved. Oracle is a registered trademark of Oracle Corporation.

# About the FastTrakExpress™ CD-ROM

FastTrak Express provides interactive certification exams to help you prepare for certification. With the enclosed CD, you can test your knowledge of the topics covered in this book with over 700 multiple choice questions.

To Install FastTrak Express:

1. Insert the CD-ROM in your CD-ROM drive.
2. From your computer, choose Start/Run.
3. Select the CD-ROM drive and Run the file called "setupfte.bat." This will launch the Installation Wizard.
4. When the Setup is finished, you may immediately begin using FastTrak Express.
5. To begin using FastTrak Express, enter the corresponding license key number of the exam you want to take (you only have to enter this number for the first time you take the exam):

| EXAM | LICENSE KEY NUMBER |
|---|---|
| 01: Introduction to SQL and PL/SQL | 285142485116 |
| 02: Database Administration | 251283858092 |
| 03: Backup and Recovery Workshop | 266182827688 |
| 04: Performance Tuning Workshop | 291381817587 |
| 05: Network Administration | 247284868193 |
| 06: Oracle8i Upgrade Exam | 214984739747 |
| 07: All in One Oracle8i DBA | 201253941449 |

(This exam contains all six (6) chapter exams combined into one exam.)

FastTrak Express offers two testing options: the Adaptive exam and the Standard exam.

## The Adaptive exam

The Adaptive exam style does not simulate all of the exam environments that are found on certification exams. You cannot choose specific subcategories for the adaptive exam and once a question has been answered you cannot go back to a previous question.

You have a time limit in which to complete the adaptive exam. This time varies from subject to subject, although it is usually 15 to 25 questions in 30 minutes. When the time limit has been reached, your exam automatically ends.

To take the Adaptive exam:

1. Click the Adaptive Exam button from the Main window. The Adaptive Exam window will appear.
2. Click the circle or square to the left of the correct answer.

**NOTE**
*There may be more than one correct answer. The text in the bottom left corner of the window instructs you to "Mark the best answer" (if there is only one answer) or "Mark all correct answers" (if there is more than one correct answer.*

   3. Click the Next button to continue.
   4. To quit the test at any time, click the Finish button. After about 30 minutes, the exam exits to review mode.

After you have completed the Adaptive exam, FastTrak Express displays your score and the passing score required for the test.

- Click Details to display a chapter-by-chapter review of your exam results.
- Click on Report to get a full analysis of your score.

To review the Adaptive exam:
After you have taken a Adaptive exam, you can review the questions, your answers, and the correct answers. You may only review your questions immediately after an Adaptive exam. To review your questions:

   1. Click the Correct Answer button.
   2. To see your answer, click the Your Answer button.

## The Standard exam

After you have learned about your subject using the Adaptive sessions, you can take a Standard exam. This mode simulates the environment that might be found on an actual certification exam.

You cannot choose subcategories for a Standard exam. You have a time limit (this time varies from subject to subject, although it is usually 75 minutes) to complete the Standard exam. When this time limit has been reached, your exam automatically ends.

To take the Standard exam:

   1. Click the Standard Exam button from the Main window. The Standard Exam window will appear.
   2. Click the circle or square to the left of the correct answer.

**NOTE**
*There may be more than one correct answer. The text in the bottom left corner of the window instructs you to Choose the Best Answer (if there is only one answer) or Mark All Correct Answers (if there is more than one correct answer).*

3. If you are unsure of the answer and wish to mark the question so you can return to it later, check the Mark box in the upper left hand corner.
4. To review which questions you have marked, which you have answered, and which you have not answered, click the Review button.
5. Click the Next button to continue.
6. To quit the test at any time, click the Finish button. After about 75 minutes, the exam exits to review mode.

After you have completed the Standard exam, FastTrak Express displays your score and the passing score required for the test.

- Click Details to display a chapter-by-chapter review of your exam results.
- Click on Report to get a full analysis of your score.

**NOTE**
*The passing score required is for this CD engine only, and does not correspond to the actual passing score required for the official exam.*

To review a Standard Exam
After you have taken a Standard exam, you can review the questions, your answers, and the correct answers.
You may only review your questions immediately after a Standard exam.
To review your questions:

1. Click the Correct Answer button.
2. To see your answer, click the Your Answer button.

# Changing Exams:

FastTrakExpress provides several practice exams to test your knowledge. To change exams:

1. Select the exam for the test you want to run from the Select Exam window.

# Technical Support

If you experience technical difficulties please call (888) 992-3131. Outside the U.S. call (281) 992-3131. Or, you may e-mail **bfquiz@swbell.net** . For more information, visit the FastTrakExpress web site at www.fasttrakexpress.com.

**WARNING: BEFORE OPENING THE DISC PACKAGE, CAREFULLY READ THE TERMS AND CONDITIONS OF THE FOLLOWING COPYRIGHT STATEMENT AND LIMITED CD-ROM WARRANTY.**

**Copyright Statement**
This software is protected by both United States copyright law and international copyright treaty provision. Except as noted in the contents of the CD-ROM, you must treat this software just like a book. However, you may copy it into a computer to be used and you may make archival copies of the software for the sole purpose of backing up the software and protecting your investment from loss. By saying, "just like a book," The McGraw-Hill Companies, Inc. ("Osborne/McGraw-Hill") means, for example, that this software may be used by any number of people and may be freely moved from one computer location to another, so long as there is no possibility of its being used at one location or on one computer while it is being used at another. Just as a book cannot be read by two different people in two different places at the same time, neither can the software be used by two different people in two different places at the same time.

**Limited Warranty**
Osborne/McGraw-Hill warrants the physical compact disc enclosed herein to be free of defects in materials and workmanship for a period of sixty days from the purchase date. If the CD included in your book has defects in materials or workmanship, please call McGraw-Hill at 1-800-217-0059, 9am to 5pm, Monday through Friday, Eastern Standard Time, and McGraw-Hill will replace the defective disc.
The entire and exclusive liability and remedy for breach of this Limited Warranty shall be limited to replacement of the defective disc, and shall not include or extend to any claim for or right to cover any other damages, including but not limited to, loss of profit, data, or use of the software, or special incidental, or consequential damages or other similar claims, even if Osborne/McGraw-Hill has been specifically advised of the possibility of such damages. In no event will Osborne/McGraw-Hill's liability for any damages to you or any other person ever exceed the lower of the suggested list price or actual price paid for the license to use the software, regardless of any form of the claim.

OSBORNE/McGRAW-HILL SPECIFICALLY DISCLAIMS ALL OTHER WARRANTIES, EXPRESS OR IMPLIED, INCLUDING BUT NOT LIMITED TO, ANY IMPLIED WARRANTY OF MERCHANTABILITY OR FITNESS FOR A PARTICULAR PURPOSE. Specifically, Osborne/McGraw-Hill makes no representation or warranty that the software is fit for any particular purpose, and any implied warranty of merchantability is limited to the sixty-day duration of the Limited Warranty covering the physical disc only (and not the software), and is otherwise expressly and specifically disclaimed.
This limited warranty gives you specific legal rights; you may have others which may vary from state to state. Some states do not allow the exclusion of incidental or consequential damages, or the limitation on how long an implied warranty lasts, so some of the above may not apply to you.
This agreement constitutes the entire agreement between the parties relating to use of the Product. The terms of any purchase order shall have no effect on the terms of this Agreement. Failure of Osborne/McGraw-Hill to insist at any time on strict compliance with this Agreement shall not constitute a waiver of any rights under this Agreement. This Agreement shall be construed and governed in accordance with the laws of New York. If any provision of this Agreement is held to be contrary to law, that provision will be enforced to the maximum extent permissible, and the remaining provisions will remain in force and effect.

NO TECHNICAL SUPPORT IS PROVIDED WITH THIS CD-ROM.